THE PENGUIN CLASSICS

FOUNDER EDITOR (1944–64): E. V. RIEU

EDITORS:

Robert Baldick (1964–72)   *Betty Radice*   *C. A. Jones*

MARIE HENRI BEYLE, known through his writings as Stendhal, was born in Grenoble in 1783 and educated there at the École Centrale. A cousin offered him a post in the Ministry of War and from 1800 onwards he followed Napoleon's campaigns in Italy, Germany, Russia and Austria. In between wars, he spent his time in Paris drawing-rooms and theatres.

After the fall of Napoleon, he retired to Italy, adopted his pseudonym, and started to write books on Italian painting, Haydn and Mozart, and travels in Italy. In 1821 he left Italy because of the political situation, and returning to Paris he finished his book *De l'Amour*. This was followed by *Racine et Shakespeare*, a defence of romantic literature. *Le Rouge et le Noir* was his second novel, and he also produced or began three others, including *La Chartreuse de Parme*, none of which was received with any great understanding during his lifetime.

Beyle was appointed Consul at Civitavecchia after the 1830 revolution, but his health deteriorated and six years later he was back in Paris and beginning a life of Napoleon. In 1841 he was once again recalled for reasons of illness, and in the following year he suffered a fatal stroke. Various autobiographical works, his *Journal*, his *Souvenirs d'Égotisme* and *Vie de Henry Brulard*, were published later, as his fame grew.

JEAN STEWART (Mrs James Pace) taught French literature at Cambridge for several years. She has translated over forty books, including La Bruyère's *Characters* for the Penguin Classics.

B. C. J. G. KNIGHT is Emeritus Professor of Microbiology of the University of Reading and an avid collector of 18th–20th century French books, especially of Stendhal and Stendhaliana. He is the translator and editor, with Jean Stewart, of *Diderot, Interpreter of Nature: Selected Writings*.

STENDHAL

THE LIFE OF
HENRY BRULARD

TRANSLATED
AND WITH AN INTRODUCTION BY
JEAN STEWART AND
B. C. J. G. KNIGHT

PENGUIN BOOKS

Penguin Books Ltd, Harmondsworth, Middlesex, England
Penguin Books Australia Ltd, Ringwood, Victoria, Australia

—

This translation first published by the Merlin Press 1958
Published in Penguin Books 1973

—

Copyright © The Merlin Press, 1958

—

Made and printed in Great Britain by
Hazell Watson & Viney Ltd
Aylesbury, Bucks
Set in Linotype Granjon

To the memory
of

HENRI MARTINEAU
25 April 1882–21 April 1958

On n'en finirait plus avec Stendhal
– Paul Valéry

INTRODUCTION

Biographical Background

1783–99. Marie Henri Beyle (Stendhal) born 23 January 1783 in Grenoble, son of Chérubin Beyle and his wife Henriette, née Gagnon, who died in childbed November 1790. Lived in Grenoble, went to Central School, passed examinations for entry to the École Polytechnique in Paris where he went on 10 November 1799. He did not attend the Polytechnique and lived at first alone and later in the house of his cousin Pierre Daru, who took Stendhal into his offices in the Ministry of War.

1800–1801. Went with the army of Napoleon over the St Bernard Pass into Italy and moved from garrison to garrison in Lombardy and various towns in Northern Italy as aide-de-camp to General Michaud. The period 1783 to 1801 is the basis of his *Vie de Henry Brulard*. April 1801 began his *Journal*. At end of 1801 obtained leave and returned to France.

1802–5. Various occupations and love affairs, interested in the theatre and tried to write a play; much reading, including in particular the Ideology of Destutt de Tracy.

1806–14. Returned to Paris from Marseille and renewed contact with his cousins Pierre and Martial Daru, important military persons. Went with Napoleonic armies to Germany, Austria, Hungary.

1810–11. Held official posts, auditeur to the Council of State, inspector of furniture and buildings of the Crown. Travelled in Italy (Florence, Rome, Naples) and had the first idea of writing an *Histoire de la Peinture en Italie*.

1812. Went with the Headquarters staff of Napoleon's army into Russia, entered Moscow, saw it in flames; was sent back to organize provisioning for the retreat from Moscow at Smolensk, Mohilev, Vitebsk.

1813. New post as commissariat officer at Sagan in Silesia. Obtained leave and went to Milan.

1814. At Grenoble appointed assistant to Count de Saint-Vallier, commissioner extraordinary of the 7th military region, to organize resistance to the Allied invasion. Allies entered Paris and Napoleon exiled to Elba. The end of Stendhal's fortunes under Napoleon.

Wrote *Vies de Haydn, Mozart et Metastase*. Went to Milan where he mainly lived for the next seven years.

1815. Stendhal remained in Italy, not returning to France during the Hundred Days when Napoleon returned from Elba; Waterloo; final exile of Napoleon to St Helena.

1816. Stendhal in Milanese society, attended La Scala in box of Lodovico de Breme, met Byron and other liberals.

1817. *Histoire de la Peinture en Italie* and *Rome, Naples et Florence* published in Paris.

1818. 4 March, beginning of his painful love for Mathilde Viscontini Dembowski, whom he called Métilde.

1819. Milan, Volterra, Grenoble; 29 December, had the idea of writing a book to express all that Métilde had made him feel. This became *De l'Amour*. The political situation in Milan became increasingly difficult for the liberals.

1820. Journeyed in Northern Italy. In Milan, occupied with the book concerning his feeling for Métilde, who treated him more and more coolly. Arrests of prominent liberals began. Rumours began to spread in liberal circles that Stendhal was an agent of the French government. First draft of *De l'Amour* sent to France.

1821. The Austrian government suspected Stendhal of being connected with the Carbonari movement. 13 June, Stendhal finally left Milan on urgent advice from friends and because he recognized the hopelessness of his love for Métilde who was treating him with ever greater coolness.

1821–30. Lived in Paris, frequented literary circles, wrote for English reviews, and published books.

1822. *De l'Amour* published.

1823. *Vie de Rossini* and *Racine et Shakespeare I* published.

1824. Journalism in French and English papers and reviews.

1825. *Racine et Shakespeare II*; *D'un nouveau complot contre les industriels*.

1826. Second, much changed, edition of *Rome, Naples et Florence*. Wrote *Armance*.

1827. *Armance* published.

1828. January, went to Milan and was immediately expelled.

1829. Published *Promenades dans Rome*.
Various short stories: *Vanina Vanini, Le coffre et le revenant* appeared in *Revue de Paris*; *Mme de Vanghel* (unpublished then).

1830–31. Wrote story *Le Philtre* and his great novel *Le Rouge et le Noir* which was published in November 1830. After the revolution of July 1830 in France, which overthrew Charles X and established Louis-Philippe and the Charter, he eventually obtained the post of French Consul at Trieste, but the Austrian Government would not accept him and he had to leave.

1831. He was then sent as French Consul at Civitavecchia, the port near Rome. He went frequently to Rome.

1832. 20 June–4 July, he wrote *Souvenirs d'Égotisme* about his life from June 1821 to November 1830.

1833. September–December on leave in Paris; returned to Civitavecchia via Lyons and Marseilles, meeting George Sand and Alfred de Musset en route for Venice.

1834. Began novel *Lucien Leuwen*, started by an idea of his friend Mme Jules Gaulthier; left unfinished.

1835. In November began his autobiographical *Vie de Henry Brulard* covering his earliest years to 1801; left unfinished when he went on leave to Paris and never revised.

1836–9. On prolonged leave in Paris. Various short stories. Travels in the centre of France: *Mémoires d'un touriste* June 1838. More journeys in S.W. and S.E. France, Switzerland, Rhineland, Holland, Belgium. Published stories *La Duchesse de Palliano, l'Abbesse de Castro*.

September 1838 had first idea of *La Chartreuse de Parme*, which masterpiece he wrote in fifty-two days, 4 November to 26 December 1838; published April 1839.

1839–42. Returned to the consulate at Civitavecchia August 1839. Began a new novel *Lamiel* (unfinished); wrote story *Don Pardo*.

March 1841 had an apoplectic stroke; given leave and returned to Paris. Died suddenly 23 March 1842 from a stroke – as he had wished.

The Life of Henry Brulard

INTROSPECTION was a paramount necessity for Stendhal: self-knowledge an obsessive, ever-unattainable ideal. In his youth, from 1800 to 1814, he had consistently kept a journal, primarily in the hope that self-analysis would lead to self-mastery and hence to success in his personal and public life. Later, when he had come to realize the futility of this project, the urge toward self-knowledge for its own sake remained; and meanwhile he had turned his observations to better account in literature, analysing his reactions as traveller in *Rome, Naples et Florence*, as lover in *De l'Amour*, and transmuting no small part of his youthful ambitious self into Julien Sorel, hero of *Le Rouge et le Noir*.

In 1832 he beguiled the tedium of his official life as French Consul at Civitavecchia, when imaginative creation seemed impossible, by sketching an autobiographical fragment covering the years 1821–30; he called this *Souvenirs d' Égotisme*. In it he wrote: 'I don't know myself, and that is what sometimes at night, when I think about it, grieves me sadly ...' and again: 'One can know everything, except oneself.' This account of his recent past, however, did not go deep enough. Three years later the desire for self-assessment, which had always haunted him, revived imperatively. Memories of childhood, boyhood and youth remained unexplored, and he now turned to probe their depths. Working with feverish concentration ('ideas gallop through me') he wrote *Vie de Henry Brulard* in four months; then, on being granted leave to return to Paris in March 1836, he put it aside and, except to add a few marginal comments, never returned to it. It breaks off in 1800, on his first visit to Italy with Napoleon's army.

What we have here, then, is an unfinished and unrevised fragment of autobiography: not so much 'remembrance of things past' as a *recherche du temps perdu*, an attempt to recall lost experience with the utmost truth and objectivity. The book has an almost unique quality of spontaneity and directness. As Jean Prévost said: '*A côté des souvenirs d'enfance des autres, c'est un tableau mutilé, en partie effacé, mais c'est le seul qui ne soit pas repeint.*' [1] (Compared with the childhood memories of others, it is a mutilated and partly obliterated picture, but it is the only one which has not been touched up.) Stendhal is of course not the only self-biographer to claim total sincerity: but unlike some others, he never indulges in justification or condemnation of his younger self, in nostalgia or sentimentality. He might indeed have said with Montaigne: '*C'est ici un livre de bonne foi, lecteur.*'

A word here about Stendhal's veracity, which is not the same as sincerity. His attitude towards facts and dates was notoriously cavalier; whether carelessly or perversely, he often deviated from strict accuracy. Thus, for instance, the fine reverie with which *Brulard* opens was in all probability (as Henri Martineau deduced from a study of the MS) not actually written three years before the rest of the book, as it purports to be; and in fact in October 1832 Stendhal was travelling in the Abruzzi and could not possibly have been standing on the Janiculum Hill in Rome. None the less, the experience has an indisputably authentic ring; he must have felt, even if he did not write on that particular date: 'I'm going to be fifty, it's high time I got to know myself.'

'The purpose of true autobiography,' Roy Pascal has written, 'must be *Selbstbesinnung*,' [2] a search for one's inner standing. It is an affair of conscience ... and has become an obligation to oneself, to one's own truth ...' This is eminently the case with Stendhal's quest for identity: an exacting one, since his was a singularly complex nature, full of paradoxes and apparent contradictions. His constant inner sincerity, his loathing of cant,

1. *La Création chez Stendhal*, Paris, Mercure de France, 1951.

2. *Design and Truth in Autobiography*, London, Routledge & Kegan Paul, 1960, p. 182.

coexisted with outward deviousness; he was a man of many masks,[1] deliberately assumed to disguise but not to supplant his real self, by way of protection against a society with which he felt at odds, and perhaps as a means of getting his own back on life for having given him a clumsy physique, a bourgeois background and a self-consciousness that could be crippling. Consider the innumerable pseudonyms he adopted, some romantic, some burlesque; and the cryptograms he played with, partly for fun but also from a real need to guard his daring thoughts from police spies and his intimate feelings from an unsympathetic world. Consider the many parts he played: student of mathematics, secretary, soldier, would-be actor, would-be playwright, would-be business man, journalist, dilettante art critic, novelist, diplomat ... And his emotional life was as chequered as his career; witness the long list of women who made him happy or desperately unhappy, and whose initials he scrawled in the dust by that Italian lake in September 1835 when he was brooding over the memories that gave rise to *Brulard*.

Consider, too, the ambiguity of some of his attitudes, the contradictory nature of some of his opinions and tastes; his political radicalism and his aristocratic sensibilities; the juxtaposition, in his books, of romantic dream and dry irony; his scathing contempt for the hypocrisy of the society around him, and the Machiavellian acceptance of a kind of counter-hypocrisy as an instrument with which to fight that society (Julien in *Le Rouge et le Noir*). Above all, there is the basic contrast between his extreme sensitivity and emotional diffidence, the 'melancholy temperament' that he recognized in himself, and the cynical wit he displayed with such bravura. 'I'm supposed to be the gayest and most unfeeling of men ...' (*Brulard*, p. 7). To this contrast a shrewd observer, Mme Virginie Ancelot, whose salon he frequented in the 1820s, bears witness: 'Beyle was moved by everything, and he experienced a thousand emotional sensations in a few moments. Nothing escaped him and nothing left him undisturbed, but his sad emotions were hidden under pleasantries,

1. Analysed perceptively by Jean Starobinski in his chapter on 'Stendhal pseudonyme' in *L'Oeil vivant*, Paris, Gallimard, 1961; and at greater length by Georges Blin in *Stendhal et les problèmes de la personnalité*, Corti, Paris, 1958.

and he never seemed so gay as on the days when he was keenly distressed. Then what an outpouring of crazy wit and wisdom!'[1] He puzzled and disconcerted most of his contemporaries, so he wrote only for the 'happy few', or for posterity: 'I shall be read in 1930.' Perhaps the truth about Stendhal must always be sought, in J. P. Richard's phrase, in 'the impassioned association of extremes and contradictions'.[2] And it is in part this heady mixture of opposites, this highly individual complexity that gives such fascination to his character and writing. *Henry Brulard* does not explain away the contradictions, which were inherent in his nature, but it does shed precious light on the problem. Here, at any rate, we have Stendhal's own attempt to 'guess what sort of man I have been' by bringing back to life the child he was.

The book tells us, primarily and vehemently, what that sensitive and original child revolted against: the drabness and mediocrity of a provincial town, the conventional and conservative ideas of his middle-class family, the bourgeois meanness, coldness and cowardice of his father Chérubin Beyle, the spitefulness of his aunt Séraphie, an embittered *dévote*, and the tyranny of the 'hypocritical' abbé Raillane, to whom his first education was entrusted. True, he exaggerated their malevolence: scholars have proved that Chérubin and Raillane were by no means as black as Stendhal painted them. But as he says (p. 68): 'I was overwrought and, I imagine, very spiteful and unfair towards my father and the abbé Raillane, I admit. But even now in 1835 I have to make a great mental effort to do it, so that I cannot judge these two men. They poisoned my childhood ...' Their harsh, repressive attitude bred in him a hatred of authority: 'All tyrannies are alike ...' which became total irreverence and political radicalism. Their insistence on moral and religious conformism seemed abject hypocrisy, for which he had nothing but loathing.

The most appalling blow to the child was the death of his pretty young mother when he was seven; his passionate love for her, frankly described in *Brulard*, is surely a gift for Freudians.

1. *Les Salons de Paris, foyers éteints* by Virginie Ancelot (1858); quoted by H. Martineau in Preface to *Souvenirs d'Égotisme*, Paris, Le Divan, 1927; and in *L'Oeuvre de Stendhal*, Paris, Albin Michel, 1952, ch. 14.

2. *Littérature et sensation*, Paris, Editions du Seuil, 1954.

And it was the shock of hearing a priest say, over her coffin, 'This is God's doing;' that made of him irrevocably an atheist.

After her death, home life would have been intolerable but for the kindness of two other members of his family: his maternal grandfather Henri Gagnon, a delightful eighteenth-century rationalist, from whom he learnt to appreciate wit and irony, clear thinking and good writing; and his great-aunt Élisabeth Gagnon, a high-minded old lady who instilled into him her own 'espagnolisme', the cult of honour and heroic energy. Both trends, at first sight incompatible, were to remain permanent characteristics of Beyle the man and Stendhal the writer, and we find their roots here in 'Henry Brulard' the boy.

The old people's affection, however, was no substitute for the companionship of other boys, which his repressive upbringing denied him. 'I was always seeing children of my own age ... going off *together*, walking or running ... and that was something I was not allowed to do.' He had two sisters, one of them, Pauline, he loved dearly; but they were too young, and he was a lonely child, 'sullen, secretive and discontented', turned in on himself and living in a world of dream and make-believe. When eventually he went to school, he 'found reality far inferior to the wild visions' of his imagination, and experienced that sort of disappointment which was to recur throughout his life, and which is echoed time and again in his books: *'n'est-ce que cela?'* (is that really all?) when the fact – school, Paris or the St Bernard Pass, or the battle of Waterloo for Fabrice, or love for Julien Sorel or Lamiel – failed to measure up to the dream.

His imagination, meanwhile, was fostered by voracious reading: he had the free run of grandfather Gagnon's library. He fell madly in love with Ariosto's heroines, while the discovery of *Don Quixote*, 'read sitting under the second lime tree along the path on that side of the flower-bed where the ground was sunk a foot deep' was perhaps 'the greatest moment of my life'. However, as though to counteract this immersion in fantasy, grandfather Gagnon's passion for astronomy instilled into the boy a respect for the exact sciences, above all for mathematics, as admitting 'no hypocrisy and no vagueness, which are my two chief aversions'. This reverence for mathematics, on the part of one who, as he tells us, could never see why $- \times - = +$ may surprise; but it has a deeper significance in connection with his attitude to language. He sought always for the exact rendering of mental experience, hating inflation and rhetoric, preferring understatement to hyperbole. When experience was too intense, too intimate, or too exalted for accurate expression, above all in moments of rapturous happiness – *bonheur fou* – he preferred to remain silent. An inveterate practitioner of language, he was acutely aware of the limitations of his medium; perhaps for this reason he failed to appreciate poetry; music, for him, communicated the ineffable more directly.

To the adolescent Stendhal, moreover, mathematics had an immediate and practical advantage : it seemed to offer the key to freedom. For if he could prove a good enough scholar to win a place at the École Polytechnique in Paris, he could shake off the dust of Grenoble for ever. And Paris seemed, by contrast, Paradise. There he would live in an attic, 'write plays like Molière' and have romantic affairs . . . He did win the place, and was duly dispatched to Paris. But once again, disillusionment ensued. 'I had adored Paris and mathematics. Paris, having no mountains, inspired in me a loathing so profound that it amounted almost to homesickness'; and mathematics, having been merely a means to an end, was now forsworn. The last few chapters of *Henry Brulard* tell vividly of the miseries and mortifications of those early days in Paris. His attic was dreary and squalid; he was lonely, depressed, and fell ill. Then his Daru cousins, who were to play an important part in his life, took pity on him and housed him; and since he firmly refused to take the Polytechnique examination, Pierre Daru procured him a clerical job in the War Ministry. Here, and in the salons to which he was introduced, he suffered the humiliation of a shy proud provincial – ill at ease and none too good at spelling – which he later attributed to his Julien Sorel.

Henry Brulard ends, however, on a happier note : his departure for Italy as a lieutenant in Napoleon's army, crossing the St Bernard Pass on horseback and discovering Italy. It breaks off as he enters Milan 'on a delightful spring morning – and what a springtime!, and what a country!'. Milan meant the revelation of happiness – freedom and beauty, music and love – for Stendhal, and he stops short on its threshold. 'How can I describe the excessive happiness that everything gave me? It's impossible.' But three years after *Brulard*, in an intense spell of creative activity, he was to transmute those feelings into high art in *La Chartreuse de Parme*, written in fifty-two days straight off.

For lovers of the great novels, *Brulard* offers precious hints of those aspects of Stendhal's nature which he was to embody in his young heroes: Julien's proud, *farouche* susceptibility, Fabrice's capacity for *le bonheur fou*, the diffident delicacy of Lucien Leuwen. Through his heroes he lived romantic adventures; they were a continuation of his youthful dreams. But Brulard has its independent merits, its own special quality, and furthermore offers particular interest as an attempt to recapture the past.

The story is told from two viewpoints: the middle-aged man musing, the child experiencing. It has thus, as Jean Prévost pointed out,[1] an involuntary secret rhythm: present alternating with past, impressions with facts, self-critical effort with the free flow of reverie. Stendhal found that the act of writing stirred up memories: he kept 'making great discoveries' as he wrote. 'These discoveries are like great fragments of fresco on a wall which, long forgotten, reappear suddenly ...' Such memories emerged as pictures, strongly tinged with emotion: 'I cannot give facts, I can only show the shadow of them ... I see pictures, I remember their effects on my heart, but the causes and the shape of these things are a blank.' Only later reflection could indicate these; and he scrupulously avoided attributing to the child the perceptions of the adult. 'Now in 1835 I discover the shape and cause of past events.' And the scrawled diagrams and sketches in the manuscript are an integral part of it: they were an aid towards total recall. They are not only 'the touchstone and pledge of this untiring quest for veracity', as V. del Litto describes them;[2] they bear witness, indeed, to the truth of memory, but they also help to stimulate and strengthen it. The fugitive recollection is pinned down by the sketch; the surrounding circumstances are arduously, uncertainly, scrutinized. Except in the last chapters of the book Stendhal made no attempt to tell a coherent story: incidents were set down as they occurred to him,

1. *La Création chez Stendhal*, op. cit.
2. V. del Litto, *Le Vie de Stendhal*, Paris, Albin Michel, 1965.

scenes and characters, faces and conversations, experience and emotion surfaced and took shape with varying degrees of distinctness. Of particular interest are the very early memories cited in Chapter 3; here the shock of the incomprehensible dressing-down that followed a childish offence must have contributed to the sharpness of the recollection.[1]

The concrete vividness with which the impressions of childhood are recorded gives the book its special flavour of authenticity. He noted remembered figures – the refugee priest, 'a big man whose eyes goggled as he ate pickled pork', the fifteen-year-old girl 'who looked rather like a white rabbit with her round red eyes'; and sensations – the 'marigold- or boxroot-yellow cover' of his mother's copy of Ovid, in which this future adept of metamorphosis read, entranced, about Daphne turning into a laurel; the odd noise of the spoon scraping against the silver bowl from which he ate his bread-and-milk, or 'the whining sound, long-drawn-out but not harsh', made by the iron pump-handle in the square, 'which gave me great pleasure'; the smell of musk in grandfather Gagnon's bookcase, where young Henri hunted out erotic novels, and the reek of Provençal cooking from the grocer's next door. Even more vividly he conveys the intense feelings with which he reacted to experience: the excitement of a visit to the theatre with his uncle to see *Le Cid* 'acted in costumes of sky-blue satin with white satin shoes'; delight in music, in landscape (which 'acted on my soul like a fiddle-bow'), passionate resentment of injustice, rebellion, rage, desolation or grief. There is surely nothing to surpass in poignancy the account of the death of 'poor Lambert' in Chapter 14, set down with a brevity that is more expressive than eloquence. As for his moments of pure happiness, now as ever he chose reticence, for fear of 'deflowering' them.

The Text

THE manuscript of *Henry Brulard*, hurriedly scribbled, illustrated with sketches and diagrams jotted down to help his recollection, and further annotated by his devoted friend and cousin Romain Colomb, lay forgotten in the municipal library at

1. cf. Esther Salaman, *A Collection of Moments*, London.

Grenoble until 1890, when Casimir Stryienski partially de-ciphered it and published the first, and faulty, edition. The present translation follows the authoritative edition of Henri Martineau published in the *Classiques Garnier* (1953, Paris: Garnier), and has been prepared as a faithful rendering of the original manuscript, including Stendhal's own marginalia, anno-tations and sketches, for the English reader.

For Henri Martineau's copious biographical and explanatory notes and for Colomb's marginalia the student is referred to: the *Garnier* edition (above); the *Pléiade* edition (Stendhal, *Oeuvres Intimes*, Paris, Gallimard, 1955); Martineau's edition of 1949 (2 vols., Paris, Le Divan, 1949) and his *Petit Dictionnaire Stendhal-ien* (Paris, Le Divan, 1948).

We have followed Henri Martineau in including within square brackets the parts of words abbreviated by Stendhal for convenience or caution. Where Stendhal has used an English word or phrase this is shown in SMALL CAPITALS. We have reproduced Stendhal's italics, and respected his variant spellings of proper names, etc.

J. S. and B. C. J. G. K.

Suggestions for Further Reading

Adams, R. N., *Stendhal: Notes on a Novelist*, Merlin Press, 1959.

Green, F. C., *Stendhal*, Cambridge University Press, 1939.

Hemmings, F. W. J., *Stendhal: Aspects of His Novels*, Oxford University Press, 1964.

Levin, Harry, *The Gates of Horn*, Oxford University Press, Section 3, 1963.

del Litto, V., *La Vie de Stendhal*, Paris, Albin Michel, 1965.

Martineau, H., *L'Oeuvre de Stendhal*, Paris, Albin Michel, 1951.

Le Coeur de Stendhal (2 vols), Paris, Albin Michel, 1952.

Petit Dictionnaire Stendhalien, Paris, Le Divan, 1948 (for biographical details of those persons mentioned in *The Life of Henry Brulard*).

Stendhal, *To the Happy Few; Selected Letters of Stendhal*, translated by Norman Cameron, London, John Lehmann, 1952; New York, Evergreen editions, 1955.

The Private Diaries of Stendhal, edited and translated by Robert Sage, Gollancz, 1955.

The Charterhouse of Parma, translated with an introduction by Margaret R. B. Shaw, Penguin Classics, 1958.

Scarlet and Black, translated with an introduction by Margaret R. B. Shaw, Penguin Classics, 1953.

Love, translated by Gilbert and Suzanne Sale, introduction by Jean Stewart and B. C. J. G. Knight, Penguin Classics.

Tillet, Margaret, *Stendhal: the Background to the Novels*, Oxford University Press, 1971.

CHAPTER I

I wAs standing this morning, 16 October 1832, by San Pietro in Montorio, on the Janiculum Hill in Rome, in magnificent sunshine. A few small white clouds, borne on a barely perceptible sirocco wind, were floating above Monte Albano, a delicious warmth filled the air and I was happy to be alive. I could clearly see Frascati and Castel Gandolfo four leagues away, and the Villa Aldobrandini where Domenichino's sublime fresco of Judith is. I can distinctly see the white wall that marks the latest restorations made by Prince F[rancesco] Borghese, the same whom I saw, colonel of a regiment of cuirassiers, at Wagram, on the day when my friend M. de la Noue had his leg blown off. A good deal farther away I see the rock of Palestrina and the white building of Castel San Pietro which was once its fortress. Below the wall against which I am leaning are the big orange trees of the Capuchins' orchard, then the Tiber and the Maltese priory, a little beyond them on the right the tomb of Cecilia Metella, San Paolo and the Pyramid of Cestius. Opposite me I see Santa Maria Maggiore and the long lines of the Palazzo di Monte Cavallo. The whole of ancient and modern Rome, from the ancient Appian Way with its ruined tombs and aqueducts to the magnificent garden of the Pincio built by the French, lies spread before me.

There is no place like this in the world, I mused, and against my will ancient Rome prevailed over modern Rome; memories of Livy crowded into my mind. On Monte Albano, to the left of the convent, I could see the fields of Hannibal.

What a magnificent view! Here it was that Raphael's *Transfiguration* was admired for two hundred and fifty years! What a contrast with the gloomy grey marble gallery where it is buried now, in the depths of the Vatican! And so, for two hundred and fifty years, that masterpiece was here, two hundred and fifty years! ... Ah! in three months I shall be fifty; can that really be so? 1783, '93, 1803 – I'm reckoning on my fingers

– and 1833 makes fifty. Is it really possible? Fifty! I shall soon be fifty; and I sang Grétry's song:

Quand on a la cinquantaine ...

This unexpected discovery did not vex me; I had been thinking about Hannibal and the Romans. Why, greater men than I have died! ... After all, I said to myself, I haven't spent my life too badly ... *spent* it? Oh, that's to say, chance has not inflicted too many misfortunes on me, for have I, in fact, had any control at all over my life?

To go and fall in love with Mlle de Griesheim; what could I hope from a young lady of noble birth, the daughter of a general who was in favour two months earlier, before the battle of Jena? Brichard was quite right when he said to me with his usual malice: 'When you're in love with a woman, you must ask yourself: What do I want to do with her?'

I sat on the steps of San Pietro and there I pondered for an hour or two over this thought: I shall soon be fifty, it's high time I got to know myself. I should really find it very hard to say what I have been and what I am.

I'm supposed to be a very witty heartless man, even a rake, and in fact I see that I've been continually involved in unhappy love affairs. I was desperately in love with Mme Kubly, Mlle de Griesheim, Mme de Diphortz, Métilde; and I never possessed any of them, and several of these love affairs lasted three or four years. Métilde filled my life completely from 1818 to 1824. And I'm not cured yet, I added, after being lost in reverie about her alone for a full quarter of an hour. Did she love me?

My feelings were tender, not ecstatic. And Menti, how profoundly wretched she made me when she left me! At this point I shuddered, remembering 15 September 1826, when I came back from England. What a year did I spend between 15 September 1826 and 15 September 1827! On the day of that dreadful anniversary, I was on the isle of Ischia. And now I noticed a definite improvement; instead of thinking of my misfortune directly, as I had a few months ago, I now thought only of the *memory* of the state of misery in which I was immersed in October 1826, for instance. This observation comforted me considerably.

What sort of man have I been? I could not say. From what

friend, however enlightened, can I hope for an answer? M. di Fiori himself could give me no opinion. To what friend have I ever said a word about my unhappiness in love?

And the strange and distressing thing about it, I said to myself this morning, is that my *victories* (as I called them then, my head being full of military matters) never gave me a pleasure even half as intense as the deep unhappiness I suffered in my defeats.

My astonishing victory over Menti did not give me a pleasure one hundredth part as intense as the pain she gave me when she left me for M. de Rospiec.

Was I, then, of a melancholy character? ... And then, as I did not know what to answer, I began unconsciously to admire once again the sublime sight of the ruins of Rome and its modern greatness: the Coliseum opposite me, beneath my feet the Palazzo Farnese with its fine arcaded gallery by Carlo Maderna, and the Palazzo Corsini.

Have I been a wit? Have I had any sort of talent? M. Daru used to say that I was an utter ignoramus; yes, but it was Besançon who told me that, and that morose fellow, formerly secretary-general, was very jealous of my lively character. But have I had a lively character?

I finally came down from the Janiculum only when the light evening mist warned me that I should soon be overtaken by that sudden most unhealthy and unpleasant chill which, in this region, follows immediately after sunset. I hurried back to the Palazzo Conti (Piazza Minerva), quite exhausted. I was wearing trousers made of white English stuff; I wrote inside the waist-band: '16 October 1832, I am going to be fifty', thus abbreviated so as not to be understood: *Imgo ingt obe5.*

In the evening when I came home, somewhat bored by the ambassador's party, I said to myself: I ought to write my life, perhaps I shall at last know, when it's finished, in two or three years' time, what sort of man I have been, gay or gloomy, wit or fool, brave man or coward, and, all things considered, happy or unhappy. I could get di Fiori to read my manuscript.

I liked this idea. Yes, but what an appalling quantity of *I*'s and *me*'s! enough to put the kindest reader out of humour. *I* and *me*; except from the point of view of talent it would be like M. de Chateaubriand, that king of egotists:

De je *mis avec* moi *tu fais la récidive . . .*[1]

I say that line to myself every time I read one of his pages.

One could, of course, write using the third person: he said, he did. But then how could one describe one's hidden emotions? That's the point, particularly, on which I should like to consult di Fiori.

I have only begun writing again on 23 November 1835. The same idea of writing MY LIFE occurred to me lately during my journey to Ravenna; to tell the truth I have often thought of doing so since 1832, but I have always been discouraged by the appalling difficulty of all those *I*'s and *me*'s, which will make people take a dislike to the author. I did not feel I had enough talent to get round this. To tell the truth, I'm quite uncertain whether I have enough talent to get myself read. I sometimes very much enjoy writing, that's all.[2]

---

1. At it again, with your I's and me's! (*Trans.*)
2. Instead of so much babble, perhaps this will do: Brulard [first version: Beyl(e)] (Marie Henry), born at Grenoble in 1786, of a good bourgeois family with pretensions to nobility, the proudest possible aristocrats nine years later, in 1792. B. was witness early in life to the meanness and hypocrisy of certain people, hence his instinctive hatred for religion.

His childhood was happy until the death of his mother, whom he lost when seven years old, after which the pr[iests] made it hell for him.

As a way of escape he studied mathematics with passion and in 1797 or '98 carried off the first prize, while five pupils who entered the École Polytechnique a month later only got second prizes. He arrived in Paris the day after the 18th Brumaire (9 Nov[ember] 1799) but took care not to present himself at the examination for the École Polytechnique. He left with the Reserve Army in an amateur capacity and crossed the St Bernard Pass two days after the first Consul. When he arrived in Milan, M. Daru his cousin, then Inspector of Army Reviews, got him into the army as *maréchal de logis* and soon after this as sub-lieutenant in the 6th Company of Dragoons, of which M. Le Baron his friend was colonel. In his regiment B., who had 150 francs pension monthly and considered himself rich, being seventeen years old, was envied and not too well received; nevertheless he obtained a fine certificate from the Administrative Council.

A year later he became aide-de-camp of the worthy Lieut.-General Michaud, took part in the Mincio campaign against General Bellegarde, correctly assessed the stupidity of General Brune, and had delightful stays in the garrisons at Brescia and Bergamo. He was obliged to leave General Michaud, for one had to be a lieutenant at least to fulfil the functions of an aide-de-camp, and he rejoined the 6th Company of Dragoons at Alba and

If there be another world, I shall not fail to go and see Montesquieu. If he says to me: 'My poor friend, you never had any talent at all,' I should be sorry but not in the least surprised. I often feel it to be so; who can see himself? It's less than three years since I discovered the reason why.

I can see clearly that many writers who enjoy great renown are detestable. What it would be blasphemous, today, to say of M. de Chateaubriand (a sort of Balzac[1]) will be a TRUISM in 1880. I have never changed my mind about that Balzac; the *Génie du Ch[ristianisme]* seemed to me ridiculous when it first appeared about 1803. Crozet was taken in on Mont-Cenis, with M. Derrien. But does awareness of another's faults constitute talent? I notice that the worst painters see one another's faults quite clearly: M. Ingres is absolutely right about M. Gros, and M. Gros about M. Ingres. (I choose those who may still be talked about in 1935.)

This was the argument which reassured me about these memoirs. Suppose I go on with this manuscript and, once written, don't burn it; I'll leave it, not to a friend who might turn pious or sell himself like that humbug Thomas Moore, to an interested party, I'll leave it to a bookseller, for instance to M. Levavasseur (Place Vendôme, Paris).

Well then, after my death this bookseller receives a fat bound volume full of this horrible writing. He'll have to get some of it copied out and then read it; if the thing seems boring to him, if people have quite stopped talking about M. de Stendhal, he'll put the bundle of papers aside and perhaps they may be redis-

---

Savigliano, Piedmont; had an almost fatal illness at Saluces: fourteen times bled with leeches; ridiculous adventure with a great lady.

Bored by his narrow-minded comrades, B. came to Gr[enoble], fell in love with Mlle Victorine M[ounier]; taking advantage of the 'Little Peace' treaty, offered his resignation and went to Paris, where he spent two years in solitude, thinking he was doing nothing but amusing himself by reading *Les Lettres Persanes*, Montaigne, Cabanis, Tracy, while in fact he was completing his education.

First version: I have always and as it were by instinct profoundly despised the bourgeois as they were in 1811, and I think that this limitless contempt has since been perfectly justified by what they have done in the Chamber of Deputies in 1831 and after.

1. J.-L. Guez de Balzac, 1597–1654. (*Trans.*).

covered two hundred years later, like the memoirs of Benvenuto Cellini.

If he prints the thing and it proves boring, people will speak of it thirty years after much as they speak today about the poem *La Navigation* by Esménard, that spy who was so often mentioned at M. Daru's lunches in 1802. And in any case that spy was, if I'm not mistaken, censor or director of all the newspapers which puffed him excessively every week. He was the Salvandy of those days, and even more impudent, if that's possible, but with many more ideas.

So my confessions will have ceased to exist thirty years after being printed if the *I*'s and *me*'s prove too boring for their readers; nevertheless I shall have had the pleasure of writing them and of searching my conscience thoroughly. Moreover, if they should succeed, I've a chance of being read in 1900 by the kind of people I love, the Mme Rolands, the Mélanie Guilberts, the . . .

For instance, today, 24 November 1835, I've just come from the Sistine Chapel, where I got no pleasure at all although I was provided with a good opera-glass for looking at the ceiling and Michelangelo's *Last Judgement*; but I was suffering from neuralgia, due to drinking too much coffee the day before yesterday at the Caetanis', for which a machine brought from London by Michel A[ngelo Caetani] was to blame. The over-perfection of this machine, the over-excellence of the coffee – a bill of exchange drawn on future happiness for the benefit of the present moment – brought back my old neuralgia, and I visited the Sistine Chapel like a sheep, *id est* without pleasure; my imagination never took flight. I admired the gold brocade drapery painted *in fresco* beside the throne, that is to say the Pope's great walnut armchair. This drapery is inscribed with the name of Pope Sixtus IV (Sixtus IIII, Papa), you think you can touch it with your hand; it's two feet away from your eyes and it still creates an illusion, after 354 years.

Feeling fit for nothing, not even for my job of writing official letters, I have had a fire lighted and I am writing this, I hope without lying, without deceiving myself, with as much pleasure as if I were writing a letter to a friend. What ideas will this friend have in 1880? how different from our own! Today, these two ideas: *the most rascally of* KINGS *and hypocritical Tartar* applied to a pair whose names I dare not write, would seem to three-quarters of my acquaintances to be monstrously rash, outrageous; in 1880 these opinions will be TRUISMS which even the Kératrys of the day won't have the face to repeat. This is something new for me: to be talking to people about whose turn of mind, education, prejudices and religion one is wholly ignorant! What an encouragement to speak the *truth*, and nothing but the *truth*; that's the only thing that matters. Benvenuto spoke the *truth* and one follows his life with pleasure, as if it had been written yesterday, whereas one skips the pages of that Jesuit Marmontel, although he took every possible precaution not to offend, like a real Academician. I refused to buy his memoirs at Leghorn, at twenty sous a volume, although I adore that kind of book.

But what infinite precautions one has to take not to lie!

For instance at the beginning of the first chapter there is something that may look like boasting; no, reader, I was not a soldier at the battle of Wagram in 1809.

You must realize that forty-five years before your time it was fashionable to have served under Napoleon. And so today, in 1835, it's quite a respectable lie to imply indirectly, without a positive lie (*jesuitico more*), that one fought at Wagram.

In actual fact, I was a sergeant and then sub-lieutenant in the 6th Dragoons when that regiment went into Italy, in May 1800 I think, and I surrendered my commission at the time of the 'Little Peace' of 1803. I was exceedingly bored by my companions and could think of nothing more delightful than to live in Paris, *en philosophe*, that was how I described it to myself, on the 150 francs a month my father gave me. I assumed that after his death I should have twice or four times as much; consumed as I was by a zeal for learning, it seemed far too much. I never became a colonel, as I might have done through the powerful protection of M. le Comte Daru, my cousin, but I think I have been far happier. I soon forgot all about studying and imitating M. de Turenne, which had been my fixed aim during the three years I was a dragoon. It had sometimes conflicted with this other idea: to write comedies like Molière and live with an actress. I already felt a mortal disgust for respectable women and the hypocrisy which seems to be indispensable to them. My monstrous laziness prevailed; once in Paris I spent six whole months at a time without visiting my relations (MM. Daru, Mme le Brun, M. and Mme de Baure). I kept saying to myself, *tomorrow*. I spent two years thus, up on a fifth floor in the rue d'Angivilliers with a fine view over the Louvre colonnade, reading La Bruyère, Montaigne and J.-J. Rousseau whose inflated style soon disgusted me. There my character was formed. I also read a good many of Alfieri's tragedies, trying to get pleasure out of them; I venerated Cabanis, Tracy and J.-B. Say; I often read Cabanis, whose vague style depressed me. I lived alone, as crazy as a Spaniard, a thousand leagues from real life. Worthy Father Jeki, an Irishman, gave me English lessons, but I made no progress. I was made about *Hamlet*.

But I'm letting myself get carried away, I'm wandering from the point, I shall be unintelligible unless I keep to the order of events, and besides, I shouldn't remember the circumstances so well.

So then, at Wagram in 1809 I was not a soldier, but on the contrary attached to the War Commissariat, a post in which my cousin M. Daru had put me, to 'rescue me from vice' as my family described it. For my solitude in the rue d'Angivilliers had ended with a year spent in Marseilles living with a charming actress who had the loftiest feelings and to whom I never gave a penny, primarily for the very good reason that my father still gave me only 150 francs a month on which to live, and this allowance was paid me very irregularly in Marseilles in 1805.

But I'm rambling again. In October 1806, after Jena, I was attached to the War Commissariat, a position despised by soldiers; in 1810, on 3 August, appointed auditeur to the Council of State, and Inspector-General of Crown Property a few days after that. I was in favour, not with the master himself, Nap[oleon] did not speak to madmen of my sort, but I was well thought of by that best of men, M. le Duc de Frioul (Duroc). But I'm rambling.

CHAPTER 2

I FELL when Napoleon did in April 1814. I came to Italy, to
lead the same sort of life as in the rue d'Angivilliers. In 1821 I
left Milan, with despair in my heart because of Métilde, and
seriously thinking of blowing out my brains. At first everything
bored me in Paris; later, I wrote to distract myself; Métilde died,
so it was useless to go back to Milan. I had become perfectly
happy, that's saying too much, but really quite passably happy
in 1830 when I wrote *Le Rouge et le Noir*.

I was overjoyed by the July days; I watched the firing from
under the pillars of the Théâtre-Français, with very little danger
to myself; I shall never forget that glorious sunshine, and the
first sight of the tricolour flag, on the 29th or 30th at about
eight o'clock, after spending the night with Commendatore Pinto,
whose niece was frightened. On 25 September I was appointed
Consul at Trieste by M. Molé, whom I had never seen. From
Trieste I came in 1831 to Civita-Vecchia and to Rome, where I
still am and where I am bored for lack of being able to exchange
ideas. I need now and then to talk, in the evening, with intelligent people, failing which I feel almost suffocated.

Here, then, are the broad divisions of my story: born in 1783,
dragoon in 1800, student from 1803 to 1806. In 1806 attached to
the War Commissariat, Intendant in Brunswick. In 1809 I was
helping the wounded at Essler or at Wagram, fulfilling missions
along the snow-covered banks of the Danube, at Linz and
Passau, in love with Mme la Comtesse Petit, asking to be sent
to Spain in order to see her again. On 3 August 1810, appointed
auditeur to the Council of State, more or less thanks to her. This
life of high favour and expense took me to Moscow, made me
Intendant at Sagan in Silesia, and led at last to my downfall in
April 1815. Personally, believe it or not, I was glad of this
downfall.

After my downfall, I turned student and writer, fell madly in
love, got my *History of Italian Painting* printed in 1817; my
father, who had become an ultra, ruined himself and died, I

think, in 1819; I go back to Paris in June 1821. I am in despair because of Métilde, she dies; I'd rather she were dead than unfaithful, I write; this comforts me, I am happy. In September 1830 I returned to the administrative rut in which I still am, thinking regretfully of my life as a writer on the third floor of the Hôtel de Valois, No. 71 rue de Richelieu.

I have been a wit since the winter of 1826; before that I had kept silent out of laziness. I believe I'm supposed to be the gayest and most unfeeling of men, and it is true that I have never said a word about the women I was in love with. In this respect I've shown all the symptoms of the melancholy temperament as described by Cabanis. I have never had much success.

But the other day, musing about life, on the lonely path overlooking the Lake of Albano, I discovered that my life could be summed up by the following names, the initials of which I wrote in the dust, like Zadig, with my walking-stick, sitting on the little bench behind the Stations of the Cross of the *Minori Osservanti* built by the brother of Urban VIII, Barberini, near those two fine trees enclosed by a little circular wall :

> Virginie (Kubly),
> Angela (Pietragrua),
> Adèle (Rebuffel),
> Mélanie (Guilbert),
> Mina (de Griesheim),
> Alexandrine (Petit),
> Angeline, whom I never loved (Bereyter),
> Angela (Pietragrua),
> Métilde (Dembowski),
> Clémentine,
> Giulia.

And finally, for a month at most, Mme Azur whose Christian name I have forgotten. And yesterday, rashly, Amalia (B[ettini]).

Most of these charming creatures never honoured me with their favours; but they literally took up my whole life. After them came my writings. Really, I have never been ambitious, but in 1811 I thought myself ambitious.

The usual condition of my life has been that of an unhappy

lover, fond of music and painting, that's to say, of enjoying the products of those arts, not of practising them unskilfully. I have sought out fine landscapes, with an exquisite sensitivity; I have travelled for that reason alone. Landscapes played on my soul like a *fiddle bow*; views that nobody else praised (the line of rocks near Arbois, as you come from Dôle by the main road, I think, was for me a tangible and manifest symbol of Métilde's soul). I see that I have loved reverie above all things, even above enjoying the reputation of a wit. I only troubled to acquire this, only made it my business to improvise in conversation for the

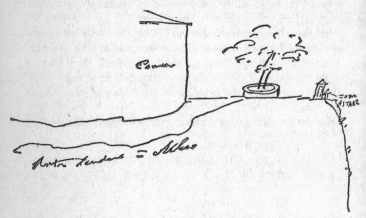

[*Monastery – Road leading towards Albano – Zadig. Astarte – Lake of Albano.*]

benefit of the company I happened to be in, in 1826, on account of the despair in which I spent the first months of that fatal year.

I learned lately, through reading it in a book (the letters of Victor Jacquemont, the Indian) that somebody had actually thought me brilliant. A few years ago I had seen more or less the same thing in a book which was then fashionable, by Lady Morgan. I had forgotten that fine quality, which has earned me so many enemies. Perhaps I had only the semblance of that quality; and my enemies are creatures too common to be judges of brilliancy; for instance how can a man like Count d'Argout be a judge of brilliancy? a man whose delight is to read daily two or three duodecimo volumes of novels fit for chambermaids! How could M. de Lamartine be a judge of wit? For one thing he hasn't any himself and, for another, he also devours two volumes of the dullest works daily. (I noticed this at Florence, in 1824 or 1826.)

The great DRAWBACK of being witty is that you have to keep your eyes fixed on the semi-fools around you, and *steep yourself in their commonplace way of feeling*. I make the mistake of attaching myself to the one who is least deficient in imagination and of becoming unintelligible to the rest, who are perhaps all the more pleased because of this.

Since I have been in Rome, I haven't been witty more than once a week and then for only five minutes at a time; I prefer reverie. The people here don't understand the subtlety of the French language enough to feel the subtlety of my remarks; they need coarse commercial travellers' wit, they are delighted with Mélodrame for instance (e.g. Michelangelo Caetani), and he is meat and drink to them. It appals me to see such a man being successful, I no longer deign to talk to people who have applauded Mélodrame. I see all the emptiness of vanity.

So two months ago, in September 1835, when I was thinking about writing these memoirs, on the bank of the Lake of Albano (at two hundred feet above the level of the lake) I wrote these initials in the dust, like Zadig:

[V. An. Ad. M. Mi. A1. Ame. Apg. Mde. C.G. Aur. (Mme Azur whose Christian name I have forgotten).]

I was in a deep reverie about these names and the astonishing stupidities and follies they made me commit (I mean astonishing to me, not to the reader; in any case I've no remorse for them).

In actual fact I possessed only six of these women whom I loved.

31

My greatest passion was either for Mélanie 2, Alexandrine, Métilde or Clémentine 4.

Clémentine was the one who caused me the greatest unhappiness when she left me. But was this unhappiness comparable with that Métilde gave me by refusing to say whether or not she loved me?

With all of these and with several others I was always a mere child; and I had scant success. But on the other hand I was deeply and passionately preoccupied with them and I still delight in the memories they have left me (some after twenty-four years, such as the memory of the Madonna del Monte at Varese in 1811). I was never enough of a ladies' man, I was concerned only with the woman I loved, and when I was not in love I was musing over the spectacle of human affairs, or delightedly reading Montesquieu or Walter Scott.

So then, as children say, I am so far from being blasé about their wiles and graces that at my age, fifty-two, at the moment of writing this, I am still spellbound by a long *chiacchierata* that Amalia had with me last night at the Valle Theatre.

In order to consider them as philosophically as possible, and to endeavour thus to strip them of the halo that disturbs my eyes, dazzles me and prevents me from seeing clearly, I shall arrange these ladies in order (to speak like a mathematician) according to their various qualities. Thus I will say, to begin with their customary passion, vanity, that two of them were countesses and one a baroness.

The richest was Alexandrine Petit, her husband and particularly she herself spent no less than 80,000 francs a year. The poorest was Mina de Griesheim, younger daughter of an impecunious general, former favourite of a ruined prince, who kept his family on his salary; or else Mlle Bereyter, actress at the Opera-Buffa.

I am trying to destroy the spell, the DAZZLING character of events, by thus considering them in military fashion. This is the only way I can hope to reach the truth about a subject which I cannot discuss with anyone. Through the diffidence of my melancholy temperament (Cabanis) I have always been incredibly, absurdly discreet in that respect. Clémentine surpassed them all as regards wit; Métilde excelled through the Spanish nobility of her feelings; Giulia, I should say, through strength of character, although on a first impression she seemed the weakest; Angela P[ietragrua] was a sublime courtesan in the Italian style, à la Lucrezia Borgia, and Mme Azur a far from sublime courtesan à la Du Barry.

I was only twice bothered about money, at the end of 1805 and again in 1806 till the month of August, because my father stopped sending me any money and that without warning me; that was the trouble. He once went five months without paying my allowance of 150 francs. Then the Vicomte and I were in great straits; his allowance was paid regularly but he always gambled all of it away the very day he received it.

In 1829 and 1830 I was in difficulties through imprudence and thoughtlessness rather than through actual lack of means, since between 1821 and 1830 I made three or four journeys to Italy, to England and to Barcelona, and at the end of that period I was only in debt for 400 francs.

My most serious lack of money drove me to the unpleasant necessity of borrowing 100 or sometimes 200 francs from M. Besançon. I paid it back after a month or two; and finally in September 1830 I owed 400 francs to my tailor Michel. Those who are familiar with the way of life of the young men of my day will consider this very moderate. From 1800 to 1830 I never owed a penny to my tailor Léger or his successor Michel (22 rue Vivienne).

My friends of those days, 1830, MM. de Mareste and Colomb, were a queer sort of friends; they would no doubt have bestirred themselves to rescue me from any great danger, but when I went out in a new coat they would have given twenty francs, the former particularly, to have had a glass of dirty water thrown at me. (Except the Vicomte de Barral and Bigillion [de Saint-Ismier] I never had any other kind of friend throughout my life.)

They were worthy people, very prudent, who had collected 12,000 to 15,000 francs salary or income through assiduous work or skill, and who could not endure to see me light-hearted and careless, happy with a blank notebook and a pen, living on not more than 4,000 or 5,000 francs a year. They would have loved me a hundred times better if they had seen me depressed and unhappy at having only half or a third of their income, whereas formerly I had somewhat shocked them when I had a coachman, two horses, a barouche and a gig, for my luxury had risen to these heights under the Emperor. In those days I had been, or had thought myself, ambitious, and what thwarted me in that respect was that I did not know what to long for. I was ashamed of being in love with the Comtesse A[lexandrine] Petit, I had as my kept mistress Mlle A. Bereyter, actress at the Opera-Buffa, I used to lunch at the Café Hardy, I was always incredibly busy. I would come back from Saint-Cloud to Paris on purpose to see one act of the *Matrimonio Segreto* at the Odéon. (Mme Barilli, Barilli, Tachinardi, Mme Festa, Mlle Bereyter.) My gig would be waiting for me at the door of the Café Hardy, for which my brother-in-law never forgave me.

All this might seem like foppishness, and yet it was no such thing. I wanted to enjoy things and to do things, but not to make a show of more enjoyment or activity than there really was. M. Prunelle, the doctor, a wit, whose good sense delighted me, a horribly ugly man who subsequently became famous as a bribed deputy and Mayor of Lyons about 1833, and who was an acquaintance of mine in those days, said of me: 'He's a rare fop.' This verdict was repeated amongst my acquaintance. They may have been right, for that matter.

My worthy brother-in-law, a regular bourgeois, M. Périer-Lagrange (a former tradesman who was ruining himself un-awares by farming in the neighbourhood of La Tour-du-Pin), lunching with me at the Café Hardy and seeing me give sharp orders to the waiters, for with all my duties to fulfil I was often in a hurry, was delighted to hear these waiters make some joke amongst themselves implying that I was a fop, which I did not in the least resent. I have always, as it were by some instinct (amply confirmed, since then, by the Chambers), profoundly despised the bourgeois.

Nevertheless I discerned, too, that only amongst the bour-geois were to be found men of energy such as my cousin Rebuffel (tradesman in the rue Saint-Denis), Father Ducros, the librarian of the town of Grenoble, the incomparable Gros (of the rue Saint-Laurent), a geometrician of the first rank and my teacher unbeknown to my male relatives, since he was a Jacobin and all my family were bigoted ultras. These three men have enjoyed all my esteem and all my love, in so far as respect and the differ-ence in our ages allowed the sort of intercourse that constitutes affection. Indeed with them I behaved as I did later with people I loved too much; I was speechless, motionless, stupid and un-gracious, sometimes giving offence through excess of devotion and lack of *self*. My self-respect, my self-interest, my very per-sonality vanished in the loved one's presence, I became trans-formed into the other person. And supposing that other was a hussy like Mme Pietragrua? But I keep anticipating. Shall I have the courage to write these confessions intelligibly? I ought to be telling a story, and I'm writing my *reflections* on certain small-scale incidents which, precisely because of their minute-ness, need to be related with extreme distinctness. How patient you will need to be, O my reader!

So then, according to me, *energy* was only to be found, in my opinion (in 1811), in that class which has to struggle with real needs.

My aristocratic friends, MM. Raymond de Bérenger (killed at Lutzen), de Saint-Ferréol, de Sinard (a pious youth who died early), Gabriel du Bouchage (a kind of swindler or unscrupulous borrower, nowadays Peer of France and a glib ex-ultra), MM. de Monval, always seemed to me to have a fear-ful respect for *convention* which struck me as very odd (Sinard, for instance). They invariably tried to be *in good taste* or *comme il faut*, as people said in Grenoble in 1793. But I was far from seeing this notion clearly. It's less than a year since I finally completed my ideas about the aristocracy. Instinctively my men-tal life has been spent in close reflection on five or six main ideas and in trying to see the truth about them.

Raymond de Bérenger was an excellent fellow and a perfect example of the maxim *noblesse oblige*, whereas Monval (who died a colonel, and generally despised, in Grenoble about 1829) was the ideal of a Deputy of the Centre. All this was quite clearly discernible when these gentlemen were fifteen – about 1798.

I only clearly see the truth about most of these things now that I'm writing them down, in 1835, to such an extent have they been surrounded until now by the glamour of youth, resulting from the extreme vividness of my sensations.

By dint of making use of the methods of philosophy, for instance by classifying the friends of my youth in their *kinds*, as M. Adrien de Jussieu does his plants (in botany), I endeavour to reach that truth which eludes me. I realize that what I took for lofty mountains in 1800 were mostly mere *molehills*; but this is a discovery which I only made very late.

I can see that I was like a skittish horse, and I owe this discovery to a remark made to me by M. de Tracy (the illustrious Count Destutt de Tracy, Peer of France, member of the French Academy and, what is worth far more, author of the Law of 3rd Prairial about the Central Schools).

I must give an example. The slightest thing, for instance a door ajar at night, would make me imagine that two armed men were lying in wait to prevent my reaching a window opening on to a gallery where I could see my mistress. A wise man like my friend Abraham Constantin would never have had such an illusion. But after a few seconds, at most four or five, my life was well and truly sacrificed, and I rushed hero-like against the two enemies, who then turned into a half-open door.

Less than two months ago something of the same sort happened to me again, this time in the realm of feelings. The sacrifice had been made and all the necessary courage assembled, when twenty hours later I noticed, on re-reading a letter I had misread (from M. Hérard), that it was an illusion. I always read very quickly things that distress me.

So then, classifying my life like a collection of plants, this is what I find:

Childhood and early education, from 1786 to 1800	15 years
Military service, 1800 to 1803 . . .	3 "
Second education, ridiculous love affair with Mlle Adèle Clozel and with her mother, who took possession of her daughter's lover. Life in the rue d'Angivilliers. To end with, a happy stay in Marseilles with Mélanie, from 1803 to 1805 .	2 "
Return to Paris, end of my education . .	1 year
Service under Napoleon, from 1806 to the end of 1814 (from October 1806 to the abdication in 1814)	7½ years

April, my adhesion, in the same number of the
Monitor which included the abdication of Napoleon. Travel, serious and terrible love affairs,
consolation through writing books, from 1814 to
to 1830 . . . . . . 15½ „

Second period of service, Consul from September 1830 to the present moment . . . 5 „

I made my début in the world through the salon of Mme de
Valserre, a pious woman with a queer chinless face, daughter
of the Baron des Adrets and a friend of my mother's. This was
probably about 1794. I had the fiery temperament and the
timidity described by Cabanis. I was extremely moved by the
lovely arms of Mlle Bonne de Saint-Vallier, I think it was she;
I can see her face and her fine arms but the name is uncertain;
it may have been Mlle de Lavalette. M. de Saint-Ferréol, of
whom I have never since heard, was my enemy and my rival;
M. de Sinard, our mutual friend, used to pacify us. All this took
place in a magnificent ground-floor apartment, looking out over
the garden of the Hôtel des Adrets, now destroyed and trans-
formed into a bourgeois dwelling, rue Neuve, at Grenoble. At
the same period began my passionate admiration for Father
Ducros (a secularized Franciscan monk, a man of the highest
merit, or so it seems to me). I had as an intimate friend my
grandfather, M. Henri Gagnon, doctor of medicine.

After all these general reflections, I'll proceed to get born.

CHAPTER 3

THE first thing I can remember is biting the cheek or forehead
of my cousin Mme Pison du Galland, wife of that witty fellow
who was a deputy in the Constituent Assembly. I can see her
now, a plump woman of twenty-five wearing a great deal of
rouge; it must have been this rouge that offended me. As she sat
in the middle of the field that was known as the Slope of the
Porte de Bonne, her cheek was exactly at my level.

'Kiss me, Henri,' she said to me. I refused, she got annoyed,

I bit her hard. I can still see the scene, but that's probably be-cause I was immediately given such a dressing-down, and never heard the end of it.

This Slope of the Porte de Bonne was covered with daisies. I used to make a bunch of these pretty little flowers. It was a field in 1786; today it's probably in the middle of the town, to the south of the Collegiate Church.

My aunt Séraphie declared that I was a monster and had an atrocious character. This aunt Séraphie had the sour temper of a pious spinster who had failed to get a husband. What had happened to her? I never discovered, we never know the scan-dalous secrets of our relatives, and I left the town for ever when I was sixteen, after having being passionately in love for three years, which had relegated me to complete solitude.

My second characteristic piece of behaviour was far more sinister.

I had been collecting rushes on the same Slope of the Porte de Bonne (Bonne de Lesdiguières). Find out the botanical name of the rush, a grass of tubular shape like a hen's feather and a foot long. I had been brought back to our house, one window of which on the first floor looked over the Grande Rue at the corner of the Place Grenette. I was making a garden by cutting these rushes into two-inch pieces, which I stuck in the gap between the balcony and the window-sill. The kitchen knife I was using slipped from my hands and fell into the street, four yards below, close to or on to a certain Mme Chénevaz. This lady was the most spiteful woman in the whole town (mother of Candide Chenevaz, who, as a young man, adored Richardson's *Clarissa Harlowe*, and subsequently became one of M. de Villèle's three hundred, was rewarded with the post of *Premier Président* at the Royal Court of Grenoble and died at Lyons *non reçu*).

My aunt Séraphie said that I had tried to kill Mme Chenevaz; I was declared to be possessed of an atrocious character, scolded by my excellent grandfather M. Gagnon, who was afraid of his daughter Séraphie, the most influential of all the pious women in the town, and scolded even by that high-minded Spanish character, my excellent great-aunt Mlle Élisabeth Gagnon.

38

I rebelled; I must have been about four years old. From that time dates my horror of religion, a horror which my reason has had great difficulty in reducing to correct proportions, and that quite recently, less than six years ago. My instinctive filial love for the republic, which in those days was fanatical, began about the same time.

I cannot have been more than five.[1]

This aunt Séraphie was my evil genius during the whole of my childhood; everyone disliked her, yet she had a great deal of influence in the family. I assume that subsequently my father was in love with her, at any rate there were long walks to the *Granaries* in a marsh below the town walls, on which I was an *unwelcome third* and always felt exceedingly bored. I used to hide when it was time to set off on these walks. This killed the small degree of affection that I felt for my father.

In actual fact I was brought up exclusively by my excellent grandfather, M. Henri Gagnon. This exceptional man had been on a pilgrimage to Ferney to see Voltaire and had been received with honour. He had a small bust of Voltaire, no bigger than one's fist, mounted on an ebony stand six inches high. (It was in queer taste, but then, the fine arts were not the strong point of Voltaire nor of my excellent grandfather.)

This bust stood in front of the desk at which he wrote; his study was at the far end of a large apartment opening on a fine terrace full of flowers. It was a rare favour for me to be admitted there, and an even rarer one to examine and to touch the bust of Voltaire.

And for all that, for as far back as I can remember, I have always supremely disliked Voltaire's writings, which have seemed to me puerile. I may say that I have never liked anything by that great man. I could not see then that he was the legislator and apostle of France, her Martin Luther.

M. Henri Gagnon wore a round powdered wig with three rows of curls, because he was a doctor of medicine, and a

1. Monsieur Gagnon bought the house next to Mesdames de Marnais and we moved. I wrote all over the plaster of the iron staples 'Henri Beyle, 1789'. I can still see that beautiful inscription which astonished my good old grandfather. Thus, my attempt on Madame Chenevaz's life dates from before 1798.

fashionable doctor among the ladies; he was even accused of having been the lover of several of them, including a certain Mme Teisseire, one of the prettiest ladies in the town, whom I don't remember ever seeing because they had quarrelled by then, but who gave me this information later on, in a peculiar fashion. My excellent grandfather, because of his wig, always seemed to

me to be eighty years old. He suffered from the vapours (like my wretched self) and from rheumatism, walked with difficulty, but on principle would never use his carriage and never wore his hat, a small three-cornered hat which he tucked under his arm and which delighted me when I could get hold of it and put it on my head, an act which was considered by the whole family to be disrespectful; at last, out of respect, I stopped playing with the three-cornered hat and the little walking-stick with its box-root knob inlaid with tortoise-shell.

My grandfather adored the apocryphal correspondence of Hippocrates, which he read in Latin (although he knew a little Greek), and Horace in Johannès Bond's edition, in horribly tiny print. He imparted to me these two passions and, in fact, almost all his tastes, but not as he would have liked, as I shall explain later.

If ever I go back to Grenoble I must get someone to look up the birth and death certificates of this excellent man, who adored me and who did not love his son M. [Romain] Gagnon, father of M. Oronce Gagnon, squadron-leader in the Dragoons, who killed his man in a duel three years ago, for which I am grateful to him; he's probably no fool. I haven't seen him for thirty-three years; he must be about thirty-five.

I lost my grandfather while I was in Germany; it may have been 1817 or 1813, I cannot recollect exactly. I remember making a journey to Grenoble to see him again. I found him very depressed; this delightful man, who had been the centre of all the *evening parties* he went to, hardly spoke at all. He said to me: 'This is a good-bye visit,' and then talked about other things; he had a horror of foolish family sentimentality.

One recollection recurs to me. In about 1807 I had myself painted in order to persuade Mme Alex[andrine] Petit to have herself painted, too; as the number of sittings was an objection, I took her to a painter opposite the Diorama Fountain who painted portraits in oil in a single sitting for 120 francs. My good grandfather saw the portrait I had sent to my sister, I think to get rid of it; his mind was already much weakened. He said on seeing this portrait: 'That's the real one!' and then relapsed into apathy and depression. He must have died soon after, at the age of eighty-two, I think.

If this date is correct he must have been sixty-one in 1789 and must have been born about 1728. He used sometimes to describe the battle of L'Assiette, an assault in the Alps vainly attempted by the Chevalier de Belle-Isle, I think in 1742. His father, a strong-minded man full of energy and honour, had sent him there as army surgeon to form his character. My grandfather was beginning his medical studies and may have been eighteen or twenty which, again, suggests 1724 as the date of his birth.

He owned an old house situated in the finest position in the town, on the Place Grenette at the corner of the Grande Rue, facing due south and having in front of it the finest square in the town, with the two rival cafés and the focus of fashionable life. There, in a first-floor apartment, very low-ceilinged but wonderfully cheerful, my grandfather lived until 1789.

He must have been rich then since he bought a superb house standing behind his own, and belonging to the de Marnais ladies. He took over the second floor of his own house in the Place Grenette and the whole corresponding floor of the de Marnais house and made himself the finest dwelling in town. He had a staircase which was magnificent for those days and a draw-ing-room which may have measured thirty-five by twenty-eight feet.

Alterations were made to the two rooms of this apartment which overlooked the Place Grenette, and among other things a *gippe* (a wall made of plaster and bricks placed edge to edge) to separate the room of my terrible aunt Séraphie, M. Gagnon's daughter, from that of my great-aunt Élisabeth, his sister. Iron staples were set in this wall and on the plaster round each of these staples I wrote: Henri Beyle 1789. I can still see these lovely inscriptions, which amazed my grandfather.

'Since you can write so well,' he told me, 'you're worthy to begin Latin.'

That word filled me with a sort of terror, and a pedant of horrible appearance, M. Joubert, tall, pale and thin, leaning on a *thorn-stick*, came to instruct me, to teach me *mura*, a mulberry. We went to buy an elementary textbook at M. Giroud's bookshop at the end of a courtyard off the Place aux Herbes. I little suspected then what a pernicious instrument was being bought for me!

At this point my misfortunes began.

But I have too long deferred telling something which must be told, one of the two or three things perhaps which will make me throw these memoirs in the fire.

My mother, Mme Henriette Gagnon, was a charming woman and I was in love with my mother.

I must hurriedly add that I lost her when I was seven.

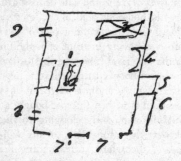

(1) My mattress – (2) Me – (3) Henriette's bed – (4) Fireplace – (5) Dark wardrobe-closet (6) Dressing-room – (7′) Big window overlooking the Rue des Vieux-Jésuites – (7) Small window – (8) Drawing-room door – (9) Way out.

When I loved her at about the age of six, in 1789, I showed exactly the same characteristics as in 1828 when I was madly in love with Alberthe de Rubempré. My way of pursuing happiness was basically unchanged; there was just this difference: I was, as regards the physical side of love, just as Caesar would be, if he came back into the world, as regards the use of cannon and small arms. I would have learned very quickly, and my tactics would have remained basically the same.

I wanted to cover my mother with kisses, and without any clothes on. She loved me passionately and often kissed me; I returned her kisses with such fervour that she was often forced to go away. I abhorred my father when he came to interrupt our kisses. I always wanted to kiss her bosom. Please be kind enough to remember that I lost her in childbed when I was barely seven.

She was plump, with a faultlessly fresh complexion, she was very pretty, and I think just not quite tall enough. Her features expressed nobility and utter serenity; she was very lively, preferring to run about and do things for herself rather than give orders to her three maids, and she was fond of reading Dante's *Divine Comedy* in the original. Long afterwards I found five or six copies in different editions in her room, which had remained shut up since her death.

She died in the flower of her youth and beauty in 1790; she must have been twenty-eight or thirty.

That was when the life of my mind began.

My aunt Séraphie dared to reproach me for not shedding enough tears. You can imagine my grief and what I was feeling! But it seemed to me that I was going to see her next day; I did not understand death.

Thus, forty-five years ago, I lost the being I loved best in the whole world.

She cannot be offended because I am taking the liberty of revealing the love I had for her; if ever I meet her again, I shall tell her about it once more. Besides, she never took any part in this love. She did not behave in the Venetian way like Mme Benzoni with the author of *Nella*. As for me, I was as criminal as possible, I was passionately in love with her charms.

One evening, when for some reason I had been put to bed on the floor of her room on a mattress, she leaped over my mattress, lively and light-footed as a doe, to reach her own bed more quickly.

Her room remained closed for ten years after her death. My

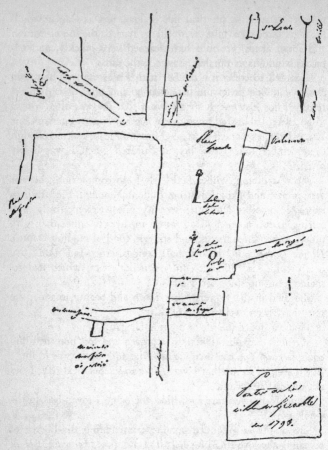

[*Part of the town of Grenoble in 1793 – Rue Lafayette – Rue Vieux-Jésuites – My father's house where I was born – Rue Saint-Jacques – La Propagation (convent) – House over which my father ruined himself – Saint-Louis (church). – South. North – Place Grenette – Incarnate Word (chapel) – Tree of Liberty. Tree of Fraternity – Old pump – Rue Montorge – M. Gagnon's first house. His second house – Grande-Rue.*]

father unwillingly granted me leave to put a blackboard of oilcloth there to study mathematics, in 1798; but no servant ever went in on pain of a severe scolding. I alone had the key. This feeling of my father's does him great honour in my opinion, now that I come to think about it.

She died, then, in her room, rue des Vieux-Jésuites, the fifth or sixth house on the left as you come from the Grande-rue, opposite M. Teisseire's house. That was where I was born; the house belonged to my father, who sold it when he began to

(1) Our house – (2) Grandfather's house – (3) The Marnais' house.

build his new street and to throw away his money. This street that ruined him was called the rue Dauphin (my father was an extreme ultra, a partisan of priests and nobles) and is now, I believe, called rue Lafayette.

I used to spend my life at my grandfather's house, which was barely a hundred yards from ours.

CHAPTER 4

I COULD write a whole volume on the circumstances of the death of so beloved a person.

That is to say: I am wholly ignorant of the details; she died in childbed apparently owing to the clumsiness of a surgeon named *Hérault*, a fool chosen, it seems, out of pique towards another *accoucheur* who was witty and talented; it was under somewhat similar circumstances that Mme Petit died in 1814. I can only describe my own feelings at length, and these will probably seem exaggerated or incredible to a spectator accustomed to the false characters found in novels (I except Fielding) or the bloodless characters found in novels based on the feelings of Parisians.

I must explain to the reader that in Dauphiné they have their own way of feeling, lively, obstinate, argumentative, such as I have met nowhere else. For people with insight, music, landscape painting and fiction should be different with every three degrees' change of latitude. For instance, the Provençal character comes to an end at Valence on the Rhône; the Burgundian character begins at Valence and gives place, between Dijon and Troyes, to the Parisian character, polite, witty, shallow, in a word much concerned with other people's opinion.

The Dauphinois character has a tenacity, a depth, a wit and subtlety that you would look for in vain in the civilization of Provence or of Burgundy, its neighbours. Where the Provençal vents his anger in atrocious insults, the Dauphinois thinks things over and argues them out within himself.

Everyone knows that Dauphiné was a state separate from France and politically half Italian until the year 1[349]. After that Louis XI, then Dauphin, having quarrelled with his father, governed the region for . . . years, and I am inclined to believe that this man of genius, with his deep nature and deep-seated timidity and his dislike of impulse, laid his stamp on the Dauphinois character. Even in my own time, according to my grandfather and to my aunt Élisabeth, who was quite typical of

46

the vigorous and generous feelings of my family, Paris was not a model; it was a far-off and unfriendly town whose influence was to be dreaded.

Now that I've tried to please my less sentimental readers by this digression, I shall tell how, on the day before my mother died, my sister Pauline and I had been taken for a walk down the rue Montorge. We came home along the houses on the left (north) side of that street; we were staying at my grandfather's house in the Place Grenette. I had been put to bed on the floor, on a mattress between the window and the fireplace, when about two in the morning the whole family came back in tears.

'But why couldn't the doctors make her better?' I asked old Marion (a regular Molière maidservant, a friend of her masters but quite ready to speak her mind to them, and who had known my mother as a young girl, had seen her married ten years before and was very fond of me).

Marie Thomasset, from Vinay, a typical Dauphinoise by nature and known by the diminutive '*Marion*', spent the night sitting beside my mattress, weeping bitterly, having apparently been told to keep me quiet. I was far more surprised than broken-hearted; I could not understand death and did not really believe in it.

'What!' I said to Marion. 'Shall I never see her again?'

'How can you see her again if they're going to take her away to the churchyard?'

'And where is the churchyard?'

'In the rue des Muriers; it belongs to the parish of Notre-Dame.'

The whole of that night's dialogue is still present in my mind, and I could easily set it down here. This was really the beginning of my emotional life; I must have been six and a half years old. In any case these dates are easy to check from certificates in the Registry Office. I fell asleep; next morning when I woke up Marion said to me : 'You must go to kiss your father.'

'What, is my little mamma dead? Shall I really never see her again?'

'Do be quiet, your father can hear you; he's there in your great-aunt's bed.'

I went to his bedside reluctantly; it was dark in the recess

47

because the curtains were drawn. I felt an aversion for my father and didn't want to kiss him.

A moment later in came the abbé Rey, a very tall frigid man, heavily pitted with smallpox, with a dull but virtuous expression, who soon afterwards became Grand Vicar. He was a friend of the family.

Believe it or not, I disliked him because he was a priest.

M. l'abbé Rey stood by the window; my father got up, put on his dressing-gown and emerged from his bed-recess with its green serge curtains. There were two fine curtains of pink taffeta figured with white which by day hid the others.

The abbé Rey embraced my father in silence. I thought my father looked very ugly, his eyes were swollen and he kept bursting into tears. I had stayed in the dark recess and I could see it all quite well.

'My friend, this is God's doing,' the abbé said at last; and this remark, made by a man I hated to another whom I did not love, made me ponder deeply.

I may seem heartless, but I was still only astonished at my mother's death. I could not understand this remark. Dare I set down what I was often told afterwards by Marion, who blamed me for it? I began to speak ill of GOD.

In any case, even supposing I were lying about my budding understanding I am certainly not lying about all the rest. If I feel tempted to lie, it will be later on, when it's a question of very serious faults. I don't believe that a child's cleverness promises superior intelligence in the man. In a sphere less subject to illusions, since after all its monuments survive, all the bad painters I have ever known produced wonderful things, promising genius, when they were eight or ten years old.

Alas, nothing is a promise of genius, although perhaps obstinacy is a sign of it.

Next day was the funeral. My father, whose face was really completely changed, dressed me in a sort of black woollen cloak which he fastened round my neck. This scene took place in my father's study, rue des Vieux-Jésuites; my father was mournful and the whole study, lined with gloomy folios, horrible to behold. The only exception to the general ugliness was the *Encyclopedia* of D'Alembert and Diderot bound in blue.

This haunt of lawyers had belonged to M. de Brenier, husband of Mme de Valserre and councillor to the High Court. Mme de Valserre, his widow and heir, had changed her name, Valserre sounding nobler and more beautiful than De Brenier. Since then she had become a canoness.

All the friends and relations forgathered in my father's study. Dressed in my black cloak, I stood between my father's knees, at 1. M. Pison senior, our cousin, a grave man but with a courtly gravity, much respected because he knew how to behave (he was fifty-five years old, thin and of a most distinguished appearance) came in and stood at 3.

Instead of weeping and showing grief he began conversing just as usual and talking about the Court (he may have meant the Law Court, that's quite likely). I thought he was speaking of foreign Courts and I was deeply shocked by his heartlessness.

A moment later in came my uncle, my mother's brother, an extremely handsome and agreeable young man dressed with the utmost elegance. He was the town's lady-killer, and he too began talking just as usual with M. Pison; he stood at 4. I became violently indignant and I remember that my father called him a frivolous man. Nevertheless I noticed that his eyes were very red, and he looked so attractive that I was somewhat pacified.

He wore his hair dressed with extreme elegance and with a scented powder; his coiffure consisted of a square pouch of black taffeta and two huge dogs' ears (as they were called six years later) such as M. le Prince de Talleyrand wears to this day.

A loud noise was heard; it was my poor mother's coffin being taken to the drawing-room before being carried away.

'Let's see now, I don't know the order of these ceremonies,' said M. Pison with an air of indifference as he stood up, and this shocked me deeply; it was my last *social* sensation. When I went into the drawing-room and saw the coffin, under its black pall, *in which my mother lay*, I was seized with the most violent despair; I realized at last what death was.

My aunt Séraphie had already accused me of being unfeeling.

I will spare the reader the tale of all the phases of my despair at the parish church of Saint-Hugues.

I was choking, I had to be taken out, I believe, because my

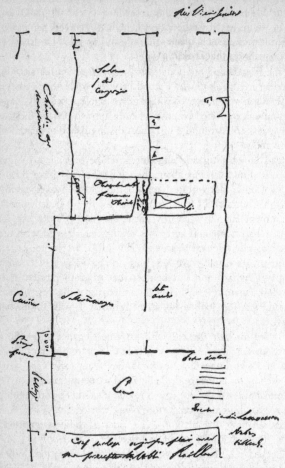

[(1) My father in an arm-chair – (2) Fireplace – (3) M. Pison – (4) My uncle. *Rue Vieux-Jésuites – My mother's room – Reception room – Small room – Housemaid's room – Drawing-room lobby – Bed – Kitchen. Kitchengarden. Furnace – Dining-room – Anteroom – Passage – Courtyard – Front door. Staircase – Lamouroux garden. Lime trees – Building where I was put with my tutor M. l'abbé Raillane.*]

grief was too noisy. I have never been able to look at that church of Saint-Hugues or the Cathedral next to it without emotion. The very sound of the Cathedral bells, when I revisited Grenoble in 1828, induced in me a bleak arid sadness devoid of tenderness, the sort of sadness that is akin to anger.

A. Baptismal fonts. *Saint Hugues – Notre Dame – Place de Tilleuls – Rue Bayard*.

When we reached the churchyard, which was in a bastion near the rue des Muriers (occupied today, or at least in 1828, by a large building, an engineers' storehouse) I behaved wildly, as

B. M. Bar[thélemy] d'Orbane – H. Me.

Marion has since told me. I wanted to stop them throwing earth on my mother's coffin, declaring that it would hurt her. But 'let us draw a veil over so dark a picture ...'

51

Owing to the complex interplay of characters within my family, the whole joy of childhood ended for me when my mother died.[1]

CHAPTER 5

Little Things Remembered from Early Childhood[2]

AT THE period when we were living in the first-floor apartment overlooking the Place Grenette, before 1790 or, to be exact, until the middle of 1789, my uncle the young lawyer had a very pleasant little apartment on the second floor, at the corner of the Place Grenette and the Grande-Rue. He used to joke with me and let me watch him take off his fine clothes and put on his dressing-gown, at nine o'clock in the evening, before supper. This was a delicious moment for me, and I would walk downstairs in front of him to the first floor delightedly, carrying the silver candlestick. My aristocratic family would have felt itself disgraced if the candlestick had not been of silver. It is true that it contained no noble wax candle, for it was customary then to use tallow. But we had this tallow sent from Briançon, with great care, packed in a case; it had to be made of goat's fat, and was ordered at the right time from a friend living in the mountains there. I can still see myself watching the tallow being unpacked and eating bread-and-milk from a silver bowl; I was always struck by the odd noise of the spoon scraping against the bottom

---

1. In my case the blackest ill-nature follows kindness and gaiety. – *Memories:* After 23 × 2 years, these are the memories which I have about happy days during my mother's lifetime: Drawing-room, suppers, captain B[eyle]. Abbé Chélan. I'm in revort. Going off to Romans. Barthélemy d'Orbane who [*word crossed out*]. M. B[arthélemy d'Orbane] teaching me to make faces.

2. Little memories to be put in AFTER THE ACCOUNT OF MY MOTHER'S DEATH: Barthélemy d'Orbane. Going off to Romans, lots of snow.

Going off to Vizille. Séraphie's hatred of the Barnave ladies whose country house we passed going to St Robert.

Little memories. To be placed in their position round about 1791. To be copied in on the left. . .

of the bowl, which was wet with milk. The relations between my family and this Briançon friend were almost those of *host and guest*, as in Homer, a natural consequence of the distrust and barbarism which were then widespread.[1]

My uncle,[2] young, brilliant and frivolous, was said to be the most attractive man in the town, to such a degree that many years later Mme Delaunay, wishing to vindicate her virtue, in spite of numerous lapses, could say: 'However, I never yielded to M. Gagnon junior!'

My uncle, I say, made game of the gravity of his father, who showed great surprise at meeting him in society wearing rich clothes for which he had not paid. 'I made myself scarce,' my uncle added as he told me the story.

One evening, in spite of everybody (but who raised objections in 1790?) he took me to the theatre. They were playing *Le Cid*.

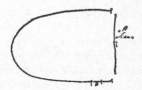

Stage. Here the Cid wounds himself – H. Henri B. aged less than six years. Disgusting theatre at Grenoble. It inspired in me the tenderest reverence. I even loved its horrid smell, in 1794, '95 and '96. This love reached frenzy at the time of Mme Kubly.

'Why, the child's crazy,' my excellent grandfather remarked when I got back; his love of literature had prevented him from objecting seriously to my visit to the theatre. So I saw *Le Cid* acted, but, I fancy, in costumes of sky-blue satin with white satin shoes.

As he recited the Stanzas, or at some other point, wielding his

1. Style; arrangement of ideas. Prepare reader's attention by a few passing words: 1st on Lambert; 2nd on my uncle in the first chapters, 17 December '35. Style. Relation of words to ideas: Dic[tionary] of the Academy, article on Saint-Marc Girardin, Ch[evalier] of König von Jean fou[tre]. Debates.

2. 20 December 1835. YESTERDAY Filarmonica: BEFORE ME Amalia Betti[ni].

sword with too much fervour, the Cid hurt himself near the right eye.

'He very nearly put out his eye,' people were saying round me. I was in the second box on the right, in the first tier.

Another time my uncle was kind enough to take me to the *Caravan of Cairo* (he found me rather in the way of his manoeuvres with the ladies, and I was well aware of this). I was beside myself with excitement over the camels. *The Infanta of Zamora*, in which a poltroon or a cook sang an arietta wearing a helmet with a rat for a crest, made me wild with delight. This seemed to me the height of comedy.

I said to myself, very vaguely no doubt and not as clearly as I am setting it down here: 'Every moment of my uncle's life is as delicious as these we are now enjoying together at the theatre. Surely the finest thing in the world is to be a charming fellow like my uncle.' It never entered my five-year-old head that my uncle might not be quite as happy as I was at seeing the caravan of camels file past.

But I went too far; instead of being simply very attentive to the ladies, I became passionate with the women I loved, but almost indifferent and above all devoid of vanity with the rest, whence my lack of success and my *fiascos*. Probably no other man at the Emperor's Court had less women than I did, although I was supposed to be the lover of the Prime Minister's wife.

The theatre, the sound of a fine deep bell (like that of the church of ... above Rolle, in May 1800, on the way to the St Bernard Pass) made, and have always made, a profound impression on my heart. Even the Mass, in which I believed so little, inspired me with solemn feelings. While still very young and certainly before my tenth year and the incident of abbé Gardon's letter, I believed that GOD despised these mountebanks. (After forty-two years of reflection I still hold that this fraud is so useful to those who practise it that there will always be someone to carry it on. The story of the medal, yesterday ... December 1835.)

I have the clearest and most vivid recollection of my grand-father's round powdered wig; it had three rows of curls. He never wore a hat.

This costume had helped, I fancy, to make him well known

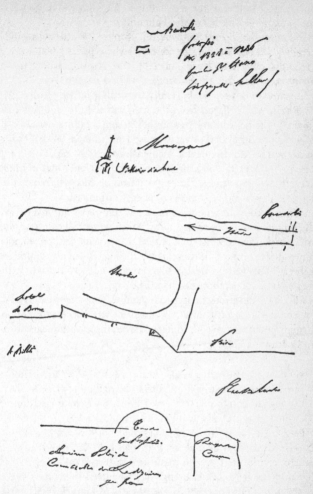

[*The Bastille fortified between 1828 and 1836 by General Haxo, that inde-fatigable braggart – Mountain. Ste Marie-on-the-hill – Pont-de-bois. The Isère – The Hotel de Bonne – Theatre. A: Box office – Prison – Place Saint-André. Tower of the Prefecture – Former palace of the Constable de Lesdiguières, I believe – Passage to the Concert Hall.*]

and respected among the common people, from whom he never took any money for his medical attention.

He was the doctor and friend of most of the aristocratic families. M. de Chaléon, the sound of whose passing-bell, tolling at Saint-Louis, I still remember; M. de Lacoste, who had an apoplectic fit in the Terres-Froides, at Le Frette; M. de Langon who came of a very noble family, according to the records; M. de Raxis, who suffered from the itch, and used to fling his coat down on the floor in my grandfather's room (grandfather scolded me, with perfect composure, because I mentioned M. de Raxis's name when speaking of this incident); M. and Mme des Adrets, Mme de Valserre their daughter, in whose salon I had my first *introduction to society*. Her sister, Mme de Mareste, seemed to me very pretty and was said to be of easy virtue.

When I knew him he was, and had been for twenty-five years, the promoter of every undertaking which served a useful purpose and which, considering the political immaturity of those remote times (1760), might be called liberal. The town owes him its Library. This was no mean achievement; it had to be bought first, then housed, then a librarian had to be paid.

He gave his protection to all young people who showed a love of study, against their parents in the first place and then in a more practical way. He quoted the example of Vaucanson to recalcitrant parents.

When my grandfather returned from Montpellier to Grenoble with his doctor's degree in medicine, he had a very fine head of hair, but public opinion informed him imperiously that unless he wore a wig nobody would trust him. An old cousin of his, Mlle Didier, who made him her heir jointly with my aunt Élisabeth and who died about 1788, had held this opinion. This worthy cousin used to give me yellow saffron-bread to eat when I went to see her on St Laurent's day. She lived in the next street to the rue Saint-Laurent; in the same street my former nurse Françoise, whom I always adored, kept a grocery. She had left my mother's service to get married. Her place was taken by her handsome sister Geneviève, to whom my father was said to have paid court.

My grandfather's room on the first floor overlooking the Place

Grenette was painted a crude green, and my father used to say to me, even in those days: 'Grandfather's a very clever man but his artistic taste isn't good.'

The French are so timid by nature that they seldom use bold colours: green, red, blue, bright yellow; they prefer indeterminate shades. Apart from this I cannot see what was wrong with my grandfather's choice. His room faced due south, he read a great deal and wanted to spare his eyes, which sometimes troubled him.

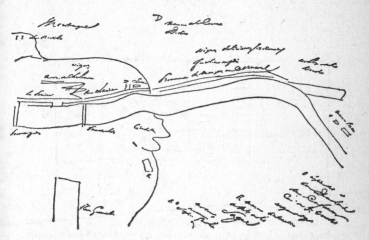

[*Mountain – The Bastille – Vineyards – Rise towards Chalemont – La Périère – Rue Saint-Laurent – D. My cousin Mme Didier's house – Delicious vines enjoying a sunny aspect. Masqueraders' parade at Carnaval – Village of La Tronche – Barral's house – Stone bridge – Wooden bridge – Citadel – Place Grenette – O. Church of M. Dumolard, my confessor, curé of La Tronche and a great Jesuit – R. Mlle de la Sagne's school; my sister, her friend Mlle Sophie Gautier.*]

But the reader, if these trivialities ever find a reader, will readily discern that all my *reasons why*, all my explanations may be badly wrong. I only have very clear mental pictures; all my explanations occur to me as I write this forty-five years after the events.

My excellent grandfather, who was in fact my real father and my close friend until I took the decision about 1796 to get out of Grenoble with the help of mathematics, often used to describe a wonderful incident.

My mother had brought me into his (green) room the day I

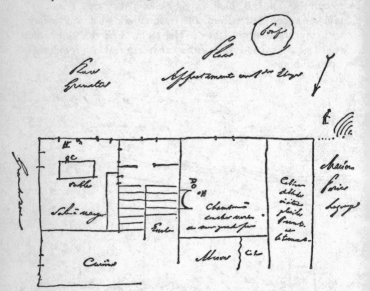

H. Me. D. M. Barthélemy d'Orbane – C. Worthy abbé Chélan – H. Me. I can't think where my aunt Séraphie and my great-aunt Élisabeth slept. I vaguely remember a room between the dining-room and the Grande-Rue. [*Place Grenette – Pump – Plan – Apartment on the first floor – Grande-Rue – Dining-room – Table – Kitchen – Staircase – Grandfather's green bedroom – Bed-recess – Closet – Study where the barometer and thermometer stood – The Perier-Lagranges' house.*]

was a year old, 23 January 1784, and was holding me up on my feet by the window; my grandfather, who was beside the bed, called me; I made up my mind to walk and I walked right up to him.

I was just beginning to talk then, and I said *hateur* for adieu. My uncle used to tease his sister Henriette (my mother) about my ugliness. Apparently I had an enormous hairless head and looked like Father Brulard, a clever monk, fond of good living

[*Detail 23 January 1783–85 – Place Grenette – Me. Grandfather – Study.
Bed-recess and bed. Place Grenette – Pump – Bedroom (uncertain) – Dining-
room – Passage – Grandfather's green bedroom – Closet – A', the top of
this partition was glazed to light the staircase. There was a door at V.*]

and very influential in his convent, an uncle or great-uncle of mine who died before my time.

I was extremely enterprising, hence two accidents described by my grandfather with terror and regret. Near the rock of the Porte-de-France I prodded a mule with a sharp pointed stick; the mule had the impertinence to plant its two hoofs against my chest and knock me over. 'That was very nearly the end of him,' my grandfather said.

I can picture the incident, but it is probably not a direct memory, only the memory of the picture I formed of the thing a very long time ago, when I was first told about it.

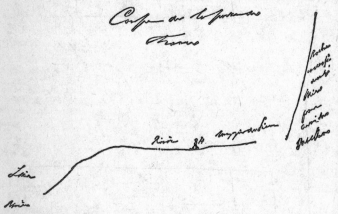

H. Where the mule kicked me. [*Cutting of the Porte-de-France – The Rabot Tower – Steep rock mined for quarrying – Store of stones. – Road – River Isère.*]

The second tragic incident was when, standing between my mother and my grandfather, I broke two front teeth in falling against the corner of a chair. My good grandfather couldn't get over his amazement. 'Between his mother and me!' he repeated as if to deplore the power of Fate.

The thing that struck me most about the first-floor apartment was that I could hear the sound made by the iron arm with which they pumped the water, a whining sound, long drawn out but not harsh, which gave me great pleasure.

Dauphinois common sense rebelled, to a great extent, against the Court. I remember very well my grandfather's departure for the State Assembly at Romans – he was then a highly respected patriot but a very moderate one; imagine Fontenelle as a tribune of the people.

On the day he left it was bitterly cold (this was the hard winter of 1789–90 – check up on this) and there was a foot of snow on the Place Grenette.

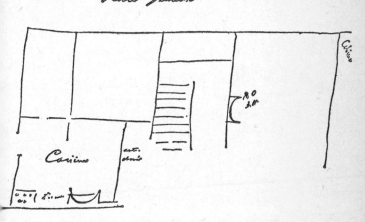

[*Place Grenette – Kitchen. Furnace – Anteroom – Closet.*]

In the fireplace of my grandfather's room a huge fire was burning. The room was full of friends who had come to see him get into his carriage. The most famous consultant lawyer of the town, its oracle in legal matters – a fine position in a town where the Parlement was held – M. Barthélemy d'Orbane, a close friend of the family, was at O and I myself at H, in front of the blazing fire. I was the hero of the moment, for I'm convinced that I was the only person in Grenoble whom my grandfather loved or was sorry to leave.

While we were standing thus M. Barthélemy d'Orbane was teaching me to make grimaces. I can still see him and myself too. This was an art in which I made swift progress, I laughed myself at the faces I made to make others laugh. They soon tried to check my growing taste for grimaces, but in vain, it has persisted to this day; I often laugh at the faces I make when I'm alone.

In the street a fop goes by with an affected expression (M. Lysi[maque] for instance, or M. le Comte . . ., Mme Del Monte's lover) I imitate his expression and laugh. My instinct is to mimic the affected movements or positions of the face rather than those of the body. At the Council of State I mimicked, without meaning to and in a highly dangerous fashion, the self-important air

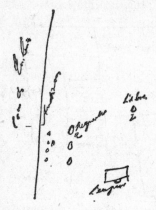

H. Me – L. Fiery abbé Louis (not yet a thief, and highly esteemed) – R. That terrible Count Regnault. [*Courtyard of the Tuileries – Audience – Regnault – a[bbé] Louis. – The emperor.*]

of the famous Comte Regnault de Saint-Jean-d'Angély standing three yards from me, particularly when, the better to hear the fiery abbé Louis, who was opposite him on the other side of the hall, he pulled down the inordinately high corners of his shirt collar. This instinct or art which I owe to M. d'Orbane has made me many enemies. To this day, that wise man di Fiori criticizes me for the irony which is concealed, or rather ill-concealed and visible against my will, at the right corner of my mouth.

At Romans my grandfather missed being elected deputy by five votes. 'I'd have died of it,' he often repeated since then, congratulating himself on having refused the votes of several country bourgeois who believed in him and used to consult him at his home in the mornings. His Fontenelle-like prudence prevented him from having any serious ambition, nevertheless he was very fond of making a speech in front of a chosen audience, for instance at the Library. I can still see myself there, listening to him in the first hall, which was full of people and seemed to me immense. But why such a crowd? What was the occasion? The picture does not tell me that. It's nothing but a picture.

My grandfather used often to tell us that at Romans his ink, which stood on his warm chimney-piece, froze on the tip of his pen. He was not nominated, but was responsible for the nomination of one or two deputies whose names I have forgotten, but he never forgot the service he had rendered them and watched them in the Assembly, where he found fault with their energy.

I was very fond of M. d'Orbane and of the fat canon his brother; I used to go and see them in the Place des Tilleuls or under the arch which led from the Place Notre-Dame to the Place des Tilleuls, quite close to Notre-Dame, where the canon used to sing. My father or my grandfather used to send the famous lawyer fat turkeys at Christmas-time.

I was also very fond of Father Ducros, an unfrocked Franciscan (from the convent that stood between the Jardin de Ville and the Hôtel de Franquières, which I remember as being apparently in the Renaissance style).

And I was fond, too, of abbé Chélan, the curé of Risset near Claix, a lean little man, all nerves and fire, with a sparkling wit, who seemed old to me but who may have been only forty or forty-five, and whose arguments at table gave me infinite amusement. He never failed to dine with my grandfather when he came to Grenoble and the dinner was much merrier than usual.

One day at supper he had been talking for three quarters of an hour, holding in his hand a spoonful of strawberries. At last he raised the spoon to his mouth.

'Abbé, you won't say your Mass tomorrow,' said my grandfather.

'Oh, excuse me, please, I shall say it tomorrow, but not today, for it's after midnight.' This dialogue delighted me for a whole month; it struck me as brilliantly witty. That's what wit consists of for a youthful nation or person, the emotion lies in the hearer; witness the witty retorts admired by Boccaccio or Vasari.

My grandfather, in those happy days, took his religion light-heartedly, and the reverend gentlemen were of the same opinion; he only became melancholy and somewhat religious after my mother's death (in 1790), and that, I imagine, through some vague hope of seeing her again in the other world like M. de

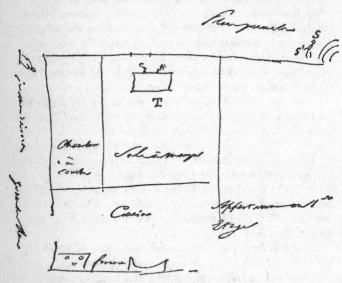

[*Place Grenette – I'm in revort. Grande-Rue – Bedroom – Dining-room – Kitchen – Furnace – First-floor apartment.*]

Broglie, who said, speaking of his charming daughter who died at the age of thirteen : 'I feel as if my daughter were in America.'

I believe M. l'abbé Chélan was dining at our house on the *Day of the Tiles*. On that day I saw the first blood that was shed by the French Revolution. A wretched journeyman hatter was fatally wounded by a bayonet thrust in the small of the back (S).

We left the table in the middle of dinner (T). I was at H and the curé Chélan at C. I shall look up the date in some chronology. The picture is as clear as possible in my mind, some forty-five years after.

A certain M. de Clermont-Tonnerre, commanding officer in Dauphiné, who was living in the Hôtel du Gouvernement, a house standing by itself overlooking the rampart (with a superb view over the hillside of Eybens, a quiet beautiful view worthy of Claude Lorraine, and an entry through a fine courtyard in the rue Neuve near the rue des Muriers) tried, I fancy, to disperse a gathering; he had two regiments, against which the populace defended itself with tiles thrown from the roof-tops, whence the name: *Day of the Tiles*.[1]

One of the subordinate officers in one of these regiments[2] was Bernadotte, the present King of Sweden, as noble a soul as Murat, King of Naples, but far cleverer. Lefèvre, the wigmaker, and a friend of my father's, has often told us how he saved the life of General Bernadotte (as he called him in 1804) when he was sharply beset down some alley. Lefèvre was a handsome and very brave man and Marshal Bernadotte sent him a present.

But all this is history, told indeed by eye-witnesses but not seen by myself. I only want to tell in future, about Russia and elsewhere, what I *have actually seen*.

My relations having left dinner before the end and I being by myself at the dining-room window, or rather at the window of a room overlooking the Grande-Rue, I saw an old woman who, holding her worn shoes in her hand, was shouting with all her might: 'I'm in revolt! I'm in revolt!'

She was going from the Place Grenette to the Grande-Rue. The absurdity of this revolt struck me forcibly: an old woman against a regiment! That same evening my grandfather told me the story of the death of Pyrrhus.[3]

I was still thinking about the old woman when I was distracted by a tragic sight at O. A journeyman hatter, wounded in the back by a bayonet thrust so I heard, was walking with

1. At Grenoble I left a water-colour landscape by M. Leroy, depicting this rising.

2. Dec[ember] 21st amended to the 22nd. Pictures by M. Bodinier. M. Girardin is right about the two columns.

3. Does this learned ending read all right? 22 Dec[ember].

great difficulty, leaning on two men over whose shoulders his arms were laid. He wore no coat, his shirt and his pale buff or white trousers were soaked with blood; I can still see him, the wound from which the blood was pouring out was in the small of his back, opposite his navel.

They were helping him to walk with difficulty as far as his room, up on the sixth floor of the Périers' house, and when he got there he died.

My relatives scolded me and took me away from the window of my grandfather's room so that I should not see this horrifying

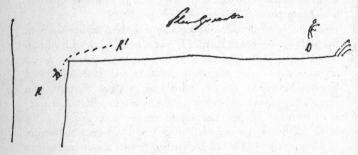

[*Place Grenette.*]

sight, but I kept going back to it. This window was very low down, on the first floor.

I saw the wretched man on every floor of the staircase of the Périers house, which was lighted by big windows overlooking the square.

This recollection, naturally, is the clearest I have retained from those days.

On the other hand I have difficulty in remembering anything about the fireworks at Fontanil (on the road from Grenoble to Voreppe) where they burnt *Lamoignon*. I was very sorry to miss the sight of a great straw dummy, dressed up; the fact is that my relatives, who were *right-thinking* and much distressed by anything which deviated from *order* (order reigns in Warsaw, said General Seb[astiani] round about 1832) didn't want me to be impressed by these proofs of the wrath or power of the people. I held the opposite view myself, at that early age; or perhaps my

66

opinion at the age of eight is masked by the very decided opinion I held at the age of ten.

On one occasion MM. Barthélemy, d'Orbane, Canon Barthélemy, M. l'abbé Rey, M. Bouvier and all the rest were talking at my grandfather's about the forthcoming arrival of M. le Maréchal de Vaux.

'His entry here will be like a ballet,' said my grandfather; this expression, which I did not understand, puzzled me very much. What could there be in common, I wondered, between an old marshal and a broom [*balai*]?

He died; the majestic sound of the bells moved me deeply. I was taken to see the *chapelle ardente* (I think it was in the Hôtel du Commandement, near the rue des Muriers, but the memory has almost faded); the sight of that black tomb, lit up by a large number of candles in broad daylight and with all its windows closed, impressed me. It was the concept of death appearing for the first time. I was taken there by Lambert, my grandfather's servant (his valet) and my intimate friend. He was a young, handsome man, very sharp-witted.

One of his friends came to tell him: 'The Marshal's daughter is nothing but a miser, the amount of black cloth she's given the drummers to cover their drums wouldn't make a pair of trousers. The drummers are grumbling, for it's customary to give enough to make a pair of trousers.' When I got home I found that my family were also talking about the miserliness of the Marshal's daughter.

Next day was a day of battle for me; I got permission, with great difficulty I fancy, for Lambert to take me to watch the procession pass. There was a huge crowd. I see myself at point H, between the main road and the Isère, near the limekiln, two hundred yards this side of the Porte-de-France and to the east of it.

The sound of the drums, muffled by the little piece of cloth that wasn't big enough to make a pair of trousers, moved me deeply. But here's quite another story: I was standing at point H, at the extreme left of a battalion of the Austrasian regiment, I think, in white coats with black trimmings, L is Lambert holding me, H, by the hand. I was six inches away from the last soldier of the regiment, S.

Suddenly he said to me: 'Stand a bit farther off so that I shan't hurt you when I fire.'

So they were going to fire! All those soldiers! They were carrying their arms reversed.

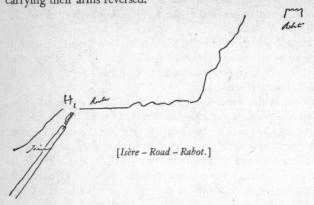

[*Isère – Road – Rabot.*]

I was dying with fright; I could see, out of the corner of my eye, the black carriage in the distance coming slowly forward over the stone bridge, drawn by six or eight horses. I shuddered as I waited for the volley. At last the officer gave a shout, and

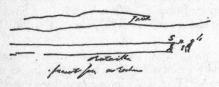

[*Isère – Battalion facing the rock.*]

immediately afterwards the volley was fired. I felt a great weight drop from me. At the same moment the crowd rushed towards the draped carriage which I was delighted to see; I seem to remember candles burning on it.

A second and maybe a third volley were fired outside the Porte-de-France, but I was hardened.

I seem to remember, too,[1] something about the departure for

1. 22 Dec[ember] 1835. Pictures by M. Bodinier, at the Albani Palace.

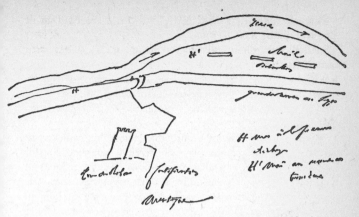

[*Isère. The Mall – Main road to Lyons – The Rabot Tower – Fortifications – Mountain – H. Myself at the first volley – H'. Myself at the second and third.*]

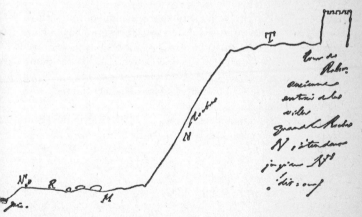

H. Me. Point from which I saw the black carriage bearing the remains of Marshal de Vaux go by, and, far worse, from which I heard the volley fired two feet away from me – R. Main road from Grenoble to Lyons and Paris – M. Store of stones – N. Rock being mined – T. Space which I saw reduced by three quarters by mining, because of the need for quarry-stones for the new building in the town. [*Isère – Rock – Rabot Tower. Former entrance to the town when the rock N stretched as far as N' (so they say).*]

Vizille (the provincial State Assembly held at the Château de Vizille, built by the Constable de Lesdiguières). My grandfather adored ancient things and I had a sublime image of this castle from the way he spoke about it. I was on the verge of conceiving a profound respect for the aristocracy, but my companions MM. de Saint-Ferréol and de Sinard, soon cured me of that.

There were mattresses fixed on to the back of the two-wheeled post-chaises.

'*Young Mounier*', as my grandfather called him, came to our house. It was only because we were forcibly separated that his daughter and I did not fall violently in love with one another, that half-hour that I spent under a carriage-gateway in the rue Montmartre, near the Boulevard, during a shower of rain, in 1803 or 1804, when M. Mounier went to take up a Prefect's duties at Rennes. (My letters to his son Édouard, Victorine's letter addressed to me. The joke is that Édouard, I fancy, believed I had gone to Rennes.)

The stiff, badly painted little portrait that can be seen in a room next to the public library at Grenoble, showing Mounier in his Prefect's dress, is a good likeness, if I'm not mistaken. A firm face, but narrow-minded. His son, of whom I saw a great deal in 1803 and in Russia in 1812 (Viazma-on-guts) is commonplace but shrewd, a sly fox, a typical Dauphinois, like the minister Casimir Perier, only the latter had now met someone even more Dauphinois than himself. Édouard Mounier has the native drawl, although he was brought up at Weimar, he's a Peer of France and a baron, and sits bravely in judgement in the Court of Peers (1835, December). Will the reader believe me if I dare to add that I would not care to change places with MM. Félix Faure and Mounier, Peers of France and my former friends?

My grandfather, a fond and zealous friend of all young people who liked to work, used to lend books to M. Mounier and took his side when his father blamed him. Sometimes, as he went down the Grand'rue, he would go into the latter's shop and speak to him about his son. The old draper, who had a great many children, and was concerned only with what could be of use, was dreadfully distressed to see this son of his waste his time reading.

Strength of character was the chief characteristic of M. Mounier junior, but his mental powers did not match his doggedness.

My grandfather used to tell us, laughing, a few years later, how Mme Borel, who was to become M. Mounier's mother-in-law, came in to buy some cloth, and M. Mounier, his father's assistant, unfolded the roll, let her feel the cloth and added: 'This cloth is sold at twenty-seven livres an ell.'

'Well, monsieur, I'll give you twenty-five for it,' said Mme Borel.

At which M. Mounier folded up the roll of cloth and put it back in the drawer with a frigid air.

'But monsieur, monsieur!' said Mme Borel in surprise, 'I'll gladly go up to twenty-five livres ten sous.'

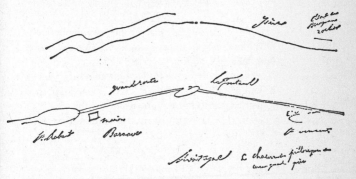

[Isère – Dent de Moirans, a rock – Main road – Le Fontanil – Saint-Robert – Barnave's house – Mountain – Saint-Vincent – C. Grandfather's picturesque cottage.]

'Madame, an honest man does not go back on his word.'

The good woman was deeply shocked.

That same love of hard-working young men, for which my grandfather incurred so much blame in those days, made him protect young Barnave. Barnave [1] was our neighbour in the country; he lived at Saint-Robert and we at Saint-Vincent (on the road from Grenoble to Voreppe and Lyons). Séraphie detested him and soon afterwards rejoiced at his death and the poverty in which his sisters were left, one of them being called, I fancy, Mme de Saint-Germain. Every time we passed through

1. 23 Dec. '35. Tired of work AFTER three hours. Desk à la Tronchin. Visit to Aracoeli.

Saint-Robert: 'Ah, there's Barnave's house,' Séraphie would say, and she treated him with an air of outraged piety. My grandfather, who was on excellent terms with the nobility, was the oracle of middle-class folk, and I suppose that the mother of the immortal Barnave, distressed at seeing him neglect his lawsuits for Mably and Montesquieu, was pacified by my grandfather. In those days our compatriot Mably had a great reputation, and two years later they re-named the rue des Clercs after him.[1]

CHAPTER 6

AFTER my mother's[2] death, my grandfather was in despair. I realize, but only now, that he must have had a character something like Fontenelle's, modest, prudent, discreet, extremely agreeable and amusing, before the death of his beloved daughter. Afterwards he often withdrew into a reserved silence. He loved nobody in the world except that daughter and myself.

His other daughter, Séraphie, bored and annoyed him; he

1. 19 December, Filarmonica, BEFORE MY CHAIR Amalia Betti[ni], WITH HER AN YOUNG MAN of Felsina . . . 20 December. Yesterday evening, Filarmonica, BEFORE MY CHAIR Amalia Betti[ni] . . . Find a place for: secret of the Rothschilds' fortune, as seen by Dom[ini]que, on 25 Dec[ember] 1835. They sell what everyone wants in way of *rentes*, and moreover have made themselves manufacturers of these (*id est*, by making loans). . . A map of Grenoble must be bought and stuck in here. I must get hold of the death certificates of my parents, which will give me dates, and the birth certificate of MY DEAREST MOTHER and my grandfather. December 1835. I alone think of them today, and with what tenderness towards my mother, who has been dead for forty-six years. So I can speak freely of their faults.
I am justified in doing the same about Mme la Baronne de Barcoff, Mme Alex. Petit, Madame la Baronne Dembowski (how long it is since I wrote that name!), Virginie, two Victorines, Angela, Mélanie, Alex[andrine], Métilde, Clémentine, Julia, Alberthe de Rub[empré], (adored for one month only).

V. 2 V. A. M. A. M. C. I. A.
$+$ $+$ $+$ $+$ $+$
A more positive man would say:
A. M. C. I. A.
My right to put down these memories: what human being does not love to be remembered by someone?

72

loved peace above all things and she was always making scenes. My good grandfather, thinking of his paternal authority, blamed himself keenly for not showing his teeth, *that's a local expression*; I retain these, reserving the right to translate them later on into Parisian French; I retain them for the present the better to remember the details that crowd into my mind. M. Gagnon respected and feared his sister, who in her youth had been fonder of another brother who had died in Paris, for which the surviving brother had never forgiven her, but with his Fontenelle-like character, amiable and peace-loving, he never betrayed this and only later did I guess it.

M. Gagnon had a sort of aversion from his son, Romain Gagnon, my uncle, a brilliant and wholly delightful young man.

It was the possession of this quality that estranged father and son, it seems to me; they were both, but in different ways, the most delightful men in the town. My grandfather's humour was

---

... [20 Dec. 1835.] Facts to be placed in position, put here so as not to be forgotten: nomination of the inspector of *mobilier* back of page 254 of this numbering. – At seven years old, began Latin, therefore in 1790.

... Facts put here so as not to forget them, to be put in their position: the reason why Omar [Rome] bores me.

The reason is, I have no society in the evening to distract me from my morning's ideas. When I was working on something in Paris, I worked till I was dizzy and couldn't do a stroke more.

But at six o'clock I had to go and dine, at the risk of disturbing the waiter for a dinner of 3 francs 50, a thing which often happened to me, and made me blush. I used to go to a salon; there, unless it was a very dull one, I was completely distracted from my morning's work, to the point even of forgetting the subject when I returned home at one o'clock in the morning.

... 20 December 1835. Morning tiredness. This is what I miss at Omar: the society is so languid (Mme Sandra, THE MOTHER OF Marietta), Countess Koven, the Princess de Da are not worth the trouble of getting into a carriage.

All this cannot distract me from my morning ideas, so when I take up my work the next day, instead of being fresh and relaxed, I feel jaded and exhausted. And after four or five days of this life, I am disgusted by my work, I have worn out my ideas by thinking of them too continuously.

I make a fortnight's trip to C[ivit]a-V[ecchi]a or to Ravenna (1835 October). This interval is too long. I've *forgotten* my work.

This is why *The Green Huntsman* languishes, this – along with the complete lack of good music – is what I dislike about Omar.

2. 2 December 1835, Mass for Bellini S[an] Lor[enzo] in Damaso.

73

restrained, and his cool subtle wit might pass unnoticed. He was, moreover, a prodigy of learning for those days (when the most comical sort of ignorance reigned). Fools or envious people (MM. Champel, Tournus the cuckold, Tourte) took their revenge by complimenting him ceaselessly on his memory. He knew, believed and quoted the accepted authorities on all sorts of subjects.

'My son has read nothing,' he sometimes said irritably. This was perfectly true, but it was impossible to be bored in a company that included M. Gagnon junior. His father had given him a charming apartment in his house and had made a lawyer of him. In a Parlement town, everybody loved chicanery and lived on chicanery and made witticisms about chicanery. I still know a lot of jokes about the *pétitoire* and the *possessoire*.

My grandfather gave his son board, lodging and an allowance of 100 francs a month, a huge sum in Grenoble before 1789, for his pocket-money; and my uncle used to buy embroidered coats worth 1,000 crowns and keep actresses.

I only had an inkling of these things, which I discerned through my grandfather's hints. I suppose that my uncle used to get presents from his rich mistresses, and with this money dressed himself magnificently and kept his poor mistresses. It should be understood that in our part of the world, in those days, it was not considered wrong to accept money from Mme Dulauron or Mme de Marcieu or Mme de Sassenage, provided one spent it *hic et nunc* and did not hoard it. *Hic et nunc* is a turn of speech that Grenoble got from its Parlement.

It happened more than once that my grandfather would turn up at M. de Quinsonnas's or at some other gathering and notice a richly dressed young man to whom everybody was listening.

'My father didn't know that coat of mine,' my uncle said, 'I would make myself scarce and hurry home to resume my modest dress-coat. When my father asked me "Please be kind enough to tell me where you got the money for those clothes?" I would reply "I've been lucky at cards." "But then why not pay your debts?" And what about Madame So-and-so who wanted to see me wearing the fine coat she'd bought me!' my uncle went on; 'I got out of it by making some sort of joke.'

I don't know whether my reader of 1880 knows a novel which is still very famous today: *Les Liaisons Dangereuses* was written at Grenoble by M. Choderlos de Laclos, an artillery officer, and depicted the morals and manners of Grenoble.

I used to know Mme de Merteuil, too; this was Mme de Montmaur, who used to give me pickled walnuts, a lame woman who lived in the Drevon house at Chevallon near the church of Saint-Vincent, between Le Fontanil and Voreppe but nearer to Fontanil. Mme de Montmaur's estate (or that rented by Mme de Montmaur) was just across the road from M. Henry Gagnon's. The rich girl who has to go into a convent must have been one Mlle de Blacons, from Voreppe. Her family was noted for its gloom, piety, correct behaviour and extreme right-wing opinions, or at least was so in 1814 when the Emperor sent me as commissaire in the 7th Military Division with that elderly senator the Comte de Saint-Vallier, one of the rakes of my uncle's period who talked to me a lot about himself and the remarkable follies committed for his sake by Mmes M. and N. whose names I have forgotten. At that time I was burning with sacred fire and thought of nothing but the means of repelling the Austrians or at least of preventing them from entering too swiftly.

Thus I witnessed Mme de Merteuil's way of life in its decline, as much as a child of nine or ten consumed by an ardent temperament can see those things which everybody avoids explaining to him.

CHAPTER 7

THE FAMILY consisted at the time of my mother's death, about 1790, of MM. Gagnon senior, aged sixty, his son Romain Gagnon, aged twenty-five, his daughter Séraphie, twenty-four, his sister Élisabeth, sixty-four; his son-in-law Chérubin Beyle, forty-three, his son Henri, seven, his daughter Pauline, four, his daughter Zénaïde, two.

These then were the characters in the dreary drama of my youth, of which I remember almost nothing but suffering and profound vexation of spirit. But let us see what these characters were like.

My grandfather Henri Gagnon (sixty years old); his daughter

Séraphie, that she-devil whose age I never discovered, might have been twenty-two or twenty-four; his sister Élisabeth Gagnon (sixty-four years old), a tall, lean, dried-up woman with a handsome Italian face and a character of extreme nobility, with the over-refinement and conscientious scruples of a Spaniard. She formed my heart in this respect and it is to my aunt Élisabeth that I owe those shocking delusions about nobility to which I fell victim during the first thirty years of my life. I presume that my aunt Élisabeth, a rich woman (for Grenoble), had remained unmarried owing to an unhappy love affair. I was told something of the sort by my aunt Séraphie in my early childhood.

My father completed the family.

Joseph Chérubin Beyle, a lawyer in the Parlement, subsequently extremely right-wing and a Chevalier of the Legion of Honour, Deputy Mayor of Grenoble, died in 1819 aged seventy-two, so I'm told, which would make him to have been born in 1747; so in 1790 he was forty-three.

He was an extremely unlikeable man, always thinking about the purchase and sale of land, excessively shrewd, accustomed to selling to peasants and buying from them, an arch-Dauphinois. Nothing could have been farther from extravagant nobility of the Spanish kind than such a character, and indeed my aunt Élisabeth had an aversion for him. He was, moreover, excessively wrinkled and ugly, and awkward and silent in the presence of women; yet he could not do without them.

This latter quality had taught him to understand *La Nouvelle Héloïse* and other works of Rousseau, of whom he spoke with adoration, and yet damned him for his impiety; for since my mother's death he had become absorbed in the most extreme and absurd devoutness. He made it his duty to recite all the Church services, there was even some talk for three of four years of his taking orders, and probably he was restrained from this by his wish to hand down his lawyer's position to me. He was going to be a *consistorial*; this was a high distinction among men of law, and he spoke of it as a young lieutenant of Grenadiers speaks about the Military Cross. He did not love me for myself but as the son who was to carry on his family.

It would have been very difficult for him to love me : (1) he saw clearly that I did not love him; I never spoke to him unless

I had to, for he was a stranger to all those fine literary and philosophical ideas which formed the basis of my questions to my grandfather and the excellent replies of that delightful old man. I saw very little of him. My passionate wish was to leave Grenoble, that's to say to leave him, and my passion for mathematics, the only means I had of leaving that town which I loathed and which I still hate, since it is here that I learned to know men, my mathematical enthusiasm drove me into absolute seclusion from 1797 to 1799. I can say that I worked during those two years and even during part of 1796 as much as Michelangelo worked at the Sistine Chapel.

After my departure at the end of October 1799 (I remember the date because on the 18th Brumaire, 9 November, I happened to be at Nemours) I meant nothing to my father except as a cadger for money; the estrangement between us increased continually, and he could not say a word without irritating me. I had an absolute horror of selling a field to a peasant by haggling for a week to gain 300 francs, which was his chief delight.

This was quite normal. His father, who bore, I believe, the great name of *Pierre* Beyle, died of gout at Claix, suddenly, at the age of sixty-three. My father, at eighteen (so it must have been about 1765), found himself with an estate at Claix yielding either 800 or 1,800 francs, a procurator's office and ten sisters to provide for, and a mother who was a rich heiress, that's to say having about 60,000 francs, and full of devilment in her capacity as heiress. She boxed my ears repeatedly in my childhood when I pulled the tail of her dog Azor (a Bolognese dog with long silky white hair). Thus money was, quite understandably, my father's great concern, whereas I have never thought about it without disgust. The very idea of money suggests cruel suffering to me, since having money gives me no pleasure, whereas the lack of it is a hateful misfortune.

I don't suppose Fate ever brought together two beings more fundamentally antipathetic to one another than my father and myself.

Hence the absence of all delight in my childhood from 1790 to 1790. That age, which everybody says is the happiest in one's life, was for me, thanks to my father, one long sequence of cruelly painful and disgusting experiences. Two devils were let loose against the wretched child that I was: my aunt Séraphie and my father, who, from 1791 onwards, was her slave.

The reader needn't worry about my tale of woe, for one thing he may skip several pages, which I beg him to do, since I am recklessly writing things that may perhaps prove very boring even for 1835, let alone 1880.

For another thing, I hardly remember anything about the wretched days of 1790–95 during which I was a poor persecuted little urchin, always being scolded at every turn and protected only by a wise old man, Fontenelle-like, who didn't want to fight for me, particularly as in case of battle his superior authority would oblige him to raise his voice, and that was what he detested above all things, and my aunt Séraphie, who had taken a dislike of me, I don't know why, was also well aware of this.

Two or three weeks after my mother's death my father and I returned to sleep in the gloomy house, I in a small varnished cot standing in my father's bed-recess. He dismissed his servants and ate his meals at my grandfather's, who refused to take any payment. I think it was for my sake that my grandfather thus inflicted on himself the constant company of a man he disliked. They had nothing in common but their feeling of deep grief. On the death of my mother, my family broke off all social relations, and to crown the dreariness of my existence we lived, thereafter, in continual seclusion.

M. Joubert, a gloomy pedant from the mountains (what they call in Grenoble a *Bet*, that's to say a lout from the mountains of Gap), M. Joubert – who taught me Latin, stupidly enough, God knows, by making me recite the rules of my elementary textbook, a thing that offended my intelligence, and I was supposed to have plenty of that – died. I used to go and have lessons with him in the small Place Notre-Dame, and I can say that I never went through it without remembering my mother and the perfect joy of the life I used to lead in her time. In those days it disgusted me to be kissed even by my good grandfather.

That fearful-looking pedant Joubert left me as a legacy the second volume of a French translation of Quintus Curtius, that insipid Roman who wrote the life of Alexander.

This dreadful pedant, five feet six inches tall, horribly thin and dressed in a dirty tattered black frock-coat was, however, not too black at heart.

But his successor, M. l'abbé Raillane, was a blackguard in every sense of the word. I don't mean to say that he had committed crimes, but one couldn't find a more arid soul, more hostile to everything decent, more utterly devoid of any feeling of humanity. He was a priest, he came from a village in Provence, he was short and lean, very prim, sallow-skinned and shifty eyed, and with an abominable smile.

He had just finished educating Casimir and Augustin Perier and their four or six brothers.

Casimir became a minister and a famous one, and, in my opinion, the dupe of Louis-Philippe. Augustin, most bombastic of men, died a Peer of France. Scipion died about 1806, slightly mad. Camille became a commonplace prefect, and has just married as his second wife a very rich woman; he's a bit mad like all his brothers. Joseph, who married a pretty and extremely affected woman and who has had some celebrated love affairs, was perhaps the most sensible of them all. Another, Amédée, I believe, having been robbed at cards in 1815 or thereabouts, chose to spend five years in the Sainte-Pélagie prison rather than pay.

All these brothers were more or less crazy; well, I believe they owed this condition to our common tutor, M. l'abbé Raillane.

Whether by cunning, by education or by priestly instinct, this man was a sworn enemy to logic and to sound argument.

My father [1] engaged him apparently out of vanity. M. Perier *milord*, father of Casimir the minister, was said to be the richest man in the neighbourhood. In fact he had ten or eleven children and he left each of them 350,000 francs. What an honour for a lawyer attached to the Parlement to engage for his son the tutor who had just left M. Perier's!

Perhaps M. Raillane had been dismissed on account of some misdeed; what inclines me to this suspicion today is that there were still three children in the Perier house who were quite young: Camille, who was my age; Joseph and Amédée, who I believe were much younger.

I know absolutely nothing about the financial arrangements

1. Dec[ember] 1825. [San] Lorenzo in Damaso, ill FOR THE champ[agne] OF YESTERDAY.

my father made with the abbé Raillane.[1] Any attention paid to money matters was considered supremely vile and base in my family. It was somehow indecent to talk about money; money was like some distressing necessity of life, unfortunately indispensable, like the privy, but which must never be spoken of. They would, however, by way of exception mention the round sums to be paid for real estate, a term which they pronounced with respect.

M. Bellier paid 20,000 crowns for his property at Voreppe. Pariset is costing our cousin Colomb over 12,000 crowns (of 3 fr.).

This reluctance to talk about money, so contrary to Parisian custom, came from goodness knows where and has become completely ingrained in my character. The only thought suggested to me by the sight of a large sum of gold is the boredom of having to protect it from thieves; this feeling has often been taken for a pose and I never mention it nowadays.

My family's sense of honour and all its lofty and extravagant feelings came from my aunt Élisabeth; these feelings reigned despotically in our house, and yet she spoke of them very seldom, once or twice a year perhaps; they were usually called forth by praise of her father. This woman, of such singular loftiness of character, was worshipped by me; she was about sixty-five years old at the time, always very neat in appearance, and her dresses, although extremely simple, were made of expensive materials. Of course I only realize these things now, on thinking about them. For instance, I don't know the expression of any of my relatives and yet their features are present to my mind, down to the slightest detail. If I can to some extent picture the appearance of my excellent grandfather, it is on account of the visit I paid him when I was already auditeur or assistant in the Com[missariat of War]. I have completely forgotten the date of this visit. My character was very slow to develop, and that's how I explain my poor memory for faces. Until I was twenty-five, nay even today, I often have to grip myself with both hands in order not to be completely swayed by the impression things make on me, and to be able to judge them rationally, on the basis of experience. But what the devil does the reader care about this?

1. Idea: perhaps if I do not correct this first draft I shall manage to escape lying through vanity. Omar, 3 December 1835.

What does he care about the whole of this work? And yet if I don't dig deep into this character of Henri, which is so hard for me to understand, I shan't be acting like an honest author anxious to say all he knows about his subject. I beg my publisher, if ever I have one, to cut all these tedious passages.

One day my aunt Élisabeth Gagnon was remembering with tender emotion her brother who had died young in Paris; we were alone one afternoon in her room which overlooked the Place Grenette. Obviously this lofty soul was answering her own thoughts, and as she was fond of me she addressed me out of politeness.

'He had so much character!' (this meant strength of will). 'Such activity! ah, how different!' (this meant how different from *the other*, my grandfather, Henri Gagnon). And immediately, correcting herself and thinking before whom she was speaking, she added: *'I've never spoken about him so much.'*

Myself: 'And at what age did he die?'

M lle Éli[sabeth]: 'At twenty-three.'

The conversation went on a long time, and at last she spoke about her father. Among a hundred other details that I've forgotten she said: 'At such and such a time, *he wept with rage when he heard that the enemy were advancing on Toulon.*'

(But when did the enemy advance on Toulon? Perhaps it was in 1736 in the war made notable by the battle of the *Assiette*, of which I've just now, in '34, seen an interestingly *truthful* engraving.)

He had wanted the militia to march. Now nothing in the world was farther from the feelings of my grandfather Gagnon, a regular Fontenelle, the wittiest and the least patriotic man I have ever known. Patriotism for my grandfather would have meant a contemptible distraction from his elegant literary ideas. My father would have promptly calculated what he could have gained by it. My uncle Romain would have said with an alarmed air: 'The deuce, this may involve me in some danger.' My old aunt's heart, and my own, would have throbbed with excitement.

Perhaps I anticipate a little as regards myself and attribute to myself at the age of seven or eight the feelings I had at nine or ten. It is impossible for me to distinguish my feelings on the same subjects at two contiguous periods.

One thing I am certain of: the solemn and forbidding portrait of my great-grandfather in its gilt frame with great six-inch-wide rosettes became dear and sacred to me as soon as I learnt of his brave and generous reaction when the enemy was advancing on Toulon.

CHAPTER 8

ON THIS occasion, my aunt Élisabeth told me that my great-grandfather was born at Avignon, a town in Provence *where oranges grow*, she told me with longing in her voice, and much nearer to Toulon than Grenoble is. I must explain that the chief splendour of our town consisted of sixty or eighty orange trees in boxes, which may originally have come from the Constable de Lesdiguières, the last important figure to have come out of Dauphiné, and which, when summer drew near, were set out with great pomp in the neighbourhood of the magnificent avenue of chestnut trees also planted, I believe, by Lesdiguières. 'Is there really a country where orange trees grow in the open ground?' I asked my aunt. I realize today that I had unwittingly reminded her of the object of her endless longing.

She told me that we had originally come from a land even more beautiful than Provence (we, that's to say the Gagnons), that her grandfather's grandfather, in consequence of some disastrous circumstance, had taken refuge in Avignon in the train of some Pope; that there he had been obliged to change his name somewhat and to hide, and had then earned his living as a surgeon.

With my present knowledge of Italy I should translate this as follows: that one M. Guadagni or Guadaniamo, having committed a slight murder in Italy, had come to Avignon about 1650 in the train of some legate or other. What struck me chiefly then was that we had come (for I considered myself a Gagnon and I never thought of the Beyles except with a distaste which I still feel in 1835) from a land where orange trees grew in the open ground. What a land of delight, I thought!

82

This notion of our Italian origin is borne out by the fact that the language of that country was held in great honour in our family, a most unusual thing in a bourgeois family of 1780. My grandfather knew and esteemed Italian, my poor mother read Dante, a very difficult thing even in our own day; M. Artaud, who spent twenty years in Italy and has just published a translation of Dante, includes no less than two mistranslations and

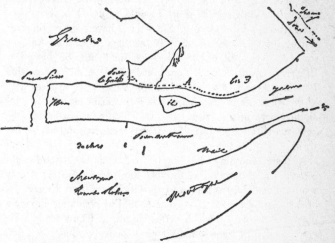

[*Grenoble – Sassenage – Drac – Stone bridge – Porte de la Graille – La Biole – Wood, B. – Isère. Island. Isère – Rock. Porte de France – The Mall – Mountain. Rabot Tower – Mountain.*]

one howler on every page. Of all the Frenchmen I know, only two, M. Fauriel who gave me the Arabian love stories, and M. Delécluze of the *Débats*, understand Dante, and yet all the scribblers in Paris constantly degrade that great writer's name by quoting him and claiming to explain him. This shocks me more than anything.

My respect for Dante is of long standing; it dates from the copies of his works that I found on the shelf in my father's bookcase that held my poor mother's books, and which were my only comfort during the days of the *Raillane tyranny*.

My horror for that man's profession and for what he taught professionally reached the verge of mania.

Would you believe that even yesterday, 4 December 1835, coming from R[ome] to C[ivita]-V[ecchi]a, I had occasion to do a great service, at little inconvenience to myself, to a young woman whom I don't imagine to be very strait-laced. On our journey she discovered my name against my will, she was the bearer of a letter of introduction to my secretary. She had a pair of very fine eyes which gazed at me not unkindly during the last eight leagues of the journey. She begged me to find her an inexpensive lodging; in short I could probably have enjoyed her favours if I'd wanted to. But while I have been writing this during the past week the dreadful memory of the abbé Raillane revived. The aquiline but rather too small nose of this pretty lady from Lyons, Mme . . ., reminded me of the abbé's; after that I couldn't bear even to look at her and I pretended to go to sleep in the coach. Even after helping her to embark, as a favour, for eight crowns instead of twenty-five, I was reluctant to visit the new quarantine station lest I be forced to see her and receive her thanks.

As there is nothing consoling but only what is ugly and loathsome in my recollections of the abbé Raillane, for the past twenty years at least I have averted my eyes with horror from the memory of that terrible period. That man should by rights have made a scoundrel of me; he was a perfect Jesuit, as I now realize. He used to take me aside when we went for walks along the Isère, from the Graille gate to the mouth of the Drac, or else just to a little wood beyond the island (A), to explain to me that I had spoken imprudently. 'But, monsieur,' I used to say to him in other words, 'it's true; it's what I feel.'

'That doesn't matter, my young friend, you must not say it, it isn't proper.' If these maxims had caught on with me I should be rich today, for three or four times Fortune has knocked at my door. (I refused, in May 1814, the post of General Director of Supplies (wheat) in Paris, under the orders of M. le Comte Beugnot, whose wife was extremely friendly towards me; next to her lover, M. Pépin de Belle-Isle, also a close friend of mine, I was perhaps the person she loved best.) So I should be rich, but I should also be a scoundrel, I shouldn't have those delightful visions of *beauty* which still often fill my head even now I'm FIFTY-TWO.

The reader may perhaps believe that I'm trying to avoid the deadly ordeal of having to talk about abbé Raillane.

He had a brother, a tailor at the end of the Grande Rue near the Place Claveyson, who was the embodiment of filthiness. There was only one shame lacking to this Jesuit; he was not dirty but on the contrary very neat and clean. He was fond of canaries, he bred them and looked after them very cleanly, but next to my bed. I cannot conceive how my father allowed anything so unhealthy. My grandfather had never entered our house after his

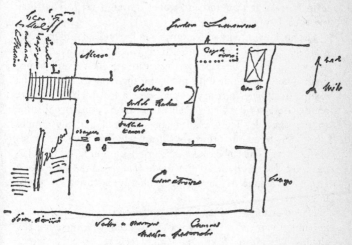

[*Fine lime tree – Lamouroux garden – Staircase joining on to the house staircase – Bed-recess – M. l'abbé Raillane's room. Work-table. Orange tree – Birds' cage. My bed – North. South – Staircase – Narrow yard –Passage – Front door – Dining-room – Kitchen – Father's house.*]

daughter's death; he would never have tolerated such a thing. My father Chérubin Beyle, as I have said, cared for me as the upholder of his name but not at all as his son.

The canaries' wire cage, fastened to wooden props which in their turn were fastened to the wall by staples in the plaster, was about nine feet long, six high and four deep. In this space some thirty wretched canaries of all colours fluttered sadly, far from the sunlight. When they were nesting the abbé used to feed them on yolk of egg, and of all that he did that was the only thing that interested me. But those confounded birds used to wake me at dawn, and soon afterwards I would hear the noise of the abbé's shovel as he tended his fire with a care that I have since recognized as characteristic of many Jesuits. But this aviary gave out a strong smell, and that two feet from my bed and in a damp dark room which never got any sunlight. We had no window over the Lamouroux garden, only a window *on sufferance* (Parlement towns are full of legal terms) which let in a bright light on to the staircase L which was shaded by a fine lime tree, although the staircase was at least forty feet above ground level. That lime tree must have been very tall.

The abbé used to fly into a quiet, sombre and spiteful rage like a phlegmatic diplomat when I ate my snack of dry bread beside his orange trees. These orange trees were a regular mania of his, even more tiresome than his mania for the canaries. Some of the orange trees were three inches and some a foot high; they stood on the window-sill which got a little sunshine during two months in the summer. The dreadful abbé declared that the crumbs which fell from our brown bread attracted flies which ate his orange trees. This abbé could have given a lesson in meanness to the most *bourgeois* of all the town *bourgeois*, the most *patet* (*patet*, pronounced 'patais', meticulously attentive to trivial interests).

My companions, MM. Chazel and Reytiers, were much less unhappy than I was. Chazel was a good fellow, quite a big boy already; his father, from the Midi, I believe, and therefore a downright brusque coarse-mannered man, who was clerk and commission agent for the Periers, cared little about Latin. Chazel used to come *by himself* (without a servant) at about ten, did his Latin exercise badly and took himself off at half past twelve, often not coming back in the evenings.

Reytiers, a pretty boy, as fair and timid as a girl, dared not look the fearful abbé Raillane in the face. He was an only son and his father was the most timid and the most pious of men. He used to arrive at eight o'clock, strictly guarded by a servant who came back to fetch him as twelve was striking at Saint-André (the fashionable church of the town, whose bells we could hear very clearly). By two o'clock the servant had brought Reytiers back with his afternoon snack in a basket. In summer about five o'clock M. Raillane used to take us for walks; in winter seldom and then at about three o'clock. Chazel being a big boy, used to get bored on the walks and would leave us very soon.

We were very anxious to go in the direction of the Île de l'Isère, for one thing the mountain looks lovely from there, and one of the *literary* vices of my father and M. Raillane was always to talk in exaggerated terms about the beauties of nature (which these fine souls must have felt very little, being preoccupied only with making money). By dint of telling us about the beauty of the Buisserate rock M. l'abbé Raillane had got us to raise our heads. But it was something quite different that attracted us to the bank near the island. There we poor prisoners could see youngsters *enjoying their freedom*, coming and going *alone* and then bathing in the Isère and a tributary stream called La Biole; an excess of happiness of which we could not envisage the possibility even in the remotest distance.

M. Raillane, like a regular Government newspaper of today, talked to us of nothing but the dangers of liberty. He could never see a child bathing without prophesying that it would end by drowning itself, thus doing us the service of turning us into cowards, in which as far as concerns myself he was completely successful. When I got my freedom two years later, I suppose about 1795, and then only by deceiving my family and telling a new lie each day, I was already thinking of leaving Grenoble at whatever cost. I was in love with Mad[ame] Kubly and swimming was no longer of enough interest for me to want to learn. Every time I got into the water Roland (Alphonse) or some other tough made me swallow a mouthful.

I can remember no dates under the horrible Raillane tyranny; I grew sullen and hated everybody. My great grief was not to be able to play with other children; my father, probably very proud of having a tutor for his son, dreaded nothing so much as to see me *go about with common children* as the aristocrats used to say in those days. One thing might provide me with a date: Mlle Marine Perier (sister of the minister Casimir Perier) came to see M. Raillane, who may have been her father-confessor, a short time before her marriage to that lunatic Camille Teisseire (a fanatical patriot who later burned his copies of Voltaire and

87

Rousseau), who in 1811, having become *sous-préfet* thanks to his cousin M. Crétet, was so astonished at the favour he saw me enjoying in the salon of Mme la Comtesse Daru (on the ground floor overlooking the garden of the Hôtel de Biron, I believe, the last house on the left in the rue Saint-Dominique, at the corner of the Boulevard des Invalides). I can still see his envious expression and his clumsy politeness to me. Camille Teisseire had grown rich, or rather his father had grown rich, making cherry ratafia, a fact of which he was greatly ashamed.

By looking through the registers in Grenoble (which Louis XVIII used to call Grelibre) for the marriage certificate of M. Camille Teisseire (rue des Vieux-Jésuites or Place Grenette, for his huge house had two entrances) and Mlle Marine Perier, I should have the date of the Raillane tyranny.

I was sullen, secretive and discontented, I used to translate Virgil; the abbé exaggerated the beauties of that poet and I accepted his eulogies much as the wretched Poles of our own day must accept the eulogies of Russian kindness in their venal newspapers. I hated the abbé, I hated my father who was responsible for the abbé's power, I hated even more the religion in whose name they tyrannized over me. I used to prove to my fellow prisoner, timid Reytiers, that all the things they taught us were so much nonsense. Where had I got these ideas from? I couldn't say. We had a large illustrated Bible bound in green with wood engravings inserted in the text, the best possible thing for children. I remember I was always looking out for absurdities in that wretched Bible. Reytiers, more timid and more devout, adored by his father and by his mother who wore a lot of rouge and had once been a beauty, used to agree with my doubts from good nature.

So, then, we were translating Virgil with great difficulty when I discovered in my father's bookcase a translation of Virgil, in four octavo volumes handsomely bound, by that scoundrel the abbé Desfontaines I believe. I found the volume that contained the second book of the Georgics, which we were murdering (we really knew no Latin at all). I hid this blessed volume in the privy, in a cupboard where they stored the feathers of the capons eaten in the house; and there, twice or thrice during our ordeal of translation, we used to go and consult Desfontaines. I fancy that the abbé discovered this because of Reytiers' cheerfulness, and there was a horrid scene. I grew more and more sombre, spiteful and unhappy. I loathed everybody, my aunt Séraphie above all.

A year after my mother's death, about 1791 or '92, it seems to me now that my father must have fallen in love with aunt Séraphie; whence the endless walks to Les Granges when they took me along to make a third but were careful to make me walk forty paces ahead of them as soon as we had passed through the Porte de Bonne. Aunt Séraphie had taken a dislike to me. I don't know why, and was always getting my father to scold me. I detested them and must have shown it, since even today when I feel a dislike for anybody the people present can always notice this immediately. I detested my younger sister Zénaïde (now Mme Alexandre Mallein) because my father made a pet of her and would lull her to sleep on his knees every evening, and because she was loudly championed by Mlle Séraphie. I covered the plaster-work in the house (coated with whitewash) with caricatures of Zénaïde the *telltale*. My sister Pauline (now Périer-Lagrange, widowed) and I accused Zénaïde of spying on us, and I believe we weren't far wrong. I always had dinner at my grandfather's but we had finished dinner as Saint-André's clock struck a quarter past one, and at two o'clock I had to leave the lovely sunshine of the Place Grenette and go to the damp cold rooms where the abbé Raillane lived in my father's house in the rue des Vieux-Jésuites. I hated this beyond anything; as I was morose and secretive I made plans to run away, but where could I get the money?

One day my grandfather said to the abbé Raillane: 'But, monsieur, why do you teach this child the celestial system of Ptolemy, which you know is wrong?'

'Monsieur, it explains everything and, besides, it has the approval of the Church.'

My grandfather could not stomach this reply and used often to quote it with a laugh; he never grew indignant about other people's business. Now, my education was my father's business, and the less M. Gagnon thought of my father's learning the more he respected his rights as a father.

But this reply of the abbé's, being frequently repeated by my beloved grandfather, finally turned me into a rabid unbeliever and the most sullen of creatures into the bargain. My grandfather understood astronomy, although he understood nothing about calculus. We used to spend summer evenings on the magnificent terrace of his apartment, from which he showed me the Great Bear and the Little Bear and talked to me poetically about the Chaldean shepherds and Abraham. Thus I acquired a certain respect for Abraham, and I said to Reytiers: 'He wasn't a scoundrel like the other people in the Bible.'

My grandfather owned, or had borrowed from the public library of which he was the founder, a quarto copy of Bruce's *Travels in Nubia and Abyssinia*. This travel book was illustrated with engravings, hence its enormous influence on my education.

I loathed all that my father and the abbé Raillane taught me. Now my father used to make me learn *Lacroix's* geography by heart and recite it, and the abbé kept this up. I was forced to know it well, but I loathed it.

Bruce, a descendant of the Kings of Scotland, so my excellent grandfather told me, inspired me with a keen liking for all the branches of learning he described. Hence my love for mathematics and eventually that idea, which I venture to call a notion of genius: *mathematics will get me out of Grenoble.*

CHAPTER 9

For all his Dauphinois canniness my father Chérubin Beyle was an enthusiast. His passion for Bourdaloue and Massillon had been succeeded by a passion for agriculture, which in turn was overthrown by his love for the trowel (i.e. for building), which he had always had, and finally by extreme right-wing politics and the passion for governing the town of Grenoble in the interests of the Bourbons. My father used to dream night and day about whatever was the object of his passion, he had considerable shrewdness and a great experience of the wiles of other Dauphinois, and I'm inclined to conclude from all this that he had some ability. But I have no clearer conception of this than of what he looked like.

My father took to going twice a week to Claix, which is a domaine (a local term meaning a small estate) of a hundred and fifty acres, I think, lying to the south of the town on a slope of the mountain, the other side of the Drac. All the land round Claix and Furonières is arid, chalky and stony. A free-thinking curé, about 1750, had the notion of cultivating the *marsh* to the west of the Claix bridge; this marshland has proved a gold-mine for the district.

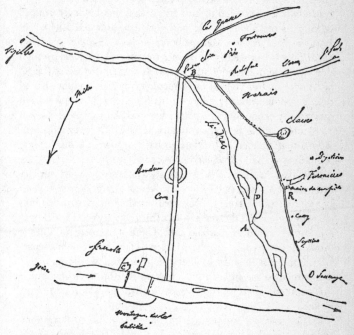

A. Wire bridge put up about 1826 – B. Pont de Claix, a remarkable semi-circular arch – C. Citadel – G. Place Grenette – D. Comboire Rock, rising sheer above the Drac which is very rapid, both rock and woods are full of foxes – R. Country house which played a most important part in my child-hood, which I revisited in 1828, when it had been sold to a general. [*Vizille – Le Gresse – Pont de Claix – Fontanieu – Meadows – Rochefort – Varces – Saint-Paul – South – Grenoble – Walk – Circular path – The Drac – Marshes – Claix – Doyatières – Furonières – My father's house – Cossey – Seyssins – Sassenage – Isère – The Bastille hill.*]

My father's house was two leagues from Grenoble; I have done the journey on foot some thousand times. It is probably owing to this exercise that my father enjoyed the perfect health which kept him going to the age of seventy-two. A bourgeois is only respected in Grenoble if he has some *property*. Lefèvre, my father's wig-maker, had some property at Corenc and used often to disappoint his customers *because he had gone to Corenc*, an excuse which was always accepted. Sometimes we took a short cut by crossing the Drac at the Seyssins ford, at point A.

My father was so full of his new passion that he never stopped talking to me about it. He sent for the illustrated Library of Husbandry or Estate Management, he '*had it come*' – as they say locally – from Paris or Lyons; I often used to look through this work, and consequently I was often taken to Claix (i.e. to our house at Furonières) on Thursday, my half-holiday. I used to walk about with my father in his fields and listen with an ill grace as he expounded his plans; however, he was so pleased to have somebody to hear the romantic tales which he called calculations that frequently I didn't go back to town till the Friday; sometimes we had left as early as Wednesday night.

I disliked Claix because I was always pestered with agricultural projects there, but I soon discovered a great compensation. I began to steal volumes of Voltaire from the forty-volume edition that my father had shelved at Claix (his property) and which was beautifully bound in marbled calf. There were forty volumes, I think, closely packed together; I used to take out two and separate all the rest slightly so that this didn't show. Besides, this dangerous work had been put away on the top shelf of the fine glass-fronted cherry-wood bookcase, which was often kept locked.

By the grace of God, even at that age I found the illustrations ridiculous, and what illustrations! ... they were those of *La Pucelle*. This miracle almost makes me believe that God intended me to have good taste and to write the *History of Painting in Italy* one day.

We always went to Claix for the *holidays*, that's to say for the months of August and September. My teachers complained that I forgot all my Latin during this interval of pleasure. Nothing revolted me more than to hear my father describe our visits to

Claix as 'our pleasure trips'. I was like a galley slave who is given a slightly lighter set of chains and forced to call them his *pleasure*.

I was overwrought and, I imagine, very spiteful and unfair towards my father and the abbé Raillane, I admit. But even now in 1835 I have to make a great mental effort to do it, so that I cannot judge these two men. They poisoned my childhood, in the full force of the word 'poison'. They had grim faces and they constantly prevented me from exchanging a word with a child of my own age. It was not until I went to the Central Schools (that admirable creation of M. de Tracy) that I came into contact with children of my own age; but not with the gaiety and carelessness of childhood. I came amongst them

secretive and ill-natured, full of ideas of revenge for the slightest punch I was given, which I resented as a grown man would an insult; in a word I had every vice short of treachery.

The worst part of the Raillane tyranny was that I was conscious of my sufferings. I was always seeing children of my own age crossing the Place Grenette, going off *together* walking or running, and that was something I was not once allowed to do. When I gave a hint of the unhappiness which consumed me, I used to be told: 'You shall have a drive in the carriage,' and Mme Périer-Lagrange (mother of my late brother-in-law), one of the gloomiest of people, took me in her carriage when she drove out for her health; she used to scold me at least as much as the abbé Raillane. She was unfeeling and devout and had, like the abbé, one of those inflexible faces that never laugh. What a substitute for a ramble with little rascals of my own age! Believe it or not, I never played at *gobilles* (marbles) and I only got a top because my grandfather pleaded for me, and his daughter Séraphie made *a scene* with him about it.

I was very sly and ill-natured, then, when I happened to discover a French edition of *Don Quixote* in the handsome bookcase at Claix. This book had pictures, but it looked old, and I loathed everything old, for my relations prevented me from meeting young people, and they themselves seemed to me extremely old. But at last I managed to understand the pictures, which amused me: Sancho Panza seated on his pack-saddle

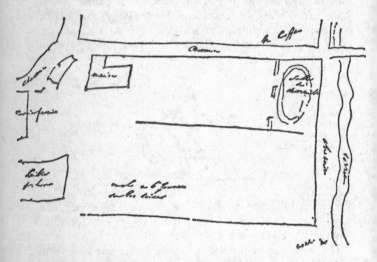

[*M. Coffe – Bath – Path – House – Arbour – Path – Torrent – North – Farmhouse – Wine-cellar – This garden measures 6 journaux of 600 fathoms.*]

held up by four stakes, Ginès de Passamont having taken away the donkey.

Don Quixote made me die of laughter. Please be good enough to remember that since the death of my poor mother I had never laughed, I was the victim of an unremitting aristocratic and religious education. My tyrants had never known a moment's inconsistency. Every invitation was refused. I often overheard discussions in which my grandfather was in favour of my being allowed to accept. My aunt Séraphie objected, referring to me in abusive terms, my father who was subservient to her answered his father-in-law with Jesuitical phrases which I knew did not commit him to anything. My aunt Élisabeth shrugged her shoulders. When a proposed outing had survived a discussion of this kind, my father would call in the abbé Raillane about some exercise which I had failed to do the day before, and which must be done exactly at the time of the outing.

Imagine the effect of *Don Quixote* in the midst of such horrible gloom! The discovery of this book, which I read sitting under the second lime tree along the path on that side of the flower-bed where the ground was sunk a foot deep, was perhaps the greatest moment of my life.

Believe it or not, my father, seeing me burst out laughing, used to come and scold me and threaten to take the book away, which he did several times, and then take me into his fields to explain his schemes for *improving* and fertilizing the soil.

Disturbed even in my reading of *Don Quixote*, I took to hiding in the arbour, a small enclosure of greenery at the eastern end of the *clos*, the small walled park.

I found an illustrated Molière; the pictures seemed to me ridiculous and I only understood *L'Avare*. I found the comedies of Destouches, and one of the absurdest of them moved me to tears. There was a love story mingled with self-sacrifice, full of generous (noble) deeds, the sort of thing that appealed to me. I've racked my memory in vain for the title of that comedy, unknown even amongst the unknown comedies of that dreary diplomat. The *Night Drummer*, which includes an idea borrowed from the English, amused me very much.

From the age of seven – and this seems to be an established fact in my mind – I had resolved to write comedies like Molière. Less than ten years ago I still remembered *how* this resolution had come about.

My grandfather was delighted by my enthusiasm for *Don Quixote*, which I described to him, for I used to tell him practically everything; this good old man of sixty-five was really my sole companion.

He lent me, unbeknown to his daughter Séraphie, *Orlando Furioso*, translated, or rather, I believe, imitated from Ariosto by M. de Tressan (whose son, now a field-marshal and in 1820 a rather dreary ultra but in 1788 a delightful young man, had played such a part in getting me to learn to read by promising me a little book full of pictures which he never gave me, a breach of faith that shocked me deeply).

Ariosto developed my character; I fell madly in love with Bradamante whom I pictured as a buxom lass of twenty-four with charms of the most dazzling whiteness.

I had a loathing for all the vulgar bourgeois details of which Molière made use to express his thought. These details reminded me too much of my own unhappy life. Not three days ago (December 1835) as two bourgeois of my acquaintance were about to enact a comic scene of petty dissimulation and semi-wrangling, I walked off ten yards in order not to hear it. I loathe such things, and this has prevented me from gaining experience. This is *no small misfortune*.

Everything that is mean and vulgar in the bourgeois way reminds me of Grenoble, everything that reminds me of Gr[enoble] fills me with horror, no, *horror* is too noble a word, with *nausea*.

Grenoble is for me like the recollection of a frightful attack of indigestion, not dangerous but horribly nauseating. Whatever is unrelievedly low and vulgar, whatever is opposed to the slightest generous impulse, whatever rejoices in the misfortune of noble and patriotic natures – that's what Grenoble means to me.

On my travels nothing surprised me more than to hear some officers of my acquaintance say that Grenoble was a charming town, sparkling with wit and where *the pretty women were unforgettable*. The first time I heard this said was at dinner at General Moncey's (now Marshal Moncey, Duke of Conegliano) in 1802 at Milan or at Cremona. I was so astonished that I asked across the table for details; I was a *rich* subaltern then, with 150 fr[ancs] a month, and full of self-confidence. My loathing for the state of sickening and continuous moral indigestion from which I had just escaped was at its height. The staff officer maintained his statement; he had spent fifteen or eighteen months in Grenoble, he declared that it was the pleasantest of all provincial towns; he mentioned Mesdames Allemand-Dulauron,

Piat-Desvials, Tournus, Duchamps, de Montaur, Mesdemoiselles Rivière (daughters of the innkeeper in the rue Montorge), Mesdemoiselles Bailly, friends of my uncle's, who kept a milliner's shop, Messieurs Drevon, the Elder and the Twin, M. Dolle from the Porte-de-France, and as regards aristocratic society (an 1800 word, since replaced by *ultra* and then by *legitimist*) M. de che[valier] de Marcieu, M. de Bailly.

Alas, I had barely heard the names of these charming people mentioned, my relatives only referred to them to deplore their folly, for they used to find fault with everything, they were *jaundiced*; this must be stressed to give some rational explanation of my misery. At my mother's death my broken-hearted relatives had severed all connection with society; my mother had been the life and soul, the gaiety of the family. My father, sullen, timid, resentful and unlovable, had the sort of character they have in Geneva (where they calculate and never laugh), and I don't think he had ever made any friends except for my mother's sake. My grandfather, a charming person, a man of the world, whose company, more than that of any other man in the town, was sought by everybody, from artisans to great nobles, from Mme Barthélemy the shoemaker's wife and a witty woman, to M. le Baron des Adrets, with whom he continued to dine once a month, cut to the heart by the death of the only creature he loved and seeing himself turned sixty, had broken with the rest of society through weariness of life. Only my aunt Élisabeth, of independent means and even wealthy (wealthy for Grenoble in 1789), had still kept a few homes to which she went for a game of cards in the evening (before supper, between seven and nine o'clock). She thus went out two or three times a week and sometimes, although full of respect for a father's rights, she took pity on me and, when my father was at Claix, she pretended to need me and took me with her as escort to visit Mlle Simon, who rouged heavily and lived in the new Jacobins' House. My kind aunt even took me once to a big supper given by Mlle Simon. I can still remember the blaze of lights and the splendour with which the table was laid; there was a centre-piece, with silver statues, in the middle of it. Next day my aunt Séraphie denounced me to my father and there was a scene. Such quarrels, always formally polite but during which unforgettably biting words were spoken, formed the sole amusement of this morose family into which my cruel fate had cast me. How I envied the nephew of Mme Barthélemy, our shoemaker's wife!

I was unhappy, but I did not see the reasons for all this; I attributed everything to the unkindness of my father and Séraphie. To be fair I should have seen them as bourgeois puffed up with pride and anxious to give their *only son*, as they called me, an aristocratic education. Such thoughts were quite beyond my age, and in any case who could have suggested them to me? My only friends were Marion the cook and Lambert my

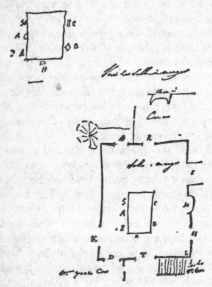

This is how we sat at table at my grandfather's, where I ate from seven years old to sixteen and a half. A. Grandfather – B. Father – C. Aunt Élisabeth – S. Aunt Séraphie – H. Me – P. The priest in hiding at our house – F. The only window in the dining-room – O. Door on to the small spiral staircase – R. Kitchen door – E. Big passage leading into the other house on the Place Grenette – M. Stove – N. Door into Lambert's room – L. Cupboard containing liqueurs, these were excellent, they were presents made to Grandfather – T. Big door on to the main staircase – D. Narrow sash-window – K. Door of Grandfather's room. [*Here is the dining-room – Fireplace – Kitchen – Dining-room – Very big courtyard – Very fine staircase.*]

98

grandfather's manservant, and Séraphie was constantly calling me away when she heard me laughing in the kitchen with them. My relatives, in their black depression, had nothing to think about but me; they glorified their nagging with the name of education and were probably quite sincere about it. Through his constant contact with me my grandfather imparted to me his reverence for literature. Horace and Hippocrates were very different men, in my eyes, from Romulus, Alexander and Numa. M. de Voltaire was a very different man from that imbecile Louis XVI whom he laughed at, or that rake Louis XV of whose loose living he disapproved; he spoke with disgust of *la* Du Barry, and the absence of the word *madame*, amidst our usual politeness, struck me very much. Voltaire was always Monsieur de Voltaire, and my grandfather always uttered the name with a smile mingled with respect and affection.

Politics cropped up presently. My family was one of the most aristocratic in the town, which meant that I immediately felt myself to be a fanatical republican. I kept seeing the fine regiments of dragoons passing on their way to Italy; I gazed at them in rapture, and my relatives execrated them. Soon the priests went into hiding, there was always a priest or two hidden in our house. The gluttony of one of the first who came, a big man whose eyes goggled as he ate pickled pork, disgusted me. (We had some excellent *pickled pork*; I used to go down to the cellar with our servant Lambert to fetch it; it was preserved in a receptacle hollowed in stone.) At home everybody ate with remarkable daintiness and fastidious good manners. I was always told, for instance, not to make any noise with my mouth. Most of these priests were common people who smacked their tongues against their palates and broke their bread messily; that was enough to fill me with repulsion for these people, who used to sit on my left hand. One of our cousins (M. Santerre) was guillotined at Lyons, and the gloom of our family and its feeling of hatred and discontent with everything was redoubled.

Formerly when I heard people speak of the naïve joys of childhood, the thoughtlessness of that age, the happiness of extreme youth – the only true happiness in life – my heart felt heavy. I never experienced any of this; and indeed that age was for me a continuous period of suffering, hatred and frustrated desire for vengeance. All my unhappiness can be summed up in a couple of phrases: I was never allowed to speak to a child of my own age, and my relatives, who were very bored because of their segregation from all society, honoured me with their continuous attention. For these two causes, at that period of life when other children are so gay, I was ill-natured, sullen, unreasonable, in short a *slave*, in the worst sense of the word, and gradually I assumed the feelings of a slave. The little happiness I managed to snatch I guarded with lies. In another respect I was absolutely like the nations of Europe today, my tyrants always spoke to me with gentle words expressing the tenderest care, and their firmest ally was religion. I had to submit to continual homilies about paternal love and the duties of children. One day, bored with my father's pathos, I told him: 'If you're so fond of me, give me five sous a day and let me live as I like. In any case you can be sure of one thing, as soon as I'm old enough I shall join up.'

My father rushed at me as if to destroy me; he was beside himself: '*You're nothing but an impious wretch*,' he said to me. Wasn't this exactly like the Emperor Nicholas and the town of Warsaw which is so much in the news as I write this (7 December 1835. Civita-Vecchia), so true is it that all tyrannies are alike.

It seems to me that, by some stroke of luck, I haven't remained ill-natured, but only disgusted for the rest of my life with bourgeois people, Jesuits and hypocrites of every sort. I was perhaps cured of my ill-nature by my successes in 1797, '98 and '99 and by consciousness of my own strength. Besides my other fine qualities I was intolerably proud.[1]

To tell the truth, thinking it over carefully, I was never cured of my irrational horror for Grenoble, rather I *forgot* it in the true sense of the word. The magnificent memories of Italy, of Milan, have blotted it all out.

But it has left me with a considerable gap in my knowledge

1. [*First Version*] When I went to the Central School (in the year V, I think), as early as the following year I won the first prizes, perhaps there is a note of this in the papers of the *Département* (since become a prefecture). When I went to the Central School, I brought all these abominable vices along with me, but I had them knocked out of me. Luckily, it seems to me that I have not remained ill-natured.

of men and things. All the details which go to make up the life of Chrysale in *L'Ecole des Femmes* :

> 'Et hors un gros Plutarque à mettre mes rabats'
> [Except for a fat Plutarch to press my neckbands in]

revolt me. If I may be allowed a metaphor *as disgusting as what I feel*, it's like the smell of oysters to a man who's had an appalling attack of indigestion from oysters.

All the facts which make up the life of Chrysale are replaced in my mind by romantic fancies. I think these blemishes in my telescope have been a help to the characters in my novels : there's a certain sort of bourgeois vulgarity which they cannot possess, and for the author it would be like talking *Chinese*, which he does not know. This term bourgeois vulgarity merely expresses a shade of meaning, it may perhaps have become very obscure by 1880. Thanks to the Press, the provincial bourgeois has become a rarity, nobody nowadays has *the manners of his status*: an elegant young man about Paris, whom I met in a very gay company, was very well dressed, without affectation, and used to spend 8,000 or 10,000 francs. One day I asked : 'What does he do?'

'He's a very busy solicitor,' I was told.

So I shall quote as an example of bourgeois vulgarity the style of my excellent friend M. Fauriel (of the Institute) in his excellent *Life of Dante*, printed in 1834 in the *Revue de Paris*. But, alas, what will have become of these things in 1880? Some clever man, who writes well, will have seized upon the profound researches of the excellent Fauriel, and the labours of that worthy conscientious *bourgeois* will be wholly forgotten. He was once the handsomest man in Paris. Mad[ame] Condorcet (Sophie Grouchy), a great connoisseur, took possession of him, the bourgeois Fauriel was fool enough to fall in love with her, and when she died, about 1820 I believe, she left him an annuity of 1,200 francs as if he had been a servant. He was deeply humiliated. I told him, when he gave me ten pages of Arab adventures for *L'Amour* : 'When you're dealing with a princess or a woman who's too rich, you've got to beat her, or else love will die out.' This remark horrified him, and he no doubt said so to little Miss Clarke who's shaped like a question mark, ?, as Pope was.

In consequence of which, soon afterwards, she had me taken to task by one of her friends, that ass M. Augustine Thierry, member of the Institute, and I dropped her flat. There was a pretty woman in that set, Mme Belloc, but she used to make love with another question mark, a black crooked creature, Mlle de Montgolfier, and really I think the poor women were quite justified.

CHAPTER 10

My Teacher Durand

I HAVE absolutely no recollection of how I was delivered from the Raillane tyranny. That scoundrel should by rights have made an excellent Jesuit of me, a worthy successor to my father, or else a loose-living soldier, a frequenter of wenches and taverns. As in Fielding, my temperament would have completely concealed the *shamefulness* of this. I should thus have become one or other of these two delightful things but for my excellent grandfather, who unwittingly imparted to me his cult for Horace, Sophocles, Euripides and all choice literature. Fortunately he despised the dull writers who were his contemporaries, and I was not corrupted by Marmontel, Dorat and similar scum. I don't know why he continually asseverated his respect for priests, from whom, actually, he felt the same repulsion as from something unclean. When he saw them established in his drawing-room by his daughter Séraphie and my father, he was perfectly polite towards them, as he was towards everybody. For the sake of something to talk about he would discuss literature, sacred writers for instance, although he had no liking for these. But for all his politeness he had the greatest difficulty in concealing the profound disgust he felt for their ignorance. 'Heavens, they don't even know their own abbé Fleury, their historian!' I overheard this remark one day, and it increased my faith in him.

I discovered soon afterwards that he rarely went to confession. He was extremely polite about religion but was not a believer. He would have been devout had he been able to believe that he would meet his daughter Henriette in heaven (M. le Duc de

Broglie said: 'I feel as if my daughter were in America'), but he was merely sad and silent. As soon as somebody came in, out of politeness he used to talk and tell stories.

M. Raillane may perhaps have been forced to go into hiding for refusing to swear loyalty to the Civil Constitution of the Clergy. Whatever its cause his disappearance was the greatest event conceivable for me, and I remember nothing about it.

This is a mental failing of mine of which I have discovered several examples since, three years ago on the esplanade of *San Pietro in Montorio* (Janiculum), there occurred to me the brilliant idea that I should soon be fifty, that it was time to think about my departure and to treat myself first to the pleasure of a backward glance. I have no recollection of the periods or of the moments when I felt too strongly. One of my reasons for believing myself brave is that I remember with perfect clarity the slightest details of the duels in which I have been involved. In the army, when it was raining and I was marching in the mud, this courage was only just sufficient, but when I had not got wet the previous night and my horse was not slithering about under me, the most perilous rashness was literally a real delight to me. My sensible comrades would turn grave and pale, or flush scarlet, Mathis would grow gayer and Farine more reasonable. It's just the same at the present moment, I never think of the possibility OF WANTING OF A THOUSAND FRANCS, which nevertheless seems to be the dominant thought, the chief obsession of those friends of my own age who are far better off than I am (for instance M. Besan[çon], Colomb, etc.); but I'm wandering from the point. The great difficulty about writing these memoirs is to remember and write down only things relative to that period of time I'm trying to hold by the forelock; for instance I'm now dealing with those obviously less unhappy days that I spent under my teacher Durand.

He was a good fellow of about forty-five, stout and round in every respect, who had a tall son of eighteen, a very pleasant boy whom I admired from afar and who later on, I believe, was in love with my sister. Nobody could have been less Jesuitical and crafty than poor M. Durand, who was moreover polite, and whose dress was strictly economical but never slovenly. To tell the truth he did not know a word of Latin, but neither did I, and this was not likely to be a bone of contention between us.

I knew by heart the *Selectae e profanis* and in particular the story of Androcles and his lion, I knew the old Testament in the same way and maybe a little Virgil and Cornelius Nepos. But if I had been given leave to take a week's holiday, written in Latin, I should not have understood a word of it. The wretched Latin of modern writers, the *De Viris Illustribus* which told about Romulus, whom I dearly loved, was unintelligible to me. Well, M. Durand was in the same case; he knew by heart the authors whom he had been explaining for the past twenty years, but when my grandfather tried once or twice to consult him over some difficulty in his Horace which was not explained by Jean Bond (a name which delighted me : in the midst of so much misery what a joy to be able to laugh at *Jambon*!) M. Durand could not even understand the point at issue.

The method, then, was a pitiful one, and if I wanted to I could teach Latin in eighteen months to a child of ordinary intelligence. But wasn't it something to have been inured to hardship for two hours every morning and three hours every evening? That's important. (Round about 1819 I taught English in twenty-six days to M. Antonio Clerichetti of Milan, who suffered under a miserly father. On the thirtieth day he *sold* to a bookseller his translation of the interrogatory of the Princess of Wales, Caroline of Brunswick, a notorious harlot whom her husband, although he was a king and lavished millions, failed to convict of having made him what ninety-five per cent of husbands are.)

I have, then, no recollection of the event which parted me from M. Raillane.

After continuous unhappiness, the result of that unkind Jesuit's tyranny, I see myself suddenly established in my excellent grandfather's home, sleeping in a small trapezoid closet along-side his bedroom and being taught Latin by the worthy Durand, who came, I fancy, twice a day, from ten to eleven and from two to three. My relatives still clung firmly to the principle of not letting me have any dealings *with common children*.[1] But

---

1. Which was nothing less than depriving me for years not only of playing, but even of exchanging a word with any child whatsoever of my own age. Insert above, under the Raillane tyranny.

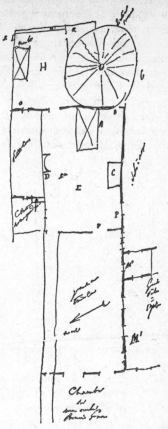

A. Grandfather's magnificent red damask bed – B. His wardrobe – C. Magnificent inlaid chest-of-drawers surmounted by a clock: Mars offering his arm to France, France wearing a cloak adorned with fleurs-de-lis, which caused a good deal of anxiety later on – F. Single window made of magnificent Bohemian glass. One pane, the top left, was cracked, and remained so for ten years – D. Fireplace – H. My room – O. My small window – RR. Cupboards – R'. My grandfather's huge cupboard. [*My bed – Spiral staircase – Small yard – Grandfather's study – Dining-room – Big gloomy courtyard. North – Big drawing-room in Italian style – Uncle Romain Gagnon's room.*]

M. Durand's lessons took place in the presence of my excellent grandfather, in winter in his bedroom at point M, in summer in the big drawing-room near the terrace at M', sometimes at M" in an ante-room which was scarcely ever used.

My recollections of the Raillane tyranny filled me with horror until 1814; about that time I forgot them, the events of the Restoration absorbed all my horror and disgust. The latter is the only feeling with which I remembered Durand's teaching *at home*, for I also followed his lectures at the Central School, but by then I was happy, at least comparatively so. I had begun to be sensitive to the beauty of the landscape consisting of the

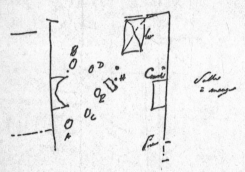

A. M. Chérubin Beyle – B. M. Gagnon – C. D. My aunts – P. M. Durand – H. Me. [*Bed – Chest-of-drawers – Door – Dining-room.*]

Eybens and Échirolles hills and the fine meadow of the *Porte de Bonne* slope seen from our classroom window, fortunately situated on the third floor of the college building; the rest was being repaired.

In winter M. Durand must have come to give me my lesson from seven to eight in the evening. At any rate, I can see myself at a small table lit by a candle, M. Durand sitting almost in a straight row with my relatives in front of my grandfather's fire, and by a half-turn to the right facing the little table (H) at which I was sitting.

That was where M. Durand began to expound Ovid's *Metamorphoses* to me. I can still see him, also the marigold- or boxroot-yellow cover of the book. I seem to remember that the frivolity of the subject matter caused an argument between Séraphie, who was being more fiendish than usual, and her father. The latter granted my wish out of love for good literature, and instead of the gloomy horrors of the Old Testament I got the loves of Pyramus and Thisbe and, above all, Daphne being turned into a laurel. This story delighted me above everything. For the first time in my life I understood that it might be pleasant to know Latin, which had been my torment for so many years.

But at this point the chronology of this important story demands: 'How many years?'

To tell the truth I don't know. I had begun Latin at the age of seven, in 1790. I suppose the year VII of the Republic corresponds to 1799 because of that riddle about the Directoire:

> Lancette
> Laitue
> Rat   [*L'an sept les tuera*]

stuck up outside the Luxembourg.

I seem to remember that I was at the Central School in the year V. I had been there for a year, for we were sitting in the big mathematics classroom when the assassination of Roberjot at Rastadt took place. It may have been in 1794 that I was construing Ovid's *Metamorphoses*. My grandfather sometimes allowed me to read the translation by, I think, M. Dubois-Fontanelle, who later became my teacher.

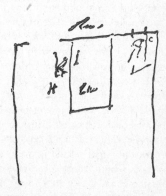

P. My father sitting at his desk C and writing – H. Me. [*Street – Table.*]

I think that the death of Louis XVI on 21 January 1793, took place during the Raillane tyranny. It's a curious fact and one which posterity will hardly credit, that my family, who were bourgeois but thought themselves on the fringe of the nobility, my father in particular who believed himself to be a ruined noble, read all the newspapers and followed the King's trial as they might have followed that of an intimate friend or a relation.

When the news of his condemnation came my family were in absolute despair. 'But they'll never dare carry out that infamous sentence,' they said. 'Why not,' I thought, 'if he's been a traitor?'

I was in my father's study in the rue des Vieux-Jésuites about seven o'clock in the evening; it was very dark, I was reading by the light of a lamp and separated from my father by a large table. I was pretending to work, but I was reading the abbé Prévost's *Memoirs of a Man of Quality* of which I had discovered a weather-beaten copy. The house shook as the post carriage rolled up, coming from Lyons and Paris.

'I must go and see what those monsters have done,' said my father, getting up.

'I hope the traitor has been executed,' I thought. Then I pondered over the extreme difference between my feelings and those of my father. I had a great fondness for our regiments which I used to watch from my grandfather's window, crossing the Place Grenette. I imagined that the King was planning to have them defeated by the Austrians. (You can see that although I was barely ten years old I was not far from the truth.) But I must confess that the interest taken in the fate of Louis XVI by M. le grand vicaire Rey and the other priests who were friends of my family's was quite enough to make me wish for his death. I held the view then that, in the words of a snatch of song that I used to sing when there was no danger of being overheard by my father or aunt Séraphie, it was one's *strict duty* to die for one's country when the time came. What mattered the life of a traitor who by means of a secret letter could bring about the massacre of one of those fine regiments that I saw crossing the Place Grenette? I was considering the issue between my family and myself when my father came back. I can still see him, in his white flannel dressing-gown which he had not taken off to go to the post station a few steps away.

'It's all over,' he said with a deep sigh, 'they've murdered him.'

I was seized with one of the keenest movements of delight I ever felt in my life. The reader may perhaps think I am cruel, but I'm just the same today at fifty-two as I was then at ten years old.

When, in December 1830, that insolent rascal Peyronnet and the other signatories to the Ordonnances were not punished by death, I said of the Parisian bourgeoisie: they mistake their moral atrophy for civilization and generosity. How, after such weakness, dare they condemn a mere murderer to death?

It strikes me that what is happening in 1835 has justified my forecast of 1830.

I was so overcome by this act of national justice that I could not go on reading my novel, certainly one of the most touching there are. I hid it, and held up before me the serious book, probably Rollin, that my father was making me read, and I closed my eyes so as to savour in peace this great event. It's exactly what I should do today, and moreover nothing less than urgent duty would induce me to go and see the traitor whom the country's interests were sending to the scaffold. I could fill ten pages with the details of that evening, but if the readers of 1880 are as poor-spirited as society people in 1835, the scene as well as the hero will fill them with profound aversion, amounting almost to what those papier mâché souls call horror. For my own part I should have far more pity for a murderer condemned to death without absolutely sufficient evidence than of a K[ING] in the same position. The DEATH OF A K[ING] who is guilty is always useful *in terrorem* to prevent the strange misconduct to which such people are driven by the ultimate madness resulting from absolute power. (Witness the love of Louis XV for the newly-made graves in country churchyards which he used to see from his carriage as he drove about near Versailles. Witness today the madness of the little Queen Doña Maria of Portugal.)

The page I have just written would shock even those who, in 1835, are my friends. I was in disgrace for my heartlessness at Mme Aubernon's in 1829, because I WISHED THE DEATH OF THE DUKE OF B[lac]as. Even M. Mignet (today Councillor of State) was horrified at me, and the hostess, whom I DID LIKE because she had a look of Cervantes, never forgave me for it; she said I was extremely immoral, and was scandalized at the baths at Aix in 1833 because Mme la Comtesse C[uri]al took my side. I can say that the approval of people whom I consider *weak* is a matter of complete indifference to me. They seem to me crazy, I'm quite sure that they don't understand the problem.

And after all, suppose I am cruel, well then, I am; there'll be many more instances of it if I go on writing.

I conclude from this recollection, which is so vividly present to me, that in 1793, forty-two years ago, my way of pursuing happiness was exactly the same as it is today, in other and more familiar terms my character was absolutely the same as today. Where one's *country* is concerned, all circumspection still seems to me *puerile*.

I should say *criminal* but for my boundless contempt for weak characters. (Example M. Félix Faure, Peer of France, First President, saying to his son at Saint-Ismier in the summer of 1828 about the death of Louis XVI: *'He was put to death by wicked men.'* This very man, sitting in the House of Peers, had just condemned those admirable young madmen who are known as the April Conspirators. For my part I should sentence them to a year's stay in *Cincinnati*, America, during which year I would give them 200 francs a month.)

The only other thing I remember equally clearly is my first communion, which my father made me take at Claix in presence of the pious carpenter Charbonot from Cossey, about 1795.

Since in 1793 the post took five whole days, possibly six, from Paris to Grenoble, the scene in my father's study may have been on 28 or 29 January 1793, at seven o'clock in the evening. At supper aunt Séraphie gave me a lecture about my *atrocious* nature, etc. I was looking at my father, he did not open his mouth, apparently for fear of being driven, and of driving me, to extremities. However cruel and atrocious I may have been, at least my family did not consider me mean-spirited. My father was too Dauphinois and too shrewd not to have discerned, even in his study (at seven o'clock), the sensations of a child of ten.

At twelve, a prodigy of learning for my age, I kept questioning my excellent grandfather, who took great delight in answering my questions. I was the only being to whom he was willing to speak about my mother. Nobody else in the family dared speak to him of that beloved being. At twelve, then, I was a prodigy of learning and at twenty a prodigy of ignorance.

Between 1796 and 1799 I paid attention only to that which would enable me to get away from Grenoble, that's to say, to mathematics. I calculated anxiously how I could spend another half-hour a day on my work. Moreover I loved, and I still love, mathematics for their own sake, as admitting no *hypocrisy* and no *vagueness*, which are my two chief aversions.

In this state of mind, what heed could I pay to a full and sensible reply by my excellent grandfather, including a comment on Sanchoniathon, an appreciation of the works of Court de Gébelin, of which my father, I don't know how, owned a fine quarto edition (perhaps there is no 12mo one), with a fine engraving representing the vocal organs of man?

At ten years old I wrote, in great secrecy, a comedy in prose, or rather the first act of one. I didn't work at it much because I was waiting for the moment of genius, that's to say that state of exaltation which possessed me, in those days, about twice a month. This work was a great secret; I have always felt as shy about my writings as about my loves. I couldn't have borne to hear anyone speak about them. I had the same feeling keenly again in 1830, when Mme Victor de Tracy spoke to me about *Le Rouge et le Noir* (novel in two volumes).

CHAPTER II

Amar and Merlino

THESE WERE two representatives[1] of the people who arrived in Grenoble one fine day and shortly afterwards published a list of 152 'notorious suspects' (of not loving the Republic, that's to say the Government and the country) and of 350 'simple suspects'. The *notorious* suspects were to be put under arrest; the *simple* ones were simply to be watched.

1. Chronology: perhaps M. Durand did not come to the Gagnon house till after Amar and Merlino.

I saw all this from below, as a child; perhaps by doing some research into the Departmental newspaper (if there was one at that time) or into the archives, one might find that the dates were all wrong; but there's no doubt about the effect on myself and my family. In any case, my father was a notorious suspect and M. Henri Gagnon a simple suspect.

The publication of these two lists caused consternation in the family. I must hasten to say that my father was only set free on the 6th Thermidor (ah! there's a date. Set free on the 6th Thermidor, three days before the death of Robespierre), and his name was on the list for twenty-two months.

This great event, then, must date from the ... of the year ... Well, what I remember is that my father was twenty-two months on the list and spent only thirty-two or forty-two days in prison.

My aunt Séraphie displayed on this occasion great courage and activity. She went to see the *members for the Département*, that's to say members of the Departmental administration, she went to see the representatives of the people, and each time she secured a respite of two or three weeks, sometimes of fifty days.

My father attributed the appearance of his name on the fatal list to an old rivalry between himself and Amar, who was a lawyer too, I imagine.

Two or three months after this trouble, about which my relatives never stopped talking in the evenings, I let fall a naïve comment that confirmed the *atrociousness* of my character. They were expressing, in polite terms, the horror they felt for the very name of Amar.

'But,' said I to my father, 'Amar put you on the list as notoriously *suspect* of not loving the Republic, whereas it seems to me *certain* that you don't love it.'

At this remark every member of the family grew red with anger, and they very nearly sent me to prison in my room; during supper, which was presently announced, nobody spoke a word to me. I pondered deeply. Nothing could be truer than what I'd said, my father took a pride in execrating the *new order of things* (this phrase was then fashionable among the aristocracy), what right had they to be angry?

This form of argument: *what right has he?* had become a habit with me ever since the first arbitrary actions that followed the death of my mother embittered my character and made me what I am.

The reader will doubtless notice that this form was rapidly conducive to intense indignation.

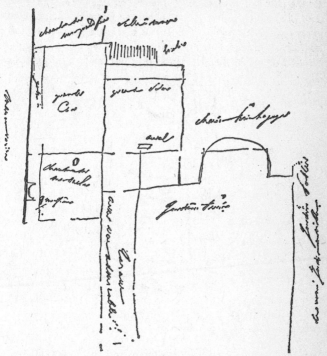

O. My uncle's room – Q. My father Chérubin B. reading Hume. [*Grand-father's room – Dining-room – Staircase – Next-door house – Gallery – Large courtyard – Large drawing-room. Altar – My uncle's room – My father – Terrace with wonderful view – Périer-Lagranges' house – Periers' garden – Public garden, called Jardin de Ville.*]

My father, Chérubin B[eyle], took up his abode in the room that was known as my uncle's room. (My charming uncle Romain Gagnon had got married at Les Échelles, in Savoy, and when he came to Grenoble every two or three months to visit his old flames he used to stay in this room, magnificently furnished in red damask – magnificently for Grenoble in 1793.)

Note, once again, the shrewdness of the Dauphinois mind. My father called it 'hiding' to go across the street and sleep at his father-in-law's, where he was known to have dined and supped for the past two or three years. The Terror, then, was very mild, and I'll boldly add very reasonable, at Grenoble. In spite of twenty years of progress, the Terror of 1815, or the reaction of my father's party, seems to me to have been more cruel. But the extreme repulsion that I feel for 1815 has made me forget the

[*My room – Staircase – Small courtyard. Smell of M. Reyboz's cooking – Grandfather's room – Large courtyard.*]

facts, and an impartial historian might perhaps hold a different opinion. I implore the reader, if ever I get one, to remember that I make no claim to veracity except in so far as *my feelings* are concerned; I have always had a poor memory for facts. Which explains, incidentally, why the celebrated Georges Cuvier always got the better of me in the arguments he sometimes deigned to have with me in his salon, on Saturdays, from 1827 to 1830.

So then my father to escape horrible persecution took up his abode in my uncle's room, O. It was in winter, for he used to say to me: '*This is an ice-box.*'

I slept beside his bed in a pretty cot made like a bird-cage, out of which I couldn't possibly fall. But this didn't last; I soon found myself in the closet next to my grandfather's room.

It strikes me now that it was only at the time of Amar and Merlino that I came to live in the closet. I was greatly bothered by the smell of cooking from M. Reyboz's, or Reybaud's, who was a Provençal grocer whose accent made me laugh. I often heard him grumbling at his daughter, who was horribly ugly, otherwise I should undoubtedly have made her the lady of my dreams. I was crazy that way, and went on being so for a long time, but I always retained the habit of perfect discretion which I have since recognized as part of the melancholy temperament, according to Cabanis.

Much to my surprise, on seeing my father at close quarters in my uncle's room, I discovered that he no longer read Bourdaloue, Massillon and de Sacy's Bible in twenty-two volumes. On the death of Louis XVI he had turned, like many others, to Hume's *History of Charles I*; as he knew no English, he read the translation by M. or président Belot, the only one there was then. Soon my father, changeable and absolute in his tastes, was all for politics. As a child I saw only the ridiculous aspect of his changeableness, today I see the reason for it. Perhaps the single-mindedness with which my father pursued his passions (or his tastes) raised him somewhat above the common run of men.

So now he was all for Hume and Smollett and wanted me to enjoy these books, as two years earlier he had wanted me to adore Bourdaloue. You can imagine how I welcomed this suggestion from the bosom friend of my enemy Séraphie.

The hatred of this pious and sour-tempered woman redoubled when she saw that I had become her father's firm favourite. There were horrible scenes between us, for I stood up to her very well; I used to argue and that was what drove her wild.

Mesdames Romagnier and Colomb, our cousins, whom I dearly loved, women of thirty-six and forty at that time, the latter being the mother of M. Romain Colomb, my best friend (who in his letter of December ..., 1835, received yesterday, takes me to task about the Preface to de Brosses, but never mind that) used to come and play cards with my aunt Élisabeth. These ladies were astonished at the scenes I had with Séraphie, which often went so far as to interrupt their game of boston, and it seemed obvious to me that they took my side against that crazy woman.

Pondering over these scenes long after they happened – which was in 1793, I fancy – I interpret them thus: Séraphie, who was quite pretty, used to make love (an Italianism to be altered) with my father and hated me passionately as constituting a moral or legal obstacle to their marriage. It remains to be seen whether in 1793 the Church authorities would have allowed a marriage between a brother-in-law and his sister-in-law. I think so; Séraphie belonged to the leading sanhedrim of the devout in town, together with her close friend, one Mme Vignon.

During the violent scenes which were repeated once or twice a week my grandfather said nothing. I've already mentioned that he had a character like Fontenelle's, but I guessed that at heart he was on my side. Seriously, what could there be in common between a spinster of twenty-six or thirty and a child of ten or twelve?

The servants, to wit Marion, Lambert at first and then the man who succeeded him, were on my side. My sister Pauline, a pretty little girl three or four years younger than I, was on my side. My second sister Zénaïde (now Mme Alexandre Mallein) was on Séraphie's side and was accused by Pauline and myself of spying on us for Séraphie.

I drew a caricature in pencil on the plaster of the big passage between the dining-room and the rooms on the Place Grenette in my grandfather's old house. It was a would-be portrait of Zénaïde, two feet high, under which I wrote: 'Caroline-Zénaïde B . . ., sneak.'

This trivial affair gave rise to a shocking scene, the details of which I can still picture. Séraphie was furious, the game of cards was interrupted. I fancy that Séraphie took the ladies Romagnier and Colomb to task. It was eight o'clock already. These ladies, justifiably offended by that madwoman's outbursts, and seeing that neither her father (M. Henri Gagnon) nor her aunt (my great-aunt Élisabeth) dared order her to be silent, decided to go home. On their departure the storm broke out with renewed fury. There was some sharp reproof from my grandfather or my aunt; to keep off Séraphie, who tried to rush at me, I took a straw chair and held it between us, and I escaped into the kitchen where I was sure that kind Marion, who adored me and detested Séraphie, would protect me.

In this recollection, side by side with the most vivid pictures I find *gaps*; it's like a fresco of which large pieces have fallen away. I can see Séraphie retreating from the kitchen and myself escorting the enemy along the passage. The scene had taken place in my aunt Élisabeth's room.

I can picture myself and Séraphie at point S. I was very fond

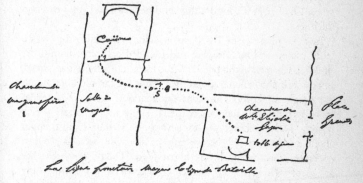

[*Grandfather's room – Kitchen – Dining-room – Mlle Élisabeth Gagnon's room. Card-table – Place Grenette – Dotted line showing the line of battle.*]

of the kitchen, which was occupied by my friends Lambert and Marion and my father's maid, who had the great advantage of not being my betters; it was only there that I enjoyed the sweetness of equality and liberty, so I took advantage of the scene not to reappear until supper-time. I seem to remember weeping with rage about the dreadful insults (impious, scoundrel, etc.) that Séraphie had flung at me, but I was bitterly ashamed of my tears.

I've been searching my mind for the last hour to find out whether this scene is true and real, together with a score of others that partially recur to me after years of oblivion as I call them forth from the shadows. Yes indeed, it is quite real, although in no other family have I ever seen anything of the same sort. It is true that I have seen few bourgeois homes, my repulsion kept me away from them and the fear that I inspired by my rank or my wit (I apologize for such vanity) may have prevented such scenes from taking place in my presence. Still, I cannot doubt the reality of the scene about my caricature of Zénaïde and of several others. I got the upper hand chiefly when my father was at Claix, which made one enemy the less, and that one the only really powerful one.

'*Disgraceful child, I could chew you up!*' my father said to me once, coming at me furiously, but he never struck me, or not more than once or twice at most.

These words: *disgraceful child*, etc., were said to me one day when I had been hitting Pauline and her cries had rung through the house.

In my father's eyes I had an atrocious character, this was a truth established by Séraphie and founded on *facts*; the murder of Mme Chenevaz, the bite on Mme Pison-Dugalland's forehead, my remark about Amar. Soon there came the famous anonymous letter signed Gardon. But some explanation is necessary in order to understand this heinous crime. It really was a naughty trick to play. I felt ashamed of it for several years when I still thought about my childhood, before my passion for Mélanie, which ended in 1805 when I was twenty-two. Today, now that the action of writing my life makes great sections of it recur to my mind, I think the Gardon venture was a very good thing.

CHAPTER 12

The Gardon Letter

THE 'battalions of Hope' or 'army of Hope' had been formed (it's odd that I cannot even remember with certainty the name of something that excited me so much as a child). I pined to belong to these battalions, which I used to see marching past. I realize now that they were an excellent institution, the only thing capable of uprooting the priestly power in France. Instead of playing at chapel, children would let their imaginations dwell on war and become used to danger. Moreover, when their country called them at the age of twenty they knew their *drill*, and instead of shuddering at the thought of the *unknown* they remembered their childish games.

The Terror was so little a terror at Grenoble that the aristocrats did not send their children to join these battalions.

A certain unfrocked abbé Gardon was in command of the army of Hope. I forged a letter; I took a piece of paper wider than it was long, in the shape of a bill of exchange – I can still picture it – and disguising my handwriting I summoned Citizen Gagnon to send his grandson Henri B ... to Saint-André so that he might be enrolled in the battalion of Hope. The thing ended with: 'Fraternal greetings, GARDON.'

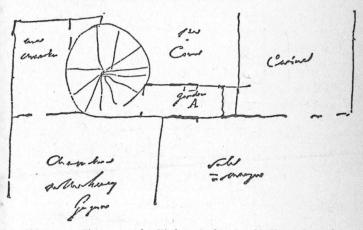

[*My room – First courtyard – Kitchen. Garden A. – M. Henry Gagnon's room – Dining-room.*]

The mere thought of going to Saint-André was the height of happiness for me. My relatives displayed great lack of intelligence; they allowed themselves to be taken in by this childish letter which must have contained a hundred improbabilities. They had to seek advice from a little hunchback named *Tourte*, a regular TOADEATER, who had wormed his way into our home by that infamous profession. But will this be understood in 1880?

M. Tourte, who had a horrible hump and was a copying clerk

in the administration of the Département, had wormed his way into the house as a sort of hanger-on, taking offence at nothing and copiously flattering everybody. I had put down my paper in a sort of ante-room between two doors, near the spiral staircase, at point A.

My relatives in great alarm summoned little Tourte to the council, since in his capacity as official scribe he was apparently familiar with Gardon's signature. He asked to look at my hand-writing, compared the two with his copying clerk's shrewdness,

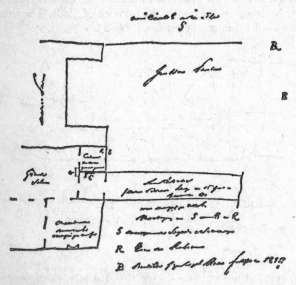

A. Altar where I served Mass every Sunday – C. Vestibule of the terrace – P. Map of Dauphiné drawn by M. de Bourcet, father of the hypocrite and grandfather of my friend at Brunswick, General Bourcet, aide-de-camp to Marshal Oudinot, since cuckolded and I believe gone mad – R. Heap of novels and other trashy books which had belonged to my uncle and reeked of amber and musk from three miles off.
[*Periers' house – Large drawing-room – Grandfather's study – My uncle's room, occupied by my father – Public garden in the middle of the town – Periers' garden – The terrace (Saracen wall fifteen feet wide and forty feet high), splendid view of mountains towards S., B. and R. – S. Seyssins and Sassenage mountains – R. Rabot Tower – B. Bastille (fortified by General Haxo in 1835).*]

and my wretched little artifice for escaping from my cage was discovered. While my fate was being discussed I had been relegated to the room that housed my grandfather's natural history collection, and which formed a lobby giving on to the terrace. Here I amused myself by *chucking into the air* (as they say locally) a ball of red clay that I had just moulded. I was in the moral position of a young deserter about to be shot. The fact of having committed a *forgery worried* me a bit.

In this terrace lobby there was a magnificent map of Dauphiné, four feet wide, hanging on the wall. My lump of clay, as it dropped down from the high ceiling, touched the precious map, which my grandfather greatly admired, and as it was very wet it left a long red streak on it.

'Oh, that's cooked my goose,' I thought. 'This is quite another matter; I've offended my only protector.' I was at the same time greatly distressed at having done something that would displease my grandfather.

At that moment I was sent for to appear before my judges, Séraphie at the head of them and by her side the hideous hunchback Tourte. I had intended to answer like a Roman, to wit, that I longed to serve my country, that it was my duty as well as my pleasure, etc., etc. But the consciousness of my offence against my excellent grandfather (the mark on the map) whom I saw pale with the fright the note signed *Gardon* had given him, weakened me and I think I made a pitiful showing. It has always been my failing to let myself be moved like a ninny by the slightest expression of meekness from the people with whom I was most angry, *et tentatum contemni*. In vain, later on, did I write this reflection of Livy's all over the place; I have never been sure of keeping up my anger.

Unfortunately, I lost my superb position through softness of heart (not of character). I had planned to threaten to go and tell abbé Gardon myself of my determination to serve my country. I made this announcement, but in a weak and timid voice. My idea scared them, but they saw that I was lacking in determination. Even my grandfather condemned me, and I was sentenced not to dine at table for three days. As soon as I heard my sentence I lost all my faint-heartedness and became a hero once more.

'I'd far rather', I told them, 'dine alone than with tyrants who never stop scolding me.'

Little Tourte tried to do his job: 'But, monsieur Henry, it seems to me . . .'

'You ought to be ashamed of yourself and hold your tongue,' I interrupted him. 'Are you a relation of mine, to speak to me like that?' etc., etc.

'But, monsieur,' he said, flushing scarlet behind the spectacles with which his nose was armed, 'as a friend of the family . . .'

'I'll never allow a man like you to scold me.'

This reference to his enormous hump suppressed his eloquence.

As I left my grandfather's room, where the scene had taken place, to go and do Latin by myself in the big drawing-room, I was in a gloomy mood. I felt confusedly that I was a weak creature, and the more I thought about it the angrier I got with myself.

The son of a notorious suspect who kept out of prison by means of successive *reprieves*, going to ask abbé *Gardon* to let him serve his country; what could my relatives say to that, with their Sunday Mass for a congregation of eighty people!

Accordingly they began to curry favour with me next day. But this affair, which Séraphie inevitably brought up against me the very next time we had a scene, set up a sort of wall between my relatives and myself. I must admit unwillingly that I began to love my grandfather less, and I immediately discerned his weakness: He's afraid of his daughter, he's afraid of Séraphie! My aunt Élisabeth alone remained loyal to me. And so my affection for her was intensified.

I remember that she opposed my hatred for my father and scolded me roundly because once, talking to her about him, I spoke of him as '*that man*'.

On which I shall make two comments:[1]

(1) My father's hatred of me and mine of him was something I took so much for granted that my memory has not deigned to retain any trace of the part he played in the dreadful business of the *Gardon* letter.

1. I feel that all this is too long, but it amuses me to see these primitive times reappearing, unhappy though they were, and I ask M. Levavasseur to cut ruthlessly, if he prints. H. Beyle.

(2) My aunt Élisabeth had a Spanish soul. Her character was the quintessence of honour. She completely transmitted to me this way of feeling, whence arose a ridiculous series of follies committed through over-scrupulousness and nobility of soul. This folly of mine only abated somewhat in 1810, in Paris, when I was in love with Mme Petit. But even today that good fellow Fiori (condemned to death in Naples in 1800) tells me: 'You spread your nets too high.' (Thucydides.)

My aunt Élisabeth, again, was wont to say of anything she admired excessively: 'It's as fine as the Cid.'

She felt, she was conscious of but never expressed, a great contempt for the *Fontenellism* of her brother (Henry Gagnon, my grandfather). She adored my mother but she never spoke of her with emotion as my grandfather did. I don't believe I ever saw aunt Élisabeth cry. She would have forgiven me for anything in the world rather than for calling my father '*that man*'.

'But how d'you expect me to love him?' I asked her. 'What has he ever done for me, except comb my head when I had ringworm?'

'He's been kind enough to take you for walks.'

'I'd far rather stay at home; I loathe the walk to the *Granges*.'

(The district near the church of Saint-Joseph, to the south-east of it, is nowadays included in the Place de Grenoble which is being fortified by General Haxo, but in 1794 it was given over to hemp fields and revolting retting-pits [pits half-full of water for steeping the hemp] in which I could make out slimy frog-spawn that filled me with horror; *horror* is the right word; I shudder when I think of it.)

Speaking to me about my mother one day my aunt happened to comment that she had not been fond of my father. This remark had a far-reaching effect on me. I was still, in my heart of hearts, jealous of my father.

I repeated this remark to Marion, who filled me with delight by telling me that at the time of my mother's marriage about 1780, she had once said to my father, who was courting her: '*Leave me alone, you horrid ugly thing.*'

I did not at that time see the shameful and unlikely character of such a remark, I only saw the meaning which delighted me.

Tyrants often make blunders, and that's perhaps the thing that has made me laugh most in all my life.

We had a certain cousin Santerre who was too lively and too much of a ladies' man and, as such, tolerably disliked by my grandfather who was far more prudent and perhaps not quite devoid of envy for the unfortunate Santerre, now getting on in years and rather poor. My grandfather professed merely to despise him on account of his former loose conduct. This poor Santerre was very tall, pitted with smallpox, with weak red-rimmed eyes; he wore glasses and a hat with a broad turned-down brim.

Every other day, I seem to remember, at any rate whenever the post arrived from Paris, he would come and bring my grandfather five or six newspapers addressed to other people which we used to read before those people.

M. Santerre used to come in the morning about eleven, he was given half a glass of wine and some bread for his lunch, and more than once my grandfather, through dislike of him, went so far as to refer in my presence to the fable of the Ant and the Grasshopper, implying that poor Santerre came to the house for the sake of his drop of wine and hunk of bread.

My aunt Élisabeth was revolted by the meanness of this reproach, and even more so was I. But the essential point about the stupidity of tyrants was that my grandfather would put on his spectacles and read all these newspapers aloud to the family. I listened to every syllable, and in my heart I made comments that were exactly the opposite of those I heard being made.

Séraphie was a fanatical bigot; my father, who was often absent from these readings, was an extreme aristocrat; my grandfather an aristocrat but a far more moderate one, hating the Jacobins chiefly for being ill-clad and ill-mannered people.

'*What a name: Pichegru!*' he would say. This was his chief objection to that famous traitor who was then conquering Holland. My aunt Élisabeth only detested death sentences.

The titles of these newspapers, which I drank in, were:

The *Journal des hommes libres*;

Perlet, the title of which I can still picture, the last word being a scrawl imitating this man Perlet's signature; thus:

The *Journal des Débats*;
The *Journal des défenseurs de la Patrie*.

Later on, I fancy, this paper, which left Paris by special messenger, would catch up the mail which had started twenty-four hours ahead of it.

I base my notion that M. Santerre did not come every day on the number of newspapers there were to read. But possibly, instead of several numbers of the same paper, there were merely a great many different papers.

Sometimes, when my grandfather had a cold, it was my job to read aloud. That was a bad blunder on the part of my tyrants! just like THE POPES founding a library instead of burning all the books as Omar did (although the authenticity of this noble deed is debated).

During all these readings, which went on, I seem to remember, for a year after Robespierre's death and which took up a good two hours every morning, I cannot remember having once shared an opinion I heard my relatives expressing. Out of prudence I held my tongue, and when I occasionally tried to speak they ordered me to keep silence instead of refuting me. I realize now that these readings were a remedy against the appalling boredom into which my family had sunk three years previously, at my mother's death, when they broke off all their social relations.

Little Tourte[1] used to take my excellent grandfather into his confidence about his love affairs with one of our relatives whom we despised as being poor and doing our nobility no credit. He was yellow, hideous, sickly-looking. He began to teach my sister

1. Put this after the note in its chronological order.

Pauline to read and I believe the brute fell in love with her. He brought to our house his brother the abbé Tourte, whose face was disfigured with *cold sores*. When my grandfather remarked that it *disgusted* him to have this abbé to dinner, I experienced the same feeling to excess.

M. Durand still came once or twice a day to our house, but I think it must have been twice, for the following reason. I had reached that incredibly stupid stage when a Latin scholar is made to write verse. The idea is to see whether he's got poetic genius, and from that time dates my horror of verse. Even in Racine, who seems to me very eloquent, I find a lot of *padding*.

To develop my poetic genius M. Durand brought along a fat duodecimo volume, the black binding of which was horribly greasy and dirty.

Such filth would have made me take a dislike even to M. de Tressan's Ariosto, which I adored, so how much more to the black volume of M. Durand, who was none too well dressed himself. This book contained a poem by a Jesuit about a fly drowning in a bowl of milk. The whole wit of it lay in the antithesis between the whiteness of the milk and the blackness of the fly, the sweetness it sought in the milk and the bitterness of death.

Lines would be dictated to me, with the epithets suppressed, for instance: Musca (*epit.*) duxerit annos (*ep.*) multos (*synonym*).

I would open the *Gradus ad Parnassum* and read all the epithets for a fly, *volucris, acris, nigra*, and I would choose one to fit my hexameters and pentameters, *nigra* for instance for *musca, felices* for *annos*.

The filth on the book and the stupidity of the ideas in it disgusted me so much that regularly every day, about two o'clock, it was my grandfather who did my verses for me, while pretending to help me.

M. Durand used to come back at seven in the evening and made me notice and admire the difference between my verses and those of the reverend Jesuit father.

Emulation is essential if one's to swallow such ineptitudes. My grandfather used to tell me about his exploits at school and I yearned for school, there at least I could have exchanged words with children of my own age.

Soon afterwards I was to have that joy: a Central School was founded, my grandfather was on the organizing committee and he appointed M. Durand as master.[1]

CHAPTER 13

My First Visit to Les Échelles[2]

I MUST tell about my uncle,[3] that delightful man who used to bring joy into our home when he came to Grenoble from Les Échelles, in Savoy, where he lived since his marriage.

Now that I am writing my life in 1835, I make many discoveries about it; these discoveries are of two kinds: (1) they are like great fragments of fresco on a wall, which, long forgotten, reappear suddenly, and by the side of these well-preserved fragments there are, as I have often said, great gaps where there's nothing to be seen but the bricks of the wall. The plaster on which the fresco had been painted has fallen and the fresco has gone for ever. There are no dates beside the pieces of fresco that remain, and now in 1835, I have to hunt for the dates. Fortunately there's no harm in an anachronism, a confusion of a year or two. After my arrival in Paris in 1799 my life became involved with public events and all dates are certain.

(2) Now, in 1835, I discover the shape and cause of past events. My uncle (Romain Gagnon) probably only came to Grenoble, towards 1795 or '96, to see his former mistresses and to have a change from Les Échelles where he was king, for Les Échelles is a small market town, inhabited at that time by peasants who had

1. Dec[ember] 14th, '35. Wrote 23 pages and finished the extremely interesting life of Costard. Costard was the Villemain, the Salvandy, the Kousin of his time in character.

2. Dictate this and have it written on the blank paper at the end of the first volume . . . join this chapter on to the end of the second volume. 18 December. To be put before 1792.

General Montesquiou grabs Savoy, therefore eight years old.

To be put at its right period before the conquest of Savoy by General Montesquiou, before 1792. Have it copied on the blank paper put at the end of the second volume.

3. Put my uncle before this journey, in his place about 1791.

127

grown rich on smuggling and farming and whose only pastime was hunting. Only at Grenoble could my uncle find the *elegances* of life, or gay pretty women, frivolous and well dressed.

I paid a visit to Les Échelles; it was like staying in Heaven, everything enchanted. The sound of the *Guiers*, a mountain torrent which flowed two hundred yards from my uncle's windows, became a holy sound for me and promptly transported me to Heaven.

Now I'm already at a loss for phrases, I shall have to work at it and re-write these pieces, as will happen again later about my visit to Milan. Where can I find words to describe perfect happiness, enjoyed with never-wearying delight by a soul sensitive to the point of ecstasy and frenzy?

I'm not sure that I shan't give up this task. I feel as if I could only paint that enchanting happiness, so pure, fresh and divine, by enumerating the woes and vexations which were completely absent from it. And that's a wretched way to describe happiness.

A seven hours' drive in a light gig by way of Voreppe, La Placette and Saint-Laurent-du-Pont brought me to the Guiers, which at that time divided France from Savoy. Savoy then had not yet been conquered by General Montesquiou, whose plume I can still picture; it was occupied about 1792, I believe. My heavenly stay at Les Échelles must have been in 1790 or '91. I was seven or eight.

It was a sudden, utter and perfect happiness, brought about in an instant by a change of setting. An amusing seven-hour journey banishes for ever Séraphie, my father, the textbook, the Latin master, the gloomy Gagnon house at Grenoble and the far gloomier house in the rue des Vieux-Jésuites.

At Les Échelles they made fun of Séraphie, of priestcraft, of everything that was so terrible and powerful at Grenoble. My aunt Camille Poncet, the wife of my uncle Gagnon, a tall and beautiful person, was the essence of good nature and gaiety. A year or two before this journey, near the Pont-de-Claix on the Claix side at point A, I had caught a brief glimpse of her white skin two inches above the knee as she was getting out of our covered carriage. Whenever I thought of her it was with ardent desire. She is still alive; I have not seen her for thirty or thirty-three years, her kindness has always been perfect. As a young woman she showed genuine sensibility. She's very like those charming women of Chambéry (whither she often went, five leagues from her home) so well described by Jean-Jacques Rousseau (*Confessions*); she had an exquisitely beautiful sister, with the clearest complexion, and with whom my uncle, I fancy used to flirt a little. I wouldn't swear that he didn't also honour with his attentions the maid-of-all-work *Fanchon*, the best and merriest of girls, though not pretty.

This journey was entirely compact of exquisite and thrilling sensations of happiness, and I could write twenty pages of superlatives about it.

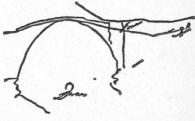

Bridge – Drac.

The difficulty, the deep regret, of describing things badly and thus spoiling a divine memory in which *the theme is so much greater than the teller*, often gives me real distress instead of the pleasure of writing. Later on, I shall quite likely not describe at all the crossing of the St Bernard Pass with the Army of the Reserve (16 to 18 May 1800) and my stay at Milan in the Casa Castelbarco or the Casa Bovara.

After all, so as not to leave my visit to Les Échelles a blank, I shall set down a few recollections which will give some idea, though extremely inaccurate, of the objects which aroused them. I was eight years old when I had this vision of Heaven.

An idea strikes me; perhaps all the unhappiness of my horrible life at Grenoble from 1790 to 1799 was really happiness, since it brought me the unsurpassable happiness of my stay at Les Échelles and my stay at Milan at the time of Marengo.

When I got to Les Échelles I was everybody's friend, everybody treated me as a bright child and smiled at me. My grandfather, that man of the world, had told me: 'You're ugly, but nobody will ever criticize you for your ugliness.'

I learned some ten years ago that one of the women who loved me best, or at any rate the longest, Victorine B[igillion], used to

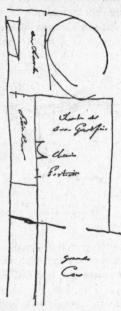

[*My room – Small courtyard – Grandfather's room. Fireplace. Portrait – Large courtyard.*]

speak of me in exactly the same terms, after an absence of twenty-five years.

At Les Échelles I made a close friend of *La Fanchon*, as they called her. I was in awe of 'auntie' Camille's beauty and, not daring to speak to her, I used to devour her with my eyes. I was taken to see MM. Bonne or de Bonne, for they made great claim to nobility. I'm not sure that they didn't even hold themselves related to the Lesdiguières.

A few years later I recognized the portrait of these worthy folk, exact in every detail, in Rousseau's *Confessions*, in the passage about Chambéry.

The elder Bonne, who farmed the estate of Berlandet, a ten-minute walk from Les Échelles, where he gave a delightful party with cakes and milk at which I rode on a donkey led by Grubillon junior, was the best of men; his brother M. Blaise the lawyer was the silliest. They made fun of M. Blaise the whole time and he laughed as much as anybody. Their brother Bonne-Savardin, a Marseilles tradesman, was very elegant, but the courtier of the family, the *roué* whom everybody considered with respect, was in the King's service at Turin and I caught only a glimpse of him.

I remember him only by his portrait, which Mme Camille Gagnon now has in her room at Grenoble (my late grandfather's room; the portrait, adorned with a red cross of which the whole family is proud, hangs between the fireplace and the little closet).

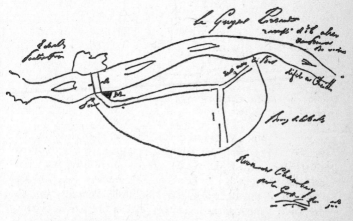

At points A A were the posts bearing the arms of Savoy, on the right bank – M. The Poncets' house where lived my uncle, Mme Poncet, Mme Camille and Mlle [Marie].
Échelles, French part. – The Guiers, a mountain stream full of islands, running towards Pont-de-Beauvoisin – Bridge – Road leading to Pont-de-Beauvoisin – Village of Les Échelles – Road to Chambéry past the grotto – Rock with grotto.]

There was a tall, good-looking girl at Les Échelles, a refugee from Lyons. (So the Terror must have begun at Lyons. This might give me a definite date. This delicious journey took place before the conquest of Savoy by G[ener]al Montesquiou, as they called him then, and after the Royalists had begun to escape from Lyons.)

Mlle Cochet was under the care of her mother but was accompanied by her lover, a handsome young man, M ..., dark and rather sad-looking. I fancy they had only just arrived from Lyons. Since then, Mlle Cochet has married a good-looking fool,

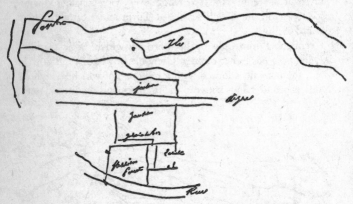

[Bridge – Island – Garden – Dyke – Garden – Wooden gallery – The Poncets' house – Stables – Street.]

a cousin of mine (M. Doyat of La Terrasse, and has had a son at the École Polytechnique. I think she may have been my father's mistress for a while). She was tall, good-natured and quite pretty, and when I knew her at Les Échelles extremely gay. She was delightful at the Berlandet party. But Mlle Poncet, Camille's sister (now Mme Blanchet, widowed) had a more delicate beauty; she spoke very little.

The mother of my aunt Camille and Mlle [Marie], Mme Poncet, sister of the Bonnes and of Mme Giroud and mother-in-law of my uncle, was the best of women. Her house, at which I stayed, was the headquarters of merriment.

This delicious house had a wooden gallery and a garden on the side of the Guiers torrent. The Guiers dyke crossed the garden obliquely.

At another party at Berlandet I rebelled out of jealousy; a young lady whom I loved had shown kindness to a rival of twenty or twenty-five. But who was the object of my passion? Perhaps this will come back to me, as many things come back to me, while I am writing. Here is the setting of the scene, which

[House – Hedge –   Steep grassy slope – Stream – The Jean-Lioud bridge – The grotto.]

I recall as clearly as if I had left it only a week ago, but without remembering what it looked like.

From B to C a slope of eight or ten feet where all the ladies were sitting. People were laughing and drinking ratafia from Teisseire (Grenoble) out of tortoise-shell snuffbox lids, as they had no glasses.

After my jealous rebellion, from point A I flung stones at the ladies. A tall fellow, Corbeau, an officer on leave, picked me up and put me into an apple tree or mulberry tree, M at point O, between two branches from which I dared not get down. I jumped and hurt myself, and ran off towards Z.

I had twisted my foot a little and I ran off limping; Corbeau, good fellow, ran after me, picked me up and carried me on his shoulders as far as Les Échelles.

He played a *patito*'s role in some sort, saying that he had been in love with Mlle Camille Poncet, my aunt, who had chosen instead the brilliant Romain Gagnon, the young lawyer from Grenoble who had just returned from exile in Turin.

On the occasion of this visit I caught a glimpse of Mlle Thérésine Maistre, sister of M. le Comte de Maistre, nicknamed Bance (and it was Bance, author of the *Voyage autour de ma chambre*, whom I saw in Rome, quite mummified, about 1832; he's nothing now but a highly polite ultra dominated by a Russian wife and still fond of painting. His genius and gaiety have disappeared; there's nothing left but his good nature).

What shall I tell about a journey to the Grotto? I can still hear the drops falling quietly from the top of the tall rocks on to the road. We went a little way into the Grotto with the ladies: Mlle Poncet was frightened, Mlle Cochet displayed greater courage. On the way back we crossed over the Jean-Lioud bridge (Lord knows what its real name was).

What shall I tell about a hunting expedition through the woods of Berland, on the left bank of the Guiers, near the Jean-Lioud bridge?

I often slipped away under the huge beeches. M ..., Mlle Cochet's lover, went hunting with ... (name and faces have escaped me). My uncle gave my father a huge dog called Berland, blackish in colour. After a year or two this reminder of a land of delight for me died; I can still picture him.

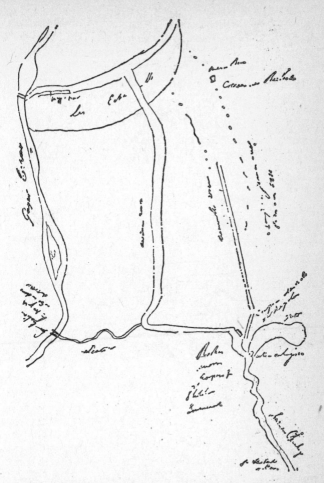

[*The Poncets' house – Les Échelles – The Bonnes' house – Slopes of Berlandet – Torrent of Guiers – Island – Old road – New road, made about 1810, which I never saw – Jean-Lioud bridge, eighty or one hundred feet above the stream – Path – Huge rocks cut by Philippe Emmanuel – Cutting in the rock made by Napoleon – Grotto – Entry to the grotto – Road to Chambéry – Saint-Thibiaud-de-Coz.*]

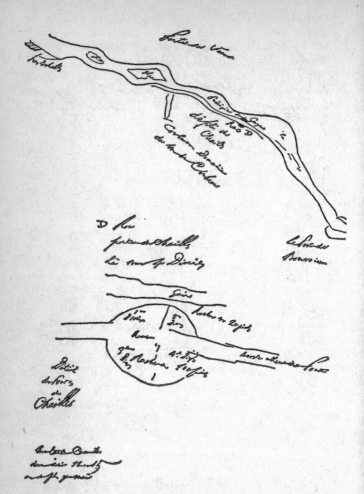

[Part of France – Les Échelles – Island – Precipices of Guiers – Island –
Bridge of Beauvoisin – Rock. Gorge of Chailles – Corbaron, M. de Corbeau's
estate – Rock, Porte de Chailles, here are four dioceses – Detail of the
Portes de Chailles: Guiers – Twenty-foot rock. – First diocese – Second
diocese – Road towards the Bridge (of Beauvoisin) – Third diocese – Fourth
diocese – Hundred-foot rock – My aunt Camille must have been twelve or
sixteen years older than me.]

I used to imagine the scenes of Ariosto taking place in the Berland woods.

The forests of Berland and the precipitous cliffs which form their outer limit on the side of Saint-Laurent-du-Pont became for me a beloved and sacred symbol. This was where I situated all the delights of Ismen in the *Jerusalem Delivered*. After I got back to Grenoble my grandfather let me read the translation

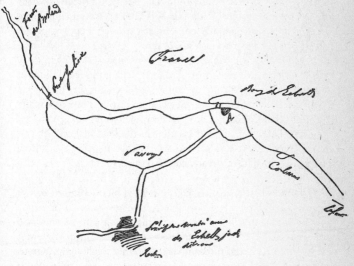

House of Mme Poncet or of my uncle who married the eldest daughter, the *heiress* (in Savoy). [*Forests of Berland – Jean-Lioud bridge – France – Village of Les Échelles – Savoy – Corbaron – Bridge (of Beauvoisin) – Rocks – Precipices formerly climbed with ladders, so they say.*]

of the *Jerusalem* by Mirabaud, in spite of all Séraphie's remarks and protests.

My father, the least elegant, the most cunning, the shrewdest, in a word the most Dauphinois of men, could not but be jealous of the amiability, the gaiety, the physical and moral elegance of my uncle. He accused him of *embroidering* (lying). Wanting to be as attractive as my uncle on this visit to Les Échelles, I tried to embroider in imitation of him.

I invented some tale or other about my textbook, the book I

used to hide under my bed so that the Latin master (was it M. Joubert or M. Durand?) shouldn't mark with his nail the lessons I was to learn at Les Échelles.

My uncle had no difficulty in seeing through the lie of an eight-or nine-year old child; I hadn't the ready wit to say to him, 'I was trying to be attractive, like yourself!' As I was fond of him, I was moved; the lesson made a deep impression on me.

They could have done anything they liked with me by *scolding* me (reproving me) in such a fair and rational way. I shudder to think about it; if Séraphie had had her brother's politeness and wit she could have made a Jesuit of me.

(Nowadays I'm *brimming with contempt*. How base, how mean the Generals of the Empire are! That's the real failing of a genius like Napoleon; to confer the highest dignities on a man because he is brave and can lead an attack. How abysmally mean and base, morally, are the Peers who have just sentenced Sergeant Thomas to prison for life, in the heat of Pondicherry, for an offence barely deserving six months in gaol! And those poor young men have already endured twenty months (18 December 1835)!

As soon as I receive my copy of M. Thiers' *History of the French Revolution* I must write on the blank pages of the 1793 volume the names of all those generals who are Peers and who have just sentenced M. Thomas, so as to have sufficient contempt for them while I read of the noble deeds that made them famous in 1793. Most of these infamous creatures are now sixty-five or seventy years old. My dreary friend Félix Faure has the infamous meanness without the noble deeds. And M. d'Houdetot! and Dijon! I could say, like Julien, 'Scum! Scum! Scum!')

Forgive this long parenthesis, O reader of 1880! Everything I'm talking about will be forgotten by that time. The generous indignation that makes my heart throb and stops me from writing will seem ridiculous. If in 1880 there is a tolerable government, the falls and rapids, the anxieties through which France will have passed in order to attain it will be forgotten, history will write one word only by the side of [Louis-Philippe's] name: *the most knavish of* K[INGS].

M. de Corbeau, who had been my friend ever since he carried me home on his back from Berlandet to Les Échelles, used to

take me trout fishing in the Guiers. He used to fish between the
Chailles gates at the foot of the cliffs of the Chailles gorge, and
the bridge of Les Échelles, sometimes by the Jean-Lioud bridge.
His line was fifteen or twenty feet long. Near Chailles, as he
whipped up his bait sharply, his white horsehair line flew up
over a tree and we beheld the trout, a three-quarter pounder –
they're the best – hanging twenty feet above the ground, at the
top of the leafless tree. What joy for me ! [1]

CHAPTER 14

The Death of poor Lambert

I'M INSERTING here, so as not to lose it, a drawing with which,
this morning, I adorned a letter I wrote to my friend R. Colomb,
who, at his age, like a prudent man, has been bitten by the mad

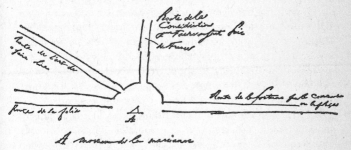

[*The way to get oneself read – The way to get oneself esteemed. Fx. Faure
gets made Peer of France – The way to go mad –. The way to make one's
fortune through trade or position – A. The moment of birth.*]

dog of Metromania, which impelled him to reproach me for
writing a preface to the new edition of De Brosses; now he
himself had also written a preface.

1. At 4.50 daylight failing; I stop work. 18 December 1835, from 2 to
4½ : 24 pages. I am so absorbed by the memories which unfold before my
eyes that I can hardly form my letters. 25 × 2 + 2 + 11 m[onths] YEARS.

This map is made in reply to Colomb, who says that I shall despise him.

I add: if there is another world I shall go and pay my respects to Montesquieu, who may perhaps say to me: 'My poor friend, you never had the slightest talent in the other world.' I shall be sorry but hardly surprised; one can't see oneself.

But my letter to Col[omb] will serve only to whitewash moneyed people; once they've attained prosperity they begin to despise those whom the public reads. The Foreign Office clerks would be delighted to cause me any little discomfiture in my profession. This disease becomes more virulent when a moneyed man, having reached the age of fifty, develops a whim to turn writer. It's like the Imperial Generals who, finding themselves unwanted under the Restoration, about 1820, took to loving music *passionately*, in other words as a *last resource*.

Let's get back to 1790 or '95. I must insist again that I don't profess to describe things in themselves but only their effect on myself. How can I help being convinced of this truth, merely by noticing that I don't remember what my relatives looked like, for instance my excellent grandfather whom I gazed at so often and with all the affection of which an ambitious child is capable.

Since, according to the barbarous system adopted by my father and Séraphie, I had no playfellow or friend of my own age, my *sociability* (my tendency to speak freely about anything) found two outlets.

My grandfather was my serious, respectable companion.

My friend, to whom I told everything, was a highly intelligent young fellow called Lambert, my grandfather's manservant. My confidences often bored Lambert, and when I pestered him too much he would give me a sharp little slap, suitable to my age. I only loved him the better for it. His chief task, which he greatly disliked, was to fetch peaches from my grandfather's estate at Saint-Vincent near Fontanil. Near this cottage, which I adored, there were some espaliers which enjoyed a sunny aspect and produced magnificent peaches. There were trellises which produced excellent *lardans* (a sort of *chasselas* grape, of which those grown near Fontainebleau are only a copy). They were all brought to Grenoble in two baskets hung at each end of a flat pole which was balanced on Lambert's shoulder, and he had to do the four-mile journey from Saint-Vincent to Grenoble in this fashion.

Lambert had ambition, he was dissatisfied with his lot, and in order to improve it he started to breed silkworms, following the example of my aunt Séraphie, who *did* silkworms at Saint-Vincent, with harmful effects to her chest. (Meanwhile I breathed more freely, the house in Grenoble under the administration of my grandfather and wise Élisabeth became pleasant to me. I sometimes ventured to go out without Lambert's indispensable company.)

Lambert, the best friend I had, had bought a mulberry tree near Saint-Joseph, and bred his silkworms in the room of a mistress of his.

While he was gathering the leaves of this mulberry tree he fell, and they brought him home to us on a ladder. My grandfather nursed him like a son. But his brain was disturbed, light no longer made any impression on his pupils, and he died after three days. In the delirium that never left him he uttered lamentable cries which pierced my heart.

For the first time in my life I knew grief. I thought about death.

The despair caused by the loss of my mother had been a frenzy in which, it seems to me, love must have played a large part. My grief at the death of Lambert was grief such as I have experienced all my life since, a thoughtful arid grief that shed no tears and could not be comforted. I was brokenhearted and nearly collapsed (for which I was sharply reproved by Séraphie) when I went ten times a day into my friend's room and gazed at his handsome face as he lay dying, breathing his last. I shall never forget his beautiful black eyebrows and that air of strength and health which his delirium only enhanced; I watched them bleeding him, after each bleeding I watched them try the experiment of shining a light in front of his eyes (a sensation of which I was reminded on the night of the battle of Landshut, in 1809, I believe).

Once in Italy I saw a picture of St John watching the crucifixion of his friend and his God which suddenly, poignantly, reminded me of what I had experienced twenty-five years earlier at the death of *poor Lambert*, as he was called by the family after

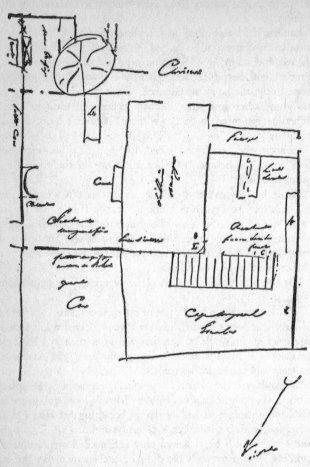

L. Cupboard where liqueurs were kept – A. Big walnut-wood cupboard for the family linen. Linen was considered with a kind of respect – B. Door to the dining-room – C. Window on to the staircase, giving a poor light, but very large and fine. [*My bed – My trapezium – Spiral stair – Kitchen – Small courtyard – Grandfather's room. Bed. Fireplace. Chest-of-drawers – Dining-room. Door – Passage – Poor Lambert's room. Lambert's bed. Window – Splendid window of Bohemian glass – Large courtyard – Well of the main staircase – North.*]

his death. I could fill five or six pages more with the *clear* recollections I have of this great grief. They nailed him in his coffin, they took him away ...

Sunt lacrimae rerum.

The same part of my heart is moved by certain of Mozart's accompaniments in *Don Giovanni*.

Poor Lambert's room was on the main staircase next to the cupboard where they kept the liqueurs L.

A week after his death, Séraphie was quite rightly incensed

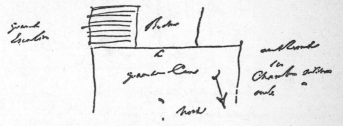

[*Main staircase – Woodshed – Large courtyard – North – On the second floor, here, my uncle's room.*]

because they served her some soup or other in a little chipped earthenware bowl (which I can still picture, forty years after the event) which had been used to receive Lambert's blood during one of his bleedings. I suddenly burst out weeping so violently that my sobs choked me. I had never been able to weep at my mother's death. I only began to be able to weep more than a year later, alone in my bed at night. Séraphie gave me a scolding when she saw me weeping over Lambert. I went off into the kitchen muttering as if to avenge myself: infamous, infamous!

My happiest moments of expansiveness with my friend took place while he was sawing wood in the woodshed, separated from the courtyard at C by a railing formed of walnut-wood posts shaped on a lathe as in garden balustrades.

After his death I used to stand in the gallery, from the second floor of which I could perfectly well see the posts of this balustrade, which it seemed to me would make superb tops. How old could I have been? This notion of tops at any rate suggests my

mental age. One thing strikes me, I could have poor Lambert's
death certificate looked up, but was Lambert his Christian name
or his surname? I fancy that his brother, who kept a little low-
class café in the rue de Bonne near the barracks, was called
Lambert too. But what a difference, good heavens! I used to

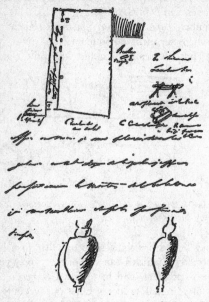

L. Place where Lambert sawed logs for my grandfather's fireplace – H.
Me. From here I stared at the wooden bars of the woodshed and gave
myself paroxysms of pain, sending all the blood to my head, opening my
mouth wide – T. Grandfather's thermometer. [*Long gallery with elegant
little windows – Privy reserved for the family – My uncle's room – Woodshed – Tops – L. Place where Lambert sawed. He laid the log thus – Rope
– Edge of the saw – C. Rope for the saw – R. Piece of wood for pulling the
rope taut.*]

think at that time that nothing could be so *common* as that
brother, whom Lambert sometimes took me to see. For it must
be confessed that in spite of the perfectly and essentially republican views I held at that time, my relatives had successfully
imparted to me their aristocratic and stand-offish tastes. I still

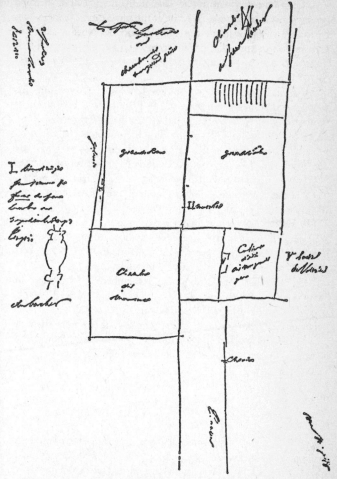

[*Two priests – Death of Lambert – The Choriers' terrace – Place from which I forced myself to remember poor Lambert by staring at the tops of the woodshed – Gallery – The 2 priests, Guillabert and . . . – Grandfather's room – Large courtyard – My uncle's room – Poor Lambert's room – Large drawing-room. My table – Grandfather's summer study – Chorier – Terrace – V. Bust of Voltaire – Magnificent view.*]

have this failing, which, for instance, prevented me, not ten days ago, from enjoying a young woman's favours. I loathe the mob (to have any dealings with), while at the same time I passionately desire their happiness as *the people*, and believe that this can only be secured by asking their opinion on an important subject. That's to say by summoning them to nominate deputies for themselves.

My friends, or rather my so-called friends, go on from this point to question the sincerity of my liberalism. I have a horror of anything dirty; now the populace is always dirty in my eyes. The only exception is in Rome, but there dirt is concealed by ferocity. (For instance the unparalleled dirtiness of the little Sardinian abbé Crobras, but my boundless respect for his energy. His five-year lawsuit with his superiors. *Ubi missa, ibi mensa.* The Caetani princes are well acquainted with these stories about M. Crobras from Sartena, I believe, in Sardinia.)

The paroxysms of love that I gave myself at point H are unbelievable. I came near to bursting a blood-vessel. I have just hurt myself *mimicking* them, at least forty years after. Is Lambert remembered today, except in his friend's heart?

I'll go farther, is Alexandrine remembered, who died in January 1815, twenty years ago?

Is Métilde remembered, who died in 1825?

Don't they belong to me, to me who love them more than all the rest of the world? I who think about her passionately, ten times a week, and often for two hours at a stretch? [1]

CHAPTER 15

MY MOTHER had had a rare talent for drawing, they often used to say in my family. 'Alas, she did everything well,' they would add with a deep sigh. After which a long sad silence. The fact is that before the Revolution, which changed everything in these remote provinces, drawing used to be taught, in Grenoble, as

1. Idea: to go and spend three days at Grenoble, and not see Crozet till the third day. To go alone and incognito to Claix, to the Bastille, to la Tronche.

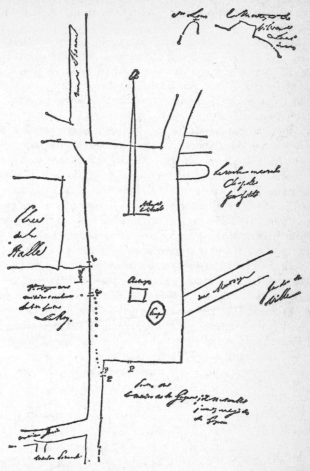

[*Place de la Halle – M. Le Roy lived here, third floor, facing south and west – Rue Vieux-Jésuites – Father's house – Tree of Liberty – Chestnut trees – Pump – Doors of M. Gagnon's house (I feel I'm swearing when I say M. Gagnon) – Saint-Louis – The Villard de Lans mountain, I believe – The Incarnate Word, a tiny chapel – Rue Montorge – Jardin de Ville.*]

absurdly as was Latin. Drawing meant making neat parallel hatchings in red chalk, to imitate engravings; little attention was paid to outline.

I often came across large heads drawn in red chalk by my mother.

My grandfather quoted this example, this all-powerful *precedent*, and in spite of Séraphie I went to learn drawing from M. Le Roy. This was a great step forward, as M. *Le Roy* lived in the Teisseire house, just before the great gate of the Jacobins, and I was gradually allowed to go there and above all to come home by myself.

This was tremendous for me. My tyrants, as I called them when I saw other children running about, suffered me to go alone from P to R. I realized that by hurrying, since they counted the minutes and Séraphie's room directly overlooked the Place Grenette, I could take a turn round the Place de la Halle, which you reached through the gate L. I was in view only while crossing from R to L. The clock of Saint-André, from which the town took its time, struck every quarter of an hour; I had to leave M. Le Roy's at half past three or four, I can't quite remember which, and be home five minutes later. M. Le Roy or rather Madame Le Roy, a mischievous creature of thirty-five, very piquant and with lovely eyes, had been specially instructed, under threat, I suppose, of losing a profitable pupil, not to let me go out before a quarter past three. Sometimes, as I went upstairs, I stopped for a whole quarter of an hour to look out of the staircase window at F, merely for the pleasure of feeling myself free; my imagination in these rare moments was no longer concerned with reckoning my tyrants' next move but began to enjoy everything.

Soon, my great preoccupation was to guess whether Séraphie would be at home at half past three when I got back. My good friend Marion (Marie Thomasset, from Vinay), a maid out of Molière, who detested Séraphie, was a great help to me. One day when Marion had told me that Séraphie was going out after coffee, about three o'clock, to visit her good friend, Mme Vignon the *boime* [hypocrite], I ventured to go into the Jardin de Ville (full of little urchins). To get there I crossed the Place

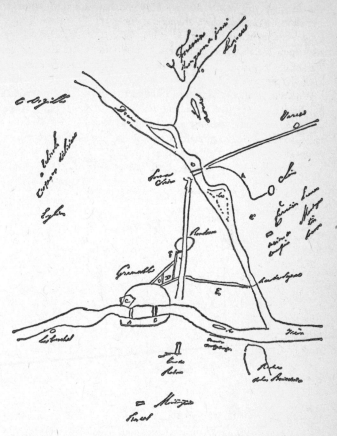

C. Citadel – A. Wooden bridge – B. Stone bridge – D. Horribly muddy road, called the hobblers' road – F. Méné road – To go to Claix, I mean to Furonières, we used to take the Méné road, from O to F, then the Cours (pronounced Cour*se*), the bridge and the paths marked R and R'. Sometimes path E, by the Canel mill and the Seyssins ferry. My friend Crozet built a wire bridge there about 1826. [*Vizille – Échirolles, delightful slopes – Eybens – La Tronche – Drac – Claix bridge – Grenoble – The Rabot Tower – Mountain – Bastille – Fontanieu (we owned meadows there) – La Gresse – North – Varces – Islands – Claix – Furonières, a hamlet – My father's house – Very high mountain – Seyssins ferry – Islands – The Isère – Way up to Saint-Martin – Rock of La Buisserate.*]

Grenette passing behind the shed where they stored chestnuts, and slipping through the archway into the garden.

I was seen, some friend or protégé of Séraphie betrayed me and there was a scene in front of the old folk that evening. I lied, quite rightly, when Séraphie asked me: 'Have you been to the Jardin de Ville?'

Whereupon my grandfather scolded me gently and politely, but firmly, for lying. I felt strongly what I could not express. Is not lying the only resource left to slaves? An old servant, who had succeeded poor Lambert, a sort of La Rancune, who faith-

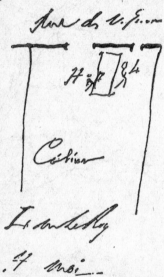

[*Rue des V[ieux]-Jésuites – Study – L. M. Le Roy – H. Me.*]

fully performed my relatives' orders and who used to say of himself, morosely, 'I'm a murderer of chamber-pots,' was instructed to take me to M. Le Roy's. I was free on the days when he had to go to St Vincent to fetch fruit.

This glimpse of liberty drove me wild. 'What can they do to me, after all?' I said to myself. 'Is there another child of my age who doesn't go out alone?'

I went to the Jardin de Ville several times; when I was seen there I was scolded, but I never answered back. They threatened to put a stop to my drawing lessons, but I went on escaping. I had had a taste of liberty and had grown fierce. My father was beginning to be absorbed in his grand passion for agriculture and he often went to Claix. I seemed to notice that in his absence Séraphie began to be afraid of me. My aunt Élisabeth, from Spanish pride, having no rightful authority, remained neutral; my grandfather, true to his Fontenelle-like character, had a

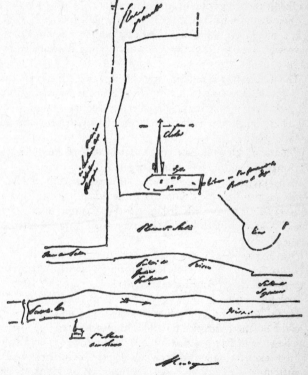

[Place Grenette – House where Mmes Colomb and Romagnier lived – Steeple. Church. Gallery reached from the offices of the dép[artement] – Tower – Place Saint-André – Rue du Palais – Palais de Justice – Parlement – Prison – Theatre – Wooden bridge – Isère – Sainte-Marie-on-the-hill – Mountain.]

horror of shouting; Marion and my sister Pauline were openly on my side. Séraphie was considered crazy by many people, for instance by those excellent women, our cousins Mesdames Colomb and Romagnier. (I learnt to appreciate them when I reached the age of reason and had some experience of life.) In those days a word from Mme Colomb made me turn in on myself, which makes me think that by using gentleness they could have made anything of me, probably a *commonplace* and thoroughly *shifty* Dauphinois. I took to resisting Séraphie and had some shocking bouts of temper myself.

'You shan't go back to M. Le Roy,' she would say.

It seems to me, thinking it over carefully, that Séraphie must have won a victory and that consequently my drawing lessons were interrupted.

The Terror was so mild in Grenoble that my father from time to time went to live in his own house in the rue des Vieux-Jésuites. I can picture M. Le Roy there, giving me a lesson at the big black table in my father's study and saying to me at the end of the lesson :

'Monsieur, tell your *dear* father that I can't continue to come for thirty-five or forty-five francs a month.'

He was referring to the *assignats,* which were steadily *tumbling down* (as they said locally) in value. But what date can I put to this very clear picture which has suddenly recurred to me? Perhaps it was very much later, at the time when I was painting in *gouache.*

Drawing and M. Le Roy were the last things I bothered about. This teacher made me draw eyes in profile and full face, and ears, in red chalk, copying other drawings, engraved, I fancy, to look like pencil.

M. Le Roy was a very polite *Parisian*, dried up and weakly, aged by the most excessive licentiousness (such is my impression, but how could I justify those words: the most excessive?) and for that matter as polite and civilized as they are in Paris, which seemed to me excessively polite, accustomed as I was to the frigid, discontented, wholly uncivilized air usually worn by shrewd Dauphinois people (see the character of Père Sorel in *Le Rouge,* but where will *Le Rouge* be in 1880? It will have vanished into outer darkness).

One evening at dusk, it was cold. I was daring enough to escape, ostensibly to join my aunt Élisabeth at Mme Colomb's. I ventured into the Jacobins' club which held its meetings in the church of Saint-André. My mind was full of the heroes of Roman history, I saw myself becoming one day Camillus or Cincinnatus or both at once; Heaven knows what punishment I'm risking, I said to myself, if one of *Séraphie's spies* (that was how I thought at the time) sees me here. The president sat at P, some poorly dressed women at F, myself at H. People clamoured to speak and spoke rather wildly. My grandfather habitually and *light-heartedly* made fun of their turns of speech. It immediately struck me that my grandfather was right and I was unfavourably impressed; these people whom I wanted to love seemed to me horribly vulgar. This high narrow church was very badly lit and I saw a great many women of the poorest class. In short I was then as I am now; I love the people and I detest their oppressors, but it would be a perpetual torture for me to have to live amongst them.

I'll borrow for a moment the language of Cabanis.[1] I have too delicate a skin, a woman's skin (later on I always had blisters after holding my sword for an hour),[2] the least thing takes the skin off my fingers, which are very well shaped; in a word the surface of my body is like a woman's. Thence comes, perhaps, my insurmountable horror of everything that looks *dirty* or *damp* or *blackish*. And there were a great many such things at the Jacobins' club at Saint-André.

When I went to Mme Colomb's an hour later my aunt, with her Spanish character, gave me a very serious look. We went out; when we were alone in the street she said to me: 'If you run away like that your father will notice.'

'He never will, unless Séraphie gives me away.'

'Let me speak ... And I'm not concerned with telling your father about you. I shan't take you to Mme Colomb's any more.'

These words uttered with great simplicity touched me, the

1. Style. These words *for a moment* are restful to the spirit. I would have cut them out in 1830, but in 1835 I regret not finding similar ones in the *Rouge*, 25 December 1835.

A fish dinner at No. 120.

2. 24 December 1835. Tramontana of nerves. *Kept:* FIRST word written on the desk *à la Tronchin.*

ugliness of the Jacobins had impressed me, I was thoughtful the next day and the following days; my idol had been shaken. If my grandfather had guessed what I was feeling, and I'd have told him everything if he had spoken to me while we were

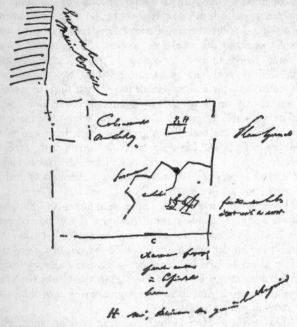

[*Staircase of the Teisseires' house – M. Le Roy's study – Place Grenette – Screen – M. Le Roy – Window with a green curtain on its lower half – Charming landscape hung on the wall at a height of six feet – H. Me, drawing my eyes in red pencil.*]

watering the flowers on the terrace, he could have made fun of the Jacobins for ever and brought me back into the bosom of the *Aristocracy* (so called at that time, now the Legitimist or Conservative party). Instead of deifying the Jacobins my imagination would have dwelt on and exaggerated the dirtiness of their hall at Saint-André.

This dirtiness left on its own was soon obliterated by some tale of a battle won which set my family groaning.

About this time, the arts took hold of my imagination, by way of the senses, as a preacher would say. In M. Le Roy's studio there was a large beautiful landscape: a steep mountain in the near foreground, adorned with tall trees; at the foot of this mountain a shallow but broad and clear stream flowed from left to right at the foot of the lowest trees. There, three women almost or quite naked were gaily bathing. They formed almost the only touch of brightness in this canvas of three and a half by two and a half feet.

This landscape, with its lovely greenery, impressed an imagina-

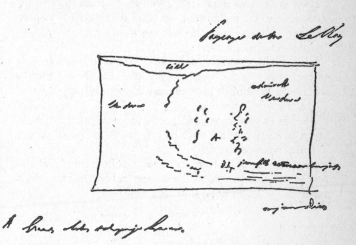

[M. Le Roy's landscape – Sky – Greenery – Admirable greenery – Water – Girls tucking up their skirts, or young goddesses – A. Great trees, the kind I love.]

tion already prepared by *Félicia* and came to represent for me the ideal of happiness. It was a blend of tender feeling and sweet voluptuousness. Just to bathe like this with charming women!

The clearness of the water contrasted wonderfully with the foul streams of *Les Granges*, full of frogs and covered with green scum. I used to think that the green plant which grows on these polluted streams was a form of decay. If my grandfather had told me: 'It's a plant, just as the *mould* which spoils bread is a plant,' my repulsion would have quickly ceased. I only overcame it completely after M. Adrien de Jussieu (that wise and natural man, so sensible and so lovable), on our journey to Naples (1832), had told me at length about these small plants which I still thought of as somehow signs of decay, although I knew vaguely that they were plants.[1]

I have only one method of preventing my imagination from playing tricks on me, and that is to go straight for the object. I saw this very clearly when I advanced on the two guns mentioned in General Michaud's certificate.[2]

Later on, I mean about 1805, at Marseilles, I had the delicious pleasure of seeing my mistress, who had an exceptionally beautiful figure, bathing in the Huveaune with its crown of tall trees (at Mme Roy's country house).

I can vividly remember M. Le Roy's landscape, which for four or five years was the *ideal* of voluptuous happiness for me. I could have exclaimed, like some ass or other in some novel of 1832: '*That's my ideal.*'

All this, as you can realize, is quite independent of the merits of the landscape, which was probably just a plateful of spinach devoid of aerial perspective.

Later on Gaveaux's opera *Le Traité Nul* initiated me into the passion that was fulfilled by the *Matrimonio Segreto*, first met at Ivrea (end of May 1800) and by *Don Giovanni*.

CHAPTER 16

I was working at a little table at point P, near the second window of the big Italian-style drawing-room, happily translating Virgil or Ovid's *Metamorphoses*, when the sinister sound of a vast crowd gathered on the Place Grenette told me that two priests had just been guillotined.

1. Today I ought to study the natural history of worms and beetles which always repel me. Towards 1810, I bought two volumes by Monsieur Duméril with this intention, but the campaign in Russia, that of 1813, and my mission with the seventh division distracted me from it. At Grenoble, however, I read a little in order to talk about it to Madame Gauthier.

2. M. Colomb must have this certificate. [*Note by Colomb:* Yes.]

This was the only blood shed at Grenoble by the Terror of '93.

This shows one of my greatest faults: my reader of 1880, remote from the fury and intensity of party feeling, will take a dislike to me when I confess that this death, which appalled my grandfather, drove Séraphie into a fury and intensified the

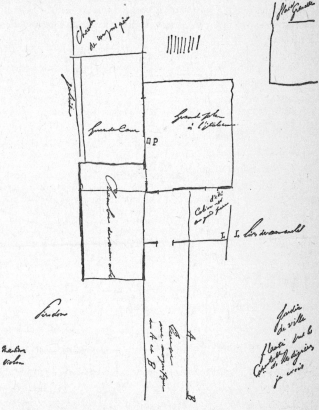

[*Mantion, violinist – Pirodon – Gallery – Grandfather's room – Large courtyard – My uncle's room – Large drawing-room in the Italian style – Grandfather's summer study – Terrace, magnificent view from A and B – Place Grenette – L. My uncle's books – Jardin de Ville laid out by the Constable de Lesdiguières, I believe.*]

haughty Spanish reticence of my aunt Élisabeth, gave me PLEASURE. Now the great word has been written.

Furthermore, and what's worse, I AM still IN 1835 THE MAN OF 1794.

(Here's another way of fixing a definite date. The register of the Criminal Court, now Royal Court, in the Place Saint-André, must give the date of the deaths of MM. Revenas and Guillabert.)

My confessor, M. Dumolard of Bourg-d'Oisans (a one-eyed and seemingly good-natured priest who became a rabid Jesuit after

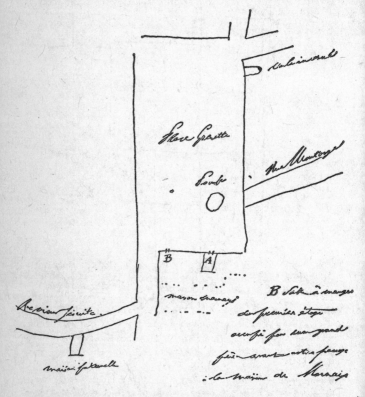

[*Rue Vieux-Jésuites – Father's house – Place Grenette – Pump – Marnais' house – Incarnate Word – Rue Montorge – B. First-floor dining-room occupied by my grandfather before we moved to the Marnais' house.*]

1815) showed me, with gestures which struck me as ridiculous, some Latin prayers in verse written by MM. Revenas and Guillabert, whom he tried hard to make me think of as important military officers.

I said to him haughtily: 'My grandad told me that twenty years ago they hanged two Protestant ministers in the same square.'

'Oh, that's very different!'

'The Parlement condemned the first two for their religion; the Criminal Court has just condemned these two for having betrayed their country.' If these were not the exact words, at any rate this was the meaning.

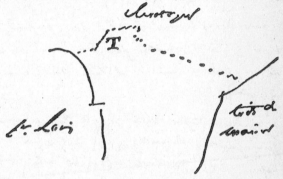

[*Saint-Louis – Mountain – Roofs of houses.*]

But I didn't yet understand that it's dangerous to argue with tyrants; they must have read in my eyes my lack of sympathy with two traitors to their country. (I thought in 1795 and I still think in 1835 that there is no crime to be *compared* with this.)

I was given a terrible scolding, my father flew into one of the worst rages against me that I can remember and Séraphie was triumphant. Aunt Élisabeth gave me a talking-to in private. But I believe, God forgive me, that I convinced her that it was the law of retaliation.

Luckily for me my grandfather did not join my enemies, and privately he entirely agreed that the death of the two Protestant ministers was just as blameworthy.

'Far more so, under the tyrant Louis XV the country was not in danger.'

I did not say tyrant but my face must have said it for me. If my grandfather, who had already taken sides against me in the battle with the abbé Gardon, had done the same thing in this business, it would have been all up between us; I'd have stopped loving him. Our talks about good literature, Horace, M. de

[*Specimen of Barnave's handwriting bound in the MS.*]

Voltaire, Chapter XV of *Bélisaire*, the finest passages of *Télémaque* and *Séthos*, which had formed my mind, would have ceased, and I should have been far more unhappy throughout the time that elapsed between the death of the two wretched priests and my exclusive passion for mathematics: spring or summer 1797.

We spent every afternoon in winter warming our legs in the sun[1] in my aunt Élisabeth's room which overlooked the Grenette

1. Terrasse Chorier to be placed. Summer trousers with the strong odour of their material. My uncle's books at the corner of the big desk in the Rue des Vieux-Jésuites. My uncle's marriage and life.

at point A. Above the church of Saint-Louis, or rather to one side of it, one could see (at T) the trapezoid form of the Villars-de-Lans mountain. As I sat there my imagination, inspired by the Ariosto of M. de Tressan, saw and dreamt of nothing but a meadow among high mountains. My scrawl at that time was very like the enclosed specimen of my illustrious compatriot's handwriting.

My grandfather was accustomed to say, as he drank his very

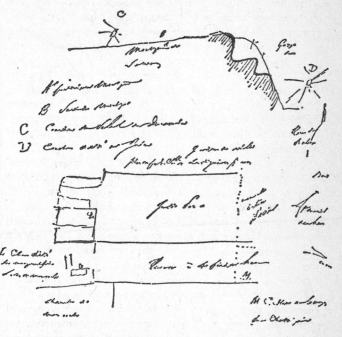

A. First mountain – B. Second mountain – C. December sunset – D. Summer sunset, June – L. Grandfather's summer study. My uncle's books – N. Study where Poncet established himself – G. Carpenter's bench beside which I used to spend my life – M. Cabinet with inlaid diamond shapes of walnut wood, in a vulgar architectural style, *à la Bernini*. [*Mountain of Sassenage – Jardin de ville planted by Constable de Lesiguières, I believe – Periers' garden – Periers' new house – Terrace 40 feet high – My uncle's room – Wide gorges – Rabot Tower – Bas[tille] – Saint-Marie-in-the-hill – North – Inn and small garden of Pirodon.*]

good coffee at about two o'clock in the afternoon with his legs stretched in the sun : 'From 15 February onwards, *in this climate*, it's *very pleasant* in the sun.'

He was fond of ideas about geology and would have been a partisan or an opponent of M. Élie de Beaumont's upheavals, which delight me. My grandfather spoke to me *with passion*, that's the important point, about the geological ideas of a certain M. Guettard, whom *I fancy* he had known.

I noticed with my sister Pauline, who was on my side, that the conversation at the best time of day, while taking coffee, always consisted of moans; they used to moan about everything.

I cannot give real facts, I can only show the *shadow* of them.

We used to spend the summer evenings from seven to half past nine (at nine o'clock the *sein* or *saint* [curfew] rang at Saint-André; the beautiful sound of that bell moved me keenly). My father, who was insensitive to the beauty of the stars (I was for ever talking about constellations with my grandfather), used to say that he was catching cold and went to talk in the next room with Séraphie.

This terrace, formed by the breadth of the so-called *Saracens'* wall which was fifteen or eighteen feet high, had a magnificent view over the mountain of Sassenage, where the sun set in winter; over the Voreppe rock, where it set in summer, and to the north-west of the Bastille on its mountain (now transformed by General Haxo) which rose above all the houses, and over the Rabot tower, which, I fancy, was the entry into the town before the Porte-de-France rock was cut through.

My grandfather spent a great deal of money on this terrace. Poncet, the carpenter, came and set up his workshop for a whole year in the natural history room for which he made whitewood cupboards; he next made boxes eighteen inches broad and two feet high of chestnut wood, full of good soil, vines and flowers. The vines climbed up from the garden of M. Périer-Lagrange, that good-natured imbecile, our neighbour.

My grandfather had had porches built, made of strips of chestnut wood. This was a great work, which was entrusted to a carpenter named Poncet, a good-natured cheerful boozer of about thirty. He became my friend for, after all, with him I enjoyed the pleasures of equality.

My grandfather watered his flowers every day, twice rather than once a day. Séraphie never came on to this terrace; this was a moment of respite. I always helped my grandfather to water his flowers and he talked to me about Linnaeus and Pliny, not from a sense of duty but with enjoyment.

This is the great, the extreme, debt I owe this excellent man. To complete my joy he had the utmost contempt for pedants (the Lerminiers, the Salvandys, the ... of today), he had the same sort of wit as M. Letronne who has just dethroned Memnon, *neither more nor less than the statue of Memnon.*[1]

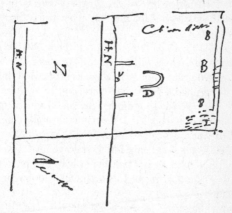

Natural history room – HN. Minerals, birds ... [*Summer study – Terrace.*]

My grandfather talked to me with equal interest about Egypt, he showed me the mummy bought through his influence for the Public Library; there the excellent Father Ducros (the first remarkable man I spoke to in my life) was infinitely obliging to me. My grandfather, strongly reproved by Séraphie with the tacit support of my father, made me read *Séthos* (a dull novel by the abbé Terrasson), which at that time seemed divine to me. A novel is like a fiddle-bow, the reader's soul is like the violin *which yields the sound.* My soul was crazy then, and I'll now tell why.

While my grandfather was reading, sitting in his arm-chair at

1. *Malade Imaginaire*, II, *v.* (*Trans.*)

D opposite the little bust of Voltaire at V, I looked at his book-case which stood at B, and opened the quarto volumes of Pliny. There I hunted out particularly the natural history of *woman*.

There was a delicious odour of ambergris or musk (which for the past sixteen years have made me feel ill, perhaps ambergris and musk have the same odour). Finally I was attracted to a pile of paper-bound books, untidily flung down at L. They were trashy novels, unbound, which my uncle had left at Grenoble when he went away to settle at Les Échelles (Savoy, near Le Pont-de-Beauvoisin). This discovery was a crucial one for my character. I opened a few of these books; they were common-place novels of 1780 but for me they represented the essence of sensual delight.

My grandfather forbade me to touch them but I kept watch for the moment when, sitting in his arm-chair, he was most busily absorbed in reading the new books of which, I don't know how, he always had a great abundance, and I would steal one of my uncle's novels. My grandfather no doubt noticed my thefts, for I see myself next installed in the natural history room, waiting for some patient to come and ask for him. On such occasions my grandfather groaned at being forced to leave his beloved studies and would go off to see his patients in his room or in the ante-room of the main apartment. In a flash I slipped into his study L and purloined a volume.

I cannot express the passion with which I read these books. After a month or two I discovered *Félicia, or My Frolics*. I went absolutely wild, the possession of a real mistress, which was then the object of all my wishes, couldn't have plunged me into such a torrent of sensual bliss.

From that moment my aim was fixed: to live in Paris and write comedies like Molière.

This became my obsession, which I hid under a deep dissimu-lation; Séraphie's tyranny had given me the habits of a slave.

I have never been able to speak of the things I adored; such speech would have seemed blasphemous to me.

I still feel this as keenly in 1835 as I felt it in 1794.

These books of my uncle's bore the address of M. *Falcon*, who at that time kept the only reading-room; he was a keen patriot profoundly despised by my grandfather and thoroughly hated by Séraphie and my father. Consequently I began to love him; he was probably the man I have respected most in all Grenoble. This former lackey of Mme de Brizon (or some other lady in the rue Neuve, at whose house my grandfather had been waited on at table by him), this lackey had a soul twenty times more noble than that of my grandfather or uncle, let alone my father or that Jesuit Séraphie. Possibly only my aunt Élisabeth could be compared with him. Falcon, who was poor, made little money and despised money-making, used to fly a tricolour flag outside his bookshop whenever the army had a victory and on Republican fête-days. He adored that Republic both during Napoleon's reign and under the Bourbons, and died in 1820 at the age of eighty-two, still poor but honest in the extreme.

I used to cast a sidelong glance at Falcon's shop as I went by. He wore a large wig, perfectly powdered, and flaunted a fine red coat with big steel buttons in the fashion of that time, which was the heyday of his beloved Republic. He was the finest specimen of the Dauphinois character. His shop was near the Place Saint-André; I remember when he moved into the Palace. He took over the shop A in the former Palace of the Dauphins where the Parlement, and afterwards the Royal Court, used to sit. I used to go through a passage at B on purpose to see him. He had a very ugly daughter, about whom my aunt Séraphie was always making jokes, accusing her of having love-affairs with the patriots who came to read the papers in her father's reading-room.

Later on Falcon settled at A'. Then I was bold enough to go and read at his place. I don't remember whether, at the time when I used to steal my uncle's books, I was bold enough to become one of his subscribers. I seem to remember by some means or another I had some of his books.

My reveries were powerfully inspired by the *Life and Adventures of Mme de . . .*, an extremely touching novel, perhaps highly absurd since the heroine was captured by savages. I think I lent this novel to my friend Romain Colomb, who remembers it to this day.

Soon I got hold of *La Nouvelle Héloïse*. I think I took it from the top shelf of my father's bookcase at Claix.

I read it lying on my bed in my *trapezium* at Grenoble, after taking care to lock myself in, and in an ecstasy of happiness and pleasure impossible to describe. Today this book seems to me pedantic; even in 1819 when I was in the throes of the most extravagant passion I could not read twenty pages of it consecutively. Stealing books became my great concern thenceforward.

I had a corner beside my father's desk in the rue des Vieux-Jésuites where I used to put the books I liked, half hidden by

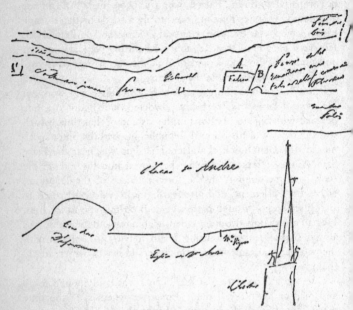

[*Isère – Wooden bridge – A – Theatre – Prison – Tribunal – A. Falcon – B. Passage of the Renaissance period with heads in relief as at Florence – Rue du Palais – Place Saint-André – Tour du Départment – Mme Vignon – Church of Saint-André – Steeple.*]

their lowly position; there were copies of Dante with curious woodcuts, translations of Lucian by Perrot d'Ablancourt (the fair but faithless ones), the Marquis d'Argens's *Correspondence of Milord All-eye with Milord All-ear,* and finally the *Memoirs of a man of quality retired from the world.*

I managed to get someone to open my father's study, which

had been deserted ever since the fatal listing by Amar and Merlino, and I made a close inspection of all the books. He had a superb collection of Elzeviers, but unfortunately I didn't understand Latin, although I knew by heart the *Selectae e Profanis*. I found a few duodecimo books above the little door which led into the drawing-room and I tried to read some articles in the *Encyclopédie*. But what was all this compared with *Félicia* and *La Nouvelle Héloïse*?

My literary confidence in my grandfather was extreme; I was quite sure he would not betray me to Séraphie and my father. Without admitting that I had read *La Nouvelle Héloïse*, I ventured to say something in its praise. His conversion to Jesuitism must have been fairly recent and instead of cross-questioning me severely he told me that M. le Baron des Adrets (the only one of his friends with whom he had continued to dine two or three times a month since my mother's death) at the time when *La Nouvelle Héloïse* came out (was it 1770?) kept his family waiting for dinner one day: Mme des Adrets sent for him a second time, and at last this unemotional man apeared in a flood of tears.

'What is the matter, my dear?' asked Mme des Adrets in great alarm.

'Ah, madame, Julie is dead!' he said, and scarcely ate anything.

I devoured the advertisements for books which arrived with the newspapers. My relatives used at that time, I think, to receive a newspaper which they shared with someone.

I got it into my head that Florian must be a sublime book, presumably because of the titles: *Gonsalvo de Cordova, Estelle*, etc. I put a three-franc piece in a letter and wrote to a Paris bookseller to send me a certain work of Florian's. It was rash, what would Séraphie say when the parcel arrived?

But after all it never did arrive, and with a louis that my grandfather had given me on New Year's Day I bought a Florian. It was out of this great man's works that I made my first comedy.[1]

1. 27 December 1835. Lacenaire is writing his Memoirs too. They say one volume was burned in the fire at the rue Pot-de-Fer.

CHAPTER 17

SÉRAPHIE's bosom friend was a certain Mme Vignon, the leading *boime* of the town. (*Boime* in Grenoble means a mealy-mouthed hypocrite, a female Jesuit.) Mme Vignon lived on a third floor in the Place Saint-André and was the wife of an attorney I believe; she was highly respected as a mother of the Ch[urch] who was able to place priests and always had some of them staying with her. What interested me was that she had a daughter of fifteen who looked rather like a white rabbit, with her round red eyes. I tried, vainly, to fall in love with her during a visit of a week or two that we made to Claix. There my father did not hide at all and always lived in his own house, the finest in the canton.

On this journey there were Séraphie, Mme and Mlle Vignon, my sister Pauline, myself and perhaps a certain M. Blanc de Seyssins, a ridiculous person who greatly admired Séraphie's bare legs. She used to go out into the garden in the mornings bare-legged, without stockings.

I was so much possessed by the devil that the legs of my bitterest enemy made an impression on me. I would willingly have fallen in love with Séraphie. I imagined myself finding a delicious pleasure in clasping this relentless enemy in my arms.

In spite of her condition as a marriageable young lady, she got someone to force open a disused door which gave access from her room to the staircase leading down to the Place Grenette; and after a shocking scene, in which I can still remember her face, she had a key made for herself. Apparently her father had refused to let her have the key to this door.

She used to let in her friends this way, and among others this Mme Vignon, a female Tartuffe, who said special prayers to the saints and whom my good grandfather would have loathed if his Fontenellish character had allowed him: (i) to feel loathing; (ii) to express it.

My grandfather used his most powerful oath against this Mme Vignon: 'May the Devil spit on your arse!'

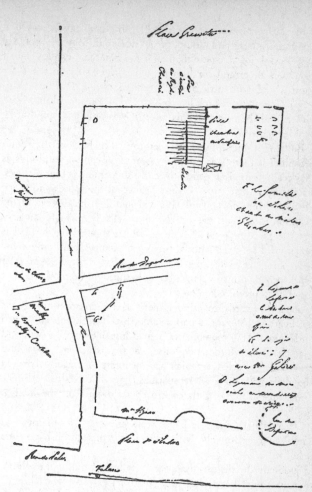

[Place Grenette – Entrance on ground-floor – Door. Séraphie's room – Staircase – Rue Vieux-Jésuites – F. The family sitting in the sun in aunt Élisabeth's room – Grand rue – Rue des Clercs, then called rue Mably. Mably and Condillac stayed here – Rue du Département – L. Lodgings of Lefèvre the barber, my father's friend – G' Here I achieved 7 with Mme Galice – O. My father's lodgings before his marriage, on the second floor – Mme Vignon – Place Saint-André – Tour du Département – Rue du Palais – Falcon.]

My father always hid in Grenoble, that is to say he stayed at my grandfather's and did not go out during the day. His political passion did not last more than eighteen months. I can see myself going on an errand for him to Allier's bookshop in the Place Saint-André with fifty francs' worth of *assignats* to buy Fourcroy's *Chemistry*, which led to his passion for agriculture. I can understand the origin of this taste; it was only at Claix that he could go about freely.

But might not all this have been caused by his love-affair with Séraphie, if there was such a love-affair? I cannot see things as they really were, I only have my childish memories. I see pictures, I remember their effects on my heart, but the causes and shape of these things are a blank. It's still just like the frescoes of the [Campo Santo] at Pisa, where you can clearly make out an arm, but the piece of fresco beside it, which showed the head, has fallen off. I see a sequence of *very clear* pictures, but I only know what things were like in so far as they affected myself. And even this aspect of things I remember only through the recollection of the effect it produced on me.

Soon afterwards my father experienced a sensation fit only for the heart of a tyrant. I had a tame thrush which usually lived under the dining-room chairs. It had lost one leg in a fight and hopped about. It defended itself against cats and dogs, and everybody protected it, which was fortunate for me, as it covered the floor with dirty white splashes. I used to feed this thrush, rather disgustingly, with cockroaches drowned in the kitchen slop-pail.

Severely kept apart as I was from any creatures of my own age, living exclusively with my elders, this childish pastime delighted me.

Suddenly the thrush disappeared; nobody would tell me how; someone must have crushed it inadvertently when opening a door. I thought my father had killed it out of spite; he discovered this, the idea distressed him, and one day he spoke to me about it indirectly and very tactfully.

I was sublime, I flushed to the whites of my eyes but would not open my lips. He urged me to answer, I remained silent; but my eyes, which at that age were very expressive, must have spoken.

That's my revenge, you tyrant, for the gentle fatherly air with which you have so often forced me to go on that detestable walk to the *Granges* amongst those fields watered by carts of night soil from the town.

For over a month I gloried in this revenge of mine. That's rather fine in a child.[1]

My father's passion for his property at Claix and for agriculture was becoming extreme. He had great *improvements* made, for instance he had the land *dug down* to two and a half feet in depth and all stones bigger than an egg removed to a corner of the field. Jean Vial, our old gardener, Charrière, Mayousse and old ..., an old soldier, performed these tasks for *fixed charges*, for instance twenty crowns (sixty francs) for working a *tière*, a strip of land enclosed between two rows of vines or maples bearing vines.

My father planted the Grandes Barres and then the Jomate where he pulled up the wild vines. He got in exchange from the hospital (which had been left it by will, I fancy, by a certain M. Gutin, a draper) the Molard vineyard, between the orchard and our own Molard. He cleared the ground, had it dug deeply and buried the *Murger* (a heap of stones seven to ten feet high) and finally levelled and planted it.

1. 20 Dec[ember] 1835, events to be placed in their correct period, put here so as not to forget them: Inspector of Crown Property, how, 1811. After the Emp[eror]'s objection I became Inspector of Crown Property, owing to my birth certificate, 2ndly owing to the Michaud certificate, 3rdly owing to the addition of a name. The mistake is not having put Brulard de la Jomate (la Jomate belonging to us). M. de Bor (Baure) was a perfectly good and well-mannered magistrate of the end of the 18th century; he liked justice and honesty and would not have committed a wrong deed except as a last resort and in self-defence. Moreover, witty, eloquent, a good talker, with a great knowledge of writers, a particular friend of M. le C[ardin]al de Beausset and M. de Villaret, Bishop (of the University), tall, thin, with malicious little eyes and an extremely long nose. He would have made an excellent and very dignified archbish[op]. He [de Baure] suffered for cash payment something which I would not have suffered for anything, to be vilified by M. le Comte Da[ru] whose general secretary he was. It was he who, to oblige Mme Petit (for I, with my scatter-brained ways and my ideas of high and open virtue shocked him twenty times a day) arranged my nomination after the Emperor's objection. Appointed to Amsterdam the [...] Sept[ember] or Nov[ember] 1811.

He used to talk to me at great length about all these plans; he had become a regular *South-country landowner*.

This sort of lunacy is often to be found south of Lyons and Tours; this mania consists of buying fields which yield 1 or 2 per cent, withdrawing for this purpose money lent at 5 or 6 per cent and sometimes borrowing at 5 per cent *to round things off*, as they say, and then buying fields that would yield 2 per cent. A Minister of the Interior who knew his business ought to launch a campaign against this mania which destroys all wealth and all that part of happiness which depends on money in the twenty Départements south of Tours and Lyons.

My father was a memorable example of this mania, which derives partly from avarice, and partly from pride and the craze for nobility.

CHAPTER 18

First Communion

THIS mania, which ended by radically ruining my father and leaving me with nothing but my share, one-third, of my mother's dowry, eased my life considerably round about 1794.

But before going further I must hastily tell the story of my first communion, which, I fancy, took place before 21 July 1794.

What consoles me a little for my impertinence in writing so many *I*'s and *me*'s is that I imagine many quite ordinary people in this nineteenth century are doing likewise. So that about 1880 there will be a flood of memoirs, and I, with my *I*'s and *me*'s, will only be like everybody else. M. de Talleyrand and M. Molé are writing their memoirs, and so is M. Delécluze.

A priest who, it must be admitted, was far less of a scoundrel than the abbé Raillane, was put in charge of that major operation, my first communion, to which my father, at that time very pious, attached the greatest importance. The abbé Raillane's Jesuitism frightened even my father, just as M. Cousin frightened even that Jesuit.

This worthy priest, apparently so good-natured, was called Dumolard and was a peasant, full of simplicity and born in the neighbourhood of La Matheysine or La Mure, near Bourg d'Oisans. Since then he has become an important Jesuit and has obtained the delightful living of La Tronche, ten minutes from Grenoble (which is like having the sub-prefecture of Sceaux for a sub-prefect who has been the tool of a minister or who married one of his illegitimate daughters).

At this time, M. Dumolard was so good-natured that I felt able to lend him a small Italian edition of Ariosto in four volumes 18mo. But it may not have been until 1803 that I lent him this.

M. Dumolard was not bad-looking, except for one eye which was always shut; to be quite honest, he was one-eyed, but his features were pleasant and expressed not only good nature but something far more ridiculous – complete and cheerful frankness. He was really not a scoundrel in those days, or rather, when I think it over, my twelve-year-old shrewdness practised only in utter solitude was quite taken in, for since then he has been one of the craftiest Jesuits in town, and moreover that superb living, within reach of the pious women of the town, testifies for him and against my twelve-year-old simplicity.

M. de Barral, Premier Président and the most indulgent and well bred of men, told me, about 1816 I suppose, as we were walking in his splendid garden of La Tronche next door to this living:

'That Dumolard is one of the most arrant rascals of the whole gang.'

'And M. Raillane?' I asked him.

'Oh, Raillane's the worst of the lot. How could your father choose such a man?'

'I swear I don't know; I was the victim, not the accomplice.'

For two or three years M. Dumolard used to come and say Mass at our house, in my grandfather's Italian-style drawing-room. The Terror, which was not much of a terror in Dauphiné, never noticed that eighty or a hundred pious women emerged from my grandfather's house every Sunday at noon. I forgot to mention that when I was quite small they made me serve at these Masses and I performed my duties only too well. I looked very modest and serious. All my life religious ceremonies have moved me deeply. For a long time I served at Mass for that villain the abbé Raillane, who used to say Mass at the [House of the Propagation of the Faith], at the end of the rue Saint-Jacques, on the left; it was a convent and we used to say Mass in the gallery.

We were so childish, Reytiers and I, that it was a great event when one day Reytiers, presumably through nervousness, wet himself during the Mass at which I was serving on a pinewood *prie-dieu*. The poor wretch tried to get rid of, mop up or absorb the wetness which, to his great shame, he had produced, by

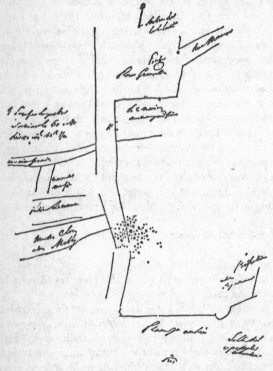

[*Tree of Liberty – Pump. Place Grenette – Rue Montorge – Grandfather's 2 houses – A'. Door through which the sixty to eighty pious women used to come out, about half-past eleven – Rue Vieux-Jésuites – My father's house – Lamouroux garden – Rue des Clercs, formerly Mably – Prefecture, formerly Département – Place Saint-André – Prison – Theatre.*]

rubbing his knee against the cross-bar of the *prie-dieu*. It was quite a scene. We often used to visit the nuns; one of them, tall and well built, I liked very much, and this was doubtless noticed since I've always been very tactless in that respect, so I did not see her again. One of the things I observed was that the Lady Abbess had a lot of blackheads on her nose, which seemed to me horrible.

The Government had made the shocking mistake of persecuting priests. The good sense of Grenoble and its mistrust of Paris saved us from the harsher consequences of this stupid action.

The priests indeed considered themselves persecuted, but sixty pious women used to come at eleven in the morning to hear Mass said in my grandfather's drawing-room. The police could not even pretend to be unaware of this. The main street was crowded with people coming away from our Mass.

CHAPTER 19

MY FATHER was struck off the list of suspects (this had been our only ambition for the last twenty-one months) on 21 July 1794, thanks to the good looks of my pretty cousin Joséphine Martin.

He then took to staying for long periods at Claix (that's to say at Furonières). My independence originated, as did the liberty of Italian towns in the eighth century, in the weakness of my tyrants.

During my father's absence I contrived to go and work in the rue des Vieux-Jésuites in the drawing-room of our flat, where nobody had set foot for the past four years.

This idea, which like all mechanical inventions was the daughter of immediate necessity, had immense advantages. For one thing I went by myself to the rue des Vieux-Jésuites, two hundred yards from the Gagnon house; for another I was safe there from the incursions of Séraphie, who, at my grandfather's, when she was more full of devilment than usual, would come and search my books and forage among my papers.

Undisturbed in the silent drawing-room where stood the fine piece of furniture that my poor mother had embroidered, I began to work with pleasure. I wrote my comedy called, I think, *M. Piklar.*

I always waited for the moment of inspiration to write.

I was only cured of this mania much later. If I had got over it earlier I should have finished my comedy *Letellier and Saint-*

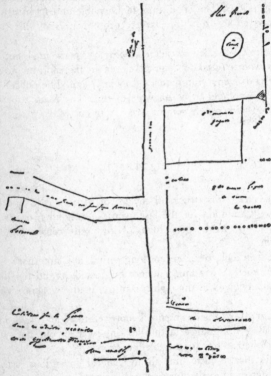

[*Place Grenette. Pump – Rue Montorge – M. Le Roy's door – Grande-Rue – First Gagnon house – Periers' house – Second Gagnon house, formerly de Marnais'. Entrance – Rue Vieux-Jésuites or Jean-Jacques Rousseau. Father's house. G. Genou – Café kept by M. Genou, father of M. de Genoude, of the Gazette de France – Rue du Département – Rue Mably – Here* SEVEN TIMES WITH *Mme Galice.*]

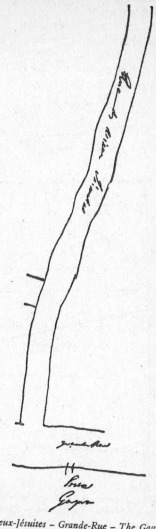

[*Rue des Vieux-*]*ésuites – Grande-Rue – The Gagnons' door.*]

Bernard which I took with me to Moscow and, what's more, brought back with me (it's among my papers in Paris). This folly seriously affected my productivity; even in 1806 I waited for the moment of genius to write.

Throughout my life I have never talked about anything to which I was passionately devoted; the least criticism would have wounded me to the heart. M. Adolphe de Mareste (born in Grenoble about 1782), who was at the time my close friend, wrote to me at Milan to give me his opinion about the *Lives of Haydn*,

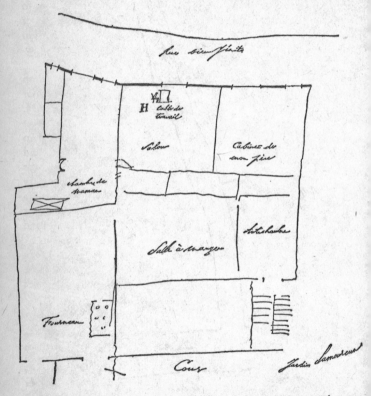

[*Rue Vieux-Jésuites – Drawing-room. Work table – Father's study – Maman's room – Dining-room – Anteroom – Furnace – Courtyard – Lamouroux garden.*]

Mozart and Metastasio. He had not the least conception that I WAS THE AUTHOR.

If, around 1795, I had spoken of my intention of writing, some sensible man would have told me: 'Write something every day for a couple of hours, genius or no genius.' Such a remark would have induced me to make good use of ten years of life which I have idiotically spent in waiting for *genius.*

My imagination had been occupied in anticipating the injuries my tyrants would do me and in cursing them; now that I was free, at H in my mother's drawing-room, I had leisure to like something. My passion was for medals modelled in plaster on moulds or hollows of sulphur. I had had a slight passion previously: my love for *épinaux,* knotty sticks cut from hawthorn hedges, I believe; and for game-shooting.

My father and Séraphie repressed both of these. My passion for thorn-sticks died under my uncle's teasing; my passion for game-shooting, based on pleasurable reveries fostered by M. Le Roy's landscape and by the vivid pictures my imagination conceived on reading Ariosto, became a craze, made me worship *La Maison Rustique* and Buffon and write about animals, and it perished only through satiety. At Brunswick in 1808 I was one of those in charge of shooting-parties where they killed fifty or sixty hares, with peasants as beaters. It horrified me to kill a doe and this horror has increased. Today nothing seems duller to me than to change a charming bird into four ounces of dead flesh.

If my father, from bourgeois nervousness, had allowed me to go shooting, I should have become nimbler, which would have been useful for me in war. I was nimble there only by an effort of strength.

I'll speak about shooting later; let's get back to the medals.[1]

1. 26 Dec[ember]. To be placed: Character of MY FATHER Chérubin B. He was not miserly at all, but a man of passions. Nothing cost too much if it satisfied his dominant passion: thus in order to have some land worked in a special way, he omitted to send me the 150 fr[ancs] a month without which I could not live in Paris. He had a passion for agriculture and for Claix, then a year or two's passion for building (the house in the rue de Bonne, which I had been stupid enough to plan with Mante). He borrowed at eight or ten per cent with the object of completing a house which some day might give a return of six. Bored with the house he gave himself up to

AFTER four or five years of the deepest and most dreary unhappiness, I was able to breathe only when I was alone behind a locked door in that apartment in the rue des Vieux-Jésuites which I had hitherto abhorred. During those four or five years my heart had been full of a feeling of impotent hatred. Without my bent for sensual pleasure I might have become, thanks to an education whose real nature those who were educating me did not suspect, a *real blackguard* or smooth insinuating scoundrel, a real Jesuit, and I should no doubt have been very rich. My reading of *La Nouvelle Héloïse* and the scruples of Saint-Preux turned me into an essentially decent person; after having read this book in tears and in an ecstasy of love, I might still act like a rogue but I should feel myself to be a rogue. Thus it was a book read in great secrecy and against the will of my relatives that made a decent man of me.

The Roman History of that woolly writer Rollin, in spite of his dull comments, had filled my head with facts revealing solid virtue (based on *utility*, not on the vainglorious honour of monarchies; Saint-Simon provides a fine piece of evidence for Montesquieu's maxim about *honour* being the basis for monarchic rule; it wasn't bad to have seen this in 1734, the period of the *Lettres Persanes*, when reason among Frenchmen was still in its infancy).

The facts I learned from Rollin, confirmed, explained and illustrated by the continuous conversation of my excellent grandfather and the theories of Saint-Preux, gave me an unparalleled feeling of repugnance and profound contempt for the com- [mandments] OF GOD AND THE CHURCH as expounded by

---

the passion for administration for the Bourbons, to the incredible extent of spending seventeen months without going to Claix, two leagues from the town. He ruined himself between 1814 and 1819, the date, I think, of his death. He loved women to excess, but timidly like a child of twelve; Mme Abraham Mallein, neé Pascal, laughed at him heartily for this.

p[riests] whom I saw every day grieving at the *victories of their country* and wishing French troops to be beaten.

The conversation of my excellent grandfather, to whom I owe everything, his veneration for those benefactors of humanity so removed from the ideas of Ch[ristianity], saved me no doubt from being caught like a fly in a spider's web by my respect for ceremonies. (I realize today that this was the original form of my love for: (1) music, (2) painting, (3) the art of Vigano.) I am inclined to believe that my grandfather was a recent convert in 1793. Perhaps he had become pious at my mother's death (1790) or else the need to have the support of the clergy in his profession as doctor may have forced him to assume a light veneer of hypocrisy at the same time as his wig with the three rows of curls. I think this the more likely, for I witnessed his friendship, which was of long standing, with M. l'abbé Sadin, the curé of Saint-Louis (his own parish); with Canon Rey and his sister, Mlle Rey, to whose house we often went (my aunt Élisabeth used to play cards there) in a little street behind Saint-André, now called rue du Département; and even with the charming, perhaps over-charming, abbé Hélie, curé of Saint-Hugues, who had baptized me and who subsequently reminded me of this at the Café de la Régence in Paris, where I used to lunch around 1803, during my real education in the rue d'Angivilliers.

It must be noted that in 1790 priests did not follow out the consequences of their theories and were far from being as intolerant and absurd as they are now in 1835. They did not mind my grandfather having his little bust of Voltaire by him as he worked, nor his conversation being, except on one single subject, just what it would have been in Voltaire's salon, while the three days that he had spent in that salon were quoted by him, whenever the occasion arose, as being the finest days in his life. He did not hesitate to tell critical or scandalous stories about priests, of which this wise and unemotional man had collected hundreds during his long and observant life. He never exaggerated and he never lied, which justifies me, I fancy, in suggesting today that intellectually he was no bourgeois; but he was liable to conceive undying hatreds on the occasion of very trivial offences, and I cannot clear his character from the reproach of being *bourgeois*.

I have met the bourgeois type even in Rome, in M 120 and

his family, particularly M. Bois, the Simonetti brother-in-law who has made money.

My grandfather had a reverence and a love for great men which certainly shocked the present curé of Saint-Louis and the present grand-vicaire of the Bishop of Grenoble, a bishop who makes it a point of honour not to return the Prefect's visit because he is a *prince* of Gre[noble], so I understand (told me, with approval by M. Rubichon, Civita-Vecchia, January 1835).

Father Ducros, that unfrocked Franciscan whom I believe to have been a man of genius, had ruined his health by stuffing birds with poisons. He suffered greatly from bowel trouble and I discovered through my uncle's jokes that he had a priapism. I could not understand this complaint, which seemed to me something quite natural. Father Ducros was very fond of my grandfather, his doctor, to whom, in part, he owed his position as librarian; but he could not help somewhat *despising* the weakness of his character, he could not bear Séraphie's incursions which frequently went so far as to interrupt conversation, disturb the party and force the guests to leave.

Characters of the Fontenelle type are very sensitive to this shade of unexpressed contempt; my grandfather therefore often tried to damp my enthusiasm for Father Ducros. Sometimes when Father Ducros came to the house with something interesting to tell, I was sent into the kitchen. I was not offended; only sorry not to hear the queer story. This philosophical man appreciated my eager attentiveness and the keen liking I showed for him, which made me never leave the room when he was there.

He used to present to his friends of both sexes gilt frames two and a half by three feet, fitted with large sheets of glass behind which he had set out six or eight dozen plaster medallions, each an inch and a half in diameter. One set displayed all the Roman emperors and empresses, another all the great men of France from Clément Marot to Voltaire, Diderot and d'Alembert. What would the M. Rey of today say at the sight of such a thing?

These medallions were prettily set off with tiny gilt-edged cardboard mounts, and scrolls of the same material filled the spaces between the medallions. This sort of ornament was very unusual at that time, and I must say that the contrast between the dull white of the medallions, with the light, delicate, clearly drawn shadows that marked the features of each portrait, and the gilt edges of the mounts with their golden-yellow colour, produced a most elegant effect.

The bourgeois people of Vienne, Romans, La Tour du Pin, Voiron, etc., who came to dine at my grandfather's, never tired of admiring these frames. I, for my part, standing on a chair,

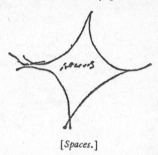

[*Spaces.*]

never tired of studying the features of those *famous men* whose lives I wanted to imitate and whose writings I longed to read.

Father Ducros wrote on the upper part of these frames, forming the letters with his gilt-edged cardboard:

FAMOUS MEN OF FRANCE

or

EMPERORS AND EMPRESSES

At Voiron, for instance, at my cousin Allard du Plantier's (he was descended from Allard the historian and antiquary), these frames were admired as much as antique medallions; I'm not

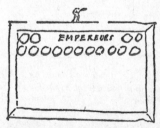

Frame of white plaster medallions made by Father Ducros, librarian of the town of Grenoble (about 1790), died about 1806 or 1816.

[Library of Grenoble – A. Librarian's big desk – B.B. Books – I fancy
they've made quite a nice museum out of the Natural History room, I saw
it in 1816 when I came about the Didier affair – Rue Neuve – Library –
Courtyard. Entry – Natural History room about 1804 – N. Portrait gallery
– P. Portrait of M. Mounier – O. Staircase to Father Ducros's nice little
apartment – E. Anteroom to the library – M. Mummy – C.C.C. Stuffed
birds – R. Antiquities.]

sure that our cousin, who wasn't very bright, didn't even think that they were antique medallions. (His father's brilliance had enervated him, as Louis XIV's did Monseigneur.)

One day Father Ducros said to me:

'Would you like me to teach you to make medallions?'

This opened Paradise to me.

I went to his apartment, a really delightful one for a man who was fond of meditation, so much so that I'd like to have one like it to end my days in.

Four small rooms ten feet high and facing south and west, with a very pretty view over Saint-Joseph, the hills of Eybens, the bridge of Claix and the mountains stretching out endlessly towards Gap. These rooms were full of bas-reliefs and medallions modelled on the antique or on tolerable modern work.

The medallions were for the most part made of red sulphur (reddened with a mixture of vermilion), which looks very handsome and impressive; in fact there was not a square foot of the surface of this apartment which did not provoke thought. There were pictures too; 'But I'm not rich enough,' Father Ducros used to say, 'to buy those I should like.' The principal picture was a snow scene, which wasn't utterly bad.

My grandfather had taken me several times into this charming apartment. As soon as I was alone with my grandfather and out of the house, out of reach of my father and Séraphie, I was perfectly cheerful. I walked very slowly, for my good grandfather suffered from rheumatism, which I imagine must have been due to gout (for I, who am his true grandson and have the same physique, suffered from gout at Civita-Vecchia in May 1835).

Father Ducros, who was well-to-do – he left his possessions to M. Navizet of Saint-Laurent, a former contractor in the chamois-leather trade – was very well served by a tall stout valet, a worthy fellow who helped in the library, and an excellent maid. I used to give them presents, at the suggestion of my aunt Élisabeth.

I was as green as could be, thanks to the miracle of my shocking solitary education and the way in which the whole family had set upon a poor child to indoctrinate him, a system which had been most thoroughly carried out because it suited the taste of my grief-smitten family.

This inexperience of the simplest things led me to make many awkward mistakes at M. Daru senior's, between November 1799 and May 1800.

Let's get back to the medallions. Father Ducros had somehow or other got hold of a number of plaster medallions. He soaked them in oil and over this poured sulphur mixed with well-dried powdered slate. When this mould was quite cold he put into it a little oil and surrounded it with a piece of oiled paper a quarter of an inch deep, from A to B, with the mould at the bottom. On to the mould he poured freshly made liquid plaster, and then,

immediately, some coarser and stronger plaster, so as to make the plaster medal one-third of an inch thick. This was what I never succeeded in doing properly. I did not mix my plaster fast enough, or rather I let the air get to it. It was in vain that the old servant Saint ... brought me powdered plaster. I found my plaster still gelatinous five or six hours after I had put it on to the sulphur mould. But the actual moulds, the most difficult part, I made immediately and quite well, only too thick. I did not spare my material.

I established my plasterer's workroom in my poor mother's dressing-closet. I always felt a sense of awe on entering her room, into which nobody had gone for the past five years, and I avoided glancing at the bed. I could never have laughed in that room, which was hung with Lyons wall-paper cleverly imitating red damask.

Although I never succeeded in making a frame filled with medallions as Father Ducros did, I was always preparing to win glory that way by making a great quantity of sulphur moulds (at B in the kitchen).

I bought a large chest containing twelve or fifteen drawers, each three inches deep, where I stored all my treasures.

I left all these things at Grenoble in 1799. From 1796 onwards I had ceased to take any interest in them; anybody might have made matches from my precious moulds (or hollows) of slate-coloured sulphur.

I read the Dictionary of Medallions in the Encyclopedia of Methods.

A clever teacher who knew how to take advantage of this taste of mine could have made me study the whole of ancient history with passionate interest; I ought to have been made to read

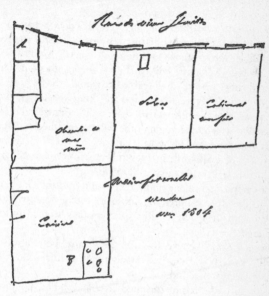

In 1816 we stayed at the corner of the rue de Bonne and the Place Grenette, where I made love to Sophie Vernier and to Mlle Eléon[ore], in 1814 and 1816, but not enough, I'd have been less bored. From here I heard David being guillotined, to the great glory of M. le duc Decazes – A. My plasterer's workshop – B. Furnace where I made my sulphur. [*Rue des Vieux-Jésuites – My mother's room – Drawing-room – My father's study – Kitchen – Father's house, sold about 1804.*]

Suetonius, then Dionysus of Halicarnassus, as my young head became able to take in serious ideas.

But the reigning taste at Grenoble in those days was for reading and quoting the epistles of a certain M. de Bonnard: I suppose he was some small Dorat, as one says small beer. My grandfather used to mention Montesquieu's *Grandeur des*

Romains with respect, but I could make nothing of it, which is not hard to believe, since I was ignorant of the events on which Montesquieu bases his splendid edifice of reflections.

I ought at least to have been made to read Livy. Instead of which I was given to read and to admire the hymns of Santeuil: '*Ecce sede tonantes . . .*' You can imagine what sort of welcome I gave to this religion of my tyrants.

The priests who dined at our house tried to repay the hospitality of my relatives by getting sentimental about the Royaumont Bible, the unctuous and honeyed tone of which filled me with profound disgust. I liked the New Testament in Latin a hundred times better; I had learnt the whole of it by heart in an 18mo. edition. My relatives, like the kings of today, wanted religion to keep me subservient, whereas I breathed only revolt.

I used to watch the Legion of the Allobroges (the one I believe, which was commanded by M. Caffe, who died at the Invalides at the age of eighty-five in November or December 1835), and my chief thought was: oughtn't I to join up?

I often went out alone and I used to go into the Gardens but I found the other children too familiar; from a distance I longed to play with them but at close quarters they seemed to me ill-mannered.

I even began, I believe, to go to the theatre, but I always had to come away at the most interesting point, at nine o'clock when I heard the curfew sound.

Every sort of tyranny revolted me, and I had no love for authority. I used to *do my exercises* (compositions, translations, verses about the fly drowned in a bowl of milk) on a pretty little walnut-wood table in the ante-room of the big Italian drawing-room, except on Sundays when the door on to the main staircase was always closed because of our Mass. I took it into my head to write on the wood of this table the names of all the assassins of princes, for instance: Poltrot, Duc de Guise, at . . . in 15[63]. My grandfather, as he helped me write my verses or rather wrote them himself, saw this list; his calm, gentle soul, so opposed to any sort of violence, was deeply distressed; he almost concluded that Séraphie must have been right when she claimed that I had an atrocious nature. Perhaps I had been induced to make out my list of assassins by the action of Charlotte Corday – 11 or 12

July 1793 – about which I was wildly excited. In those days I was a great enthusiast for Cato of Utica, and the mawkish Christian reflections of *worthy Rollin*, as my grandfather called him, seemed to me the acme of silliness.

And at the same time I was so childish that, having found in Rollin's *Ancient History*, I think, a character named *Aristocrates*, I was astonished at this circumstance and communicated my excitement to my sister Pauline, who was a liberal and on my side against Zénaïde-Caroline, who belonged to Séraphie's party and was called a spy by us.

Before or after this, I had developed a keen interest in optics,

[*Curved mirror.*]

which induced me to read Smith's *Optics* in the public library. I used to make spy-glasses with which to look at one's neighbour while appearing to be gazing straight ahead. Once again, with a little skill, they could very easily have launched me by this means into the study of optical science and made me *pick up* a fair amount of mathematics. From there to astronomy would have been but a step.

CHAPTER 21

WHEN I quite justifiably asked my father for money, for instance because he had promised it me, he used to grumble and get angry, and instead of the six francs he had promised would give me three. This shocked me to the core; fancy not keeping one's promise!

The Spanish feelings imparted to me by my aunt Élisabeth kept me up in the clouds; I thought of nothing but honour and heroism. I had not the least cunning, not the slightest skill at manoeuvring, not the least trace of smooth-tongued (or Jesuitical) hypocrisy.

This fault I have retained in spite of experience, reasoning and remorse for having been fooled innumerable times through my *espagnolisme*.

I am still just as unskilful; every day, through *espagnolisme*, I am cheated of a few centimes when I buy the most trifling thing. This vexes me so much an hour later that I've acquired the habit of buying very little. I'll deny myself for a whole year a small piece of furniture which might cost me twelve francs, because I'm convinced I should be cheated, which would annoy me, and my annoyance would outweigh the pleasure of having that piece of furniture.

I am writing this on a desk *à la Tronchin* [with an adjustable top] made by a carpenter who had never seen such a thing. I went without it for a whole year because I did not want to be cheated. At last I took the precaution of going to speak to the carpenter, not on my way back from the coffee-house at eleven o'clock in the morning, when my temper is fieriest (just as it was in 1803 when I used to drink *red-hot* coffee in the rue Saint-Honoré at the corner of the rue de Grenelle or the rue d'Orléans), but when I was tired, and my desk *à la Tronchin* only cost me four and a half crowns.

This characteristic meant that my arguments about money, always a thorny topic between a fifty-one-year-old father and a fifteen-year-old son, usually ended, on my side, in a fit of profound contempt and extreme indignation.

Sometimes, not by cunning but by pure luck, I spoke eloquently to my father about the thing I wanted to buy, and unconsciously I *fired* him (I passed on to him some of my own passion) and then, without making any difficulty, indeed quite willingly, he gave me whatever I needed. One day when the fair was on in the Place Grenette, while he was in hiding, I told him how much I wanted some of those sheets of brass the size of a playing-card, with letters cut out in them; he gave me six or seven *assignats* worth fifteen sous each, and when I came back I had spent the lot.

'You always spend all the money I give you.'

As he had given me those fifteen-sou *assignats* with as much grace as could be expected from so ungracious a character, I admitted that his reproach was quite justified. If my relatives had known how to manage me, they could have turned me into the kind of simpleton I see so often in the provinces. The indignation I have always felt, ever since my childhood and with the greatest intensity, formed my character, such as it is, in spite of them. But what is this character of mine? I should be hard put to it to say. Perhaps I shall see the truth at sixty-five, if I ever reach that age.[1]

A poor man who speaks to me in a *tragic style*, as in Rome, or in the *style of comedy*, as in France, rouses my indignation: (1) I detest being disturbed in my reveries; (2) I don't believe a word he tells me.

Yesterday, as I went down the street, a working-class woman of about forty, but quite handsome, was saying to a man who was walking beside her : *Bisogno campar* (one's got to live, after all). This remark, quite devoid of play-acting, moved me to tears. I never give anything to the poor who beg from me; I don't think this is from miserliness. When that big fellow the health officer at Civita-Vecchia told me (11 December) about a poor Portuguese in the *lazaretto* who only wants six hunks of bread a day, I immediately gave him six or eight *paoli* in cash.

1. To be placed. Concerning my character. I shall be asked : But are you a prince or an Émile, whom some [Jean] J[acques] Rousseau will take the trouble of studying and morally guiding? I will answer : All my family had a hand in my education.

After the great imprudence of having given up everything on my mother's death, I was for them the only remedy for boredom and they gave me back all the boredom I got from them. Never to speak to a child of my own age! – Writing : ideas gallop through me, if I don't note them down at once I lose them. How can I write quickly enough? That, M. Colomb, is the reason I am getting into the habit of writing badly. Omar, THIRTYEST DECEMBER 1835 on the way from San Gregorio and from Foro Boario.

As he refused for fear of getting into trouble with his superior (a vulgar peasant from Fiuminata, named Romanelli), I thought it would be more fitting for a consul to give a crown, which I did; so six *paoli* were from genuine humanity and four on account of the gold braid on my coat.

Speaking of financial arguments between father and son: the Marquis Torrigiani of Florence (a heavy gambler in his youth and one who was much accused of cheating) seeing that his three sons sometimes lost ten or fifteen louis at cards, to spare them the embarrassment of having to ask him for them, entrusted 3,000 francs to a faithful old porter with orders to hand this money over to his sons when they lost, and to ask him for more when the 3,000 francs were spent.

This is very fine in itself, and moreover the sons were touched by such behaviour and became more moderate. This marquis, an officer of the Legion of Honour, is the father of Madame Pazzi, whose beauty I admired so keenly in 1817. The story about her father's card-playing would have distressed me horribly in 1817 owing to that accursed *espagnolisme* of my character, of which I have been complaining. This *espagnolisme* prevents me from having the *genius of comedy*:

(1) I avert my eyes and my memory from anything that is mean;

(2) I sympathize, as I did ten years ago when I read Ariosto, with all sort of stories about love, about forests (the woods and their boundless silence) and about generosity.

The most commonplace Spanish story, if it contains generosity, brings tears to my eyes, whereas I avert my eyes from the character of Molière's Chrysale and still more from the basic malice of *Zadig*, *Candide*, the *Poor Devil* and other works of Voltaire, of whom the only thing I really adore is:

> *Vous êtes, lui dit-il, l'existence et l'essence*
> *Simple avec attribut et de pure substance.*

Barral (Count Paul de Barral, born in Grenoble about 1785) imparted to me at a very early age his liking for these lines, which his father, the Premier Président, had taught him.

This *espagnolisme*, which I got from my aunt Élisabeth, makes me even now, at my age, appear an inexperienced child, a mad-man *increasingly incapable of any serious business* in the eyes of that authentic bourgeois, my cousin Colomb (whose exact words these are).

The conversation of an authentic *bourgeois* about *men and life*, which is nothing but a collection of such ugly details, re-duces me to a profound SPLEEN when I am forced by some con-vention to listen to it for any length of time.

This is the secret of my aversion for Grenoble, in 1816, which at the time I was not able to explain to myself.

Even today, at fifty-two, I cannot account for the feeling of depression that Sunday induces in me; this is so acute that I may start out cheerful and contented, but after walking two hundred yards down the street I notice that the shops are shut: *Oh, it's Sunday,* I think. And immediately any inner tendency to happiness evaporates.

Is it out of envy for the contented looks of workers and bourgeois in their Sunday best?

In vain I tell myself: why, I'm wasting fifty-two Sundays a year in this way and about ten holidays as well; the thing is too strong for me and I have to fall back on stubborn work.

This defect, my aversion for Chrysale, has perhaps kept me young. It may thus be a fortunate misfortune, like that of not having had many women (women like Bianca Milesi whom I failed to possess in Paris one morning in 1829, merely through not noticing that the time was ripe – she was wearing a black velvet dress that day – somewhere in the rue du Helder or the rue du Mont-Blanc).

As I have possessed hardly any such women (authentic bour-geoises) I am not in the least blasé at fifty. I mean morally blasé, since physically, as might be expected, my senses are consider-ably blunted, so much so that I can easily go a fortnight or three weeks without a woman; that sort of fasting only troubles me in the first week.

Most of my apparent follies, particularly the stupidity of not having seized *bald-headed* opportunity (as Don *Japhet d'Arménie* calls it) on the wing, all the occasions on which I've been cheated when buying things, etc., etc., come from the *espagnolisme* im-parted to me by my aunt Élisabeth, for whom I always had the deepest respect, a respect so deep that it kept all tenderness out of my feeling for her, and, I fancy, from my reading of Ariosto when so young and with such enjoyment. (Today Ariosto's heroes seem to me mere grooms whose only merit lies in their strength, which brings me into conflict with clever people who openly prefer Ariosto to Tasso (here, M. Bontadossi, Don Philippo Ca[etani]), whereas in my opinion, when Tasso fortunately forgets to imitate Virgil or Homer, he is the most touching of poets).

In less than an hour I have just written these twelve pages, and I've stopped from time to time, to try to avoid writing anything that's not clear and that I should have to cross out.

How could my writing have been *physically* good, M. Colomb? My friend Colomb, who overwhelms me with his reproach in his yesterday's letter and the preceding ones, would face torture for the sake of his word and for my sake. (He was born in Lyons about 1785; his father, a former merchant and a very honourable man, retired to Grenoble about 1788. M. Romain Colomb has an income of 20,000 or 25,000 francs and three daughters, rue Godot-de-Mauroy, Paris.)

CHAPTER 22

The Siege of Lyons, Summer 1793

THE famous siege of Lyons, the defending general of which, M. de Précy, I was later to know so well at Brunswick, 1806-9 – he was, after M. de Tressan, my first model of a well-bred man in my early childhood – this siege of Lyons excited the whole of the South of France; I was for Kellermann and the Republicans, my relatives were for the beleaguered forces and Précy (without the *Monsieur*, as they said).

Our cousin Santerre from the Post Office, whose cousin or nephew Santerre was fighting in Lyons, used to come to the house twice a day; as it was summer we drank our morning *café au lait* in the natural history room overlooking the terrace.

It was at point H that I have perhaps experienced the keenest transports of love for my country and of hatred for the *aristocrats* (the *legitimists* of 1835) and the priests, its enemies.

M. Santerre, an employee of the Post Office, was always bringing us six or seven newspapers 'borrowed' from subscribers, who did not get them until two hours later on account of our curiosity. He would take his drop of wine and his bread, and listen to

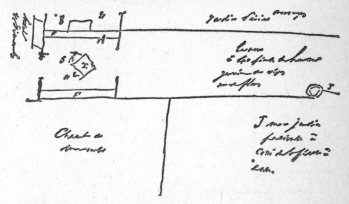

A. Natural history room – Closed cupboards containing minerals, shells – T. Breakfast table with excellent *café au lait* and very good well-baked rolls, perfect *griches* – S. M. Santerre with a broad-brimmed hat on account of his weak, red-rimmed eyes – H. Myself, avidly listening to the news – B. Study of my grandfather (M. Henry Gagnon) – L. Pile of books belonging to my uncle, smelling of musk, from which I got my education. [*Mountains – Periers' garden – The Sunday altar – Terrace 40 feet high covered with vines and flowers –]. My private garden beside the water-stone – My uncle's room.*]

the newspapers being read. Often he brought us news from Lyons.

I used to go alone on to the terrace and try to hear the guns from Lyons. I see from the *Chronological Tables*, the only book I have in Rome, that Lyons was captured on 9 October, 1793. Thus it was during the summer of 1793, at the age of ten, that I used to come and listen for the guns from Lyons; I never heard them. I looked longingly at the Méaudre mountain (pronounced Mioudre) from which they could be heard. Our worthy cousin Romagnier (cousin through marrying a certain Mlle Blanchet, a

195

[Skyline seen at sunset from my grandfather's terrace – 2 mountains – Méaudre or Mioudre at M in the valley between the two mountains A and B – V. Valley of Voreppe which I adored as being the way to Paris – S. Sunset in April, at V in summer, at D in winter. This gives 2 hours of twilight – Grenoble – Isère.]

relation of my grandfather's wife I believe) was from Mioudre, whither he used to go every two months to visit his father. On his return he used to make my heart beat wildly by telling me: 'We can hear the guns of Lyons very well, especially in the evening at sunset and when the wind's in the nor'-west.'

I gazed at point B with the keenest desire to go there, but this was a desire that I had to be careful not to express.

I should perhaps have put in this detail much earlier, but I repeat that so far as my childhood is concerned I only have very clear impressions, without *dates* or *likenesses*.

I write them down more or less as they occur to me.

I have no book and I don't want to read any books, I only make very slight use of the stupid *Chronology*, which bears the

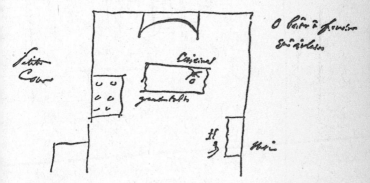

[*Small courtyard – Kitchen. Big table. Me – O. Box of powder which exploded.*]

name of that dry shrewd man, M. Loeve-Veimars. I shall do the same when dealing with the Marengo campaign (1800), with the campaign of 1809, with the Moscow campaign, and with that of 1813 when I was commissariat officer at Sagan (Silesia, on the Bober); I don't profess to be writing a history, but merely setting down my recollections in order to guess what sort of man I have been: stupid or witty, cowardly or brave, etc., etc. This is the answer to that great saying: *Gnoti seauton*.

During that summer of 1793, I got very excited about the siege of Toulon; needless to say my relatives approved of the

traitors who surrendered it; however, my aunt Élisabeth with
her Castilian pride said to me...

I watched the departure of General Carteau[x] or Cartaud,
who paraded in the Place Grenette. I can still see his name on

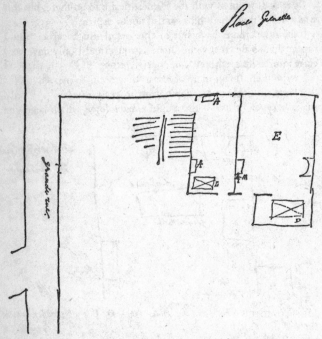

A.A. Séraphie's wardrobes – L. Her bed – E. aunt Élizabeth's room – D.
Bed and bed-recess. H. Myself reading *La Henriade* or *Bélisaire*, of which
my grandfather greatly admired the fifteenth chapter or the opening:
Justinian was growing old... 'What a picture of Louis XV's old age,' he
would say – M. Staircase and steps of the Périer-Lagranges' house, François,
the eldest son, kind and foolish, a great horseman, married my sister
Pauline during my campaigns in Germany. [*Place Grenette – Grande-Rue.*]

the waggons as they clattered slowly and noisily past on the
paving-stones along the rue Montorge, on their way to Toulon.

A great event was in store for me. It affected me very much
at the time, but it was too late; all bonds of affection were for

ever broken between my father and myself, and my aversion for the pettiness of bourgeois life and for Grenoble was thenceforward insuperable.

My aunt Séraphie had been ill for a long time. Finally, she was said to be in danger; it was my friend, kind Marion (Marie Thomasset), who uttered this momentous word. The danger grew urgent, priests flocked in.

One winter's evening, I seem to remember, I was in the kitchen about seven o'clock at night, at point H opposite Marion's cupboard. Somebody came to tell us: 'She has passed away.' I threw myself down on my knees at point H to thank God for this great deliverance.

If Parisians are as foolish in 1880 as in 1835, this reaction to

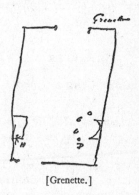

[Grenette.]

the death of my mother's sister will brand me as barbarous, cruel and atrocious.

Be that as it may, that is the truth. After the first week of requiem masses and prayers, everybody in the house felt a great sense of relief and release. I believe that even my father was relieved to be set free from that fiendish mistress, if she really was his mistress, or from that fiendish bosom friend.

One of her last actions had been, one evening when I was sitting at my aunt Élisabeth's chest of drawers, at point H reading *La Henriade* or *Bélisaire* which my grandfather had just lent me, to exclaim: 'How can anyone give such books to a child! Who gave him that book?'

My excellent grandfather, at my insistent request, had just had the great kindness to go with me, despite the cold, as far as his study adjoining the terrace, at the other end of the house, to get me this book which I had wanted very much that evening.

The whole family was sitting in a row, like a row of onions, in front of the fire at point D. People often used this expression at Grenoble: row of onions. My grandfather only replied to his daughter's insolent reproof by shrugging his shoulders and saying: 'She's a sick woman.'

I have no idea of the date of this death; I could find it from the registrar's lists at Grenoble.

I fancy that soon afterwards I went to the Central School, which Séraphie would never have tolerated. I think it must have been about 1797, and that I only spent three years at the Central School.

CHAPTER 23

The Central School

MANY years later, about 1817, I learnt from M. Tracy that he had been largely responsible for the excellent law concerning Central Schools.

My grandfather was the highly respected head of the committee whose duty it was to submit the names of teachers to the Departmental Administration and to organize the school. My grandfather adored literature and education, and for the past forty years had been the leader of every literary and liberal movement in Grenoble.

Séraphie had scolded him roundly for agreeing to serve on the organizing committee, but the founder of the Public Library owed it to his social position to be at the head of the Central School.

My master Durand, who used to come to our house to give me lessons, was to teach Latin; how could I not go to his lectures at the Central School? If Séraphie had been alive she would have found a reason, but under the circumstances my father confined himself to uttering profound and solemn words about

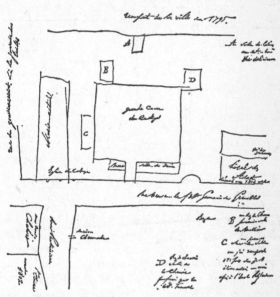

[College of Grenoble – The Claix Bridge – Snow, permanently or at least
for 8 months of the year – Mountains of Échirolles – Comboire – Magnificent
view – Ramparts of the town in 1795 – Rue du gouvernement. Here the
Day of the Tiles – College church. At present a museum – Main courtyard
of the college – 'The Round' – Art classroom – A. Latin classroom on the
second or third floor. Delicious view – Mme de Valserre – Hotel des Adrets,
destroyed about 1804 and rebuilt – Rue Neuve, the faubourg St-Germain of
Grenoble – My aunt Chalvet – Ste Claire before 1802 – Rue Pertuisière –
Cheminades' house – B. On the ground-floor, first mathematics classroom –
C. On the first floor, second classroom where I won the first prize against
seven or eight pupils admitted to the École Polytechnique a month later –
D. Ground floor, chemistry classroom, Dr Trousset as teacher.]

the moral danger of evil acquaintances. I was beside myself with joy; the school was formally opened at a meeting in the Library, at which my grandfather made a speech.

This may have been that crowded gathering in the first hall, SS, of which a picture recurs to my mind.

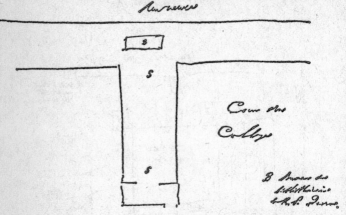

[*Rue Neuve – College courtyard – B. Desk of the librarian, the Rev. Father Ducros.*]

The teachers were MM. Durand for Latin; Gattel, general grammar and logic; Dubois-Fontanelle, author of a tragedy called *Éricia or The Vestal* and editor for twenty-two years of *The Gazette des Deux Ponts*, literature; Trousset, a young doctor, a protégé and indeed a pupil of my grandfather's, chemistry; Jay, a great braggart five foot ten tall, without any talent but good at inspiring children (getting them excited), drawing – he soon had three hundred pupils; Chalvet (Pierre-Vincent), a penniless young rake, a typical untalented author, history – and responsible for collecting school fees, part of which money he squandered in the company of three sisters, professional harlots, who gave him a fresh p[ox] of which he died soon after; finally Dupuy, the most pompous and paternal bourgeois I have even seen, was professor of mathematics, without the shadow of a shadow of any talent. He would hardly have made a surveyor, and he was appointed in the town where Gros lived! But my grandfather knew nothing about mathematics, which he hated, and moreover the pompous manner of Father Dupuy (as we called him; he called us my children) was bound to win general esteem for him at Grenoble. This man, for all his emptiness, said one important thing: '*My child, study Condillac's Logic, it is the foundation of everything.*'

To this day one couldn't say a truer thing, provided one replaced the name of Condillac by Tracy.

The joke is that I don't think M. Dupuy understood the first thing about this *Logic* of Condillac which he recommended to us; it was a very slim little duodecimo volume. But I anticipate; that's my failing, and perhaps when I read this over again I shall have to strike out all the phrases which err against chronological order.

The only man who was absolutely in the right place was M. l'abbé Gattel, a dapper trim abbé, always in female company, a real seventeenth-century abbé; but he was very serious when giving his lectures, and knew, I fancy, all that was then known about the principles according to which, guided first by instinct and secondly by convenience and analogy, different peoples formed their languages.

M. Gattel had made a very good dictionary in which he had dared to note pronunciation, and which I have always used. And finally, he was a man who knew how to work five or six hours every day, which is something tremendous in the provinces, where they do nothing but *loaf* all the time.

Parisian fools criticize the description of right and natural pronunciation. This is through cowardice and ignorance. They are afraid of appearing ridiculous if they note the pronunciation of *Anvers* (the town), *cours*, *vers*. They don't know that at Grenoble, for instance, people say: *J'ai été au Cour-ce,* or *J'ai lu des ver-ce sur Anver-ce et Calai-se*. If such speech is heard at Grenoble, an intelligent town still having some bonds with the Northern districts which have got the better of the South as regards language, what can you expect at Toulouse, Bazas, Pézenas, Digne? In such places they ought to stick up posters at the church doors, to teach French pronunciation.

A Minister of the Interior who wanted to do his job thoroughly, instead of intriguing with the king and in the Chambers like

M. Guizot, ought to ask for a loan of two million a year to bring up to the educational level of the rest of France the inhabitants of that unlucky triangle that lies between Bordeaux, Bayonne and Valence. In those parts they believe in witches, they cannot read and they don't speak French. Such regions may by a fluke produce an outstanding man like Lannes or Soult, but the bulk of the population is unbelievably ignorant. I imagine that by reason of its climate and the passion and energy this imparts to the body, this triangle of country ought to produce the finest men in France. Corsica suggests this idea to me.

That little island, with its 180,000 inhabitants, gave eight or ten remarkable men to the Revolution, whereas the Département du Nord, with 900,000 inhabitants, produced hardly one. And who that *one* might be I don't know. Needless to say, priests are all-powerful in this unlucky triangle. Civilization extends from Lille to Rennes and stops near Orleans and Tours. To the south-east, Grenoble is its brilliant boundary.[1]

The appointment of teachers to the Central School – MM. Gattel, Dubois-Fontanelle, Trousset, Villars (a peasant from the Hautes-Alpes), Jay, Durand, Dupuy, Chalvet, to name them roughly in order of their usefulness to children, the first three having some merit – cost little and was soon done, but there were big repairs to be done to the buildings. In spite of the war, everything got done in those energetic times. My grandfather was continually asking for funds from the Departmental Administration.

Lessons began in the spring, I believe, in makeshift classrooms. M. Durand's classroom had a delicious view, and eventually,

1. 31 December 1835. Omar. Began this book, of which this is the three hundred and twenty fifth page, and a hundred more : in all, four hundred, the ... 1835. Speed: 3 December 1835 I was at 93, 31 Dec[ember] at 325 : 232 in 28 days. On top of which there was the journey to Civita-Vecchia.

No work done on the days of the journey, and the d[ay] of my arrival here one or two with no writing done. Thus, 232 in 23 days, or ten pages per day, in the ordinary way eighteen or twenty pages per day, and on post days four or five or none at all.

How could I have written a good hand physically? Apart from this my bad handwriting discourages the inquisitive, 1 January 1836.

Yesterday from a quarter to twelve until five minutes past twelve at night at the house of M. Linpra [Praslin] with don Filippo by his fire. COMING from Sandre and *Rodolphe* at the Valle.

after a month, I came to appreciate it. This was on a lovely summer's day and a gentle breeze was waving the long grass on the Porte de Bonne slope, just across the way, sixty or eighty feet below us.

I was sick of hearing my relatives constantly praising the beauty of the fields, the greenery, the flowers, etc., buttercups,

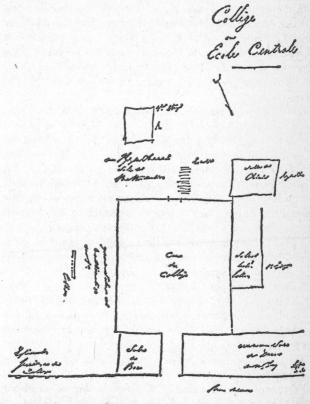

[*College or Central School – 3rd Floor – On the ground-floor, mathematics classroom. Staircase. Chemistry classroom. Ground floor – Large mathematics classroom on first floor. Blackboard – College courtyard – Literature classroom – 1st floor – Jesuits' and College Church – The round classroom. M. Jay's enormous art classroom – M. Chalvet's apartment – Rue Neuve.*]

etc., etc. These banal phrases of theirs gave me a dislike for flowers and flower-beds which still persists.

Fortunately, the magnificent view which I discovered *for myself* from one of the school windows, next door to the Latin classroom, where I used to go and day-dream all alone, overcame the profound disgust aroused by the remarks of my father and his friends the priests.

In the same way, so many years later, the rhythmic and pretentious phrases of MM. Chateaubriand and Salvandy made me write *Le Rouge et le Noir* in too clipped a style. This was very foolish, for in twenty years' time who will pay attention to the hypocritical nonsense of these gentlemen? Whereas I am taking a ticket in a lottery of which the great prize consists in this: to be read in 1935.

It was the same state of mind which made me close my eyes to the landscapes about which my aunt Séraphie went into ecstasies. I was, in 1794, like the people of Milan in 1835; the much-loathed German authorities wanted to make them like Schiller whose noble soul, so different from that of stolid Goethe, would be greatly shocked to see himself praised by such apostles.

It was a very strange experience for me to make my first appearance, in the spring of 1794 or '95, at the age of eleven or twelve in a school where I had ten or twelve companions.

I found reality far inferior to the wild visions of my imagination. These companions were not gay enough, not wild enough, and their manners were beneath contempt.

I seem to remember that M. Durand, puffed up with pride at finding himself teacher in a Central School but still goodnatured, made me translate Sallust's *De Bello Jugurtino*. Liberty produced its first fruits, I regained my common sense and lost my anger, and took a great liking to Sallust.

The whole college was full of workmen; many of the rooms on our third floor were open and I went alone there to day-dream.

Everything was surprising to me about this longed-for liberty which I had at length attained. The delight I found in it was not what I had dreamed about, those gay delightful noble companions I had imagined did not exist, but in their stead I found very selfish little scamps.

I have had the same sort of disappointment in more or less

everything throughout my life. Only the joys of ambition have been free from it; in 1811 when I was appointed auditeur and a fortnight later Inspector of Crown Property, I was drunk with satisfaction for three months at no longer being attached to the War Commissariat and exposed to envy and maltreatment from the coarse-mannered heroes who were the Emperor's hacks at Jena and at Wagram. Posterity will never realize how gross and stupid these men were away from their battlefields. And even on the battlefield, how cautious! They were like Admiral Nelson, the hero of Naples (see Colletta, and what I heard from M. di Fiori), like Nelson always reckoning what every wound would bring in the way of endowments and medals. What ignoble creatures, when compared with the lofty virtue of General Michaud or Colonel Mathis! No, posterity will never know what contemptible humbugs they were, these heroes of Napoleon's Bulletins. And how I used to laugh when I received the *Moniteur* in Vienna, Dresden, Berlin, Moscow; scarcely anybody used to be sent it in the army, for fear they would laugh at its lies. The Bulletins were engines of war, *field-works*, not historic documents.

Fortunately for poor Truth, the extreme baseness of these heroes, now Peers of France and Judges in 1835, will reveal to posterity the facts about their heroism in 1809. I make an exception only for that pleasant fellow Lasalle and for Exelmans, who since then ... But then he had paid a visit to Marshal Bourmont, the Minister of War. Moncey, too, would not have stooped to certain actions, but Suchet ... I was forgetting the great Gouvion-Saint-Cyr before age reduced him to a semi-imbecile, and this imbecility goes back to 1814. After that date he retained only his talent for writing. And in civil affairs, under Napoleon, what contemptible bastards are M. de Barante harrying M. Daru at Saint-Cloud at seven o'clock on a November morning, or the Comte d'Argout, meanly currying favour with General Sebastiani!

But, good heavens, where had I got to? To my Latin lessons in the school building.

CHAPTER 24

I HAD scant success among my companions. Today I can see that then I had a most ridiculous blend of haughtiness and longing for amusement. I responded to their most rapacious selfishness with my Spanish-style ideas of nobility. I was heart-broken when they left me out of their games, and to crown my misery I did not understand those games, in which I displayed a loftiness of soul and a fastidiousness which must have seemed sheer lunacy to the others. The only things that carry any weight with children are the cunning and quick-wittedness of a selfishness which, it seems to me, knows no bounds.

To complete my lack of success I was shy with the teacher; a word of restrained criticism uttered by a pedantic little bourgeois with a correct accent brought tears to my eyes. These tears showed cowardice in the opinion of the Gaultier brothers, Saint-Ferréol, Robert (now director of the Théâtre Italien in Paris) and particularly Odru. The latter was a peasant of great strength and even greater vulgarity who was a foot taller than any of us and whom we called Goliath; he had Goliath's grace, but he used to box our ears soundly when his dull wits finally grasped the fact that we were making fun of him.

His father [was] a rich peasant from Lumbin or some other village in the valley. (This term is used of the valley *par excellence*, the beautiful valley of the Isère, from Grenoble to Montmélian. Actually, the valley extends as far as the Moirans peak, thus:)

My grandfather had taken advantage of the passing of Séraphie to make me take courses in mathematics, chemistry and drawing.

M. Dupuy, that pompous and comical bourgeois, was, in the matter of civic importance, a sort of subordinate rival to Dr Gagnon. He grovelled before the nobility, but this advantage which he had over M. Gagnon was counterbalanced by a complete lack of those civilities and literary ideas which in those days formed the staple food of conversation. M. Dupuy, jealous at seeing M. Gagnon a member of the organizing committee and his superior, refused to accept this fortunate rival's recommendation in my favour, and I only won my place in the mathematics class by my own merit, which merit I was to find continually called in question for three successive years. M. Dupuy, who constantly (yet never too often) talked about Condillac and his *Logic*, had not a trace of logic in his head. He spoke with dignity and grace, and he had an imposing head and very civil manners.

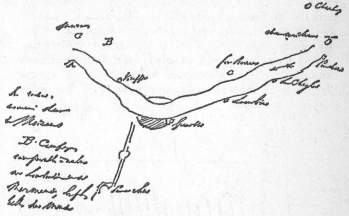

[*Chambéry – Montmeillan – Pontcharra – Fort Barraux – Le Cheylas – Lumbin – Grenoble – Voreppe – Moirans – The Claix Bridge – A Rock called Dent de Moirans – B. Landscape comparable to those of Lombardy and Marmande, the finest in the world.*]

He had had a very fine idea in 1794, namely to divide the hundred pupils who filled the ground-floor hall for the first mathematics lesson into groups of five or seven, each having a leader.

My leader was one of the *big boys*, that's to say a young man who was past puberty and a foot taller than we were. He used to spit at us, skilfully putting one finger in front of his mouth. In the army they call a character like that a *blackguard*. We complained about this blackguard, whose name I think was Raimonet, to M. Dupuy who, behaving with admirable dignity, degraded him. M. Dupuy was used to instructing young artillery officers at Valence, and had a great sense of honour (the sword-thrust kind).

We followed Bezout's dreary course of lessons, but M. Dupuy

had the intelligence to tell us about Clairaut's work and the new edition of this which M. Biot (that hard-working charlatan) had just made.

Clairaut was eminently fitted to open our minds, which Bezout tended to keep permanently blocked up. In Bezout, every *proposition* looks like some great secret learnt from a neighbouring gossip.

In the drawing class I considered that M. Jay and M. Couturier (with his broken nose) were terribly unfair to me. But M. Jay, failing any other merit, had that of bombast, and this bombast, instead of making us laugh, stimulated us. M. Jay was extremely successful and this was of great importance for the Central School, about which the priests spread slander; he had two or three hundred pupils.

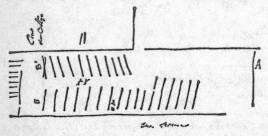

B. Benches on the rue Neuve side – B'. Benches lighted from the windows overlooking the courtyard – Y. Tall M. Jay striding about the classroom looking like a genius, with his head thrown back – A. Cupboard where models were kept. [*College courtyard – Rue Neuve.*]

These all sat on separate benches, seven or eight to a bench, and new benches had to be made every day. And what models! Inferior nudes drawn by MM. Pajou and M. Jay himself, arms and legs and everything else, more or less, were heavy and clumsy and hideous. They were like the drawings of M. Moreau in his youth, or of that M. Cochin who says such queer things about Michelangelo and Domenichino in his three little volumes on Italy.

There were large heads drawn in red chalk or engraved to look like pencil drawings. It must be admitted the artist's total ignorance of drawing was less obvious here than in the nude figures. The great merit of these heads, which were eighteen inches high, consisted in the hatchings being exactly parallel; as for copying Nature, that was never even considered.

A fellow named Moulezin, a stupid self-important ass and nowadays a rich and important bourgeois of Grenoble and no doubt one of the fiercest opponents of common sense, soon achieved immortality by the perfect parallelism of his hatchings in red chalk. He drew nudes and had been a pupil of M. Villonne (of Lyons); as for myself, a pupil of M. Le Roy, whom ill-health and Parisian good taste had prevented, while he lived, from becoming as big a charlatan as M. Villonne, a designer of printed fabrics, I never got beyond the big heads which shocked me greatly but had the advantage of being a lesson in modesty.

I needed one badly, to be quite honest. My relatives, whose product I was, congratulated themselves, in front of me, about my talent, and I thought myself the most distinguished young fellow in Grenoble.

My inferiority at games with the boys in my Latin class opened my eyes a little. The bench where we drew the big heads at H, on which I was put next to the two ridiculous-looking sons of a shoemaker (a shocking thing for M. Gagnon's grandson!) inspired me with the will to get on or die.

Here's the story of my talent for drawing: my ever-judicious family had decided, after a year or eighteen months of lessons with that well-mannered man, M. Le Roy, that I drew very well.

The fact is that I never even suspected that drawing is an imitation of Nature. I drew a head in half-relief, with a hard black pencil. (In Rome, at the Braccio Nuovo, I discovered that this was the head of Musa, Augustus's doctor.) My drawing was neat and cold, without the slightest merit, like a schoolgirl's drawing.

My parents who, for all their phrases about the beauty of the countryside and fine landscapes, had no feeling for the arts at all – there wasn't a single decent engraving in our house! – declared that I was very good at drawing. M. Le Roy was still alive, and was painting his landscapes in gouache (opaque colour) less badly than the rest.

I got leave to drop pencil-drawing and began to paint in gouache.

M. Le Roy had done a view of the bridge over the Vence, between the Buisserate and Saint-Robert, seen from point A.

I used to cross this bridge several times a year to go to Saint-Vincent, this drawing, especially the mountain at M, seemed to me a very good likeness, and I suddenly saw light : so then, first of all and above all, a drawing must look like Nature !

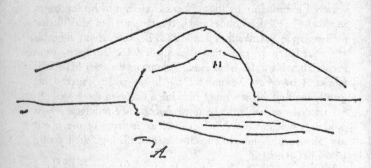

I stopped thinking about nicely parallel hatchings. After this splendid discovery I made rapid progress.

Poor M. Le Roy died, and I was sorry to lose him. Meanwhile, however, I was still a slave, and all the boys used to go to M. Villonne, who made designs for printed fabrics and had been driven out of *Commune-Affranchie*, the Enfranchised Town, by war and fear of the scaffold. Commune-Affranchie was the new name given to Lyons since its capture.

I informed my father (but by chance and without being so cunning as to think about it) of my liking for gouache, and I bought from Mme Le Roy, at three times their real value, many of her husband's gouaches.

I greatly coveted two volumes of La Fontaine's *Tales* with very delicately but clearly engraved illustrations.

'They're quite horrid,' Mme Le Roy told me, with her fine hypocritical soubrette's eyes, 'but they're masterpieces.'

I saw that I shouldn't be able to get the *Tales* thrown in for the price of the gouaches. Then the Central School opened and I forgot about gouache painting; but my discovery remained with me. One must copy Nature, and perhaps this prevented my big heads, imitated from those commonplace drawings, from being as execrable as they might have been. I remember the *Indignant Soldier* in Raphael's *Punishment of Heliodorus*; I can never see the original (in the Vatican) without remembering my copy; my quite arbitrary pencil-work, a spurious merit, was particularly skilful in the dragon on top of the helmet.

When we had achieved a tolerable piece of work, M. Jay would sit down in the pupil's place, and correct the head a little, arguing bombastically, but still arguing, and finally signing the head on the back, apparently *ne varietur*, so that it might be submitted to the competition in the middle or at the end of the year. He excited us, but he had not the least conception of *beauty*. He had, in all his life, painted nothing but one second-rate picture, a figure of Liberty copied from his wife, short, squat and shapeless. To make it look lighter he had filled up the foreground with a tombstone behind which Liberty appeared hidden from the knees down.

The end of the year came, there were examinations in the presence of the committee and I believe one member of the Département.

I only got a wretched *accessit*, and that, I suppose, merely in order to please M. Gagnon, head of the committee, and M. Dausse, another committee member who was a great friend of M. Gagnon's.

My grandfather was humiliated by this, and told me so with perfect courtesy and restraint. His simple remark made the greatest possible impression on me. He added, with a laugh: 'You were only able to show us your big bottom!'

This unflattering position had been noticeable at the blackboard in the mathematics class.

This was a board six feet by four, supported at a height of five feet by a very strong frame, and one had to climb three steps to reach it.

M. Dupuy made the pupils demonstrate a proposition, for instance the square of the hypotenuse, or this problem: a piece of work is paid seven pounds, four sous, three deniers a fathom, the workman makes two fathoms, five feet, three inches. How much will he earn?

During the course of the year M. Dupuy had always called up to the blackboard MM. de Monval, who were noblemen,

M. de Pina, a nobleman and an ultra, M. Anglès, M. de Renneville, a nobleman, and myself never or only once.

The younger Monval, a goose with a goose's face but a good mathematician (so they said at school), was massacred by brigands in Calabria about 1806, I believe. The elder, once very thick with Paul-Louis Courier, became a rotten old ultra ... He

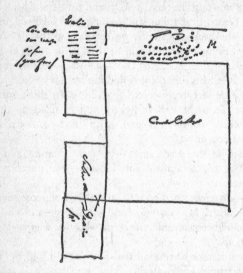

M. Mathematics classroom – D. M. Dupuy, 5 feet 8 inches tall, with his big walking-stick, in his immense armchair – M. His favourites, the aristocratic pupils – H. Myself, pining to be summoned to the blackboard and hiding so as not to be summoned to it, dying of fear and timidity – H'. My bench. [*Staircase, a death-trap, without iron railings – College courtyard – Art classroom.*]

was made a colonel and ruined a great lady of Naples in a horrid way; at Grenoble he tried to blow hot and cold about 1830, was shown up and despised by everyone. He died of this widespread and richly deserved contempt, and was highly praised by the pious (see the *Gazette* of 1832 or 1833). He was a pretty specimen, an out-and-out scoundrel.

M. de Pina was Mayor of Grenoble from 1825 to 1830, an out-and-out reactionary who, forgetting honesty in favour of his nine or ten children, collected an income of 60,000 or 70,000 francs. A gloomy fanatic and, I imagine, an out-and-out scoundrel, a real Jesuit.

Anglès, since then Prefect of Police, an indefatigable worker, a lover of order, but politically an out-and-out scoundrel, although in my view infinitely less of a scoundrel than the two aforementioned who, as scoundrels, take first prize, to my mind.

Pretty Countess Anglès was a friend of Countess Daru, in whose salon I saw her; the good-looking Count de Meffrey (from Grenoble, like M. Anglès) was her lover. The poor woman was very bored, I fancy, in spite of her husband's grand position.

That husband, the son of a famous miser and himself miserly, was the gloomiest brute and had the most tortuous and anti-mathematical of minds. Moreover, his cowardice caused a scandal; I'll tell later the story of his box on the ear, and his tail. Towards 1826 or '27 he lost his position as Prefect of Police and went off to build a fine country house in the mountains, near Roanne, where he soon after died very suddenly, still quite young. He was a gloomy brute; he had all the worst aspects of the Dauphinois character, being base, cunning, sly and attentive to the meanest details.

M. de Renneville, a cousin of the Monvals, was handsome and a stupid ass. His father was the dirtiest and proudest man in Grenoble. I've never heard speak of him since I was at school.

M. de Sinard, my friend, was good natured, he was reduced to beggary by emigration, and protected and supported by Mme de Valserre. He was my friend.

One climbed up to the blackboard and wrote, at O. The head of the pupil who was demonstrating was quite eight feet up in the air. I, being made conspicuous once a month and getting no help from M. Dupuy, who talked to Monval or M. de Pina while I did my demonstration, was consumed with shyness, and I stammered. When my turn came to climb up to the blackboard in front of the committee, my shyness was intensified, I grew confused as I looked at the gentlemen and particularly at that terrible M. Dausse, sitting beside the blackboard, to the right. I had the presence of mind to stop looking at them and pay attention to nothing but my operation, and I managed to do it correctly although I bored them. How different from what happened in August 1799! I can say that it was through my own merit that I made good at *mathematics* and in drawing, as we used to say at the Central School.

[*Slate.*]

I was stout and shortish, I wore a light grey coat. Hence the reproof.

'Why didn't you get a prize?' my grandfather would ask me.

'I hadn't time.'

During this first year, lessons had gone on for only four or five months, I think.

I used to go to Claix, still mad about game-shooting; but as I roamed the fields against my father's will, I kept brooding deeply over that remark: 'Why didn't you get a prize?'

I cannot remember whether I went for four years or only three to the Central School. I am sure of the date when I left, an examination at the end of 1799, and the Russians expected in Grenoble. The aristocrats and my relatives too, I fancy, used to say:

O Rus, quando ego te adspiciam!

I, for my part, was anxiously awaiting the examination which would get me out of Grenoble! If I ever go back there, a few searches in the archives of the Departmental Administration, at the Prefecture, will tell me whether the Central School was opened in 1796 or not until 1797.

At that time we used to count by the years of the Republic;

it was Year V or Year VI. Only long afterwards, when the Emperor stupidly willed it so, did I learn to know 1796, 1797. I saw things at close quarters in those days.

The Emperor then began to raise up the throne of the Bourbons and was seconded by the extreme and boundless baseness of M. de Laplace. It's a strange thing that poets are courageous, and learned people, so-called, are base and servile. What servility, what abasement towards authority did M. Cuvier display! It horrified even the sensible Sutton Sharpe. At the Council of State M. le Baron Cuvier always supported the meanest policy.

When the Order of the Reunion was instituted, I was in the innermost Court circles; he came *weeping*, there's no other word, to try and get it. I'll tell the Emperor's reply in due course. Bacon, Laplace, Cuvier, all sold themselves out of cowardice. M. Lagrange was less contemptible to my mind.

Secure of glory through their writings, these gentlemen hope their scientific reputations will cover up their political conduct; whether it's a question of money or of favours, they rush to feather their own nests. The celebrated Legendre, a geometrician of the first rank, on receiving the Cross of the Legion of Honour, fastened it to his coat, looked at himself in the glass and jumped for joy. The room was low, he hit the ceiling with his head and fell down half dead. What a worthy death this would have been for this successor of Archimedes!

What despicable things have they not done in the Academy of Sciences from 1815 to 1830 and since then, to get themselves decorated! It's quite unbelievable; I learnt details from MM. de Jussieu, Edwards, Milne-Edwards, and through the talk in Baron Gérard's salon. But I've forgotten most of such horrors.

A diplomat is less base, in that he openly says: 'I am going to do all that I can to get on.'[1]

1. 1 January 1836, 29 pages. I am stopping owing to lack of daylight, at a quarter to five.

Mlle Kubly, and then Victorine Bigillion. Wooden Bridge, Mem[oirs] of Duclos.

CHAPTER 25

RELEASED from tyranny, my soul began to gain some resilience. Gradually I lost my obsession by that exhausting feeling, impotent hatred.

My kind aunt Élisabeth was my salvation. She used to go almost every evening to play cards with Mme Colomb or Mme Romagnier. There was nothing bourgeois about these excellent sisters, save a certain circumspection of manner and a few habits. They had noble souls, which is a thing seldom found in the provinces, and they were deeply attached to my aunt Élisabeth.

I have not done justice to these kind cousins; they had lofty and generous souls and they had given remarkable proof of this in the important occasions of their lives.

My father, more and more engrossed in his passion for agriculture and for Claix, used to spend three or four days a week there. He was not nearly so happy in M. Gagnon's house, where he had dined and supped every day since my mother's death. He could only speak his mind to Séraphie. He stood in awe of my aunt Élisabeth's Spanish character; there had always been very little conversation between these two. His everlasting petty Dauphinois cunning and his chilling reserve did not harmonize with her noble sincerity and simplicity. Mlle Gagnon had no liking for my father who, on the other hand, was incapable of carrying on a conversation with Dr Gagnon; he was respectful and polite, Dr Gagnon was very polite, and that was all. My father thus lost nothing by spending three or four days a week at Claix. Two or three times he told me when he made me go with him to Claix how sad it was, at his age, not to have a home of his own.

When I returned in the evenings to have supper with my aunt Élisabeth, my grandfather and my two sisters, I had no fear of being severely cross-questioned. I usually said with a laugh that I had been to fetch my aunt from Mesdames Romagnier and Colomb; often, in fact, I used to accompany my aunt from their home to the door of ours, and then run off again to spend half an hour on the promenade in the Jardin de Ville, which, on a summer's evening, by moonlight, under the splendid eighty-feet-tall chestnut trees, served as a meeting-place for all the gay young people of the town.

Little by little I grew bolder, and I went more often to the theatre, where I always stood in the pit.

I watched with tender interest a young actress named Mlle Kubly. Soon I fell desperately in love with her; I never spoke to her. She was a slim, rather tall young woman, with an aquiline nose; she was pretty, slender and shapely. She still had the thinness of extreme youth, but her expression was serious and often melancholy.

Everything was new to me in that strange madness which suddenly took possession of all my thoughts. All other interests vanished for me. I scarcely recognized the feeling whose description in *La Nouvelle Héloïse* had so delighted me; still less was this the sensual pleasure of *Félicia*. Suddenly I became indifferent and quite impartial about everything else around me; this was the period when my hatred for my late aunt Séraphie died away.

Mlle Kubly played *jeune première* roles in comedy and also sang in light opera.

Obviously, true comedy was no use to me. My grandfather kept dinning into my ears the great phrase : *knowledge of the human heart*. But what could I know about the *human heart*? At the very utmost a few *forecasts* picked up in books, in *Don Quixote* particularly, the only book that did not inspire me with mistrust; all the rest had been recommended by tyrants, for my grandfather (I suppose he had been recently converted) refrained from making fun of the books which my father and Séraphie made me read.

What I wanted, therefore, was romantic comedy, i.e. drama without gloom, dealing with unhappy love affairs rather than financial misfortunes (gloomy, depressing dramas based on lack of money have always revolted me as being bourgeois and too realistic; my a . . . also is a part of Nature, as Préville is supposed to have said to some author or other).

Mlle Kubly excelled in Florian's *Claudine*.

A young woman from Savoy, who has had a child at Montenvers by a young man of fashion on his travels, dresses up as a man and, taking her baby along with her, becomes a roadsweeper on a public square in Turin. She meets her lover again; she still loves him and becomes his servant; but this lover is about to be married.

The actor who played the lover, named Poussi I believe – this name suddenly comes back to me after all these years – used to say with utterly convincing naturalness: 'Claude, Claude!' at a certain moment when he scolded his servant for speaking ill of his betrothed. That tone of voice echoes in my soul, and I can still see the actor.

For several months this work, repeatedly asked for by the public, gave me the keenest pleasure, and I would say the keenest pleasures ever given me by works of art, except that, for a long time my *chief* pleasure had been a tender admiration of the most devoted and fanatical kind. I dared not utter the name of Mlle Kubly; if someone named her in my presence I felt a strange contraction of my heart and nearly swooned; there was a kind of storm in my blood.

If someone said *la* Kubly instead of Mlle Kubly, I felt an impulse of hatred and horror that I could scarcely contain.

She sang with her poor thin little voice in *Le Traité Nul*, an opera by Gaveaux (a dull-witted creature who died insane a few years later).

This was the beginning of my love for music, which has been perhaps my most powerful and most expensive passion; it still persists at fifty-two and is keener than ever. I don't know how many leagues I wouldn't go on foot, or how many days' prison I would not endure to hear *Don Giovanni* or the *Matrimonio Segreto*, and I know nothing else for which I would make such an effort. But unfortunately for me, I detest *mediocre* music (to my mind it's a caricature of good music: for instance Donizetti's *Furioso* yesterday evening at the *Valle* in Rome. The Italians, very unlike myself, cannot endure music that is more than five or six years old. One of them said in my presence at Madame 120's; 'How can a piece of music more than a year old be beautiful?').

What a parenthesis, good heavens! When I read this over, I shall have to strike out or insert elsewhere about half this manuscript.

I learned by heart – and with what ecstasies! – that continuous jerky trickle of vinegar that was called *Le Traité Nul*.

A tolerable actor, who played the valet's role gaily (I realize today that he had the genuine insouciance of a poor devil who has only gloomy thoughts at home and throws himself into his role with delight), gave me my first notions of *comedy*, particularly at the end, when he gets up the country dance ending with '*Mathurine nous écoutait . . .*'

A landscape the shape and size of a bill of exchange, on which there was a great deal of gamboge strengthened with sepia, especially in the left foreground, which I had bought at M. Le Roy's and which I was at that time delightedly copying, seemed to me exactly the same thing as the acting of this comedian, who made me laugh whole-heartedly when Mlle Kubly was not on the stage; if he spoke to her I was moved and enchanted. It may be for this reason that even today I often get the same sensation from a picture or a piece of music. How often I have experienced this identification in the Brera museum at Milan (1814–21)!

The truth and strength of this feeling are hard to express and indeed are hard to credit.

The marriage, the intimate union, of these two arts, was for ever cemented for me when I was twelve or thirteen, by four or five months of the keenest happiness and the most intense sensuous delight, verging on pain, that I have ever experienced.

I realize now (but I realize it from Rome, at the age of fifty-two) that I had a taste for music before that thin vinegary *Traité Nul*, so typically French, with its skipping rhythms – but which I still know by heart. Here are my recollections: (1) the sound of the bells of Saint-André, particularly as they rang for the elections one year when my cousin Abraham Mallein (father of my brother-in-law Alexandre) was *président*, or merely elector; (2) the sound of the pump on the Place Grenette when the maids drew water in the evenings with the long iron handle; (3) finally, but least important of all, the sound of a flute played by some shop assistant in a fourth-floor room on the Place Grenette.

These things had already given me pleasure which, although I did not realize it, was musical pleasure.

Mlle Kubly also played in Grétry's *Épreuve Villageoise*, which was infinitely less bad than the *Traité Nul*. A tragic situation made me shudder in *Raoul, sire de Créqui*; in short, all the

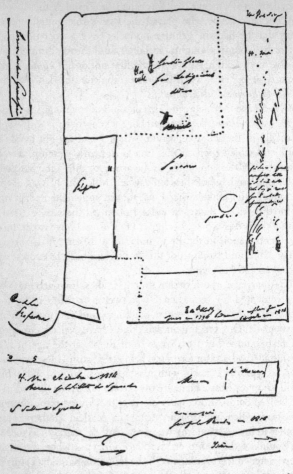

[*Grandfather's terrace – Tower of the Préfecture – Préfecture – Hercules – Garden planted by Lesdiguières, so it's said – Flower-bed – Fountain – Rue Montorge – H. Me – Avenue of chestnut trees 90 feet high – I left at Grenoble a small oil-painting by M. Le Roy which gives a good impression of this walk – Mlle Kubly – Wall in 1794, stupidly replaced by a fine railing about 1814 – H. My room in 1814 – O. Box office for entertainments – S. Theatre – Houses. Morenas' house – New quay made by the Bourbons about 1818 – Isère – La Périère.*]

wretched little operas in 1794 acquired sublimity for me through the presence of Mlle Kubly; nothing could be commonplace or mean when she appeared.

One day I had the extreme courage to ask somebody where Mlle Kubly lodged. This was probably the bravest action of my life.

'Rue des Clercs,' I was told.

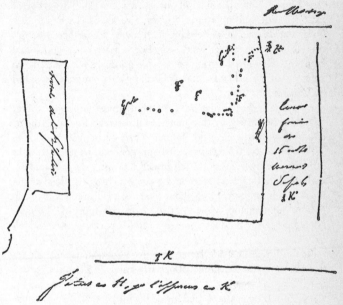

[*Hotel de la Préfecture – Railing – Railing – Rue Montorge – Terrace consisting of 15 or 20 superb chestnuts – I was at H, I saw her at K.*]

I had had the courage, much earlier, to ask if she had a lover. To which the person I asked replied, with some vulgar comment, that he knew nothing about her habits.

I used to walk down the rue des Clercs on the days when I was feeling very brave, my heart thumping; I should perhaps have collapsed if I had met her and I was greatly relieved when, having reached the end of the rue des Clercs, I was sure not to meet her.

One morning, walking by myself at the far end of the avenue of tall chestnuts in the Jardin de Ville and, as usual, thinking about her, I caught sight of her at the other end of the garden, near the wall of the Intendance, coming towards the terrace. I nearly felt faint, and at last I *took flight*, running along by the railing, by the line marked F, as if the devil were carrying me; she was, I think, at K' and I was fortunate enough not to be seen by her. Note that she did not know me at all. This is one of my most outstanding characteristics; I've always been like that (even the day before yesterday). The joy of seeing her close up, five or six yards away, was too great; it seared me, and I fled from this very real burning pain. This peculiarity inclines me to believe that in love I have the melancholy temperament described by Cabanis.

Indeed, love has always been for me the most important thing, or rather the only thing that mattered. I have never been afraid of anything save of seeing the woman I love exchange an intimate look with a rival. I feel very little anger against the rival: he's pursuing his own interest, I tell myself, but my grief is boundless and so acute that I collapse on a stone bench by the door of the house. I admire everything about the rival who's preferred to me (Major Gibory and Mme Martin, Palazzo Aguissola, Milan). No other grief produces one thousandth part of this effect on me.

At the Emperor's side I was attentive and zealous, and unlike the rest quite unconcerned about my cravat. (Example: seven o'clock in the evening, at ... in Lusace, on the 1813 campaign, the day after the death of the Duc de Frioul.)

I am neither timid nor melancholy when I write, and run the risk of being hissed; I feel full of courage and pride when I am writing a phrase which will be spurned by one of those two giants of 1835, MM. Chateaubriand or Villemain.

No doubt in 1880 some artful cautious charlatan will be in the fashion, as these gentlemen are today. But if people read this they will think me envious, and that distresses me; that contemptible bourgeois vice is, it seems to me, the most alien to my character.

Really, I am desperately jealous only of people who make love to a woman with whom I'm in love; what's more, I'm jealous even of those who made love to her ten years before me. For instance, Babet's first lover (Vienna, 1809).

'You used to receive him in your bedroom!'

'Any room was a bedroom for us, we were alone in the château and he had the keys.'

I can still feel the pain these words gave me, and yet it was in 1809, twenty-seven years ago; I can still picture pretty Babet's utter simplicity while she was looking at me.

I have certainly been getting a great deal of pleasure out of writing for the past hour, trying to describe with *real accuracy* my feelings in the time of Mlle Kubly; but who the deuce will have the courage to wade through it, to read this excessive pile of *I*'s and *me*'s? I even find it *stinking* myself. That's the weakness of this sort of writing in which, moreover, I cannot season the insipidity with any sauce of charlatanism. Dare I add: *as in Rousseau's Confessions?* No, despite the enormous absurdity of this objection, people will once more think I am envious, or rather anxious to establish a comparison, appalling in its absurdity, with the masterpiece of that great writer.

I declare once again, and once for all, that I supremely and sincerely despise M. Pariset, M. de Salvandy, M. Saint-Marc Girardin and the other braggarts, the mercenary and Jesuitical pedants of the *Journal des Débats*; but that doesn't make me think myself any closer to the great writers. I don't consider myself to have any genius, which would guarantee my worth, other than that of painting a *faithful likeness* of Nature, which appears to me so clearly at certain moments; in the second place, I am sure of my perfect honesty, of my adoration for the truth; and in the third place I am sure of the pleasure I take in writing, a pleasure which reached frenzy in 1817, at Milan, at M. Peronti's, Corsia del Giardino.[1]

1. I am always amazed at having been able to please people like M. Lemo[Molé], de Créqui, or M. de Cot ... [?] or certain gentlemen of the Faubourg Saint-Germain who were looking for certain of my works, according to what Sautelet told me about 1828. (M. Sautelet, a liberal publisher, blew his brains out about 1829 through a mixture of vanity, love and debts. He was the owner of *Le National*, and an associate of that honest, patriotic and pig-headed Paulin, still a publisher in 1836). [*But Stendhal has crossed out these lines and written across them*]: Too lengthy.

CHAPTER 26

But let's get back to Mlle Kubly. How far I was from envy, or from any thought of dreading *the imputation of envy*, or indeed from thinking of other people in any way whatsoever, at that time! Life was just beginning for me.

There was only one being in the world, Mlle Kubly; only one event, would she play that evening or the next?

What a disappointment for me when she was not playing, and some tragedy was being given!

What transports of pure, tender and triumphant joy when I read her name on the bill! I can still see that bill, the shape of it, the paper, the printed letters.

I went to read that beloved name in three or four of the places where it was billed, one after the other: at the Jacobins' Gate, under the vault of the Garden, at the corner of my grandfather's house. I did not merely read her name, I gave myself the pleasure of re-reading the whole bill. The somewhat battered type used by the bad printer who produced this bill became precious and holy to me, and for many long years I loved it more than finer lettering.

I even remember this: when I came to Paris in 1799 the beauty of the lettering shocked me, it was not that in which the name Kubly had been printed.

She went away, I cannot say at what period. For a long time I couldn't go to the theatre. I got leave to learn music, not without a struggle; my father's religion was shocked by so profane an art, and my grandfather had not the slightest taste for it.

I took a violin teacher named Mention, the most amusing fellow, who had the old traditional French gaiety mingled with bravery and love. He was very poor but he had an artist's heart; one day when I was playing worse than usual he shut the book, saying: 'I shan't teach you any more.'

I went to a clarinet teacher named Hoffmann (rue de Bonne), a worthy German; I played slightly less badly. I don't know

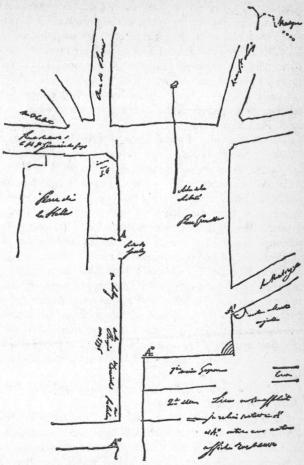

[*Mountain – Rue Saint-Louis – Rue de Bonne – M. Chabert – Rue Neuve, the f[aubour]g St-Germain of the district – Love affair with S.G. – Place de la Halle – Porte des Jacobins – M. Le Roy – Mlles Bourgeois about 1796 – M. Corréard – M. Rubichon – Tree of Liberty – Place Grenette – Rue Montorge – Vaulted passage into the garden – 1st Gagnon house – 2nd ditto. Terrace – Places where bills were posted. I read them particularly at A' and A''', besides another posted in the rue Neuve.*]

how I came to leave this teacher and go to M. Holleville, rue Saint-Louis, opposite Mme Barthélemy's, our shoemaker's wife. He was quite a fair violinist, and although rather deaf he knew when I was playing the least bit out of tune. I used to meet there M. Félix Faure (now Peer of France, Premier Président, one of those who was a judge in August 1835). I don't know how I came to leave Holleville.

Finally I went to take singing lessons, unbeknown to my relatives, at six o'clock in the morning, from a very good singer in the Place Saint-Louis.

But it was no good; I was the first to be revolted by the sounds I made. I bought Italian songs, including one on which I read *Amore,* or something of the sort, *nel' cimento*; I took this to mean *in the cement, in the mortar*. I adored these Italian songs of which I understood nothing. I had begun too late. If anything could have made me sick of music it would have been the execrable sounds that one has to make while learning it. Only the piano might have enabled me to avoid this difficulty, but I was born into an essentially unmusical family.

When, later on, I wrote about music, my friends' principal objection was on the score of this ignorance of mine. But I must say without any affectation that at that very moment I could feel subtleties in the piece that was being played of which they were unaware. It's just the same with the subtleties of expression in different copies of the same picture. I see these things as clearly *as through a crystal*. But, good Lord, what a fool people will take me for!

When I came back to life after a few months of Mlle Kubly's absence I was a different man.

I no longer hated Séraphie, I just forgot her; as for my father I wished only one thing, not to be near him. I noticed with remorse that I had not a *drop* of tenderness or affection for him.

I must be a monster, then, I said to myself. And for many years I found no answer to this objection. In my family they harped *ad nauseam* on fondness for one's relatives. These worthy folks called *fondness* the continual nagging with which they had honoured me for five or six years. I began to perceive that they were dreadfully bored and that, being too vain to resume the social relations they had rashly dropped at the time of their cruel bereavement, their only resource against boredom was myself.

But nothing had any further power to move me after what I had been feeling. I studied Latin and drawing resolutely, and I won a first prize, I don't remember for which of these two subjects, and a second prize.

I translated with pleasure Tacitus's *Life of Agricola*; this was almost the first time that I got any pleasure out of Latin. This pleasure was spoilt *amaregiato* by the blows I got from big Odru, that heavy, ignorant peasant from Lumbin, who studied with us and never understood a thing. I had some tough fights with Giroud, who wore a red coat. I was still a child for a great part of my daily life then.

And nevertheless the storm that had been raging in my mind for several months had matured me. I began to tell myself seriously: 'I must make up my mind and get out of this slough.'

I had only one means in the whole world: mathematics. But I was taught mathematics so stupidly that I made no progress; it's true that my schoolfellows made even less, if that's possible. The great M. Dupuy explained propositions to us as if they'd been a set of recipes for making vinegar.

And yet Bezout was my only resource for getting out of Grenoble. But Bezout was such a fool! He had a mind like that of M. Dupuy, our pompous teacher.

My grandfather knew a narrow-minded bourgeois named Chabert who taught mathematics privately, *in his own room*. That's what they said locally, and it fitted the man perfectly. I got leave, with some considerable difficulty, to go to this room of M. Chabert's; it was thought that M. Dupuy might be offended, and moreover there was a fee of twelve francs a month, I believe.

I replied that most of the pupils in the mathematics class at the Central School went to M. Chabert's, and that if I didn't go I should be left at the bottom of the class at the Central School. So I went to M. Chabert's. M. Chabert was a fairly well-dressed bourgeois, but he always seemed to be in his Sunday best and scared stiff of spoiling his coat or his waistcoat or his smart breeches of 'goose-dung' coloured kerseymere; he was moreover quite good-looking in a bourgeois way. He lived in the rue

Neuve, near the rue Saint-Jacques and almost opposite the ironmonger Bourbon, whose name impressed me, since it was only with signs of the deepest respect and the utmost devotion that my bourgeois relatives pronounced this name. You'd have thought the fate of France depended on it.

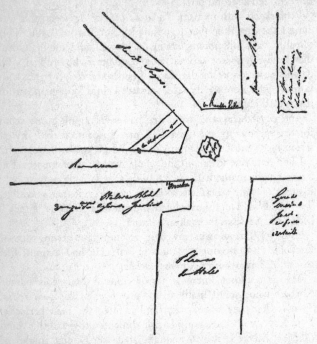

[*The St-Jacques pump – Rue St-Jacques – M. Renauld[on] the cuckold – Here ten years later stood the house built according to my plans, through which my father ruined himself – Big Jacobin monastery, built of freestone – Place de la Halle – Cornmarket, which I saw when it was still the Jacobins' church – Bourbon – Rue Neuve – M. Chabert on the 3rd floor.*]

But at M. Chabert's I encountered the same disfavour that had depressed me so at the Central School and had kept me from ever being called up to the blackboard. In a small room, among seven or eight pupils gathered round a blackboard of oil-cloth, nothing could be more humiliating than to ask if one might demonstrate at the board, in other words go up and explain for the fifth or sixth time a proposition which four or five pupils had already explained. And yet this was what I was obliged to do sometimes at M. Chabert's, otherwise I should never have *demonstrated*. M. Chabert thought me a *minus habens* and he stuck to this abominable opinion. Later on, it was extremely funny to hear him speak of my success at mathematics.

But in those early days it showed a strange lack of thought, or rather lack of intelligence, on the part of my relatives not to ask whether I was able to *demonstrate* and how many times a week I went to the board. They did not condescend to go into such details. M. Chabert, who professed profound respect for M. Dupuy, only called up to the board those who were summoned thither at the Central School. There was a certain M. de Renneville whom M. Dupuy called up to the board as being a nobleman and a cousin of the Monvals – he was a sort of imbecile, almost dumb and with staring eyes; I used to boil with indignation when I saw M. Dupuy and M. Chabert prefer him to me.

I can excuse M. Chabert; I must have been the most presumptuous and scornful small boy. My grandfather and my family proclaimed me a prodigy; hadn't they been giving me all their attention for the past five years?

M. Chabert was, in fact, less of an ignoramus than M. Dupuy. From him I learnt about Euler and his problems on the number of eggs a peasant woman brings to market when a rascal robs her of one-fifth, and then she drops half the rest, etc., etc.

This opened my mind; I caught a glimpse of what it meant to use the instrument called algebra. I'm hanged if anyone had ever told me about this; M. Dupuy was always making pompous phrases on the subject, but never told us, quite simply: it's a *division of labour* which works miracles like all divisions of labour, and allows the mind to concentrate all its strength on a single aspect of things, on a single one of their qualities.

How different it would have been for us if M. Dupuy had said to us: this cheese is soft, or it is hard; it is white, it is blue; it is old, it is new; it is mine, it is yours; it is light or it is heavy. Out of so many qualities let us consider exclusively the weight.

Whatever this weight may be, let us call it A. Now, without thinking exclusively of the cheese, let us apply to A all that we know about quantities.

This very simple thing was never told us by anybody, in that remote province; since that date, the École Polytechnique and the ideas of Lagrange will have spread their influence into the provinces.

The masterpiece of the education of those days was a little scoundrel dressed in green, mild, hypocritical and gentle, who was less than three feet high and learned by heart the *propositions* that were being demonstrated but without worrying whether he understood them in the least. This favourite of M. Chabert as well as of M. Dupuy was called, if I'm not mistaken, Paul-Émile Teisseire. The examiner for the École Polytechnique, that idiot Louis Monge, brother of the great geometrician, who made such a notorious blunder (at the beginning of the *Statics*), did not notice that Paul-Émile's whole merit lay in his astonishing memory.

He got into the Polytechnique; his complete hypocrisy, his memory and his pretty girlish face had less success there than at Grenoble; he certainly left the school an officer but was soon touched by grace and became a priest. Unfortunately he died of consumption; I should have enjoyed watching his progress. I had left Grenoble with an inordinate desire to be able some day to give him, deliberately, a mighty volley of slaps.

I seem to remember having given him one on account already, at M. Chabert's, where he had quite justifiably surpassed me with that imperturbable memory of his.

As for him, he never lost his temper over anything and bore with perfect composure the volleys of 'You *little hypocrite*!' which were showered on him from every side, and which were intensified one day when we saw him crowned with roses, playing the part of an angel in a procession.

He was about the only personality I noticed at the Central School. He made a fine contrast with the gloomy Benoît, whom I met at M. Dubois-Fontanelle's lessons on literature and according to whom the sublimest knowledge consisted in Socratic love, which Dr Clapier, the lunatic, had taught him.

It's ten years, perhaps, since I thought about M. Chabert;

gradually I remember that he was in fact much less narrow-minded than M. Dupuy, although he spoke with even more of a drawl and looked far shabbier and more bourgeois.

He had a high opinion of Clairaut, and it was a tremendous thing to have put us in contact with that man of genius and relieved us a little from the dreary Bezout. He had Bossut and abbé Marie, and from time to time he made us study a theorem in these authors. He even had in manuscript a few small things

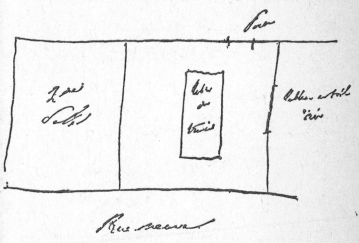

[*Door – Second classroom – Work table – Blackboard of oil-cloth – Rue Neuve.*]

by Lagrange, the sort of thing that was within our childish range.

I seem to remember that we wrote with pens in paper note-books, and on a blackboard of oil-cloth.

My disgrace extended to everything; perhaps it came from some blunder by my relatives, who may have forgotten to send a turkey at Christmas to M. Chabert or his sisters, for he had some very pretty ones, and but for my bashfulness I'd willingly have flirted with them. They had a great regard for the grandson of M. Gagnon, and moreover they used to come to Mass at our house on Sundays.

We used to go and make surveys with a graphometer and a plane-table; one day we surveyed a field next to the Chemin des Boiteuses. It was the field marked BCDF. M. Chabert made all the others draw the lines on the plane-table; eventually my turn came, but I was last or next to last, with a child after me. I was annoyed and humiliated; I pressed too hard on the pen.

'But I told you to draw a line,' drawled M. Chabert, 'and you've made a stripe.'

He was right. I think that this condition of marked disfavour

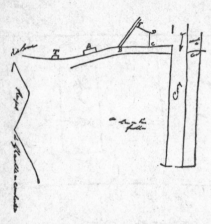

The house of that lunatic Camille Teisseire, a Jacobin who in 1811 wants Rousseau and Voltaire to be burnt – A. Hotel of the Good Wife, she's represented as headless, which struck me very much. [*Porte de Bonne – Ramparts of Grenoble to the west – Execution ground – Cours – The Canel Mill.*]

from MM. Dupuy and Chabert and of utter indifference from M. Jay at the drawing-school prevented me from becoming a fool. I had a rare predisposition to this, for my relatives, who with their gloomy bigotry were always declaiming against public education, had convinced themselves without much difficulty that by five years of unfortunately over-assiduous attention they had produced a masterpiece, and that masterpiece was myself.

One day I said to myself, but actually this was before the

Central School: 'Couldn't I be the son of some great prince, and everything that I'm told about the Revolution and the little I see of it is a fable intended for my education, as in *Émile*?'

For my grandfather, that agreeable talker, in spite of his pious resolutions, had mentioned *Émile* in my presence, spoken about *the Profession de foi du vicaire Savoyard*, etc., etc., etc., I had stolen this book at Claix, but I hadn't understood the first thing about it, not even the absurdities on the opening page, and after a quarter of an hour I'd dropped it. To do justice to my father's taste he was enthusiastic about Rousseau and sometimes talked about him, for which and for his imprudence in a child's presence he was well scolded by my aunt Séraphie.

CHAPTER 27

I HAD, and still have, the most aristocratic tastes; I'd do anything for the happiness of the people, but I would rather, I think, spend a fortnight in gaol every month than live amongst shopkeepers.

About this time I became friendly, I don't quite know how, with François Bigillion (who afterwards killed himself, I believe, from distress about his wife).

He was a simple, natural, sincere man, who never tried to imply by some ambitious answer that he knew the world, women, etc. This was our great ambition and our principal vanity at school. Each of these lads wanted to convince the rest that he had had a woman and knew the world; there was nothing like that about good Bigillion. We went for long walks together, especially towards the Rabot Tower and the Bastille. We felt uplifted by the magnificent view we enjoyed from there, particularly towards Eybens, behind which the highest Alps rise up. Rabot and La Bastille are, the one an old tower, the other a small house, situated at two very different heights, on the mountain enclosed by the town walls, which, though ludicrous in 1795, are being made good in 1836.

On these walks we used to impart to one another, with the utmost frankness, what we thought about that terrible, dark and delicious forest into which we were about to enter. I mean, of course, society and the world.

Bigillion had certain great advantages over me:

(1) He had lived in liberty since his childhood, as the son of a father who was not excessively fond of him and who knew how to amuse himself otherwise than by treating his son as a doll.

(2) This father, a well-to-do country bourgeois, lived at Saint-Ismier, a village one postal stage from Grenoble, towards the east, in a very pleasant position in the Isère valley. This worthy countryman, a lover of wine, good fare and fresh peasant girls, had rented a small apartment at Grenoble for his two sons who were being educated there. The elder was called Bigillion according to the custom of our province, the younger Rémy, a humorist, an odd fellow, a regular Dauphinois but generous, a little jealous even then of the friendship that existed between Bigillion and myself.

This friendship, based on perfect mutual trust, became intimate after one week. He had had an uncle who was a learned and, surely, a most unmonkish monk, good Father Morlon, a Benedictine perhaps, who, when I was a child, had consented, out of friendship for my grandfather, to hear my confession once or twice. I had been greatly surprised by his gentle and polite tone, so very different from the harsh pedantry of the frigid boors to whom my father usually handed me over, such as M. l'abbé Rambault.

This good Father Morlon had a great influence on my mind; he owned Letourneur's translation of Shakespeare, and his nephew Bigillion borrowed for me, one after the other, all the eighteen or twenty volumes of this work, a considerable one for a child.

I felt reborn as I read it. For one thing Shakespeare had the immense advantage of not having been praised and preached at me by my relatives, as Racine had been. They had only to praise something *enjoyable* for me to take a violent aversion to it.

To complete Shakespeare's hold on my heart, I even believe my father spoke ill of him to me.

I distrusted my family on all subjects, but in the matter of art their praises were enough to give me an overpowering dislike of the finest things. My heart, which was far maturer than my mind, felt keenly that my family praised things as KINGS praise religion nowadays, namely, with an *ulterior motive*. I felt confusedly, but very strongly and with an ardour that I have now lost, that any moral objective, any motive of self-interest, that's to say, in the artist, kills a work of art. I read Shakespeare continually from 1796 to 1799. Racine, constantly praised by my relatives, seemed to me a contemptible hypocrite. My grandfather had told me the story of his death from the loss of Louis XIV's favour. Besides, verse bored me because it stretched out a phrase and made it lose its clarity. I detested *courser* instead of a horse. I called this hypocrisy.

Living alone, as I did, in the bosom of a family that spoke with great correctness, how could I have been aware of degrees of nobility in language? Where could I have heard speech that was not elegant? I disliked Corneille less. The authors whom I loved to distraction were Cervantes's *Don Quixote*, and Ariosto in translation. Immediately after these came Rousseau, who had the double fault (DRAWBACK) of praising pr[iests] and religion and of being praised by my father. I read with delight La Fontaine's *Tales*, and *Félicia*. But these were not *literary pleasures*. That's the sort of book you read with one hand only, as Mme ... used to say.

In 1824, when I was falling in love with Clémentine and trying hard not to let my soul become absorbed by the contemplation of her charms (I remember a great struggle one evening, at Mme du Bignon's concert, at which I sat beside the celebrated General Foy; Clémentine being an ultra, never set foot in this house), when, I mean, I was writing my *Racine and Shakespeare*, people accused me of disloyalty to my earliest feelings; the real truth, as is clearly evident – and I took care not to reveal it, knowing it would not be believed – was that my first love had been for Shakespeare, and for *Hamlet* and *Romeo and Juliet* among others.

The Bigillions lived in the rue Chenoise (I'm not sure about the name), the street that comes out between the vault of Notre-Dame and a little river over which the Augustines' convent was built. There a famous bookseller lived whom I often used to visit. Beyond was the Oratory where my father had been in prison for a few days with M. Colomb, father of Romain Colomb the oldest of my friends (in 1836). Here's this street; I have almost forgotten what it was called but not what it looked like.

In this apartment, on the third floor, at B, there lived with

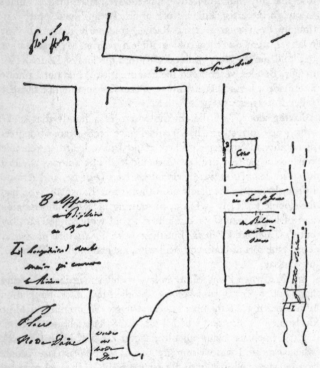

[*Place aux Herbes – Street leading to the wooden bridge – Courtyard – Rue Pont-St-Jaime – M. Belair, the dancing-master – Small river – Vault of Notre-Dame – Place Notre-Dame – B. Bigillions' apartment on the 3rd floor – L. Bookseller in the house over the river.*]

the Bigillion boys their sister, Mlle Victorine Bigillion, a very unaffected girl, very pretty, not with a Grecian beauty but, on the contrary, her looks were essentially *allobrogian*. I think this is called the Gaelic race nowadays. (See Dr Edwards and M.

238

Adrien de Jussieu; at any rate it was the latter who made me believe in this classification.)

Mlle Victorine was witty and very thoughtful, and she was the essence of freshness. Her face was in perfect harmony with the lattice windows of the apartment she occupied with her two brothers, and which was dark in spite of facing south and being on the third floor, because the house opposite was enormous. This perfect harmony struck me, or rather I felt the effect of it without understanding it.

I often had supper with the two brothers and their sister. A maid from their country district, as simple as themselves, prepared it; they used to eat brown bread, a thing that seemed incomprehensible to me who had never eaten anything but white.

Therein lay my sole advantage over them; in their eyes I belonged to a superior class; the grandson of M. Gagnon, member of the Central School Committee, was a *nobleman*, while they were bourgeois and nearly peasants. Not that they showed any trace of regret or foolish admiration; for instance they liked brown bread better than white bread, and there was nothing to stop them having their flour sifted if they wanted to eat white bread.

We lived there in all innocence, around the walnut-wood table covered with a tablecloth of unbleached holland, Bigillion the elder brother, fourteen or fifteen, Rémy, twelve, Mlle Victorine, thirteen, myself thirteen, the maid seventeen.

We made a very youthful society, as can be seen, and there were no grandparents to bother us. When M. Bigillion senior came to town for a day or two we dared not wish him elsewhere. But we felt ill at ease with him.

We may all have been a year older than that, but no more; my last two years at school, 1798 and 1799, were entirely absorbed by mathematics, with Paris as my goal; so it must have been 1797 or rather 1796; in 1796 I was thirteen.

We lived, then, like young rabbits playing about in a wood and browsing on wild thyme. Mlle Victorine was the housewife; she had bunches of dried grapes in vineleaves tied up with thread which she used to give me and which I loved almost as much as her charming face. Sometimes I asked her for a second bunch, and she often refused, saying: 'We've only eight left and they've got to last out the week.'

Once or twice every week provisions came from Saint-Ismier. That's the custom in Grenoble. Every bourgeois has a passion for his *estate*, and prefers a salad that comes from his estate at Montbonnot, Saint-Ismier, Corenc, Voreppe, Saint-Ismier or Claix, Échirolles, Eybens, Domène, etc., etc., and which costs him four sous, to the same salad bought for two sous in the Place aux Herbes. This bourgeois had 10,000 francs invested at 5 per cent with the Periers (the father and cousin of Casimir, Minister in 1832); he laid them out on an estate that yields him 2 or 2½ per cent and he's delighted. I suppose he feels repaid through satisfied vanity and the pleasure of saying with a self-important

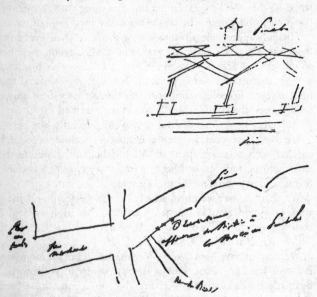

I've left at Grenoble a view of the Wooden Bridge which I bought from M. le Roy's widow. It's an oil-painting and *sbiadita*, mawkish, *à la Dorat, à la Florian*, but a good likeness as regards *the lines*, it's only the colours that are softened and 'florianized' – Rue Marchande, rightly so-called, whither came to buy or, at least to pass through, all the peasants of *the Valley* (the valley from Grenoble to Montmélian, a rich and very beautiful region). [*Wooden bridge – Isère. Place aux herbes – Rue Marchande – Bridge – Spiral staircase. Bigillions' apartment on the rise up to the Wooden Bridge – Rue du Boeuf.*]

air: *I've got to go to Montbonnot* or: *I've just come from Montbonnot.*

I was not at all in love with Victorine; my heart was still aching from Mlle Kubly's departure, and my friendship for Bigillion was so intimate that I think I had confided to him the secret of my infatuation, curtailing the story for fear of being laughed at.

He had not been horrified; he was the best-natured and simplest of creatures, and these precious qualities were combined in him with the shrewdest common sense, a family characteristic

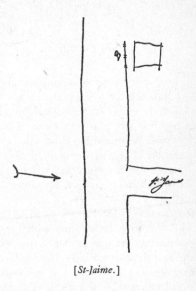

[*St-Jaime.*]

which in his case had been strengthened by conversation with Rémy, his brother and intimate friend, who lacked sensibility but whose common sense was far more ruthless. Rémy often spent whole afternoons without opening his lips.

The happiest moments of my life were spent in this third-floor apartment. Soon after, the Bigillions left that house to go and live on the Pont-de-Bois rise; or rather it was the other way round; from the Pont-de-Bois they came to the rue Chenoise, I fancy, certainly to that street into which the rue Pont-Saint-Jaime runs.

I am sure of the three lattice windows and of their position with regard to the Pont-Saint-Jaime. I am making more discoveries than ever while writing this (in Rome, January 1836). I had forgotten three quarters of these things which I hadn't thought about half a dozen times during the last twenty years.

I was very shy with Victorine, whose young bosom I admired, but I used to confide everything to her, for instance about Séraphie's persecutions from which I was just beginning to escape, and I remember she refused to believe me, which distressed me dreadfully. She implied that I was ill-natured.

CHAPTER 28

RÉMY would have frowned severely on any attempt of mine to court his sister, Bigillion made me understand, and this was the only point on which there was not perfect frankness between us. Often, towards nightfall after our walk, when I made as if to go up to see Victorine, he would bid me a hasty good-bye that vexed me considerably. I felt the need for friendship and for talking freely to someone; my heart was sore from all the unkindness to which, rightly or wrongly, I was convinced I had been subjected.

I must confess, however, that I much preferred having these simple talks with Victorine rather than with her brothers. I realize now what my feelings were at that time; it seemed to me incredible to see at such close quarters that terrible creature, a woman, moreover one with superb hair, arms that were divinely shaped though still rather thin, and a charming bosom which was often somewhat uncovered because of the extreme heat. In truth, sitting at the walnut-wood table two feet away from Mlle Bigillion with the corner of the table between us, I only talked to her brothers for propriety's sake. But for all that I had no wish to be in love; I was *scottato* (scalded), as they say in Italian, I had just experienced the fact that love is a serious and terrible thing. I did not admit it to myself, but I was conscious that on the whole my love for Mlle Kubly had probably given me more pain than pleasure.

While I had this feeling for Victorine, so innocent in language and even in thought, I forgot to hate and above all to believe that I was hated.

I fancy that after a time Rémy's brotherly jealousy was allayed; or else he went to spend a few months at Saint-Ismier. He may have seen that I was not really in love, or he may have had some affair of his own; we were all schemers at thirteen or fourteen. But even at that age boys are very subtle in Dauphiné, we haven't the light-heartedness of Parisian youngsters, and passions possess us early. Passions for trifles maybe, but the fact is that we desire things passionately.

In any case, I went at least five times a week, as soon as night fell or the curfew tolled (the nine o'clock bell of Saint-André's) to spend the evening with Mlle Bigillion.

Without saying anything about the friendship that existed between us, I was rash enough to mention this family one day at supper with my relatives, and I was severely punished for my thoughtlessness. I saw them pour scorn on Victorine's family and brothers, with the most expressive play of features.

'Isn't there a daughter? Some country miss, no doubt?'

I can only faintly recollect the terms of horrible contempt and the expression of cold disdain which accompanied them. I remember only the searing impression made on me by this contempt.

It must have been with exactly the same air of cold and mocking contempt that M. le Baron des Adrets, no doubt, spoke of my mother or my aunt.

My family, although belonging to the medical and legal professions, considered themselves bordering on the aristocracy, and my father even claimed to be a man of quality come down in the world. All the contempt which they expressed that evening during the whole of supper was based on the fact that M. Bigillion, my friends' father, was a country bourgeois and that his younger brother, a very shrewd man, was Director of the Departmental Prison on the Place Saint-André, a sort of bourgeois gaoler.

The Bigillion family had welcomed Saint Bruno to the Grande Chartreuse in . . .; this was proved beyond a doubt, and was far more worthy of respect than the *famulus* B[eyl]e, judge in the

243

village of Sassenage under the feudal lords of the Middle Ages. But Bigillion senior, that worthy pleasure-loving fellow, well-to-do in his own village, did not dine at M. de Marcieu's nor at Mme de Sassenage's, and bowed first to my grandfather as soon as he saw him afar off, and moreover spoke of M. Gagnon with the highest respect.

This sort of haughtiness amused a family which was usually dying of boredom, and lasted throughout supper. I had lost my appetite on hearing my friends treated thus, and I was asked what was the matter with me. I answered that I had had a very late snack. Lying is the only resource of the weak, and an easy one. I was furious with myself; how could I have been foolish enough to talk to my relatives about something that interested me?

Their contempt distressed me deeply and I now see the reason why: it was Victorine. Was it not true, then, that with that terrible creature, much dreaded but exclusively adored, a well-bred and pretty woman, I enjoyed almost intimate conversation every evening?

After four or five days Victorine won the day; I decided that she was more charming and better-bred than my gloomy *shrivelled* (as I put it) and unsociable relatives, who never gave supper parties, never set foot in a salon where there were even ten guests, whereas Mlle Bigillion was often invited to dinners of twenty-five guests at M. Faure's at Saint-Ismier and at her late mother's relatives' at Chapareillan. Indeed, she seemed of nobler birth because of the reception of Saint Bruno about 1080.[1]

Many years later I understood the process that was going on in my heart at that time, and for lack of a better word I called it *crystallization* (the term which so deeply shocked that great man of letters, M. le Comte d'Argout, Minister of the Interior in 1833, in an amusing scene described by Clara Gazul).[2]

It took quite five or six days to exonerate Victorine from contempt, during which time I thought of nothing else. The glorious victory over an insult set a *new fact* between Mlle Kubly and my present state. Though in my innocence I did not suspect it, this

1. Date: Saint Bruno, died in 1101, in Calabria.
2. Clara Gazul, i.e. Mérimée. (*Trans.*)

was a great point scored; between oneself and one's grief one must introduce new facts, even if it means breaking one's arm.

I had just bought a good edition of Bezout and had it carefully bound (it may still be in existence at Grenoble in M. Alexandre Mallein's, the chief tax-collector); I drew on it a wreath of foliage with a capital V in the middle. I gazed at this memorial every day.[1]

After Séraphie's death I might, through the need for love, have become reconciled with my family, but this arrogant behaviour set an infinite space between myself and them; I might have forgiven the imputation of a crime to the Bigillion family, but contempt ... ! And my grandfather was the one who had expressed it most gracefully and thus most effectively!

I took good care not to speak to my relatives about other friends I made at this period: MM. Gall, La Bayette ...

Gall was the son of a widow who loved him exclusively and respected him dutifully as master of their fortune; the father must have been some old officer. This sight, so strange to me, charmed and touched me. Oh, if only my poor mother had lived! I thought. If at least I had had relatives like Mme Gall, how I should have loved them! Mme Gall had a great respect for me as being the grandson of M. Gagnon, the benefactor of the poor to

1. On the occasion of one of my journeys (returns) to Grenoble, about 1806, a well-informed person told me that Mlle Victorine was in love. I greatly envied the happy man. I supposed it was Félix Faure. Later, another person said to me: 'Mlle Victorine, talking of the person whom she had loved for so long, said to me: "He is not handsome, but no one will ever reproach him for his ugliness ... He was the wittiest and most amiable of all the young men of my time." In a word, said this person, she meant you.' 10 J[anuar]y 1836. (Read de Brosses.)

whom he gave free medical attention and even a couple of pounds of beef to make broth. My father she didn't know at all.

Gall was pale, thin, *scraggy*, marked with smallpox, and more-over of a very cold, temperate and cautious character. He felt that he was absolute master of their small fortune and that it must not be wasted. He was simple and honest, not in the least given to boasting or lying. I think he left Grenoble and the Central School before I did, and went to Toulon to join the Navy.

That pleasant fellow La Bayette was also going into the Navy; he was a nephew or some other relation of Admiral (i.e. Rear- or Vice-Admiral) Morard de Galles.

He was as lovable and noble as Gall was worthy of respect. I still remember the charming afternoons we spent talking together at the window of his little room. It was on the third floor of a house looking out over the new Place du Département. There I shared his snack of apples and brown bread. I was avid for any conversation that was sincere and devoid of hypocrisy. To these two virtues, common to all my friends, La Bayette added great nobility of feelings and manners, and a tender-heartedness which he expressed more gracefully than Bigillion, though he lacked the latter's capacity for deep passion.

I seem to remember that he gave me good advice at the time of my love for Mlle Kubly, about whom I ventured to tell him, such was his sincerity and kindness. We pooled all our slight experience of women, or rather all our slight learning, drawn from the novels we had read. We must have been very amusing to listen to.

Soon after my aunt Séraphie died, I had read and adored the *Secret Memoirs* of Duclos, which my grandfather was reading.

I think it must have been in the mathematics classroom that I made the acquaintance of Gall and La Bayette; it was certainly there that I made friends with Louis de Barral (now the oldest and best of my friends, the person in all the world who loves me best, and I think there is no sacrifice I would not make for him).

He was very small in those days, very thin, very *scraggy*, and was said to indulge to excess in a bad habit which we all had, and the fact is that he looked like it. But his looks were redeemed in a remarkable fashion by the superb uniform of a lieutenant in the Engineers for he was what they called an 'Attached

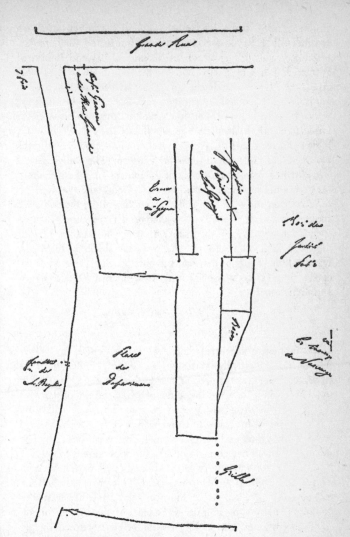

[*Grande-Rue – 7 times – Café Genou, whence M. de Genoude – M. Gagnon's terrace – Périer-Lagranges' garden – Baths – Wood of the public Garden – View over the Sassenage mountains – Railing – Place du Département – La Bayette's window.*]

Engineer'; this ought to have been a good way to win over rich families to the Revolution, or at least to mitigate their hatred.

Anglès, who has since become Count Anglès and Prefect of Police, and has been enriched by the Bourbons, was also an Attached Engineer; so was an essentially second-rate person adorned with red hair and called Giroud, not to be confused with Giroud in the red coat with whom I often used to fight. I made relentless fun of the gold-braided Giroud, who was far bigger than I; that's to say who was a man of eighteen whereas I was still a child of thirteen or fourteen. This difference of two or three years is enormous at school; it's like the difference between a nobleman and a commoner in Piedmont.

What won me over completely about Barral the first time we spoke together (I think he was then under the supervision of Pierre-Vincent Chalvet, the history master, who was very ill with the elder sister of smallpox), what won me about Barral, I say, was: (1) the beauty of his coat, the blue of which seemed to me enchanting; (2) his way of reciting those lines of Voltaire which I still remember:

> *Vous êtes, lui dit-il, l'existence et l'essence,*
> *Simple . . .*

His mother, a very great lady (*she was a Grolée*, my grandfather said respectfully), was the last of her kind to wear its costume; I can still picture her beside the statue of Hercules in the Garden in a flowered dress, i.e. of white satin adorned with flowers, which dress was tucked up into the pockets like my grandmother's (Jeanne Dupéron, widow B...) with a huge powdered chignon and perhaps a small dog under her arm. The urchins followed her admiringly at a distance, and as for myself I was taken, or carried, by faithful Lambert; I may have been three or four when I beheld this vision. This great lady had the manners of her class. M. le Marquis de Barral, her husband, ex-Président, or even Premier Président, of the Parlement, refused to emigrate. On which account he was spurned by my family as if he had been given twenty slaps in the face.

Sagacious M. Destutt de Tracy had the same idea in Paris and was forced to accept positions, like M. de Barral, who, before the Revolution, was called M. de Monferrat, or rather M. le

Marquis de Monferrat (pronounced Monferâ, the *a* very long); M. de Tracy was reduced to living on the salary of a councillor in Public Education, I believe; M. de Barral had preserved an income of 20,000 or 25,000 francs of which in 1793 he surrendered half or two thirds, not to his country but to his fear of the guillotine. He may have stayed in France through love of Mme Brémond, whom he since married. I have met M. Brémond junior in the army, where he was a major, I think, then *sous-inspecteur aux Revues* and always a man of pleasure.

I'm not saying that his father-in-law, Président de Barral (for Napoleon made him Premier Président when he created the Imperial Court) was a genius, but in my eyes he was so much the opposite of my father, and had such a dislike of pedantry and of hurting his son's feelings that when they left the house to go for a walk in the *waste lands of the Drac*, if the father said: Bonjour,

the son replied: Toujours,

the father: ... Oie,

the son: ... Lamproie,

and the whole walk was spent making rhymes and trying to catch one another out.

This father taught his son Voltaire's *Satires* (that great reformer's only perfect work, in my opinion).

This was my first glimpse of genuine *good form*, and it won me at once.

I kept comparing this father, who made up rhymes and was full of delicate consideration for his children's self-respect, with the gloomy pedantry of my own father. I had the deepest respect for M. Gagnon's learning, I loved him sincerely, I didn't go so far as to say to myself: 'Couldn't my grandfather's boundless learning be combined with the gay, kindly friendliness of M. de Barral?'

But my heart, so to speak, had a *presentiment* of this idea, which was subsequently to become a fundamental one for me.

I had already seen good form, but partly disfigured, ruined by piety, at the devout evening parties where Mme de Valserre collected, on the ground floor of the Hôtel des Adrets, M. du Bouchage (a ruined Peer of France), M. de Saint-Vallier (the great Saint-Vallier), his brother Scipion, M. de Pina (ex-Mayor of Grenoble, a thorough Jesuit, with an income of 80,000 francs and seventeen children), MM. de Sinard, de Saint-Ferréol, myself, Mlle Bonne de Saint-Vallier, whose fine arms (white and fleshy like a Venetian beauty's) moved me so strongly.

The curé Chélan and M. Barthélemy d'Orbane were also models of these good manners. Father Ducros's manners were those of genius. (The word *genius* was for me, at that time, what the word *God* is for a bigot.)

CHAPTER 29

I DID not see M. de Barral in such a favourable light at that time, he was the *bête noire* of my relatives because he had not emigrated.

Necessity making me hypocritical (a fault which I have since corrected only too well and the lack of which has done me so much harm, at Rome for instance), I mentioned to my family the names of MM. de la Bayette and de Barral, my new friends.

'La Bayette! A good family,' my grandfather said. 'His grandfather was a ship's captain and his uncle, M. de . . ., Président in the Parlement. As for Montferrat, he's a contemptible . . .'

It must be confessed that one night, at two in the morning, certain municipal authorities, M. de Barral amongst them, had come to arrest M. d'Antour, former Councillor to the Parlement, a thirty-one-year-old idiot who lived on the first floor and who spent most of his time walking up and down his big drawing-room, biting his nails. The poor devil was losing his eyesight and, moreover, was a notorious suspect, like my father. He was pious to the point of fanaticism, but apart from that there was no harm in him. It was thought shameful that M. de Barral should come to arrest someone who had served under him as Councillor when he was Président of the Parlement.

There's no denying the fact, the French bourgeois were ludicrous creatures in 1794 when I first began to understand them, when they were complaining bitterly of the arrogance of the nobility, but, amongst themselves, valuing a man solely on account of his birth. Virtue, kindness, generosity counted for nothing; rather, the more distinguished a man was the more they criticized him for lack of birth, and what birth!

About 1803, when my uncle Romain Gagnon came to Paris and stayed with me in the rue de Ménars, I did not introduce him to Mme de Neuilly, for the very good reason that this lady did not exist. Shocked to hear that there had been no introduction, my good aunt Élisabeth said:

'Something extraordinary must have happened. Otherwise Henry would have taken his uncle to see this lady; one is always glad to show that one isn't *just anybody*.'

The person who wasn't just anybody was, if you please, myself.

And when our cousin Clet, a horribly ugly man who looked like an apothecary and in fact was an apothecary (an army pharmacist), was about to get married in Italy, my aunt Élisabeth replied to criticisms about his deplorable appearance:

'He's a shoddy-looking creature, you must agree,' somebody said.

'Granted, but still he's got birth! He's cousin to the leading doctor in Grenoble; does that count for nothing?'

The character of this high-minded lady was a striking example of the saying: *Noblesse oblige*. I can think of nothing that was too generous, too noble, too difficult for her generous and disinterested nature. It is partly due to her that I speak correctly; if I let fall a vulgar word she would say: 'Oh, Henry!' and her face expressed a cold disdain the memory of which *haunted* me (pursued me for a long time).

I have known families where they spoke as well, but none where they spoke better than in my own. I don't mean to say that my family did not often make the usual eight or ten Dauphinois mistakes.

But if I used an imprecise or pretentious term, I was promptly made fun of, and my grandfather enjoyed doing this all the more because it was the only sort of fun which Séraphie's morose piety allowed the poor man. In order to avoid a mocking glance from this witty man, one had to use the simplest turns of phrase and the right word, and yet be careful not to utter a vulgar word.

I have seen children in rich Parisian families always using the most far-fetched turns of phrase, aiming at nobility of style, and the parents encouraging this attempt at pomposity. Young Parisians are apt to say *courser* instead of *horse*, hence their admiration for MM. de Salvandy, de Chateaubriand, etc.

Besides, a fourteen-year-old Dauphinois in those days had a depth of sincerity and feeling which I have never met with in a young Parisian. On the other hand we said: 'J'étais au *Cour-se* où M. *Passe-kin* (Pasquin) m'a lu une pièce de ver-*se* sur le voyage d'Anver-*se* à Calai-*ce*.'

Until I came to Paris in 1799 it never entered my head that there was any other sort of pronunciation. Subsequently I took

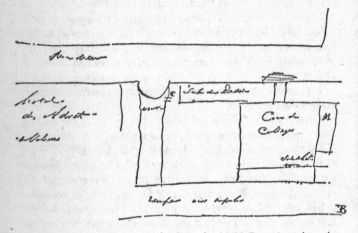

C. P.-V. Chalvet's apartment under the vault – M. M. Dupuy's mathematics classroom. [*Rue Neuve – Hotel des Adrets. Mme de Valserre – Vault – Art classroom – College courtyard – Latin classroom – Rampart. Superb view.*]

lessons from the famous La Rive and Dugazon to get rid of the last traces of my native *drawl*. I have kept only two or three words (côte, *kŏte*, instead of *kāute*, a hillock; so the worthy abbé Gattel was quite right to make a note of pronunciation in his good dictionary, a thing for which he was blamed recently by some stupid Parisian *man of letters*), and the firm and passionate accent of the South which, revealing the *strength of feeling* and the vigour with which we love or hate, immediately seems odd and therefore *almost ridiculous* in Paris.

When I talked to my friends Bigillion, Le Bayette, Gall and Barral then, I used to say *chŏse* instead of *chaūse*, *cŏte* instead of *caūte*, *Calai-ce* instead of *Kalai* (Calais).

Barral used to come from La Tronche every morning, I fancy, to spend the day at Pierre-Vincent Chalvet's, the history master's, rooms in the school building, under the vault; near B there was a rather pretty lime-tree walk, very narrow, but the limes, although pollarded, were old and bushy, and the view was delicious; there I used to walk with Barral, who had come from point C; quite near by, M. Chalvet, who was concerned about his trollops, his p[ox] and the books he was concocting and who moreover was the most casual of men, gladly let him escape.

I think that it was while walking along P that we met Michoud, who looked like an ox but was an excellent fellow (his only mistake was to die a corrupt official and councillor in the Royal Law Courts, about 1827). I'm inclined to think that this excellent man believed that honesty is only necessary between individuals and that it is always permissible to be false in one's duty as a citizen in order to pick up some money from the Government. I make a great distinction between him and his companion Félix Faure; the latter was born with a base soul, and so now he's a Peer of France and Premier Président of the Royal Law Courts at Grenoble.

But whatever may have been poor Michoud's motives for selling his country to please the Attorney-General, in 1795 he was the best-hearted, most natural and shrewdest but most simple-hearted of my friends.

I think he had learnt to read, together with Barral, at Mlle Chavand's; they often talked about their adventures in her little class. (Already the rivalries, friendships and hatreds of the great world!) How I envied them! I even believe I lied once or twice to some of my other schoolfellows, pretending that I too had learnt to read at Mlle Chavand's.

Michoud loved me until he died, and I was not ungrateful; I had the highest esteem for his good sense and kindness. Only once did we come to blows, and since he was twice my size he thrashed me soundly.

I blamed myself for losing my temper, not because of the beating I got, but because I had failed to appreciate his extreme kindness. I was mischievous and said clever things that earned me many a blow, and this same characteristic earned me in the army, in Italy and in Germany, more than that, and in Paris relentless criticism from petty writers.

When a witticism occurs to me, I'm conscious of its neatness

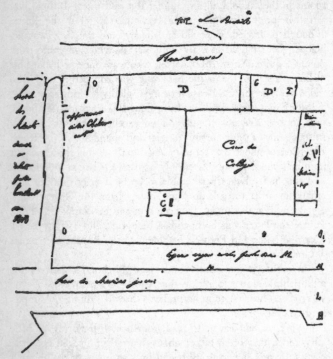

OOO. College buildings (built by the Jesuits) – P. Beginning of the avenue of old lime-trees. Limes MAIMED by pollarding – L. At a lower level, garden of M. de Plainville, Commander or Adjutant of the fortress, father of Barral's friend Plainville – C. Chemistry classroom with its two pillars and its table. Teacher M. Trousset (who shortly after died of consumption, a protégé of my grandfather's) – D. Art classroom – D'. Classroom for 'the round' with a stage at T' – G. Table where sections of a cadaver were exposed in the presence of Mlles Genèvre. [*The Bastille – Rue Neuve – Hotel des Adrets, dmolished and rebuilt by M. Trouilloud about 1808 – M. Chalvet's apartment on the first floor – College courtyard – Mathematics classroom – Waste ground enclosed by wall M – Rue des Muriers, I think.*]

and not of its unkindness. I am always surprised at its unkind implications; for instance, it was Ampère and A. de Jussieu who pointed out to me the implications of the remark I made to that rascal the Vicomte de La Passe (Civita-Vecchia, September 1831 or 1832): 'May I venture to ask your name?' for which La Passe will never forgive me.

Now, out of prudence, I shall say such things and the other day D[on] Filippo Caetani gave me credit for being one of the least spiteful men he had ever met, although my reputation was that of a man of infinite wit but great spitefulness and even greater immorality (because I wrote about women in *l'Amour* and because I can't help making fun of hypocrites, a set of men who are even more highly respected, believe it or not, in Paris than in Rome).

Not long ago Mme d'Auvers, Mme Toldi of the *Valle*, said to Prince C[aetani], as I was leaving her house: 'But that's M. de S[tendhal], who's so very witty and *so immoral*.'

An actress who has had a child by the Neapolitan Prince Leopold of Syracuse! Don Filippo, good fellow, cleared me in all seriousness of the imputation of immorality.

Even if I just tell you that a yellow gig has passed down the street I have the misfortune to give mortal offence to hypocrites and even to *fools*.

But at heart, dear reader, I don't know what I am: kind, unkind, witty or foolish. But I do know perfectly well what gives me pain or pleasure, what I desire and what I hate.

A salon full of provincials who have made money and show off their luxury is my *bête noire*, for instance. Next to that comes a salon full of marquises and bigwigs decorated with the Legion of Honour who flaunt their morality.

A salon of eight or ten people, of whom all the women have had lovers, where the talk is gay and full of anecdotes, and a light punch is drunk at half past twelve, is the place in all the world where I feel most at my ease, there in my heart of hearts I would infinitely rather hear someone else speak than speak myself. I readily fall silent out of *happiness*, and if I talk it's only to *pay my entrance fee*, a term which, used in this way, I introduced into Parisian society and which, like *fioriture* (imported be my), I keep meeting there. I must admit that I more rarely

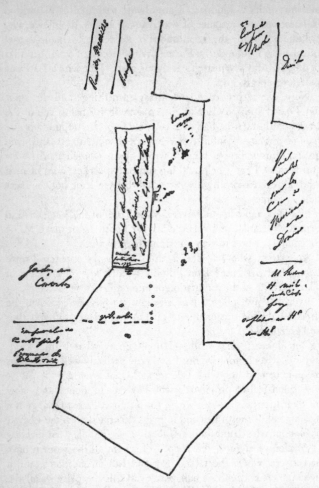

[*Rue des Muriers* – *Rampart* – *Tomb of* MY POOR MOTHER – *Demilune* –
Wonderful view over the mills of Murianette and Domène – *Provincial
Commander's house, where M. de Tonnerre was living on the Day of Tiles.
Sold, partly destroyed, about 1793. Steps* – *Raised ground and vases* –
Garden at lower level – *Wooden railing* – *Rampart 12 or 15 feet high* –
Clipped lime walk. – *M. Michoud* – *H. Myself, the day of my fight, or
rather at H' and M'.*]

256

meet *crystallization* (see *l'Amour*). But I don't insist on this in the least; if someone can find a better word, more native to the language, for the same idea, I shall be the first to applaud it and to use it.[1]

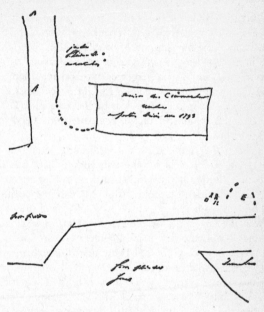

A. Avenue of clipped, stunted old lime trees (like a real poet who joins the Academy and speaks of Venus and Pomona) – H. Me – M. Michoud – E. Rising ground, 8 or 10 feet, at the foot of which was our 'home' for prisoners' base – Magnificent view over wooded hills – [*Plainvilles' garden at a lower level – Commander's house sold, partly destroyed, about 1793 – Fortifications – Demilune – Ditches full of rushes.*]

1. A sort of folly which sees every perfection and turns everything to perfection in the object affecting the lover. He's poor, ah! I love him all the more for that! He's rich, ah! I love him all the more for that!

CHAPTER 30

I REALIZE now that one quality common to all my friends was naturalness or lack of hypocrisy. Thanks to Mme Vignon and my aunt Séraphie I had conceived for this essential condition of success in present-day society a violent aversion which has done me much harm and which verges on physical repulsion. After prolonged contact with a hypocrite I begin to feel seasick (just as, a month ago, the Italian spoken by the Chevalier Tallenay forced Countess Sandre to unlace her corset, witnessed at ... November 1835).

Naturalness was not the most conspicuous quality of poor Grand-Dufay, a fellow of infinite wit, and so there was never more than a *literary* friendship between us, full of jealousy on his part and of mistrust on mine, while we both had the highest esteem for one another.

He won the first prize for general grammar the same year, I fancy, that I won the first prize for literature. But what year was it? Was it 1796 or 1795? I badly need the archives of the Prefecture; our names were printed on a bill *in folio* and posted up. By the wise law of M. de Tracy (which I'll copy out later), the examinations were accompanied by great pomp. Were not the hopes of the country involved? It was a lesson for the member of the Administration of the Département, a moral product of the despotism of Mme du Barry, as much as for the pupil.

What was one to do, in 1796, with all men over twenty? To save the country from the harm they were disposed to do it and wait, somehow or other, for their DEATH?

This is sad to say, but none the less true. What a relief for the ship of State, in 1836, if all men over fifty were suddenly gathered to their fathers! Except, of course, *the King, my Wife and I.*

During one of the numerous illuminations which took place every month between 1789 and 1791, a *bourgeois* stuck up a transparency which was inscribed:

Long Live
The King
My Wife and I

Grand-Dufay, the eldest of four or five brothers, was a thin skinny little creature with a big head, his face badly pitted with smallpox and yet very red, his eyes brilliant but sly and with something of the disturbing vivacity of a wild boar. He was wily and never rash in his talk, always seeking to praise but in the most moderate terms possible. You'd have thought him a member of the Institute. Moreover, quick-witted, with an admirable grasp of things, but even at that early age devoured by ambition. He was the eldest son and the spoilt child (as we say here) of a mother of like character, and not without reason: the family was a poor one.

What an admirable Plougoulm (i.e. an Advocate-General bought by the powers that be, and adept at whitewashing the most infamous injustices) Dufay would have made!

But he did not live long, and at his death in Paris about 1803 I found myself guilty of one of the worst feelings of my life, one of those which have made me most reluctant to go on with these memoirs. I had forgotten it since 1803 or 1804, the time of this man's death. It's strange how many things I have remembered since I began writing these confessions. They occur to me suddenly, and I think I judge them with impartiality. I keep seeing the *better course* which I did not take. But who the deuce will have the patience to read such things?

When I go out in the street wearing a new well-cut coat, my friends would pay a crown to have somebody throw a glass of dirty water over me. That's badly put, but the fact is true (except, of course, for the excellent Comte de Barral, who's a character like La Fontaine).

Where will a reader be found who, after four or five volumes of *I*'s and *me*'s, won't long for a bottle of ink, rather than a glass of dirty water, to be thrown at me? And yet, O reader, all the harm lies merely in those seven letters B, R, U, L, A, R, D which make up my name. Suppose I had written *Bernard* this book would merely be a novel written in the first person, like the *Vicar of Wakefield*, which rivals it in innocence.

At any rate the person to whom I bequeath this posthumous work will have to get all the details abridged by some hack editor, the M. Amédée Pichot or the M. Courchamps of the day. It has been said that you never go so far in an *opera d'inchiostro* as when you don't know where you are going, and if it were always so the present memoirs, which depict a *man's heart*, to talk like MM. Victor Hugo, d'Arlincourt, Soulié, Raymond, etc., etc., would be a very fine thing indeed. The *I*'s and *me*'s were torturing me last night (14 January 1836) while I was listening to Rossini's *Moses*. Good music makes me think with greater intensity and clarity about what's on my mind. But that's only when the moment of *judging* it is over, and it's so long since I passed *judgement on Moses* (1823) that I forget what my verdict was and I no longer think about it, I'm merely the *Slave of the Ring*, as in the *Arabian Nights*.

Memories throng as I write. I've just noticed that I have left out one of my most intimate friends, Louis Crozet, now Chief Engineer, and a very good Chief Engineer, at Grenoble, but buried alive – like the *Baron buried opposite his wife*[1] – and thereby, drowned in the narrow egotism of a petty, jealous bourgeois community in a small town in our mountain region (La Mure, Corps or Le Bourg d'Oisans).

Louis Crozet was cut out to be one of the most brilliant of men in Paris, and in any salon he would have beaten Koreff, Pariset, Lagarde and myself as well, if one may mention oneself. Pen in hand he would have been a wit of the same sort as Duclos, author of the *Essai sur les Moeurs* (but this book may perhaps be dead by 1880), the man who, according to d'Alembert, *had the most wit in a given time*.

I think it was *at Latin* (as we said), in M. Durand's class, that I made friends with Crozet, who was then the ugliest and most ungainly child in the whole Central School; he must have been born about 1784.

He had a round pallid face, badly pitted with smallpox, and very bright little blue eyes, the rims of which were damaged and roughtened by this cruel disease. The whole effect was completed

1. Verse from *The Man of the Day*:
    As good as dead, though still in life,
    Here lies the Baron opposite his wife.

by a slight air of sulky pedantry; he walked badly as if his legs were crooked. All his life he was the very reverse of elegant, and unfortunately he always aimed at elegance, and with all this he had a quite divine wit. (La Fontaine.)

His feelings were rarely moved, but, when they were, he loved his country passionately and I imagine he was capable of heroism if need be. He would have been a hero in a deliberative assembly, a *Hampden*; for me, that is to say everything. (See the *Life of Hampden* by Lord King or Dacre, his great-grandson.)

To conclude, he was the most intelligent and sagacious of all the Dauphinois I have known, and he had that boldness mingled with timidity which is needed to shine in a Parisian salon; like General Foy, he grew animated as he talked.

He was most useful to me through the aforementioned quality *sagacity*, of which I was wholly devoid by nature and with which, it seems to me, he succeeded in partially inoculating me. I say partially, for I always have to force myself to attain it. And if I discover anything I am apt to exaggerate my discovery to myself and see nothing else.

I excuse this defect of my mind by calling it *the necessary and sine qua non effect of extreme* sensibility.

When an idea takes possession of me too violently in the middle of the street, *I fall down*. Example : in the rue de Richelieu near the rue des Filles-Saint-Thomas, my only fall in five or six years, caused, about 1826, by this problem : Should M. de Belleyme, in the interests of his ambition, get him appointed deputy, or should he not? This was at the time when M. de Belleyme, Prefect of Police (the only popular magistrate under the elder branch of the Bourbons), was clumsily seeking to become a deputy.

When ideas occur to me in the middle of the street I'm always on the point of bumping into a passer-by, falling down or getting run over by the carriages. Somewhere near the rue d'Amboise, one day in Paris (one example among a hundred), I was looking at Dr Edwards without recognizing him. That's to say there were two reactions : one told me : There's Dr Edwards; but the second, preoccupied with thought, did not add : I must say good day and talk to him. The doctor was greatly surprised but not offended; he did not think I was acting the genius (as would have done MM. Prunelle, former Mayor of Lyons, the ugliest man in France, Jules-Césare Boissat, the most foppish, Félix Faure and many another of my acquaintances and friends).

I was fortunate enough to see a great deal of Louis Crozet in Paris in 1800, in Paris from 1803 to 1806, and in Plancy where I went to visit him and stable my horses during some mission or other of the Emperor's; finally, we slept in the same room (Hôtel de Hambourg, rue de l'Université) the night of the fall of France in 1814. He was smitten with indigestion in the night, out of grief, whereas I, who was forfeiting everything, considered the thing rather as a spectacle. And besides I was annoyed about the Duke of Bassano's stupid correspondence with me when I was in the 7th Military Division with that old *dodderer,* M. le Comte de Saint-Vallier.

I was also still annoyed, I confess it to the shame of my intelligence, about the way the Emperor had behaved with the deputation from the legislative body, which included that emotional and eloquent idiot Lainé, from Bordeaux, as well as that *heartless* man, quite unsullied by any sensibility, called Roederer.

Crozet and I, in order not to waste our time in enthusiastic gossip about La Fontaine, Corneille or Shakespeare, wrote what we called *Characters* (I'd like to see one of them today).

They consisted of six or eight folio pages describing (under a fictitious name) the character of somebody we both knew, to a jury composed of Helvétius, Tracy and Machiavelli, or Helvétius, Montesquieu and Shakespeare. Those were the writers we admired at that time.

Together we read Adam Smith and J.-B. Say, and then we dropped this science because we found in it obscure and even contradictory points. We were first-class mathematicians, and Crozet, after his three years at the École Polytechnique, was so good at chemistry that he was offered a place comparable to that of M. Thénard (now a Peer of France but according to us, at that time, a man of no genius; we adored nobody but Lagrange and Monge; even Laplace seemed to us hardly more than an *illuminating mind* capable of explaining and enlightening but not of inventing). Crozet and I read Montaigne, and Letourneur's

Shakespeare I don't know how many times (although we knew English very well).

We had five- or six-hour sessions of work after taking coffee at the Hôtel de Hambourg in the rue de l'Université, with its view over the Museum of French Monuments, that charming and almost perfect creation which the contemptible B[ourb]ons have destroyed.

Perhaps I showed some conceit just now in calling myself an excellent mathematician. I never learnt differential and integral calculus, but at one period I spent my whole time thinking with great pleasure about the art of finding equations, about what I would call, if I dared, the metaphysics of mathematics. I won the first prize (and without any favouritism, on the contrary my haughtiness had antagonized people) against eight young men who, a month later, at the end of 1799, were all admitted to the École Polytechnique.

I must have had six or eight hundred work-sessions of five to six hours each with Louis Crozet. This earnest studying with furrowed brow we called *swotting*, a term used at the École Polytechnique. These sessions were my real literary education; it was with the keenest delight that we sought thus to explore truth, to the great horror of Jean-Louis Basset (now Baron de Richebourg, auditeur, former sub-prefect, former lover of a rich woman of the Montmorency family, and a fop without any wit but also without malice). This creature, four feet three inches high and in despair at being named Basset, lived with Crozet at the Hôtel de Hambourg. His only merit, as far as I know, was to have got a bayonet thrust in the chest, perhaps through the lapel of his coat, one day when from the pit we stormed the stage of the Théâtre-Français in honour of Mlle Duchesnois (but good Lord, I'm going too far afield) – an excellent actress in two or three roles, who died in 1835.

We made no allowances for each other, Crozet and I, when we worked together, we were always afraid of letting vanity lead us astray, since we found no other of our friends capable of arguing with us on these topics.

These friends were the two Bassets, Louis de Barral (my close friend, a close friend of Louis Crozet too), Plana (Professor at Turin, member of all the Academies and all the Orders of that country). Crozet and Plana, both friends of mine, were a year behind me in mathematics; they were learning arithmetic while I had reached trigonometry and the elements of algebra.

CHAPTER 31

MY GRANDFATHER did not at all like M. Dubois-Fontanelle; he behaved with deliberately cultivated vanity and the ruthlessness of a member of high society towards numberless people about whom he spoke in pleasant words but whom he did not in the least like.

I imagine he was afraid of being despised and held of little account as a man of letters by poor M. Dubois, who had written a tragedy which has had the honour of sending his bookseller to the galleys. The play in question was *Éricie or The Vestal*; obviously the same as *Éricie or The Nun*, or the *Mélanie* of that scheming fellow Laharpe, whose frigid genius had, I imagine,

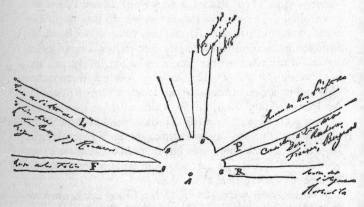

A: Moment of birth – B: Roads taken at 7 years old, often unconsciously. It is supremely absurd to try, at 50, to leave road R or road P for road L. Frederick II never got himself read, and since the age of 20 he's been dreaming of road L. [*Road to public esteem – Road taken by good Prefects and State Councillors: MM. Daru, Roederer, Français, Beugnot – Road to money: Rothschild – Road to the art of getting oneself read: Tasso, J.-J. Rousseau, Mozart – Road to Madness.*]

264

stolen this subject from poor M. Dubois-Fontanelle, who was always so poor that he had adopted a horribly tiny handwriting to save paper.

Poor M. Dubois had gone to Paris when fairly young and *in love with the Beautiful*. Continuous poverty forced him to cultivate the useful; he never reached the rank of first-class *humbugs* such as Laharpe, Marmontel, etc. Necessity obliged him to accept the political editorship of the *Journal des Deux-Ponts*; and worse still, he married a great fat German woman, an ex-mistress of Maximilian-Joseph, King of Bavaria, then Prince Max and a colonel in the French army.

His eldest daughter, daughter of the King, married a certain Renauldon, a conceited person exactly cut out to be the Mayor of a large provincial town. And indeed he was a good mayor from 1800 to 1814, I believe, and moreover outrageously cuckolded by my cousin Pellat, that king of fools, who was disgraced on this account and forced to leave the district, with a place in the Tax Department procured him by the charitable financier Français (of Nantes) who was powerful under the Empire and who procured a place for Parney. I knew him well about 1826 as a scribbler calling himself M. Jérôme. All these clever people, disappointed in their ambitions, took up literature as a last resource. Through their knowledge of intrigue and their political friends they obtained the semblance of success, and in actual fact made themselves *ridiculous*. I have seen, of this sort, M. Roederer, M. Français (of Nantes), and even the Comte Daru when, with his poem *Astronomy* (published after his death) he made himself a free Associate of the Academy of Sciences. These three men of great intelligence and shrewdness, and certainly in the first rank of State Councillors and Prefects, had never seen that little geometrical figure invented by myself, a mere auditeur, a month ago.

If, when he came to Paris, poor M. Dubois, who called himself Fontanelle, had been given a pension of 100 louis on condition that he wrote (like Beethoven in Vienna in 1805), he would have cultivated the *Beautiful*, in other words, would have imitated not Nature, but Voltaire.

Instead of this he was obliged to translate Ovid's *Metamorphoses* and, still worse, some English books. This worthy man gave me the idea of learning English and lent me the first volume of Gibbon, and I noticed on this occasion that he pronounced it: *Té istory of té fall.* He had learnt his English with the aid of a dictionary, without a teacher, because of his poverty.

I did not learn English till many years later, when I had the idea of learning by heart the first four pages of the *Vicar of Wakefield* (Ouaikefilde). I think this was about 1805. Some-

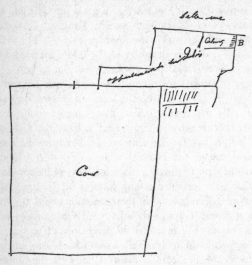

[*Fine view – Apartment of M. Dubois. Closet – Courtyard.*]

body had the same idea in Scotland, I believe, and I only discovered this in 1812 when I picked up a few copies of the *Edinburgh Review* in Germany.

M. Dubois-Fontanelle was almost crippled with gout, his fingers had grown shapeless, he was polite, obliging, helpful, and moreover his character had been broken by constant misfortune.

The *Journal des Deux-Ponts* having been taken over by the Revolutionary army, M. Dubois-Fontanelle did not on that account became an *aristocrat*, but, strangely enough, always remained a *French citizen*. This will seem obvious in 1880, but was nothing less than a miracle in 1796.

Witness my father who, at the Revolution, was lucky enough

to gain status by his talents, became Deputy Mayor and acting Mayor of Grenoble, and Chevalier of the Legion of Honour, and yet abhorred the very Revolution which raised him from the mire.

M. Fontanelle, poor and honourable, abandoned by his newspaper, arrived in Grenoble with his fat German wife, who, in spite of her previous trade, had vulgar manners and little money. He was only too glad to become a teacher with board and lodging, and even went to live in his apartment at the south-west corner of the school courtyard before it was finished.

At B was his fine octavo Kehl edition of Voltaire, the only one of his books that this excellent man would never lend. His books were annotated in his own writing, fortunately almost illegible without a magnifying glass. He had lent me *Émile* and was greatly worried because beside J.-J. Rousseau's crazy announcement: 'The death of Socrates is that of a man, that of J[esus]-C[hrist] is that of a God' he had gummed a slip of paper containing a highly sensible and unrhetorical comment which drew the opposite conclusion.

This inset slip of paper would have done him great harm, even in my grandfather's eyes. What would have happened if my father had seen it? About the same time my father refused to buy Bayle's *Dictionary* at the sale of the property of our pleasure-loving cousin Drier, in order not to jeopardize my religious faith, and he told me so.

M. Fontanelle was too much broken by misfortune and the character of that she-devil his wife to be an enthusiast; he had not the slightest spark of fire like the abbé Ducros, and so he had practically no influence on my character.

It seems to me that I went to his classes with that little Jesuit Paul-Émile Teisseire, with fat good-natured Marquis, a rich young man from Rives or Moirans, with good-natured Benoît, who sincerely believed he was a Plato because Dr Clapier had taught him to love (after the fashion of the Bishop of Clogher).

This did not horrify us because our relatives would have been horrified at it; but it surprised us. I realize today that what we set our hearts on was victory over that dread creature, a charming woman, the judge of a man's merit, rather than pleasure. We found our pleasure everywhere. Gloomy Benoît made no proselytes.

Soon fat *Marquis*, distantly related to me I think, ceased to understand any of the lessons, and he left us. I fancy we also had with us one Penet, a Gautier or two, *minus habens* without importance.

For this course of study, as for all the rest, there was an examination in the middle of the year. I had a decided advantage over that little Jesuit Paul-Émile, who learnt everything by heart and who frightened me for that reason, for I have *no memory at all*.

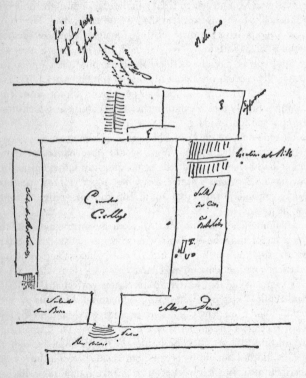

D. M. Dubois' armchair – H. Me – T. Table round which the 8 or 10 pupils sat. [*Superb view over Eybens – Fine view – Private staircase built for the Jesuits – F. Apartment – Library staircase – Mathematics classroom – College courtyard – Literature classroom – 'The Round' classroom – Art classroom – Steps – Rue Neuve.*]

That's one of the great defects of my mind: I keep on brooding over whatever interests me, by dint of examining it from different mental points of view I eventually see something new in it, and I *alter its whole aspect*.

I point and extend the tubes of my glasses in all ways, or retract them, to borrow the image used by M. de Tracy (see his *Logic*).

That little rascal of a Paul-Émile, with his honeyed insincere tone, made me very scared of this examination. Luckily a certain M. *Teste-Lebeau* from Vienne, member of the Departmental Administration, pressed me with questions. I was obliged to invent answers and I won the day over Paul-Émile who only knew by heart the summary of the lessons in the course.

In my written composition there was even some sort of idea about J.-J. Rousseau and the praises he deserved.

All that I learnt at M. Dubois-Fontanelle's lessons seemed to me to be learning that was superficial or *false*.

I thought I had *genius* – where the devil had I picked up that idea? – genius for the profession of Molière and Rousseau.

I sincerely and supremely despised the talent of Voltaire; I considered it *puerile*. I sincerely admired Pierre Corneille, Ariosto, Shakespeare, Cervantes, and paid lip-service to *Molière*. My difficulty was to reconcile them all.

My ideas about literary beauty are basically the same as in 1796, but every six months they improve or, if you prefer, they alter a little.

This is the *only thing I've worked at all my life*.

All the rest has merely been *bread-and-butter* work, added to a touch of vanity at being able to earn it as well as the next man; except the *Intendancy* at Brunswick, after the departure of Martial. Here there was *the attraction of novelty* and the blame expressed by M. Daru about the Intendant of Magdebourg, M. Chaalons, I fancy.

My literary ideal consists more in enjoying the works of others and in assessing them, pondering over their merit, than in writing myself.

About 1794, I was foolishly awaiting the moment of *genius*. Something like the voice of God speaking from *the burning bush* to Moses. This silliness made me waste a lot of time, but may perhaps have prevented me from being satisfied with the *semi-commonplace* as are so many writers of talent (for instance M. Loeve-Veimars).

When I begin to write I no longer think of my literary ideal, I am beset with ideas which I feel urged to note down. I imagine M. Villemain is beset by the forms of sentences; and what is known as a poet, a Delille or a Racine, by forms of verse.

Corneille was excited by forms of repartee: like Émilie to Cinna – '*Hé bien! prends-en ta part et me laisse la mienne . . .*'

And since my idea of perfection changes every six months, it's impossible for me to note what it was around 1795 or 1796 when I was writing a play the name of which I have forgotten. The chief character may have been called Picklar and may have been taken from Florian.

The only thing I see clearly is that for the past forty-six years my ideal has been to live in Paris, in a fourth-floor room, writing a play or a book.

The innumerable mean actions and the worldly wisdom necessary to get a play performed prevented me from writing one, much against my will, and only a week ago I was bitterly regretting it. I have sketched out more than twenty plays, always too detailed and too deep, too unintelligible for an audience of fools like M. Ternaux with which the Revolution of 1789 has filled the pit and the boxes.

When, with his immortal pamphlet *What is the Third Estate? We are on our knees, let us arise,* the abbé Sieyès struck the first blow at the political aristocracy, he founded without knowing it the aristocracy of literature. (This idea occurred to me in November 1835, while making a preface for de Brosses which shocked Colomb.)

CHAPTER 32

I HAD, then, a certain notion of literary beauty in my head in 1796 when I went to M. Dubois-Fontanelle's lessons, and it was very different from his. The most striking feature of this difference was my adoration for the tragic and simple truthfulness of Shakespeare, in contrast to Voltaire's *pompous puerility*.

I remember amongst other things that M. Dubois used to recite to us with enthusiasm certain lines of Voltaire's or his own which contained the words: '*twist the knife ... in the wound.*' This word *knife* shocked me to the core, profoundly, because it did not follow my rule, my love for simplicity. Today I can see the *reason* for this. All my life I have felt things keenly but I only see the reason why long afterwards.

Only yesterday, 18 January 1836, the feast of the *catedra* of Saint Peter, as I came out of Saint Peter's at four o'clock and turned back to look at the dome, *for the first time in my life* I looked at it as I look at any other building, and I saw the iron balcony round the tambour. I said to myself: I'm seeing it as it is for the first time, hitherto I've looked at it as one looks at the woman one loves. I liked everything about it (the tambour and the dome, that is), how could I have found any fault in it?

And so I'm led, by another path and from a different angle, to awareness of that defect which I noted earlier in this veracious story of mine, *lack of sagacity*.

Good Heavens, how I'm rambling! So then I had my own inward doctrine when I followed M. Dubois's lessons, I learnt all that he taught me only as a *useful falsehood*. When he blamed Shakespeare, particularly, I blushed inwardly.

But I learnt this literary doctrine *all the better* for not being enthusiastic about it.

One of my misfortunes has been never to please those people about whom I was most enthusiastic (for instance Mme Pasta and M. de Tracy); apparently I must have loved them in my own way and not in theirs.

Similarly I often make a failure of expounding a theory which I *adore*, somebody contradicts me, tears spring to my eyes and I can't go on speaking. I would say if I dared: '*Ah, you're breaking my heart!*' I remember two examples that struck me particularly:

My praise of Correggio, in relation to Prud'hon, when talking to Mareste in the Palais-Royal, and going on a picnic with MM. Duvergier de Hauranne, that nice fellow Dittmer and that horrid fellow Cavé.

Secondly, talking about Mozart to MM. Ampère and Adrien de Jussieu on the way back from Naples in 1832 (a month after the earthquake which damaged Foligno).

From a literary point of view, M. Dubois's course of lectures (since printed in four volumes by his grandson Ch. Renauldon) was useful to me by giving me an over-all picture of the field of literature and preventing my imagination from exaggerating the unknown regions of it such as Sophocles, Ossian, etc.

This course was very useful to my vanity in that it definitely confirmed other people in the opinion which set me among the seven or eight most intelligent boys in the school. I fancy, however, that Grand-Dufay was placed before me; I've forgotten the names of the others.

M. Fontanelle's golden age, the period of which he spoke with emotion, was that of his arrival in Paris, about 1750. Everybody was talking about Voltaire then and the works that he was constantly sending from Ferney. (But was he then at Ferney?)

All this fell flat for me, who loathed Voltaire's *puerility* and his *mean envy* of Corneille; it seems to me that I had already at that time noticed the parsonical tone of Voltaire's *Commentary* in the fine edition of Corneille illustrated with engravings which filled one of the upper shelves of my father's glass-fronted bookcase at Claix, that bookcase of which I stole the key and in which, I fancy, I had discovered *La Nouvelle Héloïse* a few years earlier, and certainly, since then, *Grandisson*, which I read in floods of tears in a second-floor attic of the Claix house, where I thought myself secure.

M. Jay, that big braggart, so worthless a painter, had a remarkable gift for exciting the most violent emulation in our hearts, and I now consider that the most important gift for a teacher. How differently I thought in 1796! Then I worshipped genius and talent.

A temperamental person, doing everything *on impulse*, as a man of genius usually does, would never have had three hundred and fifty to four hundred pupils, as did M. Jay.

In short, the rue Neuve was crowded when we came out of his

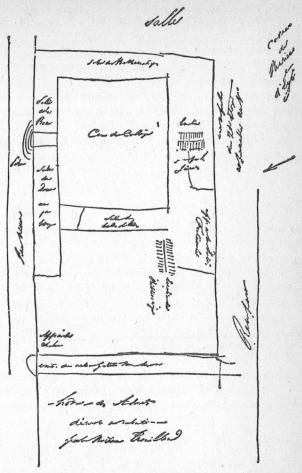

[Classroom – Hillsides of Murianette and Eybens – View, superb from the second floor and fair from the first – Rampart – Mathematics classroom – 'The Round' classroom – Steps – Rue Neuve – Art classroom on 1st floor – College courtyard – Literature classroom – Private staircase for Jesuits – M. Dubois-Fontanelle's apartment – Library staircase – M. Chalvet's apartment – Vault over the little empty street – Hotel des Adrets demolished and rebuilt by Trouilloud the notary.]

class, which increased the master's self-important and bombastic manner.

I was delighted, as if I had secured the finest and most difficult promotion possible, when towards the middle of one year, I think, M. Jay said to me with his majestic, paternal air:

'Now then, Monsier B ..., take your portfolio and go along and draw from the round.'

The word *monsieur*, so often heard in Paris, was very seldom used in Grenoble when speaking to a child, and always surprised me when addressed to myself.

I don't know whether I owed this promotion to some remark of my grandfather's to M. Jay or to my own merit in making neat parallel hatchings in the life class to which I had recently been admitted. The fact is that it surprised me and everybody else.

Admitted among the twelve or fifteen pupils drawing from *the round*, my work in black and white chalk, copies of the heads of Niobe and Demosthenes (as we called them) surprised M. Jay, who looked scandalized at finding I had as much talent as the rest. The most gifted pupil in this class was one M. Ennemond Hélie (since then a notary in the Law Court); he was the most frigid of men, and was said to have been in the army. His work was somewhat in the style of Philippe de Champagne, but he was a man and not a child like the rest of us, and it was unfair to let him compete with us.

Soon, at the round, I won a prize. Two or three of us won it and drew lots, I got the *Essay on Poetry and Painting* by the abbé Dubos, which I read with the keenest pleasure. This book harmonized with innermost feelings of which I was myself unconscious.

Moulezin, a typical timid provincial, devoid of any ideas and very careful, excelled in making beautifully parallel hatchings with a well-sharpened piece of red chalk. A man of talent, in M. Jay's place, would have told us, pointing to Moulezin: 'Gentlemen, this is what not to do.' Instead of which Moulezin was the rival of Ennemond Hélie.

Clever Dufay did very original drawings, according to M. Jay; he distinguished himself particularly when M. Jay had the excellent idea of making each of us pose in turn for the study of heads. We also had that fat lout Hélie, nicknamed *le bedot* (stupid, clumsy) and the two Monvals, whose favoured position in the mathematics class had followed them to the drawing class.

One day when there were two models, big Odru from the Latin class was blocking my view, so I boxed his ears as hard as I could, at O. A moment later, when I was back in my place at H, he pulled my chair from behind and made me fall on my behind. He was a grown man, a foot taller than me, but he hated me very much. I had drawn on the staircase of the Latin class-

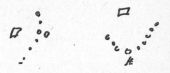

room, with the help of Gauthier and Crozet I fancy, a great life-size caricature of him, under which I had written: Odruas Kambin. He used to blush when we called him Odruas, and he said Kambin instead of *quand bien*.

It was immediately decided that we must duel with pistols. We went down into the yard, and when M. Jay wanted to intervene we took flight. M. Jay went back into the other room. We went out, but the whole school followed us. We had about two hundred followers.

I had begged Diday, who happened to be there, to be my second; I was very agitated but full of eagerness. I don't know how it happened that we went towards the Graille Gate, considerably hindered by our retinue. We had to have pistols, which wasn't easy to arrange. Eventually I got hold of a pistol eight inches long. I could see Odru walking twenty yards away from me and showering insults on me. They wouldn't let us get near one another; he could have killed me with a blow from his fist.

I didn't reply to his insults but I was trembling with rage. I don't say that I should have been exempt from fear if this duel had been arranged in the ordinary way: four or five people going off together in cold blood at six in the morning, in a cab, to somewhere a good three miles out of the town.

The guard at the Graille Gate was on the point of standing to arms.

This procession of urchins, ridiculous and very awkward for us, shouted ever more loudly: '*Will they fight? Won't they fight?*' whenever we stopped for any reason. I was very much afraid of being thrashed by Odru, who was a foot taller than his seconds or mine. I remember only Maurice Diday as my second (he's since become a contemptible ultra, Mayor of Domène, and writes *misspelt* ultra letters to the newspapers). Odru was furious.

At last, after pursuing us for an hour and a half, as night was drawing on, the young rascals left us a little peace between the Porte-de-Bonne and the Porte Très-Cloîtres. We went down into the fosse of the town, ten feet deep, which was laid out by Louis Royer, or perhaps we stopped on the edge of this fosse.

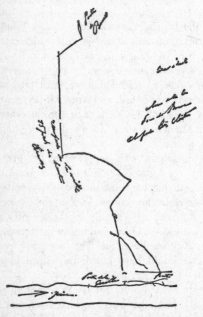

[*Porte de Bonne – Town ramparts 15 feet high. Terraces – Porte de la Graille – Bridge – Isère – Duel fought here or else between the Porte de Bonne and the Porte Très-Cloîtres.*

There the pistols were loaded, and a fearful number of paces, twenty perhaps, were measured out, and I said to myself: now's the time to be brave. I don't know why, but Odru was to have fired first; I stared at a small trapezoid piece of rock that rose behind him, A, the same that could be seen from my aunt Élisabeth's window, beside the roof of the Saint-Louis Church.

I don't know how it happened that we did not fire. Probably

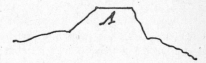

the seconds had not loaded the pistols. I seem to remember not having to aim. Peace was declared, but we didn't shake hands, far less embrace each other. Odru, in a towering rage, would have thrashed me.

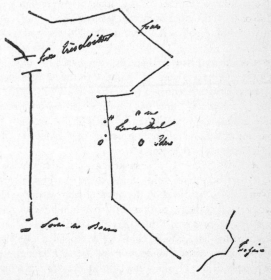

[*Porte Très-Cloîtres – Ditches – Port de Bonne – Trapezium – H. Me – O. Odru.*]

In the rue Très-Cloîtres, walking beside Diday, my second, I said to him : 'So as not to be frightened while Odru was aiming at me, I looked at the little rock above Seyssins.' [T.]

'You must never say that, you must never mention such a thing,' he said, scolding me severely.

I was greatly surprised and, when I thought it over, greatly shocked by this reprimand.

But the very next day I felt horribly remorseful at having let the affair be settled. It offended all my Spanish day-dreams; how could I dare admire the *Cid* after not fighting? How could I think about *Ariosto's* heroes? How could I admire and criticize the great figures of Roman history, about whose doughty deeds I read so often in the work of that unctuous Rollin?

As I write this I feel as if I were touching the scar of a healed wound.

I have not thought twice about this duel since my other duel, about Babet, arranged with M. Raindre (a major or colonel in the light artillery) in Vienna, in 1809.

This was the thing, I now see, which caused me most remorse throughout my early youth, and which really accounted for my presumptuousness (almost insolence) in the duel in Milan, at which Cardon was my second.

In the Odru affair I was surprised, agitated, unresisting, distracted by the fear of being thrashed by the gigantic Odru, and from time to time was on the point of being afraid. During the two hours that the procession of the two hundred boys lasted, I was saying to myself : 'When they've paced out the distance, that's when the danger will begin.' What appalled me was the thought of being carried home *on a ladder*, as I had seen poor Lambert carried. But I had not the faintest idea, for one moment, that the affair would be settled.

When the great moment came, while Odru was aiming at

me, and it seems to me that his pistol misfired several times, I was studying the outline of the little rock T. The time did not seem long to me (as it did at the Moskowa to that very brave and excellent officer *Andréa* Corner, my friend).

In a word I was not play-acting, I was perfectly natural, not boastful but very brave.

This was a mistake on my part, I should have *swaggered*; having genuinely resolved to fight I might have won a reputation in our town where people used to duel a great deal, not like the Neapolitans of 1836 whose duels produce very few corpses or none at all, but like brave men. In contrast with my extreme youth (it must have been in 1796, when I was thirteen, or perhaps 1795) and my habits of aloofness, like a young aristocrat, if I had had the intelligence to talk a bit I should have won an admirable reputation.

M. Châtel, an acquaintance and neighbour of ours in the Grande-Rue, had killed six men. In my time, that's to say between 1798 and 1805, two of my acquaintances, the younger Bernard and big-mouthed Royer, were killed in duels, M. Royer at forty-five feet, at dusk in the waste land of the Drac, near the place where the wire bridge has since been built.

That fop Bernard (son of another fop, since then Judge of the Supreme Court of Appeal, I believe, and an ultra), that fop Bernard received, at the Canel mill, a little sword-thrust from that pleasant fellow Meffrey (M. Meffrey, Tax-Collector General, husband of the Duchesse de Berry's obsequious lady-in-waiting and since then the fortunate heir of fat Vourey). Bernard fell dead, M. de Meffrey fled to Lyons; the quarrel was almost an *affair of caste*, Mareste, who was, I think, Meffrey's second, told me about it.

In any case, I developed a profound remorse:

(1) On account of my *espagnolisme*, a defect which I still have in 1830, as di Fiori has recognized and which he describes, after Thucydides, as 'spreading one's nets too high'.

(2) Lack of swagger. In moments of great danger I am natural and simple. This was good form at Smolensk, in the eyes of M. le Duc de Frioul. M. Daru, who had no love for me, wrote in the same terms to his wife, from Vilna I imagine, after the retreat from Moscow.

But in the eyes of the vulgar herd I have not played the brilliant role that was within my reach.

The more I think about it, the more it seems to me that this quarrel must have been in [17]95, and long before my passion for mathematics, my friendship with Bigillion, and my affectionate feelings for Mlle Victorine.

I had the greatest respect for Maurice Diday:

(1) Because my excellent grandfather, a friend, possibly an intimate friend of his mother's, praised him highly.

(2) I had seen him several times in his artilleryman's uniform, and he had gone to join his regiment farther away than Montmélian.

(3) Last but not least, he had the honour to be in love with Mlle Létourneau, perhaps the prettiest girl in Grenoble and the daughter of indubitably the gayest, most carefree and philosophical man there, the man who was most severely criticized by my father and my relatives. Indeed, M. Létourneau was most unlike them; he had ruined himself little by little and had married a certain Mlle Borel, I believe, sister to the mother of Victorine Mounier, who was the cause of my giving up the military profession and taking refuge in Paris.

Mlle Létourneau was one of those beauties of generous build (like Tiarini's figures in the *Death of Cleopatra* or *of Antony* in the Louvre). Diday subsequently married her but soon had the misfortune to lose her after six years of love; it was said that he was stunned by this, and retired into the country at Domène.

After my mid-year prize for 'drawing from the round', which shocked all the fawners who were more favoured than myself at M. Jay's court, but which nobody dared say I had not deserved, my place *at drawing*, as we said, was changed. I'd have thrown myself into the fire to win a prize at the end of the year, and I think I must have got one, otherwise I should remember the disappointment of having failed.

I won the first prize for literature, with applause, and an *accessit* or second prize for mathematics, which was a hard one to win. M. Dupuy had a marked dislike of my mania for arguing.

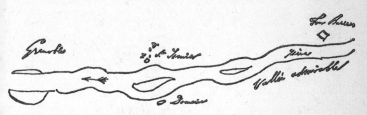

V. M. Bigillion's house – F. M. Faure's house. [*Grenoble – St Ismier – Fort Barraux – Isère – Wonderful valley – Domène.*]

Every day he summoned to the blackboard, calling them *tu*, MM. de Monval – the Monvaux as we called them – because they were noblemen (he himself had pretensions to nobility), Sinard, Saint-Ferréol, who were noblemen, good Aribert who was his protégé, the pleasant Mante, etc., and myself as seldom as possible, and when I was there he did not listen, which humiliated and disconcerted me considerably, since he never took his eyes off the others. In spite of this my love for mathematics, which was beginning to be serious, made me expound to him any difficulty that struck me while I was at the blackboard, H, M. Dupuy being in his huge sky-blue arm-chair, at D; my indiscretion obliged him to answer and therein lay the mischief. He always asked me to expound my problems to him in private, maintaining that it wasted the time of the class.

He commissioned worthy Sinard to remove my doubts. Sinard, who was much cleverer but an honest fellow, would spend an hour or two denying these doubts, then understanding them, and eventually would confess that he didn't know what to answer.

It strikes me that all these good folk, except Mante, took mathematics to be merely a matter of memory. M. Dupuy looked really sold when I won that triumphant first prize in the literature class. My examination, which took place, like all the others, in presence of the members for the Département, the members of the Examining Committee, all the teachers and two or three hundred pupils, was amusing for these gentlemen. I spoke well, and the members of the Departmental Administration, surprised at not being bored, paid me compliments and, when my examina-

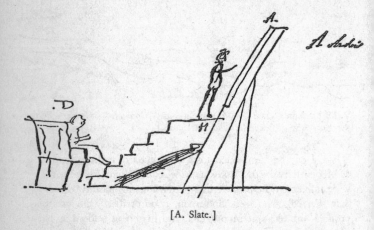

[A. Slate.]

tion was over, said to me: 'Monsieur B., you have won the prize, but for our enjoyment please be kind enough to answer a few more questions.'

I think this triumph came before the mathematics examination and won me a place and a self-confidence which in the following year obliged M. Dupuy to call me frequently to the blackboard.

If ever I go back to Grenoble I must have a search made in the archives of the Prefecture for the years 1794–9 inclusive. The printed report of the prize-giving will give me the date of all these trifling events, the memory of which recurs to me with pleasure after so many years. I was climbing the hill of life then, and my imagination was afire as I pictured the joys to come ... Now I am going downhill.

After that triumphant August my father no longer dared offer such stubborn opposition to my passion for shooting game. With a bad grace he let me take his gun, and even a heavier gun of large bore which had been made to order for the late M. Rey, his brother-in-law the notary.

My aunt Rey was a pretty woman whom I used to visit in a pretty apartment in the Palace courtyard. My father did not want me to make friends with Édouard Rey, her second son, a notorious scamp who frequented the lowest rabble. (Today he is Colonel of Artillery Rey, a consummate Dauphinois, wilier and more deceitful than four attorneys of Grenoble put together and moreover monstrously cuckolded, a very unpleasant fellow, but who must be a good colonel in that highly specialized branch of the army. It seems to me that in 1831 he was in service at Algiers. He has been the lover of M. P.)

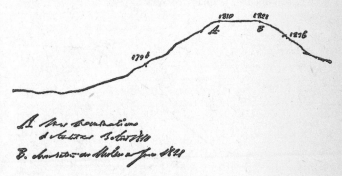

[*A. My nomination as auditeur, 3 August 1810 – B. My return from Milan in June 1821.*]

CHAPTER 33

I KEEP making great discoveries about myself as I write these memoirs. The difficulty now is, not to find and to tell the truth, but to find somebody to read it. Perhaps the pleasure of these discoveries and the judgements and assessments which follow them will decide me to go on; the idea of being read is fading more and more. Here I am at page 501 and I haven't yet left Grenoble!

This picture of a heart's upheavals would make a big octavo volume even before I reach Milan. Who would read such trifles? It would take a great painter's gift to paint them well, and I loathe almost equally descriptions in the manner of Walter Scott and the bombast of Rousseau. I ought to have a Mme Roland for a reader, and even then perhaps the lack of description of the charming shady trees along our Isère valley would make her fling the book down. How much there is to tell, for anyone who should have the patience to describe correctly! What beautiful clumps of trees, what vigorous and luxuriant vegetation in the plain, what pretty chestnut woods on the hillsides and, above them, what an impression of grandeur is conferred on the whole scene by the eternal snows of Taillefer! What a sublime bass to this lovely melody!

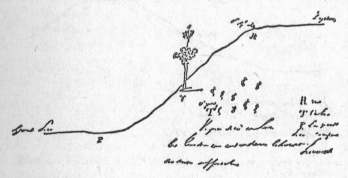

[*Doyatières – Big field – Vineyard from which the thrush flew off on hearing me come near – H. Me – T. The tree – P. The big field, comparatively horizontal.*]

I think it was that autumn that I had the delicious pleasure of shooting a thrush, in the path through the vineyard above the big field, exactly opposite the round white summit of the Taillefer mountain. This was one of the keenest pleasures in my life. I had just been rambling through the vineyard of Doyatières, I was entering the narrow path, between two very high thick hedges, which runs down to the big field from H to P, when suddenly a big thrush flew out, with a little cry, from

284

the vines at T′, right towards the top of the tree T, a cherry tree I think, very tall and slender and with sparse foliage.

I saw him, I fired from a more or less horizontal position, for I hadn't gone downhill yet. The thrush fell, making a thud as it hit the ground which I can hear to this day. I went down the path, wild with delight.

I went home, and told a cross-grained old servant who was something of a sportsman: 'Barbier, your pupil is worthy of you!'

The man would far rather have had a twelve-sou piece, and in any case didn't understand a word I was saying.

As soon as I am moved I lapse into *espagnolisme*, imparted to me by my aunt Élisabeth, who still used to say: 'As fine as the Cid.'

I was plunged deep in dreams as I wandered, gun in hand,

[*Doyatières – Big field.*]

among the vines and timber woods round Furonières. As my father, who always tried to cross me, forbade my shooting or at most tolerated it unwillingly out of weakness, I hardly ever went shooting with real sportsmen. Sometimes I went fox-hunting among the precipices of the Rock of Comboire with Joseph Brun, our woodsman. There, lying in wait for the fox, I scolded myself for day-dreaming so deeply that I should have had to be aroused if the animal had appeared. He did appear one day, fifteen feet away, trotting gently towards me; I fired and saw nothing. I had missed him completely. I had such a terror of the dangerous precipices overlooking the Drac that I was pre-occupied, that day, with the perils of my homeward journey; one

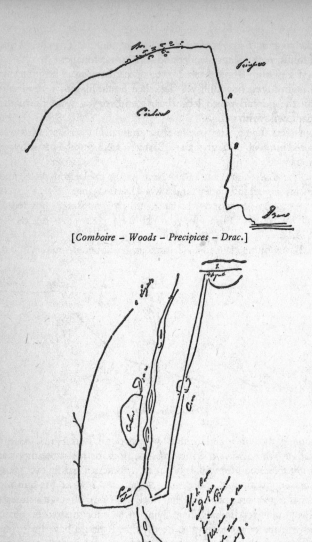

[*Comboire – Woods – Precipices – Drac.*]

[*Isère – Porte de Graille – The Cours – Seyssins – Drac – Comboire – Pont-de-Claix – See M. de Bourcet's map of Dauphiné. (It was in the terrace sitting-room on the left.)*]

had to creep over ledges like A and B, looking down at the Drac roaring past at the foot of the rock. The peasants with whom I went (Joseph Brun and his son, Sébastien Charrière, etc.) had watched their flocks of sheep on these steep hillsides from the age of six, and barefooted; when necessary they took off their shoes. For me, there was no question of taking off mine, and I went amongst those rocks twice or thrice at most.

I was completely terrified the day I missed the fox, far more than when I was held up in a field of *hemp* in Silesia (campaign of 1813) all alone, and saw eighteen or twenty Cossacks ad-

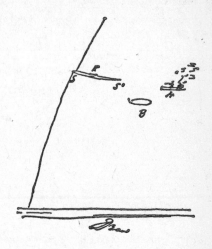

vancing towards me. On that day at Comboire I looked at my watch, a gold one, as I do on all great occasions so that I may at least remember the time clearly, and as M. de Lavalette did when he was being sentenced to death (by the Bourbons). It was eight o'clock, I had had to get up before dawn, which always leaves me confused for the rest of the morning. There I was, day-dreaming about the beautiful scenery, about love and probably also about the dangers of my journey home, when the fox came trotting towards me. His bushy tail made me recognize him for a fox, for at first sight I had taken him for a dog. At S the path may have been two feet wide, and at S′ two inches, the fox had to make a leap to cross from S' to H, and when I fired he jumped into some brushwood at B, five or six feet below us.

The paths which are possible and passable, even for a fox, are very few on this precipice; three or four sportsmen hold them, another sets on the dogs, the fox goes off and most likely runs into one of the sportsmen.

One shoot about which these sportsmen were always talking was the chamois shoot at the *Peuil de Claix*, but my father had strictly forbidden this and none of them ever dared take me there. I think it must have been in 1795 that I had that real fright among the rocks of Comboire.

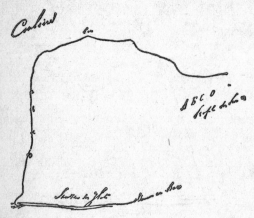

[*Comboire – Woods – A.B.C.O. Outline of the paths – Path of the Islets, leading to the ferry.*]

Soon after, I killed my second thrush (*tourdre, turdus*) but a much smaller one than the first, at nightfall, when I could barely make it out, on a walnut tree in M. de la Peyrouse's meadow, I think, above *our Pelissone* (*id est:* our Pelissone vineyard).

I killed my third and last on a little walnut tree by the side of the road to the north of our *little orchard*. This thrush, a very small one, was almost vertically above me, and almost fell on my nose. It fell on to the dry-stone wall, and with it fell great drops of blood which I can still see.

This blood was a symbol of victory. It was not until Brunswick in 1808 that pity disgusted me with shooting; today it seems to me an inhuman and disgusting sort of murder, and I would not kill a gnat needlessly. The last quail I killed at Civita-Vecchia, however, did not arouse my pity. Partridges, quails, hares, seem to me like chickens, born to be put on a spit.

If you consulted them before they were hatched out in the incubators at the end of the Champs-Elysées they would probably not refuse.

I remember the delicious sensation I had one morning, going out with Barbier before dawn and finding a beautiful moon shining and a warm breeze. It was the time of the vine harvest, and I have never forgotten it. That day I had extorted from my father permission to go with Barbier, his factotum for the management of the farm on his *estate*, to a fair at Sassenage or Les Balmes. Sassenage is the cradle of my family. They were judges or *beyles* there, and the *elder branch* (after all, Louis-Philippe talks about 'the eldest of my race') was still established there in 1795, with an income of 15,000 or 20,000 f[rancs] which, but for a certain law of the 13th Germinal, would, it seems to me, have come to me in its *entirety*. My patriotism was not shaken by this; it's true that at that age, not knowing what it was *to be in need* and to have to do unpleasant work to earn one's livelihood, money meant nothing to me but the satisfaction of one's whims; now, I had no whims, never going into society and never seeing *any woman*; money therefore meant nothing to me. At most, I would have liked to buy a double-barrelled gun.

In those days, I was like a great river about to plunge down a waterfall, like the Rhine above Schaffhausen, which still flows smoothly but which is about to rush down in an immense cascade. My waterfall was my love of mathematics, which at first as a means of leaving Grenoble, that embodiment of the bourgeois way of life and literally of *nausea*, and later for its own sake, absorbed me entirely.

Game-shooting, which led me to read with a feeling of *compassion* the *Maison Rustique* and to make extracts from Buffon's *History of Animals*, the bombast of which shocked me even at that early age as being closely akin to the hypocrisy of my father's priests, game-shooting was the thing that excited me next to mathematics.

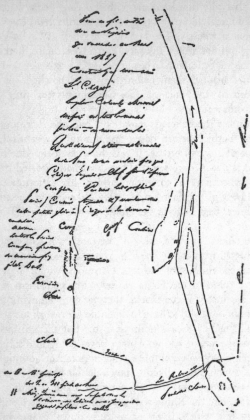

[*Wire bridge, called the Seyssins bridge, which replaced the ferry about 1827, built by my friend Louis Crozet; contemptible Monval, despised by everybody (and praised by* La Quotidienne *when he died), was a shareholder in this bridge and did not want Crozet, chief engineer, to complete the test. By means of an engraving the Periers (Casimir, Augustin, etc.) tried to take away this small fame from Crozet and give it to one of his nephews. In everything, the Periers are deceitful, scheming, dishonest, contemptible and mean – Le Rondeau – Cours – Drac – La Robine – Claix bridge – Drac – Comboire – Cossey – Cossey – By-road – Furonières – Claix – Road – From B to B' precipices two or three hundred feet deep – H. Me. I had a superb view over the hills of Échirolles and Jarry, and my gaze surveyed the whole valley.*]

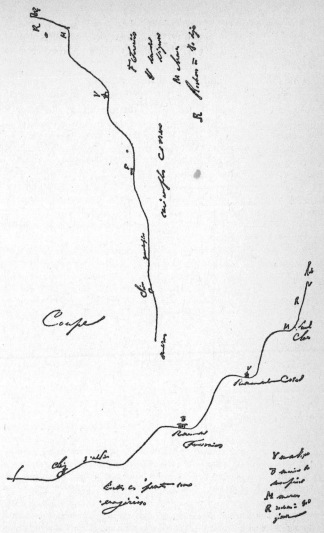

[*Cutting – Rocks – Peuil de Claix – Plateau on the hillside – Plateau of Furonières – Big field – Claix – All these slopes are exaggerated – V. M. de Vignon – My father's house – M. Marshes – R. Rock at a slope of 80°.*]

I did go as often as I could to see Mlle Victorine Bigillion, but I think that during those years she stayed for long periods in the country. I often saw a good deal of Bigillion, her elder brother, of La Bayette, Gall, Barral, Michoud, Colomb, Mante;[1] but my heart was given to mathematics.

One more story, and then I shall be bristling with x's and y's.

There was a conspiracy against the Tree of Fraternity.

I don't know why I conspired. This tree was an unfortunate young oak, very slender and at least thirty feet high, which had

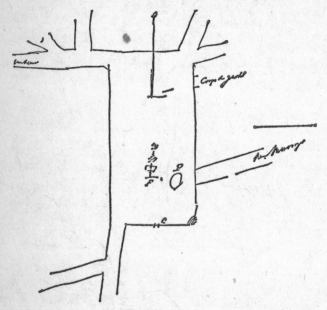

F. was this tree which may have had only a cluster of leaves at the top of its trunk – P. was the pump – C. the door of my grandfather's house, so often referred to, the first floor of which house was occupied by Mlles Codé, pious ladies. [*Rue Neuve – Guard-house – Rue Montorge.*]

1. I made friends with Mante, a hard and very dry young man, and through him with Treillard his friend. Mante later, at Paris in 1804, almost dragged me into the Moreau conspiracy, but he made me read Tracy and Say (Rue de l'Échelle, the younger P . . .'s house) and the second as much as the first.

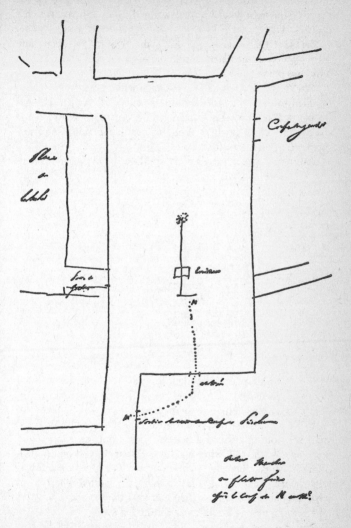

[*Place de la Halle – Porte des Jacobins – Guard-house – Notice-board –
Entrance – Exit on the night of the pistol shot – The way we went or rather
ran off after firing it, from M to M'.*]

been transplanted, to its great regret, into the middle of the Place Grenette, a good way below the Tree of Liberty, which I dearly loved.

The Tree of Fraternity, possibly the rival of the other, had been planted immediately beside the chestnut-shed, opposite the windows of the late M. Le Roy.

I don't know on what occasion, a white placard had been fastened to the Tree of Fraternity on which M. Jay had painted in yellow, and with his usual talent, a crown, a sceptre, some chains, the whole in the attitude of conquered things and surmounted by an inscription.

The inscription consisted of several lines, and again I remem-

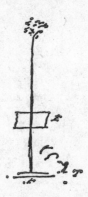

ber nothing about it, although it was the thing I conspired against.

This is surely a proof of the principle that a little passion increases one's intelligence, and a great deal extinguishes it. What were we plotting against? I have no idea. I only remember, and that vaguely, the following maxim: It's our duty to do as much harm as we possibly can to the thing we hate. And even this is very vague. Apart from this I haven't the least recollection of what we hated and why we hated it, only the picture of the fact, and nothing more, but that most distinctly.

The idea was mine alone, and I had to impart it to the rest, who at first were unenthusiastic: 'The guard-house is so close!' they said; but finally they were as resolute as myself. The conspirators were: Mante, Treillard, Colomb and I, and perhaps one or two more.

Why didn't I fire the pistol? I don't know. I think Treillard or Mante must have done it.

We had to get hold of this pistol; it was eight inches long. We loaded it to the muzzle. The Tree of Fraternity may have been thirty-six or forty feet high, the placard was fixed ten or twelve feet up, and I fancy there was a railing round the tree.

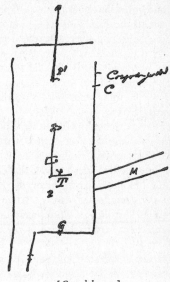

[*Guard-house.*]

We were in danger from the guard-house at C, the soldiers from which often walked about the unpaved stretch from P to P'.

Passers-by coming from the rue Montorge or the Grande-Rue might stop us. The four or five of us who did not shoot were watching the soldiers from the guard-house; this may have been my post as being the most dangerous, but I don't remember at all. Others were watching the rue Montorge and the Grande-Rue.

About eight o'clock on a pitch-dark but not very cold night – it was in autumn or spring – the square was deserted for a moment, and we strolled about nonchalantly and gave the word to Mante or Treillard. The shot was fired and made an appalling noise, the silence had been deep and the pistol loaded to bursting-point. In an instant the soldiers from the guard-house were upon us. I think that we were not alone in hating the inscription and the possibility of an attack had been expected.

The soldiers were almost touching us, we took refuge in the doorway of my grandfather's house, G, but we could be seen quite clearly; everybody was at the windows, and many people brought candles and lights shone out.

This door G, on to the Place Grenette, communicated by a narrow passage on the second floor with the door G' on to the Grande-Rue. But everybody knew about this passage.

To escape, then, we followed the line FFF. Some of us also escaped, I fancy, through the tall Porte des Jacobins, which inclines me to believe that there were more of us than I said. Prié may have been with us.

Myself and one other, Colomb perhaps, were the most keenly pursued. '*They've gone into this house,*' we heard someone shout quite close to us.

We did not go on up to the passage above the second floor; we rang sharply at the first-floor apartment on the Place Grenette, which had been my grandfather's and was now let to Mlles Codé, deeply devout old milliners. Fortunately they opened the door, and we found them very frightened by the pistol shot and reading the Bible.

Briefly we told them: we're being pursued, say that we've spent the evening here. We sat down, and almost immediately there came a violent ring at the bell, while we sat there listening to the Bible reading, I even believe one of us was holding the book.

The police officers came in. I don't know who they were; apparently I can hardly have looked at them.

'Have these citizens spent the evening here?'

'Yes, *messieurs* – yes, citizens,' the poor terrified pious creatures corrected themselves. I believe their brother M. Codé, an old clerk who had been employed at the hospital for the past forty-five years, was with them too.

These policemen or zealous citizens must have been very

short-sighted or very favourably disposed towards M. Gagnon, who was venerated by the whole town, from M. le Baron des Adrets to Poulet the cookshop keeper, for our agitation must have made us look very odd amidst these poor pious women who were beside themselves with fear. Perhaps their fear, which was equal to our own, may have saved us, for the whole party must have looked equally scared.

The officers repeated their question two or three times: 'Have

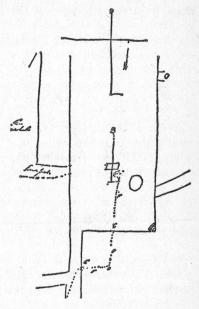

[*Place de la Halle – Porte des Jacobins.*]

these citizens spent the whole evening here? Has nobody come in since you heard the pistol shot?'

The miracle, as we realized afterwards, was that these Jansenist old maids consented to tell a lie. I think they yielded to this sin from veneration for my grandfather.

The officers took our names and finally cleared out. We cut short our civilities to the old ladies. We listened carefully, and when we could no longer hear the officers we went out and continued our way up towards the passage.

Mante and Treillard, who were more agile than us and had gone in by the door G before us, told us next day that when they reached the other door, G', they found it blocked by two guards. The young gentlemen began to talk about the kindness of the ladies with whom they had spent the evening, the guards did not ask them a single question, and they took themselves off.

Their story seems so real to me that I couldn't say whether it was not Colomb and myself who went out talking about the kindness of these ladies.

It seems more likely that Colomb and I went back into the house, and then that he left half an hour later.

The joke was the discussions which took place between my father and aunt Élisabeth about the presumed authors of the revolt. I think I told the whole story to my sister Pauline, who was my friend.

Next day at the Central School, Monval (since then a colonel, and much despised), who disliked me, said to me: 'Well, so you and your gang fired at the Tree of Fraternity?' The greatest treat was to go and look at the placard, which was riddled with shot.

The sceptres, crowns and other conquered attributes were painted on the south side, facing the Tree of Liberty. The crowns, etc., were painted bright yellow on paper stretched over a canvas, or on a canvas prepared for oil painting.

I haven't given a thought to this affair for fifteen or twenty years. I must confess that it seems to me very fine. In those days I often used to repeat with enthusiasm, and I repeated again not four days ago, the line in *Horace*:

Albe vous a nommé, je ne vous connais plus!

This act was quite in keeping with that admiration. The strange thing was that I didn't fire the pistol myself. But I don't think it was from shameful prudence. It seems to me, although I perceive the thing dimly and as if through a fog, that Treillard, who had just come up from his village (Tullins, I believe), insisted on firing the shot as if to establish his right to be one of us.

As I write this, the image of the Tree of Fraternity rises before my eyes, my memory is making discoveries. I think I can see the Tree of Fraternity surrounded by a two-foot wall faced with ashlar and supporting an iron railing five or six feet high.

Jomard was a rascally priest, like Mingrat later, who got himself guillotined for poisoning his stepfather, a certain M. Martin from Vienne, I believe, a former *Member for the Département*, as they said. I saw this scoundrel tried and then guillotined. I was on the pavement in front of the shop of M. Plana the pharmacist.

Jomard had let his beard grow, his shoulders were covered with a red cloth to show that he was a parricide.

I was so close that after the execution I could see drops of blood forming on the edge of the knife before they fell. This horrified me, and for I don't know how many days after, I was unable to eat beef.

CHAPTER 34

I BELIEVE I have dealt with everything I wanted to speak about before starting on the last story I shall have to tell about things in Grenoble; I mean the story of my plunge in mathematics.

Mlle Kubly had long been gone and I retained only a tender memory of her, Mlle Victorine Bigillion was spending much of her time in the country, the only books I enjoyed reading were Shakespeare and the *Memoirs* of Saint-Simon, then in seven volumes, which I later bought in a twelve-volume edition in Baskerville type; this was a passion which has lasted like my physical passion for spinach and which I feel quite as strongly, to say the least, at fifty-three as I did at thirteen.

I loved mathematics all the more because of my increased contempt for my teachers, MM. Dupuy and Chabert. In spite of the grandiloquence and urbanity, the suave and dignified air that M. Dupuy assumed when he spoke to anyone, I had enough shrewdness to guess that he was infinitely more of an ignoramus than M. Chabert. M. Chabert, who in the social hierarchy of the bourgeoisie of Grenoble stood so far below M.

Dupuy, sometimes on a Sunday or a Thursday morning would take a volume of Euler or ... and resolutely tackle difficulties. Nevertheless he always reminded one of an apothecary who

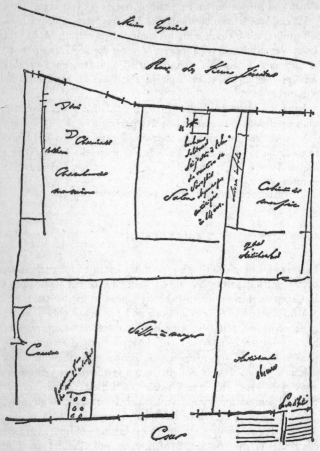

H. Myself swotting at abbé Marie. [*Teisseires' house – Rue des Vieux-Jésuites – My mother's room. Me. Cheminade. Picture – Drawing-room. Solitary happiness. Here I was safe from being plagued by Séraphie. Foretaste of misanthropy at 14 years old – My father's study. Folio books – Second anteroom – Kitchen. Furnace for sulphur moulds – Dining-room – Dark anteroom. Front door – Courtyard.*]

knows good prescriptions, but nothing showed how these *prescriptions* were derived from one another, there was no *logic*, no philosophy in that head of his; automatically, whether through education or through vanity, perhaps because of his religion, worthy M. Chabert hated the very name of such things.

Thinking as I do today, I wondered quite unfairly, a couple of minutes ago, how it happened that I failed to see the remedy at once. I had no one to turn to, my grandfather out of vanity had an aversion for mathematics, which was the only exception to his almost universal learning. People used to say respectfully in Grenoble that that man, or rather *Monsieur Gagnon, never forgot anything he had read*. Except mathematics, was the only answer his enemies could give. My father detested mathematics for religious reasons, I think; he only forgave them a little because they showed one how to *draw a plan of one's estates*. I was always making him copies of the plan of his properties at Claix, Échirolles, Fontagnieu, Le Cheylas (a valley near . . .), where he had just done a good stroke of business.

I despised Bezout as much as I did MM. Dupuy and Chabert.

There were actually five or six good mathematicians at the Central School who were admitted to the École Polytechnique in 1797 or '98, but they did not deign to explain my difficulties, which perhaps I could not set out clearly enough, or which more probably puzzled them.

I bought, or received as a prize, the works of the *Abbé Marie* in one octavo volume. I read this book as eagerly as a novel. I found in it truths set out in new ways, which pleased me very much and rewarded me for my trouble, but there was nothing actually new.

I don't mean that there was not really something new in it, which I may have failed to understand; I had not learned enough to see it.

In order to ponder undisturbed I had established myself in the drawing-room, furnished with twelve fine arm-chairs embroidered by my poor mother, which was only opened once or twice a year to be dusted. I found this room conducive to meditation; in those days I still remembered the lovely supper parties my mother used to give there. At ten o'clock sharp, the guests would adjourn from the brilliantly lighted drawing-room to the dining-room, where an enormous fish awaited them. This was my father's luxury; he still retained this instinct even after he had lapsed into devoutness and agricultural speculation.

It was on the table, T, that I wrote the first act or all five acts of my drama, which I called a comedy, while I waited for the moment of genius, much as if I expected an angel to appear to me.

My enthusiasm for mathematics may have had as its principal basis my loathing for hypocrisy, which for me meant my aunt Séraphie, Mme Vignon and their priests.

In my view, hypocrisy was impossible in mathematics and, in my youthful simplicity, I thought it must be so in all the sciences

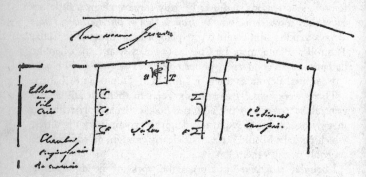

FF. Big arm-chairs embroidered by my mother (Mme Henriette Gagnon) – T. Her son's work-table – H. Me at work. [*Rue Vieux-Jésuites – My mother's room, always shut up. Blackboard of oil-cloth – Drawing-room – My father's study.*]

to which, as I had been told, they were applied. What a shock for me to discover that nobody could explain to me how it happened that: minus multiplied by minus equals plus $(- \times - = +)$! (This is one of the fundamental bases of the science known as *algebra*.)

Not only did people not explain this difficulty to me (and it is surely explainable, since it leads to truth), but, what was much worse, they explained it on grounds which were evidently far from clear to themselves.

M. Chabert, when I pressed him, grew confused, repeating his *lesson*, that very lesson against which I had raised objections, and eventually seemed to tell me: 'But it's the custom; everybody accepts this explanation. Why, Euler and Lagrange, who presumably were as good as you are, accepted it! We know you're very clever (which meant: we know you won first prize for *literature* and spoke well in front of M. *Teste-Lebeau* and the other Members for the Département). It seems you want to draw attention to yourself.'

As for M. Dupuy, he treated my timid objections (timid because of his pompous way of speaking) with a haughty smile that verged on aloofness. Although much less clever than M. Chabert, he was less bourgeois, less narrow-minded, and perhaps estimated more correctly his own knowledge of mathematics. If I could see these gentlemen for a week at the present time, I should immediately know what to think of them. But I always have to come back to that.

Brought up like a hot-house plant by relatives whose despair made them even more narrow-minded, having absolutely no contact with me, I felt things keenly at fifteen, but I was far less capable than another child of judging men and seeing through their various pretences. So really I don't put much trust in all the judgements with which I have filled the preceding 536 pages. The only part that's undoubtedly true is my *feelings*, only to reach the truth one must raise what I have said to four sharps.

[*Four sharps.*]

I express my feelings with the coldness of a man of forty whose senses are blunted by experience.

I distinctly remember that when I spoke of my difficulty about *minus multiplied by minus* to one of the *brilliant pupils* he laughed in my face; all of them were more or less like Paul-Émile Teisseire and learnt things by heart. I often saw them ending their demonstrations at the blackboard by saying: '*It is thus evident,*' etc.

It's far from evident to you, I used to think. But to me the things in question were evident and could not be doubted, however hard one tried.

Mathematics deals only with one small aspect of things (their quantity), but on this point (and that's its charm) it only says what is certain; it speaks the truth, and almost the whole truth.

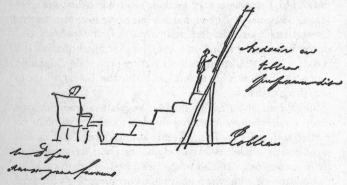

[*Slate, or rather blackboard – Blackboard – M. Dupuis in his big armchair.*]

In 1797, at fourteen years old, I imagined that higher mathematics, which I never learnt, covered all, or almost all, aspects of things, and that thus if I went on I should succeed in learning certain indubitable facts, which I could prove to myself as I chose, about *everything*.

It was a long time before I convinced myself that my objection about $- \times - = +$ simply couldn't enter M. Chabert's head, that M. Dupuy would never reply to it save by a haughty smile, and that the *brilliant ones* to whom I put my questions would always make fun of me.

I was reduced to what I still say to myself today: It must be true that $- \times -$ equals $+$, since evidently, by constantly using this rule in one's calculations one obtains results *whose truth cannot be doubted*.

My great worry was this:

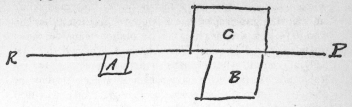

Let RP be the line separating the positive from the negative, all that is above it being positive, all that is below negative; how, taking the square B as many times as there are units in the square A, can one make it change over to the side of square C?

And, to use an awkward comparison which M. Chabert's pronounced Grenoblois drawl made even more clumsy, let us suppose that the negative quantities are a man's debts; how, by multiplying a debt of 10,000 francs by 500 francs, can this man have, or hope to have, a fortune of 5,000,000 francs?

Are M. Dupuy and M. Chabert hypocrites like the pr[iests] who come to say [Mass] at my grandfather's, and can my beloved mathematics be a fraud? I didn't know how to reach the truth. Oh, how eagerly I would have listened then to one word about logic, or the art of *finding out the truth*! This would have been the right moment to explain M. de Tracy's *Logic* to me! I might have become a different man; I should have had a far better mind.

I concluded, with my wretched little powers, that M. Dupuy might indeed be a deceiver, but M. Chabert was a conceited bourgeois who couldn't admit the existence of objections which he had not considered.

My father and my grandfather had the folio *Encyclopedia* of Diderot and d'Alembert, which is, or rather was, a work costing 700 or 800 francs. It takes a great deal to make a provincial lay out so much capital on books, from which I conclude today that before I was born my father and my grandfather must have been completely on the side of the *philosophes*.

My father was always sorry to see me looking through the *Encyclopedia*. I have the utmost trust in this book on account of my father's aversion for it and the definite hatred which it inspired in the priests who frequented the house. Rey, grand-vicaire and canon, a great papier mâché figure five feet ten inches tall, used to make a peculiar grimace as he mispronounced the names of Diderot and d'Alembert. This grimace gave me a deep, secret delight; I am still extremely liable to that sort of pleasure. I tasted it sometimes in 1815 when I saw noblemen refusing to admit the courage of Nicolas Buonaparte, as that great man was then called, and yet back in 1807 I had passionately hoped that he would not conquer England, for then where could one escape to?

I therefore tried to consult d'Alembert's mathematical articles in the *Encyclopedia*; their self-complacent tone, the absence of any cult for truth shocked me deeply, and moreover I understood very little of them. How ardently I worshipped truth in those days! How sincerely I believed it the queen of that world into which I was about to enter! I could not conceive of its having any other enemies but priests.

If $- \times - = +$ had distressed me, you can imagine what gloom possessed my soul when I opened *Statics*, by Louis Monge, brother of the illustrious Monge, who was to come and examine us for the École Polytechnique.

At the beginning of geometry textbooks we read: *Lines are called parallel when, if produced to infinity, they would never meet.* And at the beginning of his *Statics*, that egregious ass Louis Monge writes something like this: *Two parallel lines can be considered as meeting if produced to infinity.*

I thought I must be reading a catechism, and a very clumsy one at that. In vain I asked M. Chabert for an explanation.

'My boy,' he said, assuming that fatherly air which suits the foxy Dauphinois so ill, an air like Édouard Mounier's (Peer of France in 1836), 'my boy, you'll learn that later on'; and the monster, going up to his oil-cloth blackboard and drawing on it two parallel lines very close together,

———————————————

———————————————

said to me: 'Surely you see that they can be said to meet at infinity.'

I nearly gave it all up. A confessor who was skilful and a good

Jesuit could have converted me at that moment by commenting on this remark as follows: 'You see that everything is fallacious, or rather that there is nothing false and nothing true, everything is a matter of convention. Adopt the convention which will get you the best reception in society. Now the rabble is patriotic and will always defile that side of the question: become an aristocrat like your relatives, and we'll find some means to send you to Paris and introduce you to influential ladies.'

CHAPTER 35

IF THIS had been said enthusiastically, I should have become a scoundrel and by now, 1836, I should be extremely rich.

At thirteen, my picture of society was based exclusively on the *Secret Memoirs* of Duclos and the *Memoirs* of Saint-Simon in seven volumes. Supreme happiness consisted of living in Paris and writing books on 100 louis a year. Marion told me that my father would leave me more than that.

I think I said to myself: *true or false, mathematics will get me out of Grenoble*, out of this mire that makes me sick.

But this argument seems to me rather too advanced for my age. I went on with my work – it would have been too distressing to interrupt it – but I was deeply disturbed and depressed.

At last, as luck would have it, I saw a great man and I did not become a scoundrel. Here, once again, *the tale is greater than the teller*. I shall try not to exaggerate.

Adoring mathematics as I did, I had for some time past heard speak of a young man, a dyed-in-the-wool Jacobin, a great and fearless sportsman, who understood mathematics far better than MM. Dupuy and Chabert but did not teach it professionally. Only, as he was not at all rich, he had given some lessons to that sly-minded fellow Anglès (later Count and Prefect of Police, and made rich by Louis XVIII at the time of his loans).

But I was timid; how could I dare approach him. And besides his lessons were horribly expensive, twelve sous a lesson, how could I pay? (This charge seems too ridiculous, it may have been twenty-four or forty sous.)

I told all this, out of the fullness of my heart, to my kind aunt Élisabeth, who may then have been eighty years old but whose good heart and even better mind, if that's possible, were those of a woman of thirty. She generously gave me a number of six-franc pieces. But it was not the money that distressed my aunt, whose soul was full of the most legitimate and sensitive pride, but the fact that I had to take these lessons *without my father's knowledge*; to what well-founded and justifiable reproaches was she not exposing herself? Was Séraphie still living? I can't swear

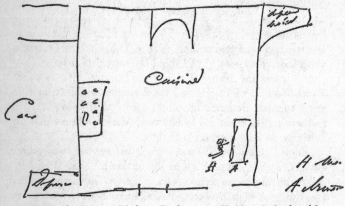

[*Courtyard – Pantry – Kitchen – Dark pantry – H. Me – A. Cupboard.*]

to the contrary. And yet I must have been quite a child at the time of aunt Séraphie's death, for when I heard of it, standing in the kitchen beside Marion's cupboard, I fell on my knees to thank God for so great a deliverance.

This event, the six-franc pieces so nobly given me by my aunt Élisabeth, to enable me to take lessons in secret from that dreadful Jacobin, prevented me from ever becoming a scoundrel. To see a man made on the model of the Greeks and Romans, and then wish to die rather than not be like him, took but an instant: *punto* (*Non sia che un punto*. Alfieri).

I don't know how, timid as I was, I made contact with M. Gros. (Here the fresco has fallen away, and I should only be a contemptible romancer, like Don Rugiero Caetani, if I undertook

308

to fill the gap. Allusion to the frescoes of the Campo Santo at Pisa and their present condition.)

Without knowing how I got there, I can see myself in the little room which Gros occupied in Saint-Laurent, the oldest and poorest district of the town; it is a long narrow street huddled between the mountain and the river. I did not go into this little room alone, but who was my fellow student? Was it Cheminade? This I have utterly forgotten; the whole attention of my mind must have been fixed on Gros. (This great man died so long ago that I think I can omit the Monsieur.)[1]

He was a young man with darkish blond hair, very active but very stout; he may have been twenty-five or twenty-six; his hair was very curly and fairly long, he wore a dressing-gown, and he said to us: 'Citizens, what shall we start with? Let's see what you know already.'

'Why, we know quadratic equations.'

And, like a sensible fellow, he began showing us how to do these equations, that's to say forming the square of $a+b$, for instance, which he made us raise to the second power: $a^2 + 2ab + b^2$, supposing the first member of the equation to be the beginning of a square, the complement of this square, etc., etc.

This was a glimpse of Heaven for us, or at least for me. At last I saw the reason for things; this wasn't one of those Heaven-sent apothecary's prescriptions for solving equations.

I felt a keen delight, like that of reading an enthralling novel. It must be admitted that everything Gros told us about quadratic equations was, more or less, in that dreadful book by Bezout, but there we did not deign to see it. It was so wretchedly set out that I couldn't bother to pay attention to it.

At the third or fourth lesson we went on to cubic equations, and here Gros was completely new. It seems to me that he transported us straight away to the extreme frontier of science, face to face with the difficulty to be overcome, or before the veil which had to be lifted. For instance he showed us one after the other the various ways of solving cubic equations, the first attempts of *Cardan* perhaps, then improved methods, and finally the present method.

1. To be placed: Races at la Grande-Chartreuse, at Sarcenas.

We were greatly surprised that he did not make us each in turn demonstrate the same proposition. As soon as we had really understood one thing he went on to the next.

Although there was absolutely nothing of the charlatan about Gros, he achieved the effect of that quality which is as useful to a teacher as to an army general; he took possession of my whole soul. I adored and respected him so much that I may have displeased him. I have so often encountered this unwelcome and surprising reaction that my memory may be at fault when I attribute it to the best of my passionate admirations. I

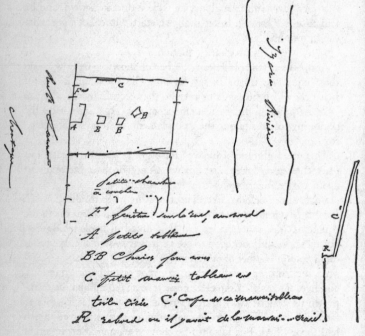

[*Mountain – Rue Saint-Laurent – River Isère – Small bedroom – F. Window on to the street, looking north – A. Small table – BB. Our chairs – C. Bad little blackboard of oil-cloth – R. Ledge where there was some bad chalk that crumbled in one's fingers when one wrote on the board. I've never seen anything so wretched.*]

310

displeased M. de Tracy and Mme Pasta by admiring them too enthusiastically.[1]

One day of important news we talked politics during the whole lesson, and at the end of it he refused to take our money. I was so used to the money-grabbing ways of Dauphinois teachers, MM. Chabert, Durand, etc., that this straightforward action intensified my admiration and my enthusiasm. I think there were three of us on this occasion, possibly Cheminade, Félix Faure and myself, and I think too we had each put down a twelve sou piece on the small table A.

I remember hardly anything about the last two years, 1798 and 1799. My passion for mathematics absorbed my time so entirely that, as Félix Faure told me, I wore my hair too long then, so much did I *grudge* the half-hour that must be wasted on getting it cut.

Towards the end of summer 1799 my patriotic citizen's heart was deeply grieved at our defeats in Italy, Novi and the rest, which caused my relatives keen delight, mingled, however, with anxiety. My grandfather, who was more reasonable, hoped that the Russians and Austrians would not reach Grenoble. But to tell the truth I can hardly speak about my family's wishes except by supposition, for the hope of leaving home shortly and my keen straightforward love for mathematics absorbed me so deeply that I paid very little attention to what my relatives were saying. I felt, although perhaps I did not formulate it clearly to myself: as things stand with me now, what do I care about such drivel!

Soon a selfish dread began to mingle with my patriotic grief. I was afraid lest, on account of the approach of the Russians, there would be no examination held in Grenoble.

Bonaparte landed at Fréjus. I accuse myself of sincerely wishing that this young Bonaparte, whom I pictured as a handsome youth like a colonel in a comic opera, might make himself King of France.

The term suggested to me nothing but ideas of brilliance and nobility. This stupid mistake was the fruit of my still more stupid

1. 29 J[anuar]y 1836. Rain and cold weather, a walk to San Pietro in Montorio where I'd had the idea of this towards 1832.

education. My relatives behaved like lackeys with regard to the King. The very names King and Bourbon brought tears to their eyes.

I don't know whether I experienced this absurd feeling in 1797, while revelling in the story of the battles of Lodi, Arcole, etc., etc., which distressed my relatives, who for a long time tried not to believe in them; or whether I experienced it in 1799 on hearing the news of the landing at Fréjus. I incline towards 1797.

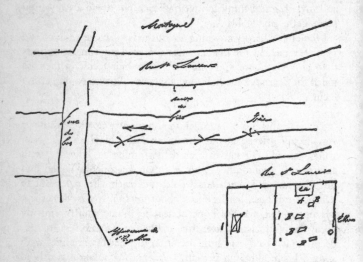

[*Mountain – Rue Saint-Laurent – Gros' house – Wooden bridge – Isère – Bigillions' apartment – Rue St-Laurent – Table – Blackboard.*]

Actually the approach of the enemy meant that M. Louis Monge, examiner for the École Polytechnique, did not come to Grenoble. We should have to go to Paris, we all told ourselves. But, I wondered, how could I get leave from my relatives for such a journey? To go to that modern Babylon, the city of corruption, at sixteen and a half! I was extremely worried, but I remember nothing distinctly.

The examinations on M. Dupuy's course of lectures were held, and resulted in a triumph for me.

I won the first prize over the heads of eight or nine youths,

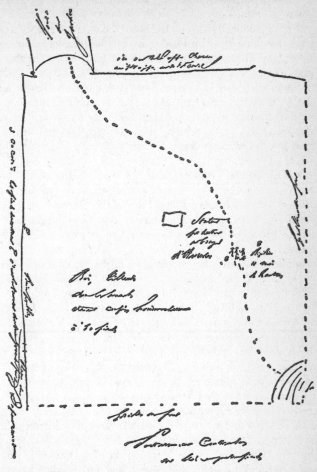

[*Garden vault – Here on the second floor Charvet's apartment, on the first M. Faure's – Bronze pedestrian statue of Hercules – B. Bigillion – H. Me. A. 2 others – Iron railings – Trees, limes whose branches were cut horizontally at thirty feet – Iron railings – Gate – Flower-bed at a level three or four feet lower – Public baths – Place du Département – On this side, twenty feet from this wall P, was my grandfather's terrace.*]

most of them older and enjoying greater favour than myself, all of whom two months later were received as pupils at the École Polytechnique.

I spoke eloquently at the blackboard, because I was speaking on a subject about which I had reflected with passionate interest for at least fifteen months, and which I had studied for three years (this to be verified, from the opening of M. Dupuy's course in the ground-floor hall of the Central School). M. Dausse, an obstinate and learned man, asked me the most difficult questions, the ones most likely to embarrass me. He was a man of terrible appearance and never encouraged one. (He looked like Domeni-coni, an excellent actor whom I've been admiring at the *Valle* in January 1836.)

M. Dausse, chief engineer, a friend of my grandfather (who was present, delightedly, at my examination) added to the first prize a quarto volume of Euler. Possibly this present was given me in 1798, a year at the end of which I again won the first prize for mathematics. (M. Dupuy's was a two- or even a three-year course.)

Immediately after the examination, in the evening, or rather the evening of the day when my name was billed so gloriously ('But in view of the way in which Citizen B ... answered, of the accuracy, the brilliant facility ...' this was the final effort of M. Dupuy's diplomacy: under pretext of not injuring my seven or eight schoolfellows, of spoiling their chances of admission to the École Polytechnique, he had gone so far as to award them the first prize, but M. Dausse, who was as obstinate as the devil, had some such phrase as the above inserted in the report and consequently printed), I see myself walking among the trees in the Jardin de Ville, between the Statue of Hercules and the gate, with Bigillion and two or three others wild with excitement at my triumph, for everybody considered it fair and it was obvious that M. Dupuy had no love for me; the rumour that I, who was privileged to attend his course, had been taking lessons from that Jacobin Gros, was not likely to endear me to M. Dupuy.

So, as we walked that way, I said to Bigillion, philosophizing as was our wont:

'At such a moment one could forgive all one's enemies.'

'On the contrary,' Bigillion said, 'one should go up to them and crush them.'

It's true that my delight had gone to my head a little, and I was making arguments in order to conceal this, and yet at bottom this reply marks the profound common sense of Bigillion, more down to earth than I was, and at the same time it marks that exaltation *à l'espagnole* to which I've unfortunately been a prey all my life.

I remember circumstances: Bigillion, my schoolfellows and I, had just been reading the notice with the phrase about myself.

Under the archway there was posted up on the door of the Concert Hall the report on the examinations, signed by the members of the Administration of the Département.

After this triumphant examination I went to Claix. I was in urgent need of rest. But I had one desperate worry, about which I brooded in the little wood of Doyatières and amongst the thickets of the Chemin des Ilots, alongside the Drac and on the 45 degree slope of the hillside of Comboire (I only carried my gun for form's sake). Would my father give me the money to take the plunge into that new Babylon, that centre of immorality, at sixteen and a half?

Here once again excess of passion, of emotion, has destroyed all recollection. I have no idea how my departure was arranged.

I was supposed to be examined a second time by M. Dupuy; I was worn out, exhausted with work, my strength was really at breaking-point. To revise arithmetic, geometry, trigonometry, algebra, conic sections, statics, so as to undergo a fresh examination, was an appalling task. I was really at the end of my tether. This new effort which in fact I had been expecting, but only in December, would have made me take a violent dislike to my beloved mathematics. Fortunately the laziness of M. Dupuy, who was busy harvesting his grapes in Noyarey, came to the aid of my own laziness. He told me, calling me *tu*, which was his great token of favour, that he was well aware of what I knew, that a fresh examination was unnecessary, and with a dignified and priestly air he gave me a superb certificate certifying an untruth, namely that he had made me undergo a fresh examination for my admission to the École Polytechnique and that I had passed it extremely well.

My uncle offered me two or four gold louis, which I refused. My excellent grandfather and my aunt Élisabeth probably gave me presents about which I have no recollection.

It was settled that I should travel with a certain M. Rosset, an acquaintance of my father's returning to Paris, where he had settled.

What I'm going to tell is not very nice. When I was about to leave, and was waiting for the carriage, I said good-bye to my father under the windows of the houses opposite the rue Montorge.

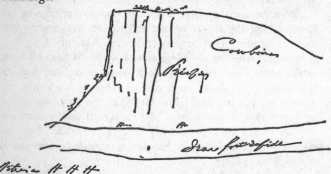

[*Comboire – Precipices – Drac, flowing very fast – I was at H H H.*]

He was weeping a little. The only impression made on me by his tears was that he looked very ugly. If the reader is revolted by this, let him deign to remember the hundreds of forced walks to *les Granges* with aunt Séraphie, walks which I was forced to take *for my own pleasure*. It was this hypocrisy which irritated me most and which made me conceive such a loathing for that vice.

Emotion has driven away absolutely every recollection of my journey with M. Rosset from Grenoble to Lyons, and from Lyons to Nemours.

It was at the beginning of November 1799, for at Nemours, twenty or twenty-five leagues from Paris, we heard of the events of the 18th Brumaire (or 9 November 1799) which had occurred the day before.

We heard of them in the evening, I understood very little

about them, and I was delighted that young General Bonaparte was going to be King of France. My grandfather used to talk frequently and with enthusiasm about Philippe-Auguste and Bouvines; I pictured any King of France as being like Philippe-Auguste, Louis XIV, or that voluptuary Louis XV, of whom I had read in the *Secret Memoirs* of Duclos.

Voluptuousness was in no way detrimental to the picture I had conceived. My fixed idea when I arrived in Paris, the idea to which I recurred four or five times a day and particularly at nightfall, at that moment of reverie, was that a pretty woman, a Parisian woman far more beautiful than Mme Kubly or my poor Victorine, would have a carriage accident in my presence or run into some great danger from which I should rescue her, and I should proceed to become her lover. My argument was a hunter's argument: I should love her with such rapture that I'm bound to find her!

This madness, which I never confessed to anyone, lasted for possibly six years. I was somewhat cured of it only by the aridity of the Court ladies at Brunswick amongst whom I started my career in November 1806.

CHAPTER 36

Paris

M. ROSSET deposited me in an hotel at the corner of the rue de Bourgogne and the rue Saint-Dominique; the entrance was in the rue Saint-Dominique. The idea was that I should be close to the École Polytechnique, which I was supposed to be entering.

I was amazed to hear the bells chiming the hours. The surroundings of Paris had seemed to me horribly ugly – there were no mountains! This disgust increased rapidly during the following days.

I left the hotel and for economy took a room on the Quincunx of the Invalides. I was looked after and shown around a little by the *mathematicians* who had entered the École the year before. I had to go and see them.

This was literally the first visit I paid in my life.

M. Daru, a man of the world, about sixty-five years of age, must have been dreadfully shocked by my gaucherie, which must have been singularly devoid of charm.

I had come to Paris with the firm intention of becoming a seducer of women, what I should today call a *Don Juan* (after Mozart's opera).

M. Daru had for a long time been secretary-general to M. de Saint-Priest, Intendant of Languedoc, which now, I believe, comprises seven Départements. It may be remembered from history books that the notorious Bastille, that gloomy tyrant, had been Intendant or rather King of Languedoc from 1685 to about 1710. It was a district having *États*, and this vestige of public discussion and liberty called for a clever secretary-general under an Intendant like M. de Saint-Priest, a sort of grandee, who may have been Intendant between 1775 and 1786.

M. Daru, a native of Grenoble, son of a bourgeois claiming noble birth, but poor out of pride, like the rest of my family, was a self-made man, and without stealing had collected some four or five hundred thousand francs. He had steered a skilful course through the Revolution, without letting himself be blinded by the love or hatred he might have had for prejudice, for the nobility or for the clergy. He was a man whose sole passion was for the profit to be derived from vanity or the vanity to be derived from what was profitable; I saw him from too far beneath him to discern which. He had bought a house in the rue de Lille, no. 505, at the corner of the rue de Bellechasse, in which, modestly, he only occupied the small apartment over the carriage gateway.

The first floor, at the end of the courtyard, was let to Mme Rebuffel, wife of a merchant of great ability, a man of warm feelings and character, quite the reverse of M. Daru. M. Rebuffel, M. Daru's nephew, got on with his uncle because he was by nature pliable and all things to all men.

M. Rebuffel used to come every day to spend a quarter of an hour with his wife and his daughter Adèle, and otherwise lived in his business and brokerage house in the rue Saint-Denis, with Mlle Barbereu his partner and mistress, an active, vulgar woman of thirty or thirty-five, who had every appearance of being unfaithful to her lover, making scenes and giving him a lively time of it.

I was greeted with affection and open-heartedness by the excellent M. Rebuffel, while M. Daru senior received me with affectionate and devoted remarks about my grandfather which made my heart ache and left me speechless.

M. Daru was a tall rather handsome old man with a big nose, which is quite uncommon in Dauphiné; he had a slight squint and a rather shifty look. With him was a dried-up little old woman, a regular provincial, who was his wife; he had married her long ago for the sake of her considerable fortune, and moreover she dared not open her mouth in front of him.

Mme Daru was kind at bottom, and very polite, with a dignified little air suitable to the wife of a provincial sub-prefect. Moreover I have never met a being more completely innocent of all celestial fire. Nothing in the world could have aroused noble or generous feelings in her soul. For such people, the most selfish sort of prudence, on which they pride themselves, replaces any wrathful or generous feeling.

The same prudent, reasonable but unlovable disposition was characteristic of her eldest son, M. le Comte Daru, Minister and Secretary of State under Napoleon, who had so much influence on my life, of Mlle Sophie, subsequently Mme de Baure, who was deaf, and of Mme Le Brun, now Marquise de Grave. Her second son, Martial Daru, had neither brains nor wit, but he was good-hearted and could not possibly have done any harm to anybody.

Mme Cambon, the eldest daughter of M. and Mme Daru, may perhaps have had a lofty character, but I caught only a glimpse of her; she died a few months after my arrival in Paris.

Need I point out that I am sketching the characters of these people as I have seen them since? The final outline, which seems to me the true one, has made me forget all previous outlines (to use a term of drawing).

I remember only certain impressions of my first entry into M. Daru's drawing-room.

For instance I can clearly see the little dress of red printed calico worn by a nice little girl of five, M. Daru's grand-daughter, with whom he played just as Louis XIV, old and bored, did with

Mme la Duchesse de Bourgogne. This nice little girl, without whom a gloomy silence would often have reigned in the little drawing-room in the rue de Lille, was Mlle Pulchérie Le Brun (today Mme la Marquise de Brossard, a very imperious woman, so they say, the size of a barrel, and who rules her husband with a rod of iron, M. le Général de Brossard, who himself rules over the Département of Drôme).

M. de Brossard is a spendthrift who lays claim to the highest nobility, a descendant of Louis le Gros I believe, a braggart, an intriguer who is quite unscrupulous as to the means by which he tries to restore his permanently chaotic finances. In sum: the character of an impoverished nobleman, an unpleasant character and one which usually involves a host of misfortunes. (I call a man's *character* his habitual manner of pursuing happiness, or, in clearer but less significant terms: *the sum total of his moral habits.*)

But I'm wandering from the point. I was far from seeing things, even physical things, so clearly in December 1799. I was all feeling, and this excess of feeling has left me with only a few very clear pictures, but no explanation of the hows and whys.

What I see very clearly today, and what I felt vaguely in 1799, is that on my arrival in Paris two things which I had constantly and passionately desired suddenly dwindled to nothing. I had adored Paris and mathematics. Paris, having no mountains, inspired in me a loathing so profound that it amounted almost to homesickness. Mathematics had become for me nothing more than the framework of last night's firework display (a thing I saw at Turin, the day after Midsummer Night 1802).

I was tormented by these changes of which, at sixteen and a half, I naturally could not see the *why* nor the *how*.

Actually, I had only loved Paris out of deep loathing for Grenoble.

As for mathematics, it had only been a means to an end. I even hated it a little in November 1799, for I was afraid of it. I was determined not to take an examination in Paris, like the seven or eight pupils who had won first prize after me at the Central School, and who had all passed. Now if my father had taken the least trouble he could have forced me to take this examination; I should have entered the École and I could no longer have *lived in Paris writing comedies*.

Of all my passions, this was the only one I still retained.

I cannot conceive, and this idea occurs to me for the first time thirty-seven years after the events, as I write this I cannot conceive how it was that my father did not force me to take the examination. He probably trusted to the extreme passion for mathematics with which he had seen me possessed. Moreover my father was only moved by what was close by him. Nevertheless I was madly afraid of being forced to enter the École, and I awaited with extreme impatience the announcement of the beginning of the course. In the *exact sciences* it is impossible to start a course at the third lecture.

Let's turn to the impressions I still remember.

I see myself taking medicine, alone and forlorn in a cheap room I had rented on the quincunx of the Invalides at the far end, between the end of the rue de l'Université and that of the rue Saint-Dominique (on that side of the quincunx), a stone's throw from the Emperor's Civil List mansion where I was, a few years later, to play such a different role.

My profound disappointment at finding Paris so unpleasant had upset my stomach. The mud of Paris, the absence of mountains, the sight of so many busy people driving swiftly past in fine carriages, whereas nobody knew me and I had nothing to do, made me profoundly unhappy.

Any doctor who had taken the trouble to study my condition, which was certainly not a complicated one, would have given me an emetic and ordered me to go out every three days to Versailles or Saint-Germain.

I fell into the hands of one who was an arrant quack and even more of an ignoramus, an army surgeon, a very thin man, living in the neighbourhood of the Invalides, at that time a very poor district, and whose job it was to attend to students of the École Polytechnique who were suffering from *blennorrhagie*. He gave me some black medicine which I took, alone and deserted, in my room which had only one window seven or eight feet up, like a prison. I see myself there, sadly sitting by a little iron stove, with my cup of tisane on the floor beside me.

But my greatest misery, in this state, was the constantly recurring thought: 'Good Heavens, what a disappointment! What is there to hope for?'

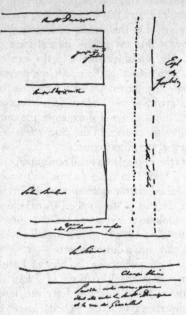

[*Esplanade des Invalides – Avenues of trees – Rue Saint-Dominique – Lodging-house where I lived – Rue de l'Université – Palais Bourbon – Quay, at that time unpaved and very muddy – The Seine – Champs-Elysées – Perhaps our lodging-house was between the rue Saint-Dominique and the rue de Grenelle.*]

CHAPTER 37

IT MUST be admitted that this was a great, a shocking disillusionment. And it was a young man of sixteen and a half, one of the least reasonable and the most susceptible to emotion that I have ever met, who experienced it!

I trusted nobody.

I had heard the priests of Séraphie and my father *glory in* the ease with which they led, that's to say deluded, so-and-so or such-and-such a group of people.

R[eligion] appeared to me a black powerful machine; I still had a certain belief in h[ell] but none in its priests. The pictures of h[ell] that I had seen in the illustrated octavo B[ible] bound in green parchment, and in my poor mother's editions of Dante, horrified me; but the p[riests] did not. I was far from seeing religion as it really is, a powerful organization and one with which it is highly profitable to be connected, as witness my contemporary and compatriot young Genou, who, barelegged, often brought me my coffee at the Café Genou at the corner of the Grand'rue and the rue du Département and who, for the past twenty years in Paris, has been M. de Genoude.

I had nothing to fall back on but my common sense and my belief in Helvétius's *Esprit*. I say *belief* deliberately, for, brought up as I was in a vacuum, as it were, obsessed with ambition, and barely emancipated by being sent to the Central School, I inevitably found in Helvétius *the forecast of the things I was going to encounter*. I had confidence in this long-term forecast because two or three little predictions, as witnessed by my own short experience, had been confirmed.

I was not, like most of my companions, crafty, shrewd and suspicious, able to get the best of a sixpenny bargain by excessive cunning and suspicion, counting the number of sticks in the bundles of firewood provided by the landlord, like my friends the *Monvals*, whom I had just met again in Paris where they had been at the École for the past year. I walked the streets of Paris like a passionate dreamer, gazing at the sky and always on the point of being run over by a cab.

In a word, *I was not adept in the affairs of life* and consequently I could not be appreciated, as some newspaper of 1836 says this morning in the characteristic style of a journal trying to disguise the nullity or puerility of its thought by the unusualness of its style.

To have seen this truth about myself would have meant that I was adept in the affairs of life.

The Monval brothers used to give me very sage advice about saving myself from being robbed of two or three sous a day, and their ideas revolted me; they must have thought me an idiot halfway to the lunatic asylum. It's true that out of pride I seldom expressed my thoughts. I fancy it was the *Monvaux* or some other students who had come to the École a year previously who found me my room and my cheap doctor.

Was it Sinard? Had he died of consumption at Grenoble the year before, or did he die there only a year or two later?

In the midst of these friends, or rather these children, so full of common sense and haggling over three sous a day with the landlord, who made eight sous a day legitimately and stole three more from each of us poor wretches, eleven sous all told, *I was plunged into involuntary ecstasies, into interminable reveries, into infinite inventions* [1] (as the newspaper says pompously).

I had my list of the bonds which conflict with passions, for instance: *priest* and *love*, *father* and *love of one's country*, or *Brutus*, which seemed to me the key to the sublime in literature. I had invented the whole thing. I have forgotten it for about twenty-six years; I shall have to come back to it.

I was constantly in a state of profound emotion. What can I love if I dislike Paris? I told myself: 'A charming woman will have a carriage accident ten paces away from me; I shall come to her aid and we shall adore one another, she will understand my soul and see how different I am from the *Monvaux*.'

But being deadly serious, I used to give myself this answer two or three times a day, and especially *at nightfall*, which even now is often, for me, a moment of tender emotion; I feel ready to embrace my mistress (when I've got one) with tears in my eyes.

At that time I was a being in a constant state of emotion, never thinking, save in rare moments of anger, about preventing our landlady from robbing me of three sous' worth of *firewood*.

Dare I say it? But it may not be true; *I was a poet*. Not, indeed, one like that amiable abbé Delille whom I met two or three years later, through Cheminade (rue des Francs-Bourgeois, in the Marais); but like Tasso, like a hundredth part of Tasso, please forgive my pride. I had no such pride in 1799, I could not write a line of verse. It's only during the past four years that I've said

---

1. *Chatterton* by M. Vigny, p. 9.

to myself that in 1799 I must have been nearly a poet. I needed only the audacity to write, a *vent* by which *genius* might escape.

First *poet* and then *genius*, is that all?

'*His sensibility has grown too keen; that which touches others lightly wounds him to the quick.*' Such I was in 1799, such I still am in 1836, but I have learnt to hide all this under an irony unnoticed by the common herd, but correctly discerned by Fiori.

'*Affection and tenderness play an overwhelming and disproportionate part in his life, his excessive enthusiasms lead him astray, his sympathies are too sincere, those whom he pities suffer less than he does.*'

This describes me literally. (Apart from its pompousness and SELF-IMPORTANCE this newspaper is quite right.)

What distinguishes me from these silly self-important journalists *who carry their heads like the Holy Sacrament* is that I have never thought that society owed me the slightest thing. Helvétius saved me from such egregious stupidity. *Society rewards the services it can see.*

The mistake and misfortune of Tasso lay in thinking: 'What! cannot the whole of Italy, which is so rich, provide a pension of 200 sequins (2,200 francs) for its poet?' I read this in one of his letters.

For lack of Helvétius, Tasso could not see that the hundred men, out of ten million, who understand that sort of *Beauty* which is not merely an imitation or an improvement of that *Beauty* which the vulgar herd already understand, will need twenty or thirty years to convince the twenty thousand next most sensitive souls that this new sort of Beauty is really beautiful.

I must point out that there is an exception to this when party spirit is involved. M. de Lamartine has written about two hundred fine lines in his life. The ultra party, around 1818, being accused of *stupidity* (they were nicknamed M. de la Jobardière), he, in his wounded vanity, praised the work of some nobleman with all the vehemence of a stormy lake bursting its banks.[1]

I have never, then, had the idea that men were being unjust towards me. I find wholly ridiculous the unhappiness of all our

1. True. Power claims to be a stranger to intelligence of which it is jealous (*Chatt[erton]*).

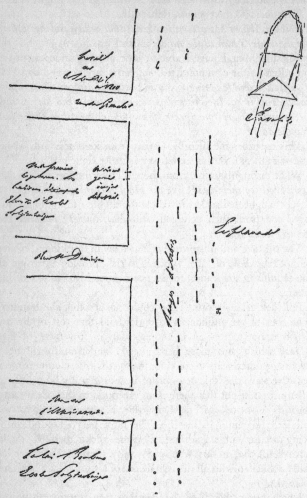

[*Invalides – Esplanade – Row of trees – Civil List mansion in 1810 – Rue de Grenelle – Lodging-house where I started off. My first lodging – The inmates were students at the École Polytechnique – Rue St-Dominique – Rue de l'Université – Palais Bourbon – École Polytechnique.*]

so-called poets who subsist on this idea and who blame the contemporaries of Cervantes and of Tasso.

I think my father allowed me at that time 100 or 150 francs a month. This was riches; I had no thought of needing money, consequently I never thought about money.

What I did need was somebody to love me, some woman.

I had a horror of whores. What would have been simpler than to pick up a pretty girl for a louis in the rue des Moulins, as I would today?

I was not short of louis. No doubt my grandfather and great-aunt Élisabeth had given me some, and I had certainly not spent them. But the smile of some loving heart! The glances of Mlle Victorine Bigillion!

All the sprightly tales, exaggerating the corruption and greed of whores told me by the mathematicians who at that time played the part of friends around me, made me sick.

They spoke of the *pierreuses*, the cheap whores on the flag-stones two hundred paces from the door of our wretched house.

What I needed was a friend. M. Sorel sometimes invited me to dinner, and so did M. Daru, I suppose, but these men seemed to me so remote from my sublime ecstasies, I was so shy, out of vanity, particularly with women, that I never spoke.

A woman? a girl? says Cherubino. Except as regards beauty I was Cherubino, I had very curly black hair and eyes that flashed terrifyingly.

The man I love, or *My lover is ugly, but nobody will ever criticize him for his ugliness, he's so intelligent*! That's what Mlle Victorine B[igillion] said, about that time, to Félix Faure, who only discovered a long time afterwards of whom she was speaking.

He was teasing his pretty neighbour, Mlle Victorine B[igillion], one day about her indifference. I fancy that Michel or Frédéric Faure, or Félix himself, would have liked to make love to Mlle Victorine.

F[éli]x Faure, Peer of France, Premier Président of the Royal Law Courts at Grenoble, a contemptible creature, *physically worn out*.

Frédéric Faure, a subtle Dauphinois, devoid of any generous feeling or any wit, died a captain of artillery at Valence.

Michel, shrewder still, more Dauphinois still, and maybe not very brave, a captain of the Imperial Guard, whom I knew in Vienna in 1809, master of the workhouse at Saint-Robert near Grenoble (from whom I drew M. Valenod in the *Rouge*). Bigillion, a very good-hearted man, honest and very thrifty, chief clerk of the County Court, killed himself about 1827, distressed, I believe, at being a cuckold but without any anger against his wife.

I don't want to describe myself as an unhappy lover on my arrival in Paris, November 1799, nor indeed as a lover at all. I was too preoccupied with society, and with what I was going to do in society, about which I knew nothing.

This problem was my mistress; hence my idea that love, before one has entered a profession and made one's entry into society, cannot be as devoted and whole-hearted as it is with someone who thinks himself familiar with society.

Nevertheless I often dreamed with rapture about our Dauphiné mountains; and Mlle Victorine used to spend several months every year at the Grande-Chartreuse, where her ancestors had received Saint Bruno in 1100. The Grande-Chartreuse was the only mountain I knew; I think I had already been there once or twice with Bigillion and Rémy.

I remembered Mlle Victorine with tender affection, but I never doubted for an instant that a Parisian girl would be a hundred times superior to her. And yet my first impression of Paris aroused supreme dislike.

This profound dislike, this disillusionment, combined with my worthy doctor made me rather ill, I believe. I could no longer eat anything.

Did M. Daru senior have me looked after in this first illness of mine?

I have a sudden picture of myself in a room on the third floor overlooking the rue du Bac; this lodging was reached through the Passage Sainte-Marie, now so much altered and improved. My room was an attic, and the last floor on the sordid staircase.

I must have been very ill, for M. Daru senior brought in the famous Dr Portal, whose face terrified me. He wore a resigned look as if he were seeing a corpse. I was given a nurse, which was something quite new for me.

I have since learnt that I was threatened with dropsy of the chest. I think I was delirious, and I spent quite three weeks or a month in bed.

I fancy Félix Faure came to see me. I think he told me, and on thinking it over I'm sure of it, that in my delirium I exhorted him, as being a good fencer, to go back to Grenoble and challenge to a duel those who should jeer at us for not having entered the

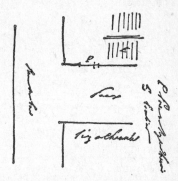

[*Rue du Bac – Passage – Ground floor – P. Ground floor door – G. Staircase.*]

École Polytechnique. If I ever speak again to the man who tried the April prisoners, I must ask him about our life in 1799. That cold-hearted, timid and selfish creature is sure to remember things clearly and besides, he must be two years older than myself and must have been born in 1781.

I can see two or three pictures of my convalescence.

My nurse cooking my beef broth by my fireside, which seemed to me *sordid*; and I was strongly warned not to catch cold; as

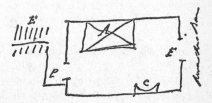

A. Bed in which I nearly died – E. Sordid staircase – C. Fireplace – F. Attic window overlooking the rue du Bac. [*Rue du Bac.*]

I was supremely bored with being in bed, I paid heed to the warnings. I was shocked by the physical details of living in Paris.

Without any interval after my illness, I can see myself lodged in a room on the second floor of M. Daru's house, no. 505, rue de Lille (or rue de Bourbon when there are Bourbons in France). This room overlooked four gardens, it was rather large, and partly an attic; the [ceiling] between the two windows sloped at an angle of 45 degrees.

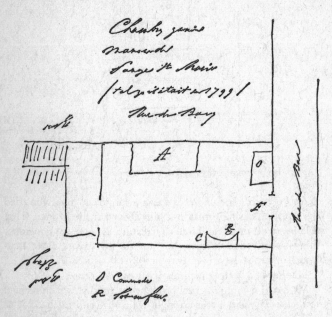

[*Furnished room, attic. Passage Ste-Marie (as it was in 1799, rue du Bac) – Rue du Bac – 3rd floor – O. Chest of drawers – R. Beef broth.*]

This room suited me very well. I made a notebook of paper to write plays on.

It was at this time, I believe, that I ventured to go to M. Cailhava's to buy a copy of his *Art of Comedy* which I could not find at any bookseller's. I unearthed this old Gascon in a room in the Louvre, I think. He told me that his book was badly written, which I bravely denied. He must have taken me for a lunatic.

I never found more than one idea in that confounded book, and that was not Cailhava's own but was, in fact, Bacon's. But isn't it something to have one idea, in a book? This one was a definition of *laughter*.

My passionate cohabitation with mathematics left me with an ardent love for good *definitions*, without which everything is only approximate.

CHAPTER 38

BUT once I had the art of comedy on my table, I seriously discussed this great question : should I become a composer of operas, like Grétry ? or a writer of comedies?

I hardly knew my notes (M. Mantion had dismissed me as unworthy to play the violin), but I told myself : notes are only the art of writing down one's ideas, the essential thing is to

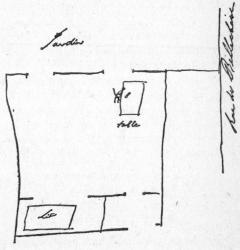

[*Garden – Rue de Bellechasse – Table – Bed* .]

have them. And I thought I had. The odd thing is that I still think so, and I often feel sorry I did not leave Paris and go to be Paisiello's servant in Naples. I have no taste for purely instrumental music, even the music of the Sistine Chapel and of the choir of the Chapter-house at St Peter's gives me no pleasure (this opinion confirmed 18 January 1836, the day of the *Catedra* of San Pietro).

Only vocal melody seems to me the product of genius. However learned a fool may become, he can never, to my mind, discover a fine melody, such as: *Se amor si gode in pace* (Act I, and perhaps Scene I, of the *Matrimonio Segreto*).

When a man of genius takes the trouble to study melody, he attains the fine instrumentation of the quartet in *Bianca e Faliero* (by Rossini) or the duet in *Armida* by the same composer.

In the heyday of my love of music, at Milan between 1814 and 1821, when on the morning of a new opera I went to collect my book of words at the *Scala*, I could not help making up all the music as I read it, singing the arias and duets. And dare I say it? Sometimes that evening I used to think my own melody *more noble* and *more tender* than that of the maestro.

As I was, and still am, totally unlearned, and knew no way of setting down the melody on a piece of paper so as to be able to correct it without fear of forgetting the original tune, it was like the first idea of a book that occurs to me. It is a hundred times more intelligible after I have worked on it. But still this first idea is something that can never be found in the books of mediocre writers. Their strongest phrases seem to me like *Priam's stroke: without strength*.

For instance I made up a charming tune, it seems to me, and I've seen the accompaniment to it, to these lines by La Fontaine (criticized by M. Nodier as lacking in piety, but that was in 1820 under the B[ourbon]s):

> *Un mort s'en allait tristement*
> *S'emparer de son dernier gîte;*
> *Un curé s'en allait gaiement*
> *Enterrer ce mort au plus vite.*

This is perhaps the only tune that I have written to French words. I hate being obliged to say *gi-teu, vi-teu*. The French seem to me outstandingly untalented for music, just as the Italians are astonishingly untalented for dancing.

Sometimes, when I am talking nonsense to myself on purpose, to make myself laugh, to provide jokes for the other side (which I am often perfectly conscious of within myself), I wonder: how could I ever have any talent for music like Cimarosa's, since I'm a Frenchman?

I answer: through my mother, whom I take after, I may perhaps be of Italian blood. The Gagnoni who fled to Avignon after murdering a man in Italy may perhaps have married the daughter of a man attached to the Vice-Legate.

My grandfather and my aunt Élisabeth had obviously Italian faces, with aquiline noses, etc.

And now that five years of continuous residence in Rome have made me more closely acquainted with the physical structure of the Romans, I can see that my grandfather had exactly the same figure, head and nose as a Roman.

What's more, my uncle Romain Gagnon had unmistakably an almost Roman head, except for his complexion, which was very good.

I have never known a beautiful song made by a Frenchman; the best of them do not rise above the crudity appropriate to a *popular* song, namely one that has to please everybody, such as:

> *Allons, enfants de la patrie ...*

by Captain Rouget de Lisle, which was made up in one night at Strasbourg.

This song seems to me infinitely better than anything else that ever came out of a French head, but by its very nature inferior to Mozart's:

> *Là ci darem la mano,*
> *Là mi dirai di sì ...*

I must confess that I find perfect beauty in the songs of only two composers: Cimarosa and Mozart, and I'll be hanged if I can honestly say which of the two I prefer.

When my ill luck has introduced me to two boring salons, it's always the one I have just left that seems to me the dreariest.

When I have been listening to Mozart and Cimarosa, it's always the one I've heard last which seems to me slightly preferable to the other.

Paisiello seems to me like a thin second-wine (*piquette*), which is quite pleasant and can even be drunk for choice and with pleasure at times when the full wine seems too strong.

I might say the same about some tunes by certain composers inferior to Paisiello, for instance: *Senza sposo non mi lasciate, signor governatore* (I don't remember the lines) out of the *Cantatrice Villane* by Fioravanti.

The worst of this *piquette* is that after a short while it seems *insipid*. You can only drink one glass of it.

Almost all authors have sold themselves to religion when they write about the races of men. The very few honest men confuse proven facts with hypotheses. It is when a science is in its infancy that a man who knows nothing about it, like myself, can venture to speak about it.

So I say that it is useless to expect a hound to have the intelligence of a spaniel, or a spaniel to tell you that six hours ago a hare passed this way.

There may be individual exceptions, but the general truth is that spaniels and hounds each have their own talent.

The same thing probably holds good about men.

What is certain, having been witnessed by myself and Constantin, is that we saw a whole section of Roman society (120, Bactacia, seen in 1834, I believe) which is exclusively preoccupied with music and can sing the finales of Rossini's *Semiramide* and the most difficult music extremely well, spend a whole evening waltzing to country-dance tunes, badly played as regards time, it must be admitted. Romans, and indeed Italians in general, are remarkably untalented for dancing.

I have put the cart before the horse on purpose not to disgust the Frenchman of 1880 when I venture to make him read that his forebears of 1830 were supremely untalented for judging or executing vocal music.

The French have become learned in this sphere since 1820, but they are still barbarians at heart; I need no further proof than the success of Meyerbeer's *Robert le Diable*.

They are less insensitive to German music, Mozart's excepted.

What a Frenchman enjoys in Mozart is not the terrible originality of the *song* in which Leporello invites the statue of the Commendatore to supper, but it is rather the accompaniment. Moreover, this essentially and pre-eminently *vain* creature has been told that this *duet* or *trio* is sublime.

A piece of rock containing iron, seen on the surface of the ground, may make one think that by digging a shaft and deep galleries one will succeed in finding a satisfactory quantity of metal, but then perhaps one will find nothing at all.

I was like that about music in 1799. Chance has led me to try to note down the sounds of my soul in printed pages. Laziness and the absence of an opportunity to learn the boring physical side of music, namely how to play the piano and set down my ideas, were largely responsible for this decision, which would have been quite different if I had found an uncle or a mistress who loved music. As for my passion, it has remained unaltered.

I would walk ten leagues through the mire, the thing I hate most in the world, to hear a good performance of *Don Giovanni*. If anybody quotes an Italian phrase out of *Don Giovanni*, immediately my tender memories of the music recur to me and take possession of me.

I have only one objection, but that not easy to understand: do I enjoy music as a *symbol*, as a reminder of the happiness of youth, or *for its own sake*?

I incline to the latter view. *Don Giovanni* delighed me before I had heard Bonoldi exclaim (at the Scala, Milan) through his little window:

> *Falle passar avanti,*
> *Di che ci fanno onor?*

But this subject is a tricky one, I'll return to it when I get involved in the discussions on art during my stay at Milan, from 1814 to 1821, which was so exciting and on the whole, I can say, the *flower of my life*.

Do I enjoy the aria: *Tra quattro muri*, sung by Mme Festa, as a symbol or for its intrinsic merit?

Doesn't *Per te ogni mese un pajo* from the *Pretendenti delusi* delight me as a symbol?

Yes, I'll grant the *symbolism* in the case of these two latter, but then I never acclaimed them as masterpieces. But I don't think there was anything symbolic about my feeling for the *Matrimonio Segreto*, which I heard sixty or a hundred times at the Odéon, sung by Mme Barilli, was it in 1803 or 1810?

Certainly no *opera d'inchiostro*, no work of literature gives me so keen a pleasure as *Don Giovanni*.

However, folio 14 of the new edition of de Brosses, which I read recently, in January 1836, came pretty near to it.

One great proof of my love for music is that Feydeau's comic operas make me *sour-tempered*.

When I had at my disposal my cousin Mme de Longueville's box, I could only sit through half a performance. I go to this theatre every two or three years, when my curiosity gets the better of me, and I come out before the second act, like the Vicomte,

> *'Le Vicomte indigné sortait au second acte'*

sour-tempered for the rest of the evening.

French opera, until 1830, soured me even more effectively, and I disliked it completely again in 1833, with Nourrit and Mme Damoreau.

I have spread myself on this subject because one is always a bad judge of one's own passions or tastes, particularly when these tastes are fashionable ones. There is not an affected young man in the Faubourg Saint-German, for instance M. de Blancmesnil, who does not profess to be mad about music. For my part, I loathe all *sentimental French music*. The *Panseron* puts me in a rage; it makes me hate the thing I love most passionately.

Good music sets me dreaming with delight about whatever is filling my heart at the moment. Hence the delicious moments I enjoyed at La Scala between 1814 and 1821.

CHAPTER 39

STAYING at M. Daru's was nothing; I had to dine there, which bored me to death.

I hated the cooking in Paris almost as much as its lack of mountains, and presumably for the same reason. I did not know what it was to be short of money. For these two reasons, I hated nothing worse than these dinners in M. Daru's tiny apartment.

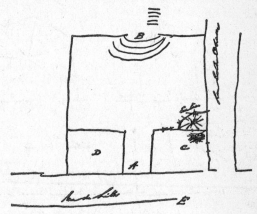

A. Carriage entry – B. Steps to porch. Spiral staircase to first floor. The whole of the first floor, A.C.D., M. Daru's apartment. The same space on the second floor, apartment of his sons MM. Pierre and Martial Daru – E. Steps leading to the staircase by which I went up to my room. [*Rue de Lille – Rue de Bellechasse – Staircase.*]

As I have said, it was situated above the main entrance.

It was in this drawing-room and this dining-room that I endured cruel sufferings while getting that education *through other people* from which my relatives had so judiciously protected me.

Polite and ceremonious manners, scrupulously observant of all the proprieties, even today freeze me and reduce me to silence. If in addition there is a suggestion of religiosity and a tendency to declaim about the great principles of morality, I'm done for.

You can imagine the effect of this poison in January 1800 applied to an inexperienced organism which, in its extreme attentiveness, absorbed every drop of it.

I would arrive in this drawing-room at half past five, I fancy, for dinner. There I would shudder at the prospect of having to

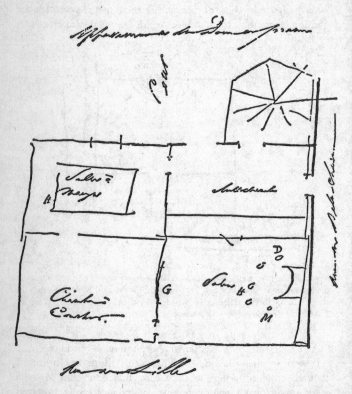

HH. Me – M. Mme Daru's armchair – D. M. Daru, senior – G. Big looking-glass with sofa in front of it. [*M. Daru's apartment on the first floor – Courtyard – Dining-room – Anteroom – Bedroom – Drawing-room – Rue de Bellechasse – Rue de Lille.*]

give my hand to Mlle Sophie, or Mme Cambon, or Mme Le Brun, or Mme Daru herself, and conduct them to table.

Mme Cambon gradually succumbed to an ailment which even then gave her a very yellow tinge. Mme Le Brun is now, in 1836, Marquise de Grave; Mlle Sophie has likewise become Mme de Baure. We have long since lost M. and Mme Daru

[*505 rue de Lille – My room – Hall – Anteroom – Bedroom – Drawing-room.*]

senior. Mlle Pulchérie Le Brun is Mme la Marquise de Brossard, in 1836. MM. Pierre and Martial Daru have died, the former about 1829 and the latter two or three years earlier.

At table, sitting at point H, I did not enjoy a single morsel I ate. I had a supreme dislike of Parisian cookery, and still have after so many years. But this annoyance meant nothing at my age, as I realized when I was able to go out to a restaurant.

It was the moral constraint that was killing me.

339

It was not, as in Grenoble, a feeling of injustice and of hatred for my aunt Séraphie.

If only I'd had nothing worse than that sort of unhappiness! It was far worse; it was the continual consciousness of things that I wanted to do and which were out of my reach.

[*Mme Daru – M. Daru, I think.*]

Imagine the extent of my misery! I who thought myself a combination of Saint-Preux and Valmont (in *Les Liaisons Dangereuses*, that imitation of *Clarissa* which has become the provincials' breviary), I, who, convinced of my own boundless capacity for loving and being loved, thought that only opportunity was lacking, I seemed to myself second-rate and awkward in every respect, among people whom I considered gloomy and depressing; how much worse would I have been in an agreeable salon!

So this was Paris, for which I had so longed!

Nowadays, I cannot imagine how I failed to go off my head between 10 November 1799, and 20 April, or thereabouts, when I left for Geneva.

I'm not sure that besides dinner I wasn't obliged to be present at luncheon too.

But how can I convey my folly? My picture of society was based solely and absolutely on the *Secret Memoirs* of Duclos, the three or seven volumes of Saint-Simon then published, and on novels.

I had only seen society, and then only in a very narrow sense, at Mme de Montmaur's, who was the original of Mme de Merteuil in *Les Liaisons Dangereuses*. She was old then, rich and lame. That I am sure of; as for morals, she objected to my being given only half a pickled walnut when I went to see her at *Le Chevallon*; she always insisted on my being given a whole one. 'It makes children so unhappy,' she would say. That's all I witnessed of her morals. Mme de Montmaur had rented or bought the house of the *Drevons*, young men-about-town who were close friends of my uncle R. Gagnon and who had practically ruined themselves.

These details about Mme de Montmaur, the original of Mme de Merteuil, may be out of place here, but I wanted to show by the story of the pickled walnuts the extent of my knowledge of society.

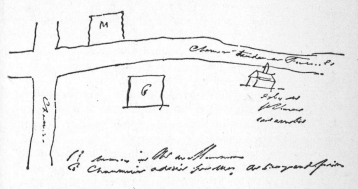

[*Path – Path leading to Fontanil – Church of St-Vincent, I think – M. Mme de Montmaur's house – G. My grandfather's cottage, which I adored.*]

That's not all, there's worse to follow. I often felt ashamed, even guilty, of the silence that too often reigned at the court of a bored, despotic old bourgeois like M. Daru senior.

This was my main grief. I thought a man should be a passionate lover and at the same time bring joy and liveliness into any social group in which he found himself.

And moreover this universal joyfulness, this art of pleasing everybody, ought not to be founded on the art of flattering all tastes and foibles. I had no inkling of all that side of the art of pleasing, which would no doubt have disgusted me; the amiability for which I longed was the pure joy of Shakespeare's comedies, the amiability that reigns at the court of the exiled Duke in the forest of Arden.

This pure, this light and airy amiability at the court of a bored, dissolute old prefect, who was also, I believe, devout ! ! !

Nothing could be more absurd, but my unhappiness, although based on *absurdity*, was none the less very real.

These silences, when I was in M. Daru's drawing-room, distressed me dreadfully.

What part did I play in this salon? I never opened my mouth there, according to what Mme Le Brun, Marquise de Grave, has since told me. Mme la Comtesse d'Oraison told me recently that Mme Le Brun is fond of me; I must ask her for some information about the sort of figure I cut in M. Daru's drawing-room on my first appearance there, at the beginning of 1800.[1]

I was dying of constraint, disappointment and dissatisfaction with myself. Who could have told me that the greatest joys in my life would fall to my lot five months later?

Fall is the right word, they fell from Heaven; but none the less they sprang from my own heart, and this was indeed my sole resource during the four or five months that I spent in my room at M. Daru senior's.

All the agonies of the drawing-room and dining-room disappeared when, alone in my room overlooking the gardens, I said to myself: 'Shall I become a composer of music, or else write comedies like Molière?' I felt, very vaguely indeed, that I did not know enough about the world or about myself to make up my mind.[2]

I was distracted from these lofty thoughts by another problem,

1. Dominique's folly. Dates: 4 March 1818. Beginning of a great musical phrase, *Piazza delle Galline*. It did not really end till rue du Faubourg Saint-Denis, May 1824–September 1826, San Remo.

2. *Sacrifice made:* Countess Sandre (8–17 February 1836). What is fine about this character is that the sacrifice was made at the Alibert Ball, on Tuesday, 16 February, when don F. spoke to me. The quarrel [between us] had lasted since the English Ball of 8 February 1836. (I learn through T. Human and M E.) I have only known my character since I have studied it, pen in hand, at fifty-three [years old]. I am so different from what I was twenty years ago that it seems to me that I am discovering things about someone else.

From 7th to 17th, nothing done, it seems to me. Rom[an]elli and Carnaval (Carnaval and first a long letter of fourteen closely-written pages about the Rom[ane]lli affair).

far more down to earth and far more urgent. M. Daru, like the punctilious man he was, could not understand why I did not enter the École Polytechnique, or, if this year was wasted, why I did not keep up my studies so as to sit for the next season's examinations in September 1800.

This stern old man gave me to understand, with great politeness and restraint, that we should have to have the matter out. It was precisely this restraint and politeness, so new to me, who heard myself addressed as Monsieur by a relative for the first time in my life, which gave rein to my crazy timidity and imagination.

I can explain this now. Basically, I understood the question very well, but these polite and unusual preliminaries made me suspect unknown and appalling abysses from which I should be unable to escape. I felt terrified by the diplomatic manners of the cunning ex-prefect, although I was quite unable at that time to call them by their proper name. All this made me incapable of upholding my opinion by words.

My complete lack of a college education made me like a ten-year-old in all social relations. The mere sight of so imposing a personage, of whom his whole family, including his wife and his eldest son, stood in awe, talking to me *tête-à-tête* and behind closed doors, made it impossible for me to utter two consecutive words. I realize today that that face of M. Daru senior, with its slight squint, exactly represented for me:

Lasciate ogni speranza, voi ch'entrate.

Not to see it was the greatest joy it could give me.

Extreme agitation always takes away my memory. Possibly M. Daru senior said to me something like this: 'My dear cousin, you ought to make up your mind within the next week.'

In my excessive timidity, anguish and *disarray*, as they say in Grenoble and as I used to say then, I fancy I wrote out beforehand the conversation I wanted to have with M. Daru.

I remember only one detail of that terrible interview. I said, expressing myself rather less clearly: 'My relatives leave me more or less free to make up my own mind.'

'That is only too obvious,' replied M. Daru in a tone that was rich in feeling and that struck me forcibly, coming from a man of such restraint and so given to periphrases and diplomacy.

This remark struck me, all the rest is forgotten.

I was very pleased with my room overlooking the gardens, between the rue de Lille and the rue de l'Université, with a glimpse of the rue Bellechasse.

The house had belonged to Condorcet, whose pretty widow was then living with M. Fauriel (now Member of the Institute, a real scholar who loved learning for its own sake, which is very rare in that body).

Condorcet, in order not to be harassed by society, had had a long wooden ladder made by which he climbed up to the third floor (I was on the second) into a room above mine. How this would have impressed me three months earlier! Condorcet, author of that *Sketch of Future Progress* which I read through enthusiastically two or three times!

Alas, my heart was changed. As soon as I was alone and undisturbed, and had shaken off my timidity, the same profound feeling revived:

'Is Paris no more than this?'

This meant: the thing I've longed for so much, as the supreme good, the thing to which I've sacrificed my life for the past three years, bores me. It was not the three years' sacrifice that distressed me; in spite of my dread of entering the École Polytechnique next year, I loved mathematics; the terrible question that I was not clever enough to see clearly was this: Where, then, is happiness to be found on earth? And sometimes I got as far as asking: Is there such a thing as happiness on earth?

Paris was completely ruined in my estimation by *having no mountains*.

The finishing touch was *having clipped trees in its gardens*.

However, as I am glad to note today (1836), I was not unfair towards the lovely green colour of these trees.

I felt, rather than said to myself clearly: their shape is deplorable, but what delicious greenery, forming a mass of charming mazes along which one's fancy roams! The latter detail is today's. At the time I felt things without clearly distinguishing their causes. Sagacity, which has never been my strong point, was totally lacking in me. I was like a skittish horse that sees not what is really there but imaginary obstacles or dangers; the good thing about it was that my courage rose, and I marched proudly on against the greatest perils. I am still like this today.

The more I walked about Paris, the more I disliked it. The Daru family were very kind to me. Mme Cambon used to compliment me on my coat *à l'artiste*, olive green with velvet lapels.

'It suits you very well,' she told me.

Mme Cambon kindly took me to the Museum with some of the family and a certain M. Gorse or Gosse, a stout common fellow who was rather attentive to her. She herself was pining away with grief at having, the previous year, lost her only daughter at the age of sixteen.

We left the Museum, and I was offered a place in the cab; I went home on foot through the mud and, flattered by Mme Cambon's kindness, I had the splendid idea of calling at her house. I found her *tête-à-tête* with M. Gorse.

However I was conscious of the extent, or part of the extent, of my stupidity.

'But why didn't you come in the carriage?' Mme Cambon asked me, astonished.

I disappeared after ten minutes. A fine impression I must have made on M. Gorse. I must have been a strange problem to the Daru family; the answer must have varied between: *he's mad* and *he's an idiot.*

CHAPTER 40

MADAME Le Brun, now Marquise de Grave, has told me that all the inmates of that little salon were astonished at my utter silence. I held my tongue instinctively, feeling that nobody would understand me; were these the sort of people to whom I could speak of my tender admiration for Bradamante? This silence, the result of chance, proved to be the best policy, it was the sole means of preserving a modicum of personal dignity.

If I ever meet that intelligent woman again, I shall have to question her closely to find out what I was like in those days.

I honestly don't know. I can only note the degree of happiness experienced by this organism. As I have constantly gone more deeply into the same questions ever since, how can I tell at what stage I was then? The well was ten feet deep, every year I've gone five feet deeper, and now that it's a hundred and ninety feet deep how can I picture what it was like in February 1800, when it was only ten feet?

My cousin Mure (head clerk in the Ministry of Commerce when he died), that most prosaic of beings, was admired because, after coming back to M. Daru's, no. 505, rue de Lille, about ten o'clock in the evening, he would go out again on foot to eat a certain kind of little pasty in the Carrefour Gaillon.

This simplicity, this naïve greed which today would strike me as ridiculous in a sixteen-year-old boy, overwhelmed me with amazement in 1800. I don't know that I didn't even go out one evening myself, into that abominable Parisian damp which I loathed, to eat some of those little pasties. I did this partly for the pleasure but mainly for the glory of it. I got less than no pleasure and less than no glory, apparently; if anybody noticed, they must have thought it a contemptible imitation. It never occurred to me simply to admit the reason for my behaviour; I might then have seemed original and naïve myself, and perhaps my ten o'clock escapade would have raised a smile in that family of bored people.

The illness which obliged Dr Portal to climb the stairs up to my third-floor room in the Passage Sainte-Marie, rue du Bac, must have been a serious one, for I lost all my hair. Of course I bought a wig, and of course my friend Edmond Cardon threw it up on to the lintel of the door, one evening, in his mother's drawing-room.

Cardon was very slender, very tall, very well brought up, very rich, with perfect manners, an admirable puppet, son of Mme Cardon, lady's maid to Queen *Marie-Antoinette*.

What a contrast between Cardon and myself! And yet we formed a close friendship. We were friends at the time of the battle of Marengo; he was then aide-de-camp to Carnot, Minister of War; we wrote to one another until 1804 or '05. In 1815 this elegant, noble, charming creature blew his brains out on seeing Marshal Ney, his relative by marriage, arrested. He was in no way implicated himself, it was sheer passing madness, caused by an excess of courtier's vanity at acquiring a marshal and prince as his cousin. Since 1803 or '04 he had called himself Cardon de Montigny; he introduced me to his wife, who was rich and elegant with a slight stammer, and who seemed scared of the ferocious energy of this Allobrogian highlander. The son of this good and lovable creature is known as M. de Montigny and is a councillor or auditeur at the Royal Law Courts in Paris.

Ah! how glad I should have been of a word of good advice then. How glad I should have been of it in 1821! But I'll be hanged if anyone ever gave it me. I got it about 1826, but then it was really too late, and besides it went too much against my habits. I have seen clearly since then that it's the *sine qua non* in Paris, but then there would have been less truth and originality of thought in what I write.

How different it would have been if M. Daru or Mme Cambon had said to me in January 1800: 'My dear cousin, if you want to have some standing in society, you must get twenty people to find it in their interest to speak well of you. Consequently, choose a salon, go there without fail every Tuesday (if that's the day), and make a point of being amiable, or at least very polite to each of the people who frequent this salon. You'll be somebody in society, and you can have hopes of pleasing some charming woman when you've won the support of two or three salons. After ten years' loyalty, these salons, if you choose them in our social rank, will get you anywhere you want. The essential thing is constant and loyal attendance every Tuesday.'

That is what I've always lacked. That was what M. Delécluze of the *Débats* meant when he exclaimed, about 1828: 'If only you'd worked a little harder!'

This worthy man must have been very much obsessed by this truth, for he was madly jealous of certain remarks of mine which, to my great surprise, made quite an impression, for instance, at his own home: 'Bossuet . . is *serious tosh*.'

In 1800 the Darus used to cross the rue de Lille and go up to the first floor to visit Mme Cardon, former lady's maid to Marie-Antoinette, who was delighted to enjoy the protection of two official War Commissioners of such high standing as the Darus, one an organizing Commissioner and the other, Martial Daru, an ordinary Commissioner. That is how I explain their acquaintance today, and I'm wrong to do so, since for lack of experience I could not judge of anything in 1800. I therefore beg the reader not to linger over these explanations which I let fall in 1836; this is fiction, with a greater or less degree of probability, but it's no longer history.

So then I was, or thought I was, very well received in Mme Cardon's salon in January 1800.

We used to dress up to act charades there, and there were endless jokes. Poor Mme Cardon did not always come; such crazy behaviour jarred with the grief from which she died a few months later.

M. Daru (later Minister) had just published *La Cléopédie*, a little poem in Jesuitical style, that's to say in the style of the Latin poems writting by Jesuits about 1700. It strikes me as fluent and insipid, but I haven't read it for at least thirty years.

M. Daru, who, basically, was not intelligent (but I'm guessing that now, as I write this) was too proud of being president of four literary societies at once. This sort of idiocy was rife in 1800 and was not so pointless as it seems to us today. Society was being reborn after the Terror of '93 and the near-terror of the following years. It was M. Daru senior who told me, with quiet joy, about this fame of his eldest son's.

As he was coming home from one of these literary societies, Edmond, dressed up as a girl, accosted him in the street some twenty yards from home. It was really funny. Mme Cardon still had the sense of fun in 1788; it would shock our prudery in 1836.

M. Daru, as he came home, found himself being followed up the stairs by the young woman, who was taking off her petticoats. 'I was astonished,' he told us, 'to see that our neighbourhood was so polluted.'

Shortly afterwards he took me to one of the meetings of one of those societies over which he presided. This one met in a street which has since been demolished to enlarge the Place du Carrousel, near that part of the new gallery, on the north side of the Carrousel, which is next to the axis of the rue Richelieu, forty paces farther west.

It was half past seven in the evening, the rooms were brightly lit. The poetry revolted me, it was so unlike Ariosto and Voltaire! It was insipid and bourgeois (how well schooled I was already!), but I gazed with admiration and longing at the bosom of Mme Constance Pipelet, who read some verse. I have told her about it since; she was then married to a poor wretch of a surgeon who suffered from a hernia, and I talked to her at Countess Beugnot's when she was Princess of Salm-Dyck, I fancy. I shall describe her marriage, preceded by a couple of month's stay with her lover at Prince Salm's castle, in order to see whether she didn't dislike it too much; and the Prince was not taken in, but knew all about it and put up with it, very sensibly.

I went to the Louvre, to work under *Regnault* the painter of *The Education of Achilles*, a dull picture engraved by the excellent Berwick, and I was a pupil in his academy. All the money that had to be paid out for portfolios, chair-fees, etc., astonished me; I was quite ignorant of all such Parisian customs and, to tell the truth, of every conceivable custom, and I must have seemed miserly.

Everywhere I went I took with me my appalling disappointment.

To think that Paris, which I had pictured as the sovereign good, seemed to me dull and hateful! I disliked everything about it, down to its cooking, which was unlike that of my home, that home which had seemed to me the sum of all that was bad.

The last straw was that my dread of being forced to pass an examination for the École made me hate my beloved mathematics.

I fancy that M. Daru senior, that terrible man, said to me: 'Since, according to the certificates you have, you're so much better than your seven schoolfellows who have been accepted, you could even now, if you were accepted, catch up with them easily enough in the courses they are following.'

M. Daru spoke to me like one who is used to wielding influence and having exceptions made for him.

Something, fortunately for me, must have held in check M. Daru's insistence on my resuming the study of mathematics. My relatives no doubt proclaimed me a prodigy in every sphere. My excellent grandfather adored me and, besides, I was essentially his handiwork; I had had no other teacher than himself, except for mathematics. He used to do my Latin compositions with me, he used to do, almost alone, my Latin verses about a fly meeting a *black* death in *white* milk.

That was the kind of wit shown by the Jesuit father, author of the poem which I had to re-write. But for the authors I read secretly I should probably have had the same sort of wit and have admired Comte Daru's *Cléopédie* and the wit of the French Academy. Would that have been a pity? I should have won success between 1815 and 1830, reputation and money, but my writings would have been far duller and far *better written* than they are. I think that the affectation that is called good writing in 1825–36 will seem highly ridiculous around 1860, as soon as France, set free from political revolutions every fifteen years, has time to consider the pleasures of the mind. The strong violent government of Napoleon (to whose person I was so devoted) lasted only fifteen years, 1800–15. The nauseating government of those idiotic Bourbons (see Béranger's songs) also lasted fifteen years, 1815–30. How long will a third government last? Any longer?

But I'm wandering from the point; our descendants will have to forgive these digressions; we hold the pen in one hand and the sword in the other (as I write these words I await the news of Fieschi's execution and the new ministry of March 1836, and I have just set my professional signature to three letters addressed to Ministers whose names I don't know).

Let's get back to January or February 1800. I really had as much experience as a child of nine, and probably the devil's own pride. Moreover, what was far more valuable, I had sensible ideas on all points, I had read an enormous amount, I adored reading, and a new book, unfamiliar to me, would comfort me for everything.

But the Darus, despite the success of the author of a translation of Horace, were not at all a literary family, but one composed of those courtiers of Louis XIV that Saint-Simon describes. The only thing they appreciated about M. Daru, the eldest son, was the fact of his success; any literary discussion would have been a political crime, since it would have tended to cast doubts on the glory of the house.

It is one of the misfortunes of my character that I forget my successes and retain a deep remembrance of my follies. I wrote home about February 1800: 'Mme Cambon rules over the realm of mind and Mme Rebuffel over that of the senses.' A fortnight later I was profoundly ashamed of my style and of my action.

It was untrue, and, far worse, it was ungrateful. It there was one place in which I felt less ill at ease and more natural, it was the salon of that excellent and pretty woman, Mme Rebuffel, who lived on the first floor of the house in which I had a room on the second. I fancy my room was just above Mme Rebuffel's drawing-room. My uncle Gagnon had told me how he had seduced her at Lyons by admiring her pretty foot and persuading her to put it up on a trunk so that he might see it better. On one occasion, but for M. Bartelon, M. Rebuffel would have surprised my uncle in an unequivocal situation. Mme Rebuffel, my cousin, had a daughter Adèle who gave promise of being very intelligent, but I fancy that she has not kept her promise. After having loved each other a little, as children do, hatred, and then indifference, replaced our childish feelings and since 1804 I have completely lost sight of her. I learnt from the newspapers in 1835 that her foolish husband, Baron Auguste Pétiet, the same man who gave me a sabre-wound on the left foot, had just left her a widow with one son at the École Polytechnique.

Was it in 1800 that Mme Rebuffel had as a lover M. *Chieze*, a somewhat starchy gentleman from Valence in Dauphiné, a friend of my family's in Grenoble, or was it only in 1803? Was it in 1800 or 1803 that the excellent Rebuffel, that good-hearted and intelligent man, whom I shall never cease to respect, took me to dinner in the rue Saint-Denis at the transport business that he ran with one Mlle Barberec, his associate and mistress?

What a difference it would have made to me if my grandfather Gagnon had thought of recommending me to M. Rebuffel instead of to M. Daru! M. Rebuffel was the nephew of M. Daru, although only seven or eight years younger, and on account of his political or rather administrative importance – being Secretary General for the whole of Languedoc, seven Départements – M. Daru presumed to tyrannize over M. Rebuffel, who, in the conversation he reported to me, displayed a divine mixture of respect and firmness. I remember comparing the tone he assumed to that of J.-J. Rousseau in his *Letter to Christophe de Beaumont, Archbishop of Paris*.

M. Rebuffel could have made anything he liked of me; I would have been a wiser man if chance had set me under his direction. But it was my destiny to have to fight for everything. What an ocean of violent sensations I have had in my life, and especially at this period!

I experienced a great many on the occasion of the little incident I'm about to tell, but in what direction? What did I desire so passionately? I cannot remember.

M. Daru the eldest son (I shall call him Count Daru, in spite of the anachronism; he only became Count about 1809, I believe, but I'm accustomed to call him so), Count Daru, then, if I may be allowed to call him that, was in 1800 General Secretary to the Ministry of War. He was killing himself with work, but it must be admitted that he never stopped talking about it and was always cross when he came to dinner. Sometimes he kept his father and the whole family waiting for an hour or two. He

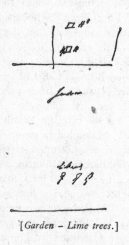

[*Garden – Lime trees.*]

would turn up at last, red-eyed and looking like an overworked ox. He often went back in the evening to his office; actually, everything was having to be reorganized, and the Marengo campaign was being secretly prepared.

I shall shortly be born, as Tristram Shandy says, and the reader will escape from these puerilities.

One fine day, M. Daru senior took me to one side and made me shudder by saying to me: 'My son will take you to work with him at the Ministry of War.' Probably, instead of thanking him, I maintained an unfriendly silence because of extreme shyness.

Next morning, walking along beside Count Daru, whom I admired but who terrified me, and I've never been able to get used to him, nor he, I fancy, to me, I can see myself walking along the rue *Hillerin Bertin*, which was very narrow in those days. But where was this War Ministry to which we were going together?

All I can see is my place at my desk, at H or H', and at whichever desk I was not occupying sat M. Mazoïer, author of the tragedy of *Theseus*, a feeble imitation of Racine.

CHAPTER 41

AT THE far end of the garden there were some wretched closely clipped limes behind which we used to go to make water. They were the first friends I had in Paris. I felt sorry for them, being clipped like that! I contrasted them with the fine limes at Claix which were lucky enough to live among the mountains.

But would I have liked to go back to those mountains?

Yes, I think so, provided that my father hadn't been there and that I could have lived there with my grandfather, most certainly, but in freedom.

That is how low my extreme passion for Paris had fallen. And sometimes I told myself that the real Paris was invisible to me.

The tops of the lime trees at the Ministry of War turned red. M. Mazoïer probably quoted Virgil to me:

Nunc erubescit ver.

That's not quite right, but I'm trying to remember it as I write, for the first time in thirty-six years. Actually, I had a horror of Virgil, as being a favourite with the priests who used to come and say Mass and talk to me about Latin at home. In spite of all rational efforts on my part, for me Virgil has never recovered from the effects of such bad company.

The lime trees budded, and at last put out leaves; I was deeply touched, I really had some friends in Paris.

Each time I went to make water behind those lime trees at the bottom of the garden, my soul was *refreshed* by the sight of these friends. I still love them after thirty-six years of separation.

But are these good friends still in existence? There has been so much building in that district! Perhaps the Ministry where I took up my official pen for the first time is still a Ministry, in the rue de l'Université, opposite that square whose name I don't know?

There M. Daru set me down at a desk and told me to copy a letter. I shan't say anything about my spidery handwriting, far worse than it is today, but he discovered that I wrote *cela* with two l's: *cella*.

So much for the man of letters, the brilliant *humanist* who discussed the merits of Racine and who had won all the prizes at Grenoble.

Now, *but only now*, I am amazed at the kindness of the whole Daru family. What could they have done with so proud and so ignorant a creature?

The fact remains, however, that I attacked Racine most effectively in my conversations with M. Mazoïer. There were four of us clerks there, and the two others, I fancy, listened to me as I skirmished with M. Mazoïer.

I had a theory in my head that I wanted to set forth under the title: *Filosofia nova*, a half-Italian, half-Latin title. I had a genuine, heartfelt, passionate admiration for Shakespeare, although I knew him only through the clumsy and pompous phrases of M. Letourneur and his associates.

Ariosto, too, had great power over my feelings (but the Ariosto of M. de Tressan, father of that kindly clarinet-playing captain who had helped to get me to learn to read, who by 1820 was an extreme contemptible ultra and a camp commandant).

It seems clear that what saved me from having the bad taste to admire Count Daru's *Cléopédie* and, later on, abbé Delille, was that inner doctrine founded on the true pleasure, the deep, considered pleasure amounting to *happiness*, that I had got from Cervantes, Shakespeare, Corneille and Ariosto, and a hatred for the puerility of Voltaire and his school. On that theme, when I dared to speak, I was positive to the point of fanaticism, for I had no doubt that any healthy-minded man, not spoilt by a bad literary education, would think like myself. I have learnt from experience that most people allow any natural artistic sensibility they may possess to be directed by the author who is in fashion; it was Voltaire in 1788, Walter Scott in 1828. And who is it today, 1836? Fortunately, no one.

This love for Shakespeare, Ariosto and after them the *Nouvelle Héloïse*, lords of my literary affections when I came to Paris at the end of 1799, preserved me from the bad taste (*Delille minus his charm*) which reigned in the Daru and Cardon salons, and which was the more dangerous for me, the more contagious, in that Count Daru was himself an author, currently writing, and a man admired in other respects by everybody, including myself. He had just been appointed chief *organizer*, I believe, of that army in Switzerland which under Masséna had just saved France at Zürich. M. Daru senior kept repeating to us that General Masséna told everybody, speaking to Count Daru: 'There's a man whom I can introduce to my friends and to my enemies.'

And yet Masséna, whom I know well, was as thievish as a magpie, which means a thief by instinct; they still talk about him in Rome (the *monstrance* of the Doria family, at Santa Agnese, Piazza Navona, I believe), while M. Daru never stole a centime.

But good heavens, how I'm running on! I cannot bring myself to talk about Ariosto, whose characters – like grooms, and *as strong as street-porters* – bore me so much today. Between 1796 and 1804 Ariosto did not arouse the *appropriate sensation* in me. I took the tender and romantic passages quite seriously. Without my realizing it, they opened up the only path through which emotion could reach my soul. It is only *after a comic passage* that my feelings can be deeply moved.

Hence my almost exclusive love of *opera buffa*, hence the gulf which separates my soul from that of M. le Baron Poitou (see, at the end of the volume, the preface to de Brosses which annoyed

Colomb) and from all the common herd of 1830 who only recognize *a brave man by his moustache*.

Only in *opera buffa* can I be moved to tears. *Opera seria*, by deliberately setting out to arouse emotion, promptly prevents me from feeling any. Even in real life a beggar who asks for alms with piteous cries, far from arousing my compassion, makes me consider, with the utmost philosophical severity, the advantages of a penitentiary.

A poor man who does not say a word to me, who does not utter lamentable and *tragic* cries as they do in Rome, and who crawls along the ground eating an apple, like the cripple I saw a week ago, touches me immediately, almost to the point of tears.

Hence my complete aversion to tragedy, and my aversion, amounting to *irony*, to tragedy in verse.

I make an exception for that great and simple man, Pierre Corneille, to my mind immensely superior to Racine, that supple well-spoken courtier. The rules or so-called rules of Aristotle were a hindrance, as was verse, to that original-minded poet. Racine seems original to the Germans, the English, etc., only because they have never yet had a witty court like that of Louis XIV, who forced all the rich and noble people of the country to spend eight hours every day together in the drawing-rooms of Versailles.

In course of time *Englishmen, Germans, Americans* and other such people, given to money-making and anti-logical day-dreaming, will come to understand Racine's courtier-like skill; even the most innocent of his ingénues, Junie or Aricie, is steeped in the guileful ways of a respectable harlot; Racine was never able to create a Mme de la Vallière, his young women are always extremely artful and perhaps physically virtuous, but certainly not morally so. Perhaps by 1900 the Germans, the Americans and the English will come to assess the courtier-like intelligence of Racine. A century later, maybe, they will come to feel that he never succeeded in creating a La Vallière.

But how will such weak eyes be able to perceive a star so close to the sun? The admiration of these *polite and miserly louts* for that civilization which gave a charming veneer even to the Maréchal de Boufflers (died about 1712), who was a fool, will prevent them from feeling the utter lack of simplicity and naturalness in Racine, and from understanding that line of Camille:

Tout ce que je voyais me semblait Curiace.

That I should write this at the age of fifty-three is perfectly natural, but what impresses me is that I should have felt it in 1800, that I should have had a sort of horror of Voltaire and the crude affectation of Alzire, together with my contempt, verging on hatred, and with very good reason – for r[eligion]; I, a pupil of M. Gagnon, who was so pleased with himself for having spent three days at Ferney as Voltaire's guest, I who had been brought up to worship the little bust of the great man, mounted on an ebony pedestal.

Who's on the ebony pedestal now, the great man or myself?

In a word, I admire my standards as they were in February 1800, when I spelt *cella* with two l's.

M. le Comte Daru, so immensely superior to myself and to so many others as a hard-working man, as a *consulting lawyer*, lacked the necessary intelligence to suspect the value of one so proud and so crazy.

M. Mazoïer, the clerk who sat next to me and who apparently was less bored by my blend of craziness and pride than by the stupidity of the other two clerks who earned 2,500 francs, had a certain respect for me, and I was indifferent to him. I considered anyone who admired that *supple courtier Racine* as incapable of seeing and feeling that *true beauty* which in my opinion lay in the simplicity of Imogen's cry:

> ... Now peace be here,
> Poor house that keep'st thyself!

The insults M. Mazoïer offered to Shakespeare and with what scorn in 1800!! moved me to the point of tears in that great poet's favour. Later, nothing made me adore Mme Dembowski so much as the criticism made of her by the more prosaic Milanese. I can name that charming woman; who else thinks of her today? Am I not alone in doing so, perhaps, now that she has been gone from this earth eleven years? I argue in the same way about the Comtesse Alexandrine Petit. Now, after twenty-two years, am I not her best friend? And when this work appears (if there should ever be a publisher not afraid to waste his time and his paper!) when this shall appear after my own death, who will still have a thought for Métilde and Alexandrine? And, in spite of their feminine modesty and that horror of being in the public eye that I have noticed in them, if they see this book published, from wherever they are, will they not be glad?

But who to dumb forgetfulness a prey is not glad, after so many years, to have his name pronounced by the lips of a friend?

But where the deuce had I got to? To my desk, where I was writing *cella*.

If the reader should have a vulgar soul, he will imagine that the object of this long digression is to conceal my shame at having

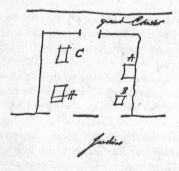

Lime trees at the end of the garden – I was at desk H or H' and M. Mazoïer at the other. The two common clerks at A and B. [*Big corridor – Garden.*]

written *cella*. He is wrong, I am quite a different man. The mistakes made by the man of 1800 are discoveries which I make, for the most part, as I write this. I only remember, after so many years and happenings, the smile of the woman I loved. The other day I had forgotten the colour of one of the uniforms I used to wear. Now, have you any experience, kind reader, of what a uniform means in a victorious army, sole object of a whole nation's attention, like the army of Napoleon!

Today, thank heaven, the tribune has put the army in the shade.

Decidedly, I can't remember the street where that office was in which I took up the administrator's pen for the first time. It was at the end of the rue Hillerin-Bertin, which then lay between garden walls. I see myself walking solemnly beside Count Daru as he went to his office, after the gloomy, chilly luncheon at no. 505, at the corner of the rue Bellechasse and the rue de Lille, as the good writers of 1800 used to say.

How different it would have been for me if M. Daru had said to me: 'When you have a letter to write, think well about what you want to say, and then about the shade of reproof or of command which the minister who will sign your letter will want to convey. When you've made up your mind, write boldly.'

Instead of this I tried to imitate the form of M. Daru's letters; he repeated the word *indeed* too frequently and I stuffed my letters full of *indeeds*.

It was a far cry from this to the great letters that I made up in Vienna in 1809, when I had a horrible pox, responsibility for a hospital for 4,000 wounded (*l'oiseau vole*),[1] one mistress whom I slept with and another whom I adored! I brought about the whole change myself by taking thought; M. Daru never gave me any other advice than his anger when he crossed out my letters.

That good fellow Martial Daru was always on joking terms with me. He used often to come to the War Office; it was like a *Court* for a military commissioner. He was responsible for order at the Val-de-Grâce Hospital, I fancy, in 1800, and no doubt M. le Comte Daru, the best brain in that Ministry in 1800 (and that's not saying much), knew all about the Reserve Army. The vanity of every member of the Corps of Military Commissioners was in a ferment about the creation of the Corps, and still more about the design of the uniform of the *Inspecteurs aux Revues*.

I think I saw, at that time, General Olivier with his wooden leg, who had recently been appointed *Inspecteur en chef aux Revues*. This vanity, which reached a peak in the matter of

1. The name of the director of the hospital was Philippe Loiseau. (*Trans.*)

braided hats and red coats, was the main topic of conversation in the Daru and Cardon homes. Edmond Cardon, encouraged by a clever mother who openly flattered Count Daru, had been promised a post as assistant in the War Commissariat.

Good Martial Daru soon dropped me a hint that I myself might wear that delightful uniform.

It strikes me, as I write, that Cardon wore it, a royal blue coat with gold braid on the collar and cuffs.

At this distance, where questions of vanity are concerned (this passion is a secondary one for me), things imagined and things seen become confused.

Martial, that excellent fellow, having thus come to see me at my office, discovered that I had sent out a letter to other offices containing the word *information*.

'The deuce!' he said, laughing, 'so you're sending that sort of letter round already!'

Apparently this meant that I, the meanest supernumerary, had usurped the privilege of, at least, a Deputy Chief Clerk.

About this word *information*, for instance, the office in charge of *pay* gave the information relating to *pay*, the office in charge of *clothing* that relating to *clothing*; take the case of an officer of the 7th Light Horse responsible for his men's clothing, having to return 107 francs from his pay, being the cost of some serge improperly received by him; I needed information from the two above mentioned offices in order to write the letter which M. Daru, Secretary-General, was to sign.

I am convinced that very few of my letters reached M. Daru; M. Barthomeuf, a vulgar man but a good clerk, was then at the start of his career as Private Secretary (that's to say, as clerk paid by the War Ministry); he worked in the office where M. Daru used to write and had to endure his strange vagaries and the excessive work which this man, ruthless towards himself and others, exacted from all who came near him. I should very soon have been affected by the contagious *terror* that M. Daru inspired, and I have never lost that feeling about him. I was excessively sensitive by nature and the harshness of his words was beyond all bounds or reason.

For a long time, however, I was not important enough to be slated by him. And now that I consider the matter sensibly, I see that I was never really ill-treated by him. I did not suffer one hundredth part of what M. de Baure, formerly Advocate-General at the Parlement of Pau, had to endure. (Was there such a Parlement? I have no book at Civita-Vecchia to look this up, but so much the better; this book, made solely out of my own memories, will not be made out of other books.)

I realize that between M. Daru and myself there was always something like a piece of the gun-carriage torn off by the enemy's cannon-ball and acting as *padding* on the body of the gun hit by that cannon-ball (as at Tessin in 1800).

I had Joinville for padding (now Baron Joinville, Military Intendant of the 1st Division, Paris) and after him M. de Baure. A most unfamiliar idea now occurs to me: perhaps M. Daru was being considerate to me? It's quite possible. But my *terror* of him was always so great that the idea only occurs to me in March 1836.

Every one at the War Ministry used to shudder at they went into M. Daru's office, for my part I was scared even to look at the door. No doubt M. Daru read that feeling in my eyes, and, being the sort of man I now know him to be (a *timid* character for whom terror inspired in others formed a *rampart*) he must have been flattered by my fear.

Coarse-grained people, such as I took M. Barthomeuf to be, must have been less affected by the strange words with which that *raging bullock* berated anyone who came near him at times when he was overwhelmed with work.

With this *terror* he ruled the seven or eight hundred clerks at the War Office, the leaders of whom, fifteen or twenty self-important people, most of them devoid of talent, having been appointed chief clerks, were soundly slated by M. Daru. These creatures, far from shortening and simplifying things, often tried to make them more complicated even for M. Daru (AS MAKES EVERY DAY WITH ME MY GREEK).[1] I must admit that this is calculated to infuriate a man who sees, lying on the left side of his desk, twenty or thirty urgent letters to answer. And I have often seen on M. Daru's desk a pile, a foot high, of such letters, asking for instructions, and written moreover by people who

1. Allusion to his Greek chancellor at the Consulate, Civitavecchia, 1836. (*Trans.*)

would be delighted to be able to say: 'I did not receive Your Excellency's instructions in time ...' and with the prospect of Napoleon flying into a rage at Schoenbrunn and talking about *negligence*, etc.

CHAPTER 42

My relations with M. Daru, thus begun in February or January 1800, ceased only with his death in 1828 or 1829. He was my benefactor in so far as he employed me in preference to many others, but I have spent many rainy days, my head aching because the stove was too hot, writing from ten in the morning till an hour after midnight, and that under the eyes of a furious man who was always angry because he was *always frightened*. It was like the *Ricochets* of his friend Picard; he was in mortal dread of Napoleon and I was in mortal dread of him.

At Erfurt in 1809, as we shall see, occurred the *nec plus ultra* of our labours. M. Daru and I had been responsible for the whole of the general administration of the army for seven or eight days; there was not even a copying clerk. Amazed at his own achievements, M. Daru only lost his temper two or three times a day; it was a real pleasure-party. I was angry with myself for being upset by his harsh words. They made no difference at all to my prospects of advancement, and in any case I have never worried about advancement. Today I realize that I tried as far as possible to keep away from M. Daru, if only by a half-closed door. I simply could not stand his harsh remarks about those present and absent.

When I wrote *cela* with two l's at the War Office at the end of the rue Hillerin-Bertin, I was still far from knowing the full extent of the harshness of M. Daru, that volcano of insults. I was in a state of amazement, I had barely as much experience as a child of nine, and yet I had just completed my seventeenth year on 23 January 1800.

What made me most wretched was the incessant and dreary conversation of the clerks who were my companions, which prevented me from working and thinking. For more than six weeks, by four o'clock I was quite stupefied by it.

Félix Faure, who had been my fairly intimate school friend at Grenoble, did not share my crazy day-dreams about Love and the Arts. This lack of craziness is what has always taken the edge off our friendship and made it no more than a lifelong companionship. Today, he is a Peer of France, Premier Président, and without too much remorse, I suppose, he condemns to imprisonment for twenty years the crazy April conspirators for whom six months would have been too great a punishment considering the perjury OF THE K[ING], and condemns to death that wise man Morey, a second Bailly, who was guillotined on 19 March 1836, guilty perhaps, but not proved guilty. Félix Faure would refuse if he were asked to commit an injustice in five minutes' time, but if his vanity, the most bourgeois vanity I know, is allowed twenty-four hours, if the K[ing] asks him for the head of an innocent man, he will find reason to grant it. Selfishness and a complete lack of the least trace of generous feeling, combined with a disposition as gloomy as that of an Englishman, and the dread of going mad like his mother and sister, make up the character of this schoolfellow of mine. He is the most contemptible of my friends and the one who has made the largest fortune.

How much more generous were Louis Crozet and Bigillion! Mareste would have done the same things, but without deceiving himself, for the sake of his own advancement, in the Italian fashion. Edmond Cardon would have done the same things, bemoaning their necessity and disguising them with the utmost possible grace. D'Argout would have done them courageously, thinking of his personal danger and overcoming that fear. Louis Crozet (chief engineer at Grenoble) would have risked his life heroically rather than condemn to twenty years' imprisonment a generous-hearted fool like Kersausie (whom I never saw), for whom six months in gaol would have been too great a punishment. Colomb would refuse even more categorically than Crozet, but he might be deceived. And so almost the most contemptible of all my friends is Félix Faure, Peer of France, with whom I lived in close contact in January 1800, from 1803 to 1805, and from 1810 to 1815–16.

Louis Crozet told me that Faure's talents were barely even mediocre, but his perpetual melancholy gave him a certain dignity when I knew him in the mathematics class, about 1799, I fancy. His father, who was born very poor, had made a tidy fortune administering the Exchequer, and had a fine estate at Saint-Ismier (two leagues from Grenoble on the Barraux-Chambéry road).

But it strikes me that my severe criticism of that contemptible Peer of France may be taken for *envy*. Shall I be believed when I add that I should scorn to change my reputation for his? Ten thousand francs and to be safe from prosecution FOR MY FUTURS WRITINGS would be my *Marshal's baton*, an imaginary one it's true.

Félix Faure introduced me, at my request, to Fabien the fencing master in the rue Montpensier, I believe, the street of the gigs, near the Théâtre-Français, behind Corazza's place near the passage opposite the fountain and the house in which Molière died. There I fenced, in the same room as several Grenoblois, although not with them.

Among others, two dirty great scoundrels (inwardly dirty, I mean, not outwardly, and scoundrels in their private affairs rather that in affairs of State), MM. Casimir Perier, subsequently Minister, and Duchesne, member of the Chamber of Deputies in 1836. The latter not only stole ten francs when gambling at Grenoble about 1820 but was caught in the act.

Casimir Perier was at that time probably the handsomest young man in Paris; he was sombre and wild and there was a look of madness in his fine eyes.

I mean madness literally. Mme Savoye de Rollin, his sister, famous for her piety and yet not ill-natured, had gone mad and for several months had uttered remarks worthy of Aretino, and in the most outspoken, undisguised terms. This is strange; where could a pious lady of the best social standing have picked up some dozen words which I dare not write down here? One explanation of this charming behaviour is that M. Savoye de Rollin, a man of infinite wit, a freethinking philosopher, etc., etc., and a friend of my uncle's, had become impotent through excesses a year or two before his marriage to the daughter of Perier *milord*. This is the name they gave in Grenoble to that witty man, a friend of my family, who heartily despised good society and who left 350,000 francs to each of his ten or twelve children, all to a greater or less extent bombastic, stupid or crazy. They had had the same tutor as myself, that deep unfeeling scoundrel, the abbé Raillane.

M. Perier *milord* never thought of anything but money. My grandfather Gagnon, who was fond of him in spite of his Protestant attitude to *good society* which greatly irritated M. Gagnon, used to tell me that M. Perier on entering a drawing-room could not resist calculating, with his first glance, exactly how much the furniture had cost. My grandfather, like all orthodox people, attributed humiliating admissions to M. Perier *milord*, who fled the best society in Grenoble like the plague (around 1780).

One evening my grandfather met him in the street: 'Come with me to see Mme de Quinsonnas.'

'There's one thing I must confess to you, my dear Gagnon; one feels out of place in good society if one has gone for any length of time without frequenting it and has grown used to bad company.'

I suppose the good society of the ladies of the Présidents of the Parlement of Grenoble, Mmes de Sassenage, de Quinsonnas, de Bailly, contained too great an element of alloy or *affectation* for a man of so lively a mind as M. Perier *milord*. I think I should have been very bored in the society where Montesquieu shone in 1745, at Mme Geoffrin's or Mme de Mirepoix's. I recently discovered that the wit of La Bruyère's first twenty pages (which, in 1803, formed my literary education after I had read Saint-Simon's praise in the three- and seven-volume editions) exactly represents what Saint-Simon means by 'infinitely witty'. Now in 1836 these first twenty pages seem childish, empty, in very good taste no doubt, but really not worth the trouble of writing. The style is admirable, inasmuch as it does not spoil the thought, which has the misfortune to be *sine ictu*. These twenty pages were perhaps witty until 1789. Wit, so *delicious* to the taste that appreciates it, does not endure. As a fine peach spoils in a few days, so *wit* spoils in a couple of hundred years, and much more quickly if there has been a revolution in the relations between the classes of society, in the distribution of power within that society.

Wit should be five or six degrees above the level of the ideas on which the intelligence of the public is based.

If it be eight degrees higher, *it gives that public a headache* (a defect of Dominique's talk when he is excited).[1]

To make my thought more explicit I'll say that La Bruyère was five degrees higher than the average intelligence of the Ducs de Saint-Simon, Charost, Beauvilliers, Chevreuse, La Feuillade, Villars, Montfort, Foix, Lesdiguières (old Canaple), Harcourt, La Rocheguyon, Humières, and of Mmes de Maintenon, de Caylus, de Berry, etc., etc., etc.

La Bruyère must have been on a level with intelligent people about 1780, at the time of the Duc de Richelieu, Voltaire, M. de Vaudreuil, the Duc de Nivernais (reputed to be Voltaire's son), when that dull Marmontel passed for a wit, in the time of Duclos, Collé, etc., etc.

In 1836, save from the point of view of literary art or rather of *style*, and with the specific exception of his judgements on Racine, Corneille, Bossuet, etc., La Bruyère remains below the intellectual level of a company such as might meet at Mme Boni de Castellane's, and which might consist of MM. Mérimée, Molé, Koreff, myself, Dupin the elder, Thiers, Béranger, the Duc de Fitz-James, Sainte-Aulaire, Arago and Villemain.

But really, wit is in short supply; everybody saves up all his strength for his profession, which ensures his rank in society. *Ready-money* wit, unforeseen even by the speaker, wit like Dominique's, alarms the proprieties. If I'm not mistaken, *wit* is going to take refuge among ladies of easy virtue, such as Mme Ancelot (who has not more lovers than Mme de Talaru, the first or the second), but with whom one dares go farther.

What a terrible digression *for the benefit* of the readers of 1880! But will they understand the allusion *for the benefit*? I doubt it; the town-criers will by then have some other expression with which to sell the King's speeches. What's an allusion, once one has *explained* it? – a tedious witticism like one of *Charles Nodier's*.

I want to paste in here an example of the style of 1835. M. Gozlan writes in *Le Temps* . . . [not in the MS.].

The gentlest, the most genuinely youthful of all those gloomy Grenoblois who learnt fencing from the elegant Fabien was undoubtedly M. César Pascal, son of an equally delightful father,

1. Dominique, i.e. Stendhal. (*Trans.*)

and to whom Casimir Perier, when he became Minister, awarded the cross, giving the post of Receiver-General of Auxerre to his natural brother, the amiable Turquin, and a similar post at Valence to Casimir's own nephew, M. Camille Teisseire.

But, for all his semi-knavery in trade, M. Casimir Perier had one Dauphinois quality, he knew how to *will*. The breath of Paris, which weakens and corrodes the faculty of *will*, had not yet penetrated our mountains in 1800. I can bear faithful witness to that as regards my schoolfellows. Napoleon and Fieschi had the faculty of *will* which is lacking in M. Villemain, M. Casimir Delavigne, M. de Pastoret (Amédée), brought up in Paris.

At the home of the elegant Fabien I convinced myself that I had no talent for arms. His assistant, gloomy Renouvier, who killed himself, I think, after having killed his last surviving friend by a sword-thrust in a duel, informed me politely of my lack of talent. I have been fortunate enough always to duel with pistols, but I could not foresee that good fortune in 1800 and, bored with always being too late in parrying in tierce and in quarte, I resolved, if need be, to rush straight at my adversary. This has made things awkward for me in the army, every time I wore a sword at my side. At Brunswick, for instance, with the Grand Chamberlain von Münchhausen, my clumsiness might have sent me *ad patres*, but luckily he was not brave that day, or rather he was anxious not to endanger himself. In the same way I had no talent for the violin, and on the contrary a strange natural talent for shooting partridges and hares; and at Brunswick I killed a crow at forty yards with one shot, from a carriage going at full trot, which won me the respect of the aides-de-camp of General Rivaud, that very courteous man (*Rivaud de la Raffinière*, detested by the Prince of Neuchâtel, Berthier, subsequently Commanding Officer at Rouen and, about 1825, an ultra).

I was also lucky enough to score a *banco-zettel* at Vienna, on the Prater, in a duel arranged against M. Raindre, Colonel or Major in the Light Artillery. That doughty hero wasn't one at all.

Really, I've worn a sword all my life without knowing how to handle it. I have always been stout and short of breath. My plan has always been: 'Are you ready?' and a straight lunge.

In the days when I used to fence with César Pascal, Félix Faure, Duchesne, Casimir Perier and two or three other

Dauphinois, I went to see Perier *milord* (in Dauphiné they cut out the *monsieur* when there's a nickname). I found him in an apartment in one of his fine houses, formerly belonging to the Feuillants (near what is today the Rue Castiglione). He lived in one of the apartments which he could not let. He was the gayest and most companionable of skinflints. He went out with me, wearing a blue coat which had a brownish stain, eight inches across, on the tail.

I could not understand how so apparently delightful a man (rather like my cousin Rebuffel) could let his sons Casimir and Scipio die of hunger.

The firm of Perier accepted, at 5 per cent, the savings of various servant girls, doorkeepers and small landowners, sums of 500 or 800 francs, seldom as large as 1,500. When the *assignats* came in and a gold louis was worth only 100 francs, the firm paid out to all these poor wretches; several of them hanged or drowned themselves.

My family considered this behaviour disgraceful. It doesn't surprise me, coming from financiers, but why, once they had made millions, didn't they find some honest excuse for compensating the servant girls?

My family were most correct about money matters; they found great difficulty in forgiving one of our relations who paid back in *assignats* a sum of 8,000 or 10,000 francs, lent to his forebears in notes from Law's bank (1718–93, I believe).

I should be writing a novel if I tried to note down here the impression made on me by things in Paris, an impression so greatly altered since.

CHAPTER 43

I DON'T know whether I said that at his father's request, M. Daru took me to two or three of those literary societies of which his father was so delighted to see him president. I admired there the figure and particularly the bosom of Madame *Pipelet*, wife of a poor devil of a surgeon afflicted with hernia. I knew her a little subsequently, when she had become a Princess.

M. Daru used to recite his verses with a good-natured air which seemed to me very strange on that stern flushed face, and I stared at him in astonishment. I told myself that I ought to imitate him, but felt no inclination to do so.

I remember the profound boredom of Sundays when I wandered about at random. So that was the Paris that I had so longed for! The lack of mountains and woods made my heart ache. Woods were closely bound up with my daydreams of tender and devoted love, as in Ariosto. The men all seemed to me *prosaic* and commonplace in their ideas about love and literature. I was careful not to tell anyone about my dislike of Paris. So I did not discover that the centre of Paris is only an hour away from a fine forest which was full of deer in the time of the kings. How delighted I would have been in 1800 to see the Forest of Fontainebleau where there are a few miniature rocks, the woods of Versailles, Saint-Cloud, etc., etc. Probably I would have thought that these woods were too much like a garden.

Assistants to the War Commissioners were to be appointed. I realized this from Mme Cardon's increased assiduities towards the Daru family and even towards myself. M. Daru went to see the Minister one morning with the report on this question.

My anxiety fixed in my mind the picture of the office where I sat awaiting the result. I was in a different office, and my table

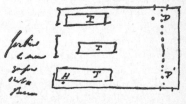

[*Garden. Just like the other office.*]

now stood in a very large room: myself H, T.T.T. tables occupied by various clerks. M. Daru came in along the line DD' after seeing the Minister; he had had Cardon and M. Barthomeuf appointed, I think. I wasn't jealous of Cardon, but I was of M. Barthomeuf for whom I had always had an aversion. While

369

waiting for the decision I had written on my hand-rest in capital letters: UNKIND RELATIVE.

Note that M. Barthomeuf was an excellent clerk, all of whose letters M. Daru signed (that's to say M. Barthomeuf presented twenty letters, M. Daru signed twelve of them, signed six or seven more with corrections and sent back one or two to be re-written).

Of mine he barely signed half, and what letters they were! But M. Barthomeuf had the mind and the appearance of a grocer's assistant and, except for Latin authors whom he knew as well as he knew the *Regulations About Pay*, was incapable of saying one word about the relation of literature to human nature and the way it affects man; I, for my part, had a perfect grasp of the way Helvétius explains the behaviour of Regulus; I frequently applied his theories in the same way myself, I had gone far beyond *Cailhava* in the art of comedy, etc., etc., and I therefore considered myself M. Barthomeuf's superior or at least his equal.

M. Daru ought to have had me appointed and then made me work really hard. But luck has led me by the hand on five or six great occasions of my life. Really I owe a little statue to *Fortune*. It was extremely lucky for me that I was not made an assistant with Cardon. I did not think so then, I sighed a little as I looked at his fine, gold-braided uniform, his hat, his sword. But I hadn't the slightest feeling of jealousy. I must have understood that I hadn't got a mother like Mme Cardon. I had seen her pestering M. Daru (Pierre) to an extent that would have made the most phlegmatic of men lose his temper. M. Daru kept his, but his wild-boar's eyes were a picture. At last he told her in my presence: 'Madame, I have the honour of promising you that, if any assistants are appointed, your son shall be one of them.'

Mme Cardon's sister, I believe was Mme Auguié whose husband was in the Postal service and whose daughters were then close friends of citizeness Hortense Beauharnais. These young ladies were brought up by Mme Campan, a schoolfellow and probably a friend of Mme Cardon.

I used to laugh and display such charm as I had in 1800 with the Auguié girls, one of whom soon afterwards, I fancy, married General Ney.

They seemed to me gay and pretty, I must have been an odd sort of creature, perhaps these girls were intelligent enough to see that I was *odd* and not *commonplace*. In short, they made me welcome, though I don't know why. What an admirable salon to have frequented! That's what M. Daru senior ought to have explained to me. This truth, a basic one in Paris, was only glimpsed by me for the first time twenty-seven years later, after the famous battle of San Remo. Fortune, to which I owe so much, has introduced me into several of the most influential salons. I refused a position worth millions in 1814, in 1828 I was intimately connected with MM. Thiers (lately Minister of Foregn Affairs), Mignet, Aubernon, Béranger. I was highly esteemed in that salon. I thought M. Aubernon a bore, Mignet devoid of wit, Thiers too impudent a chatterer; I liked only Béranger, but I did not visit him in prison, lest I should seem to be flattering the authorities, and so I let Mme Aubernon take a dislike to me as an immoral man.

And Mme la Comtesse Bertrand in 1809 and 1810! What a lack of ambition I had, or, rather, what laziness!

I have few regrets for lost opportunities. I might have twenty thousand instead of ten; I might be an Officer in the Legion of Honour, instead of *chevalier*; but I should have spent three or four hours a day on that ambitious pettifoggery which is honoured with the name of politics, I should have done many rather mean things, I should be Prefect of Le Mans (in 1814 I was going to be appointed Prefect of Le Mans). The only thing that I miss is living in Paris, but I should have grown weary of Paris in 1836 just as I am weary of my solitude among the barbarians of C[ivit]a-V[ecchi]a.

All in all, the only thing I regret is not having bought stocks with Napoleon's gratuity in 1808 and 1809.

M. Daru senior was nevertheless wrong not to have said to me: 'You ought to try to make yourself agreeable to Mme Cardon and her nieces, the Auguié girls. With their patronage you would be made a War Commissioner a couple of years earlier. Never breathe a word even to Daru about what I've just told you. Remember that you can only get on by way of the salons. Work hard in the morning, and frequent salons in the evening; my business is to act as your guide. For instance, to begin with, acquire the merit of being assiduous. Never miss one of Mme Cardon's Tuesdays!'

It would have needed all that chatter to be understood by a lunatic whose thoughts were on *Hamlet* and *Le Misanthrope* rather than on real life. When I was bored in a *salon* I stayed away the following week and only reappeared after a fortnight. What with the candour of my glance and the extreme depression and exhaustion which *boredom* causes me, I must obviously have forwarded my interests considerably by these absences. Besides, I always called a fool *a fool*. This habit brought me a *host of enemies*. Ever since I became witty (in 1826) there's been a spate of epigrams and of the *sort of remark you cannot forget*, as kind Madame Mérimée said to me one day. I ought to have forfeited my life ten times and yet I got only three wounds, of which two were mere scratches (*nioles*) on my left hand and foot.

The salons I frequented from December to April 1800 were: Mme Cardon, Mme Rebuffel, Mme Daru, M. Rebuffel, Mme Sorel I believe, whose husband had chaperoned me on my journey. They were all kindly, useful and obliging people, who took a detailed interest in my affairs and even cultivated me on account of M. (Count) Daru's reputation, which was already outstanding. They bored me, because they were not at all romantic or literary; (CUT THERE), I dropped them completely.

My cousins Martial and Daru (the Count) had been through the Vendée campaign. I never met anybody more devoid of patriotic feeling, and yet they had run the risk of being assassinated twenty times over at Rennes, Nantes and throughout Brittany; thus they did not worship the Bourbons, they spoke of them with the respect due to the unfortunate, and Mme Cardon used to tell us more or less the truth about Marie-Antoinette: kind, narrow-minded, very haughty, very much given to love affairs, and highly contemptuous of that journeyman locksmith named Louis XVI, so different from the charming Comte d'Artois. Moreover Versailles was a regular Bedlam and nobody, except perhaps Louis XVI on rare occasions, ever made a promise or a vow to the people save with the intention of breaking it.

I think I remember at Mme Cardon's a reading of the *Memoirs* of her schoolfellow Mme Campan, very different from the silly homily that was printed around 1820. Several times it was two in the morning when we walked back down the street; I was in my element, I who adored Saint-Simon, and I talked in a way that hardly matched my customary foolishness and exaltation.

I adored Saint-Simon in 1800 as I do in 1836. Spinach and Saint-Simon have been my only lasting tastes, next, however, to my taste for living in Paris with a hundred louis a year, writing books. In 1829 Félix Faure reminded me that I used to say this to him in 1798.

The Daru family were at first wholly taken up by the decree about organizing the Corps of Inspectors – a decree frequently corrected, I fancy, by M. (Count) Daru – and next by the nominations of Count Daru and of Martial; the former was made Inspector and the latter a sub-Inspector, both wearing gold-braided hats and red coats. This handsome uniform shocked military men, although they were far less vain in 1800 than two or three years later when virtue would have been ridiculed.

I think I have exhausted my first stay in Paris, from November 1799 to April or May 1800, I've even been too garrulous; I shall have to delete some things. Except for Cardon's fine uniform (gold-embroidered collar), Fabien's fencing-school and my lime trees at the bottom of the garden at the War Ministry, all the rest comes back to me only through a cloud. No doubt I often saw Mante, but I've no recollection of it. Was it at this time that Grand-Dufay died at the Café de l'Europe on the Boulevard du Temple, or in 1803? I can't say.

At the War Ministry MM. Barthomeuf and Cardon were Assistants, while I was greatly piqued and no doubt highly ridiculous in the eyes of M. Daru. For I wasn't really competent to write the simplest letter. Martial, that excellent fellow, was always on joking terms with me and never let me realize that as a clerk I lacked common sense. He was fully occupied with his love affairs with Mme Lavalette and Mme Petiet for whose sake his brother Count Daru, that man of sense, had behaved most ridiculously. He had tried to win the heart of that bad fairy with verses. I learnt all this a few months later.

All these things, so unfamiliar to me, were a cruel distraction from my thoughts about literature or about romantic love, which then came to the same thing. On the other hand my aversion to

Paris was decreasing, but I was absolutely crazy; what seemed to me true in that sphere one day seemed false the next. My head was completely at the mercy of my heart. But at least I never confided in anyone.

For thirty years at least I have forgotten that most ridiculous period of my first journey to Paris; knowing that I could call it up, I never let my thoughts dwell on it. It's barely a week since I began thinking about it again; and if there's any prejudice in what I'm writing it's against the Brulard of those days.

I don't remember whether I cast sheep's eyes at Mme Rebuffel and her daughter during this first visit, and whether we had suffered the loss of Mme Cambon while I was in Paris. I only remember that Mlle Adèle Rebuffel told me some strange particulars about Mlle Cambon, whose companion and friend she had been. Mlle Cambon, having a dowry of twenty-five or thirty thousand francs a year, which seemed enormous at the end of the Republic in 1800, experienced the fate of all too-highly-favoured people and fell victim to the most stupid sort of ideas. I suppose they had to marry her off at sixteen or at least make her take plenty of exercise.

I haven't the least recollection of my departure for Dijon and for the Reserve Army, excess of joy has absorbed it all. Count Daru, then Inspector of Reviews, and Martial Daru, sub-Inspector, had left before me.

Cardon did not follow us immediately, his clever mother wanted to make him take another step. He soon turned up in Milan as aide-de-camp to Carnot, Minister of War. Napoleon had made use of that great citizen to *wear him out* (*id est:* make him unpopular and ridiculous, if possible. Soon Carnot relapsed into an honourable poverty of which Napoleon felt ashamed only in 1810, when he had ceased to be afraid of him).

I have no recollection of my arrival at Dijon, any more than of my arrival in Geneva. The picture of these two cities then has been obliterated by the fuller pictures left in my mind by later journeys. No doubt I was wild with joy. I had with me some thirty volumes in stereotype. The idea of their being an improvement and a *new invention* made me adore these volumes. Being very sensitive to smells I spent my life washing my hands when I had read an old book and the bad smell had given me a prejudice against Dante and the fine editions of that poet collected by my poor mother, the thought of whom was always dear and sacred to me, and in 1800 was still in the forefront of my mind.

When I arrived in Geneva I was crazy about *La Nouvelle Héloïse*, and my first errand was to see the old house where J.-J. Rousseau had been born in 1712 and which I found in 1833 transformed into a splendid house, the picture of all that is useful and commercial.

At Geneva there were no coaches and I found the first signs of that disorder which apparently reigns in the army. I had been recommended to someone, apparently to a French War Commissioner left in charge of travel and transport. Count Daru had left a sick horse and I waited for its recovery.

Here, at last, my recollections begin again. After several delays, one morning at about eight o'clock my enormous portmanteau was fastened on to this young Swiss horse, a light bay, and a little outside the Lausanne Gate I got on horseback.

This was for the second or third time in my life. Séraphie and my father had always been opposed to my riding, fencing, etc.

This horse, which had not left its stable for a month, after about twenty paces galloped away, left the road and dashed towards the lake through a field planted with willows; I think the portmanteau was hurting it.

CHAPTER 44

I was dying of fright, but I had made my sacrifice, and the greatest dangers would not have stopped me. I stared at my horse's shoulders and the three feet between me and the ground seemed a bottomless precipice. As a crowning absurdity, I believe I was wearing spurs.

My frisky young horse was thus galloping at random amongst the willows when I heard somebody calling me: it was Captain Burelviller's shrewd and careful servant who came up, shouting to me to loosen the bridle, and finally managed to stop the horse after it had been galloping about in all directions for at least a quarter of an hour. I think that among countless other fears I had dreaded being carried into the lake.

'What do you want?' I said to the servant when he had at last succeeded in pacifying my horse.

'My master wishes to speak to you.'

I immediately thought of my pistols; it was probably someone who wanted to arrest me. There were a great many people going along the road, but all my life I have always seen what I imagined rather than reality (like a *skittish horse*, M. le Comte de Tracy told me seventeen years later).

I went back proudly to the captain, whom I found kindly waiting on the main road.

'What do you want with me, monsieur?' I asked him, expecting to have to fire.

The captain was a tall fair man of middle age, thin, with a mocking knavish look, not at all attractive, quite the contrary. He explained that as he went out by the gate M ... had said to him:

'There is a young man there going off to join the army on that horse; he has never ridden before and has never seen the army. Be good enough to take him with you for the first few days.'

Still expecting to lose my temper and thinking about by pistols, I looked at Captain Burelviller's straight and immensely long sword; I fancy he belonged to the heavy cavalry: blue coat, silver epaulettes and buttons.

I believe that for a crowning absurdity I had a sword; now I come to think about it, I'm sure I had.

As far as I can judge, this M. de Burelviller took a liking to me; he looked like a great rascal, and may perhaps have been expelled from one regiment and have been trying to get himself attached to another. But all this is conjecture, like the appearance of the people I knew in Grenoble before 1800. How could I have told?

M. de Burelviller answered my questions and taught me to ride my horse. We would do the day's journey together, collect our billeting orders together, and this went on till we got to the

Casa d'Adda, Porta Nova, at Milan, on the left as you go towards the gate.

I was absolutely drunk, wild with happiness and joy. And now began a period of enthusiasm and perfect happiness. My joy, my rapture, only decreased a little when I became a dragoon in the 6th regiment, and even that was only an eclipse.

I did not understand that I was then at the height of such happiness as a human being can find here below.

Nevertheless such is the truth. And that was four months after having been so miserable in Paris when I had realized, or had thought I realized, that Paris was not itself the height of happiness.

How can I express the rapture I felt at Rolle?

I may perhaps have to re-read and correct this passage, contrary to my intention, for fear of being insincere and artificial like J.-J. Rousseau.

As the sacrifice of my life to my fortune had been made and completed, I was excessively bold on horseback, but for all my boldness I kept asking Captain Burelviller: 'Am I going to kill myself?'

Luckily my horse was Swiss, and as peaceful and reasonable as a Swiss; if he had been Roman and treacherous he would have killed me a hundred times over.

Apparently M. Burelviller took a liking to me, but he made it his business to educate me in all sorts of ways; and between Geneva and Milan, during a journey of four or five leagues a day, he was to me what an excellent tutor must be to a young prince. Our life consisted of pleasant conversation, mingled with singular incidents that were not without some slight danger; consequently the remotest hint of boredom was impossible. I dared not mention my fantasies nor speak of *literature* to this dried-up roué of twenty-eight or thirty who seemed the very antithesis of emotion.

As soon as we reached our halting-place I would leave him, duly tipping his servant to look after my horse, and so I could go off and day-dream in peace.

I think it was at Rolle, where we arrived early, that, drunk with happiness from reading *La Nouvelle Héloïse* and from the thought of visiting Vevey, possibly mistaking Rolle for Vevey,

I suddenly heard a full peal of majestic bells ring out from a church standing on the hillside a quarter of a league above Rolle or Nyon, and I climbed up to it. I saw the beautiful lake spread out before my eyes, the sound of the bells was an enchanting music which accompanied my ideas and made them seem sublime.

I believe this was my nearest approach to *perfect happiness*.

Such a moment as this makes life worth living.

Later on I shall tell of similar moments, when the basis of happiness was perhaps more real; but was the sensation as keen, the rapture of happiness as perfect?

What can one say of such a moment without lying, without lapsing into fiction?

At Rolle or Nyon, I don't know which (check up on this, the church surrounded by eight or ten big trees can easily be identified), at Rolle, precisely, the happy period of my life began, it may have been 8 or 10 May 1800.

My heart still throbs as I write this, thirty-six years afterwards. I lay down my paper, I roam about my room and then return to write. I would rather leave out some genuine detail than lapse into the execrable fault of ranting, as is the fashion.

At Lausanne, I think, M. Burelviller was pleased with me. A Swiss captain, retired though still young, was Town Councillor. He was some ultra who had escaped from Spain or from some other Court; as he performed the disagreeable task of distributing billeting orders to the rascally French, he picked a quarrel with us and went so far as to say, speaking of the *honour* we had to serve our country: 'If there is any honour . . .'

No doubt my memory is exaggerating the remark.

I laid my hand on my sword and tried to draw it, which proves that I had a sword.

M. Burelviller restrained me.

'It's late, the town is crowded, we've got to find billets,' were roughly his words, and we left the Town Councillor, ex-captain, after having told him what we thought of him.

Next day, as we were riding along the road to Villeneuve, M. Burelviller questioned me about my swordsmanship.

He was amazed when I confessed my utter ignorance. I think

he made me take my guard the first time we stopped to let our horses piss.

'And what would you have done if that rascally aristocrat had called us out?'

'I'd have rushed at him.'

I must have said it exactly as I thought it.

Captain Burelviller thought highly of me after that, and told me so.

My perfect innocence and complete sincerity must have been very obvious to give value to what in any other circumstance would have been such arrant bluff.

He began teaching me a few principles of sword-play at our evening halts.

'Otherwise you'll get yourself run through like a . . .'

I've forgotten the simile.

I think it was at Martigny, at the foot of the Great St Bernard Pass, that I remember seeing this: handsome General Marmont in a State Councillor's uniform, royal blue trimmed with sky-blue, making a whole artillery regiment file past. But how was it that he wore that uniform? I don't know, but I can still see it.

I may perhaps have seen General Marmont in the uniform of a general and put that of a State Councillor on him later. (He is at Rome, near here, in March 1836, he is the *traitor* Duke of Ragusa, in spite of the lie told me not twelve days ago by Lieutenant-General Despans on my own hearth at the very place where I'm writing this now.)

General Marmont was on the left of the road, about seven in the morning just outside Martigny; it must have been 12 or 14 May 1800.

I was as gay and lively as a young colt, I considered myself as Calderon did on his Italian campaigns, I considered myself as a curious onlooker seconded to the army to see things but destined to write plays like those of Molière. If I took a job later on it would be to earn my living, not being rich enough to wander about the world at my own expense. All I asked was to see great things.

Thus it was that, with even greater joy than usual, I gazed at Marmont, that handsome young favourite of the First Consul.

Because the Swiss in whose houses we had stayed at Lausanne,

Villeneuve, Sion, etc., etc., had painted a dreadful picture of the Great St Bernard Pass, I was even gayer than usual; gayer's not the right word, I was happier. My pleasure was so keen, so intimate, that it grew thoughtful.

Without knowing why, I was extremely sensitive to the beauty of scenery. As my father and Séraphie, like the regular hypocrites they were, had sung the praises of Nature, I thought that I loathed Nature. If anyone had told me about the beauties of Switzerland I should have felt sick, I used to skip phrases of that sort in Rousseau's *Confessions* and *Héloïse*, or rather, to be precise, I skimmed through them. But the beauty of those phrases touched me in spite of myself.

I must have felt extreme delight as I went up the St Bernard but, on my word, if it hadn't been for Captain Burelviller's precautions, which often seemed to me extreme and almost ridiculous, I might have died at the outset.

Please remember my highly ridiculous education. In order not to let me run any risk my father and Séraphie had prevented me from riding on horseback and, as far as they could, from going shooting. At most, I went walking with a gun, but never on any real shooting-party which involved hunger, rain, excessive fatigue.

Moreover Nature has given me the delicate nerves and the sensitive skin of a woman. A few months later, I was unable to hold my sword for a couple of hours without having my palm covered with blisters. At the St Bernard Pass I had the physical constitution of a girl of fourteen; I was seventeen and three months, but no spoilt son of a great nobleman had ever had a more effeminate upbringing.

In the opinion of my relatives military courage was a Jacobin quality, they prized only the sort of pre-Revolutionary courage that had won the Cross of Saint-Louis for the head of the rich branch of our family (Captain Beyle de Sassenage).

Thus, except as regards my moral character, which I had formed by reading the books prohibited by Séraphie, I was a complete milksop when I arrived at the St Bernard Pass. What would have become of me if I hadn't met M. Burelviller, but had gone on alone? I had money, but I hadn't even thought of engaging a servant. Dazed by my delicious day-dreams based on

Ariosto and on *La Nouvelle Héloïse*, I paid no heed to any prudent advice; it seemed to me bourgeois; contemptible and odious.

Hence the disgust I feel, even in 1836, for *comic* incidents which necessarily involve some low character. They arouse in me a disgust amounting to horror.

An odd disposition for a successor to Molière!

All the sage advice, then, of the Swiss landlords had gone unheeded by me.

When we had reached a certain height it grew bitterly cold, a penetrating mist surrounded us and the road had been snow-covered for a long time, This road, a narrow path between two dry stone walls, was full of melting snow eight or ten inches deep, and under that loose pebbles (like those at Claix, irregular polygons with their angles slightly blunted).

From time to time a dead horse made mine rear; soon, which was far worse, he stopped rearing altogether. Really, he was a wretched hack.

CHAPTER 45

The St Bernard Pass

THINGS grew worse at every step. I made my first acquaintance with danger; the danger was not very great, it must be admitted, but for a girl of fifteen who had hardly got wet by the rain ten times in her life!

The danger, I say, was not great but it was within myself; the circumstances diminished a man's importance.

I shan't hesitate to do myself justice, I was consistently cheerful. If I day-dreamed, it was about the phrases by which J.-J. Rousseau might have described those frowning snow-covered mountains rising to the skies, their peaks continually hidden by great grey clouds racing past.

My horse kept threatening to stumble, the captain cursed and looked gloomy, and his careful servant, who had become friendly to me, had grown very pale.

I was soaked to the skin, we were constantly being obstructed and even halted by groups of fifteen or twenty soldiers slogging up.

Instead of the feelings of heroic friendship which I attributed to them as a result of day-dreaming for six years about heroes, based on the characters of Ferragus and Rinaldo, I caught a glimpse of embittered and ill-natured egoists who often swore angrily at us when they saw that we were on horseback while they were on foot. They nearly tried to steal our horses from us.

This glimpse of human nature distressed me, but I quickly put it aside to enjoy this thought: so now I'm witnessing something difficult!

I don't remember all this, but I remember some later dangers more clearly, when I was much closer to 1800, for instance at the end of 1812 on the march from Moscow to Koenigsberg.

At last, after an enormous number of zigzags which seemed

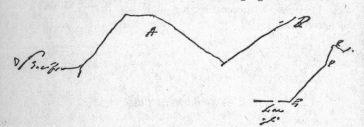

[*Precipice – Frozen lake.*]

to me to go on to infinity, I caught sight, on the left in a hollow between two huge pointed rocks, of a low house almost covered by a passing cloud.

This was the Hospice! Here, like the rest of the army, we were given a glass of wine which seemed to me an ice-cold *red-coloured decoction*.

I only remember the wine, no doubt we were also given a piece of bread and cheese.

I seem to remember going inside, or else the stories I was told about the inside of the Hospice produced a picture which for the past thirty-six years has *taken the place of the real thing*.

Herein lies that risk of falsehood of which I have been aware since I started thinking about this truthful journal, three months ago.

For instance I can clearly picture the journey down. But I won't conceal the fact that five or six years later I saw an engraving of it which struck me as a very good likeness, and now I remember *nothing but* the engraving.

That's the danger of buying engravings of the fine pictures you see on your travels. Soon you remember only the engraving, and your real recollection is destroyed.

That's what happened to me about the Sistine Madonna in Dresden. Müller's fine engraving has destroyed it for me, whereas I can perfectly well picture the bad pastels by Mengs in the same gallery in Dresden, of which I have never seen an engraving anywhere.

I can clearly see myself having difficulty in holding my horse

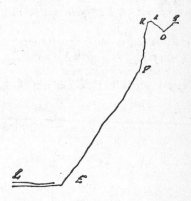

by its bridle; the path consisted of great solid rocks standing like this. From A to B was about three or four feet, D a precipice thus. L a frozen lake on which I saw fifteen or twenty fallen horses or mules; from R to F the precipice seemed to me almost vertical, from P to E it was very steep. The devil of it was that my horse had to set his four feet down close together in the straight line at point O where the two rocks forming the path met; and then the jade nearly fell; to the right there was no great danger, but to the left! What would M. Daru say if I lost his horse for him? And besides all my belongings, and probably the greater part of my money, were in the huge portmanteau.

The captain was swearing at his servant for injuring his second horse, and was hitting his own horse on the head with a cane; he was a very violent man, and really he was not paying the slightest attention to me.

To crown our misfortunes I believe a piece of artillery wanted to pass, and we had to make our horses jump on to the right bank of the road; but I wouldn't like to swear to this incident, which is in the engraving.

I remember very well our long journey down and round that cursed frozen lake.

At last, near Étroubles, or just before it, near a hamlet called Saint-Oyen, the scenery began to grow less austere.

This was a delicious sensation for me.

I said to Captain Burelviller: 'So that's the St Bernard?'

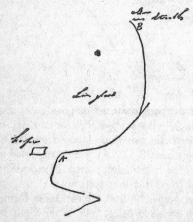

[*On the way to Étroubles – Frozen lake – Hospice.*]

I think he was angry with me, he thought I was lying (as we used to say, I was making a fool of him).

I seem to remember that he called me a conscript, which I took for an insult.

At Étroubles, where we spent the night, or at Saint-Oyen, my happiness was extreme, but I was beginning to understand that it was only when the captain was feeling cheerful that I dare venture my comments.

I said to myself: I'm in Italy, that's to say in the land of *Zulietta*, whom J.-J. Rousseau met in Venice, I'm in Piedmont in the land of Mme Bazile.

I was well aware that such ideas would have been even more impermissible to the captain who, I think, had once described Rousseau as a rascally scribbler.

I should be forced to romanticize and try to imagine the feelings of a young man of seventeen, wild with happiness on escaping from his monastery, if I wanted to speak of my sensations between Étroubles and the Fort of Bard.

I have forgotten to say that I had brought my virginity with me from Paris, it wasn't till I got to Milan that I was able to get rid of this treasure. The funny thing is that I can't distinctly remember with whom.

The strength of my timidity and of my feelings has completely destroyed my *recollection*.

As we travelled the captain gave me riding lessons, and in order to get on faster he kept hitting his horse on the head with a cane so that it bolted. My horse was a lazy cautious hack. I had to spur him violently to get him going. Fortunately he was very strong.

My wild imagination, whose secrets I dared not betray to the captain, led me to press him with questions about horsemanship. My requests were far from modest.

'And when a horse backs till it's standing near a deep ditch, what do you do then?'

'The deuce! you hardly know how to sit, and you ask me about things which puzzle the best riders!'

No doubt some round oath accompanied this reply, for it remains graven on my memory.

I must have bored him heartily. His prudent servant warned

me that he used to give his horses to eat at least half the bran he made me buy to *refresh* my own. This prudent servant offered to change to my service; he would have managed me as he liked whereas the terrible Burelviller bullied him.

This handsome speech of his made no impression on me. I fancy I imagined that I owed an infinite debt of gratitude to the captain.

Besides, I was so happy as I gazed at these beautiful landscapes and at the triumphal arch in Aosta that I had only one wish to make, namely that such a life might go on for ever.

We thought the army was forty leagues ahead of us. Suddenly we came upon it, held up before the Fort of Bard.

This is roughly the shape of the valley.

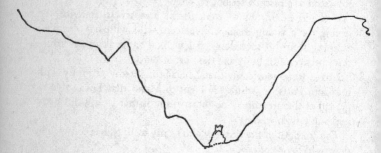

I see myself bivouacking half a league from the fort, on the left of the high road.

Next morning I had twenty-two gnat-bites on my face and one eye completely closed up.

Here my recollection becomes confused.

It seems to me that we were held up two or three days in front of the Fort of Bard.

I dreaded the nights on account of those frightful gnat-bites, and there was time for these to be partially healed.

Was the First Consul with us?

Was it, as I seem to remember, while we were in this little plain below the fort that Colonel Dufour tried to take it by storm? And that two sappers tried to cut the chains of the drawbridge? Did I see the cannon-wheels being bound with straw, or is it just the recollection of the story that comes to my mind?

The appalling gunfire, among such lofty rocks and in so narrow a valley, drove me wild with excitement.

At last the captain said to me: 'We're going over a mountain on the left. There's our road, C.'

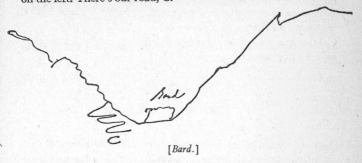

[*Bard.*]

I have learnt since that the name of this mountain is Albaredo.

After half a league I heard the following advice being passed by word of mouth: 'Hold your horse's bridle with only two fingers of the right hand, so that if he goes over the precipice he won't drag you with him.'

'The deuce! so there's danger!' I said to myself.

The road, or rather the path, newly and faintly marked-out with pick-axes was as shown at C, and the precipice at D, the rampart at R.

We stopped on a little platform.

'Ah, now they're aiming at us,' said the captain.

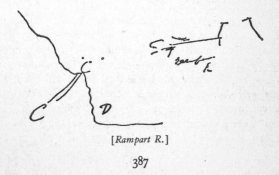

[*Rampart R.*]

'Are we within range?' I asked the captain.

'So the fellow's scared already?' he asked crossly. There were seven or eight people present.

This remark was like the crowing of the cock to St Peter. I can remember that I went close to the edge of the platform so as to be more exposed, and when he started off along the road I lingered a few minutes to show my courage. That's how I came under fire for the first time.

This was a kind of virginity which had weighed as heavily on me as the other sort.

CHAPTER 46

THAT evening, when I thought about it, I could not get over my astonishment. *'What, was that really all?'* I said to myself.

All my life I have been liable to this rather foolish astonishment and to this exclamation; I think it is due to imagination. I have made this discovery, as well as many others, in 1836, while writing this.

In parenthesis – I often say to myself, although without regrets: how many fine opportunities have I missed! I might be rich, or at least comfortably off! But I realize in 1836 that my greatest pleasure is *reverie*, but reverie about what? Often about things which bore me. The active steps which have to be taken to acquire an income of 10,000 francs are impossible to me. Moreover one has to flatter, to offend nobody, etc. Such a project is practically impossible for me. Ah well! M. le Comte de Canclaux was lieutenant or sub-lieutenant in the 6th Dragoons at the same time as myself; he was said to be a clever fellow, a schemer, never missing an opportunity of pleasing those in authority, etc., etc., taking no single step without a motive, etc., etc. General Canclaux, his uncle, had pacified the Vendée, I believe, and was not lacking in influence. M. de Canclaux left the regiment to take up a career as consul; he probably had all the qualities which I lack, and he is now consul at Nice just as I am at C[ivit]a-V[ecchi]a. This ought to comfort me for not being a schemer or even shrewd, prudent, etc. I have had the rare pleasure all my life of doing more or less what I enjoyed doing, and I've got quite as far as a man who is cold, shrewd, etc. M. de Canclaux received me politely when I passed through Nice in 1833. He may have the advantage over me of being wealthy, but he probably inherited his wealth from his uncle, and moreover he is burdened with an elderly wife. I would not change with him; I mean I should not like to have my soul in his body.

I must not, therefore, complain about fate. I had execrable luck from seven years old to seventeen, but since passing over Mount St Bernard (at 2,491 metres above sea-level) I have had no cause to complain of luck, but rather, much to be thankful for.

In 1804 I longed for 100 louis and my liberty; in 1836 I long, passionately, for 6,000 francs and my liberty. Anything more than that would do little for my happiness. This is not to say that I should not enjoy a taste of 25,000 francs and a fine well-sprung carriage; but I might get more annoyance from the thefts of the coachman than pleasure from the carriage.

My happiness consists in not having to administrate; I should be very miserable if I had an income of 10,000 francs invested in lands and houses. I should very promptly sell it all at a loss or at least at three quarters of its value, to buy an annuity. Happiness, for me, consists in giving orders to nobody and receiving none, so I think I did well not to marry Mlle Rietti or Mlle Vidau. – End of parenthesis.

I remember that I felt extreme pleasure on entering Étroubles and Aosta. Why! was the St Bernard Pass *nothing more than that*? I kept saying to myself. I even made the mistake of saying it out loud sometimes, and at last Captain Burelviller rated me, in spite of my innocence, taking it for bluff (*i.e. bravado*). Often my naïve remarks have had the same effect.

A ridiculous or merely exaggerated comment has often been enough to spoil the most beautiful things for me: for instance at Wagram, beside the gun, when the grass caught fire, that swaggering colonel, a friend of ours, who said: *'It's a battle between giants!'* The impression of grandeur was wiped out irremediably for that whole day.

But good heavens! Who's going to read all this? What high-falutin' nonsense! Shall I ever get back to my story? Does the reader know now whether he's got to 1800, to a crazy boy's first steps in the world, or to the wise reflections of a man of fifty-three?

I noticed before leaving my rock that the gunfire from Fort Bard made an appalling din; this was *sublimity*, although somewhat too close to danger. One's soul, instead of experiencing pure enjoyment, was still somewhat concerned with self-control.

Once and for all, I warn the brave man, perhaps the only one, who has the courage to read me, that all such fine thoughts date

H. Me – B. Village of Bard – CCC. Cannons firing on LLL – XX. Horses fallen off the path LLL faintly marked along the edge of the precipice – P. Precipice at an angle of 95° or 80°, 30 or 40 feet deep – P'. Other precipices, 70° or 60°, and an infinite amount of brushwood. I can still see the bastion CCC, that's all that is left of my fright. When I was at H I could see neither dead nor wounded, only horses at X. My own horse which was frisking and whose bridle I held with two fingers only, according to the rule, caused me much bother.

from 1836. I should have been amazed by them in 1800; perhaps in spite of my sound knowledge of Helvétius and Shakespeare I should not have understood them.

I have a clear and very serious recollection of the rampart from which this heavy fire had opened on us. The commander of this small fort, with its *providential* position as the fine writers of 1836 would say, thought he was holding up General Bonaparte.

I think we were billeted that night with a curé, who had

already suffered greatly at the hands of the twenty-five or thirty thousand men who had passed through before Captain Burelviller and his pupil. The captain, who was selfish and ill-natured, swore at him; I seem to remember feeling sorry for the curé; I spoke to him in Latin to allay his fears. This was a great sin and was, on a smaller scale, the crime of that vile rascal Bourmont at Waterloo. Fortunately the captain did not hear me.

The grateful curé taught me that *Donna* meant woman, *cattiva* bad, and that I must say: *quanto sono miglia di qua a Ivrea?* when I wanted to know how many miles it was to Ivrea.

That was how I began to learn Italian.

I was so moved by the number of dead horses and other remnants of the army which I found between Fort Bard and Ivrea that I have retained no distinct recollection of this. This was the first time I experienced that sensation which has since become so familiar: finding myself between the columns of one of Napoleon's armies. The immediate sensation absorbed everything, exactly as my remembrance of that first evening when Giulia treated me as a lover. My remembrance is only a fiction made up for the occasion.

I can still picture the first sight of Ivrea from three quarters of a league away somewhat to the right, and to the left in the distance mountains, perhaps the Monte Rosa and the mountains of Bielle, perhaps the Resegone of Lecco which I was later to adore so intensely.

It was becoming difficult, not to obtain a billet from the terrified inhabitants, but to protect that billet from the parties of three or four soldiers who prowled about plundering. I seem to remember having a sword in my hand to guard one of the doors of our house when mounted chasseurs wanted to carry it off to make a bivouac.

That evening I experienced a sensation I shall never forget.

I went to the theatre in spite of the captain who, rightly assessing my childishness and my ignorance about weapons, my sword being too heavy for me, was doubtless afraid that I might get myself killed at some street-corner. I wore no uniform, which is the worst possible thing when you're among the columns of an army, etc., etc.

Finally I went to the theatre; they were playing Cimarosa's *Matrimonio Segreto*, and the actress who played Carolina had a front tooth missing. This is all that remains of a sublime happiness.

I should lie and romanticize if I tried to describe that in detail.

My two great actions of (1) having crossed the St Bernard Pass and (2) having been under fire, disappeared in a flash. That seemed to me to be low and vulgar. I experienced something of the same sort of enthusiasm as at the church above Rolle, but far purer and keener. The pedantry of Julie d'Étanges embarrassed me in Rousseau, whereas everything was divine in Cimarosa.

In the intervals of my enjoyment I said to myself: 'And I have to pursue a vulgar calling instead of devoting my life to music!!'

The answer came quite good-temperedly: 'I've got to live, I'm going to see the world, become a brave soldier, and after a year or two I shall come back to music, *my only love*.' I uttered these pompous words to myself.

Life began again for me, and all the disappointment I had suffered in Paris was buried for ever.

I had just seen clearly where happiness lay. It strikes me today that my great unhappiness must have taken this form: I haven't found happiness in Paris where for so long I believed it to lie; where can it be, then? Could it perhaps be among our mountains in Dauphiné? Then my relatives must have been right, and I should do better to go home.

That evening at Ivrea destroyed Dauphiné for ever in my mind. But for the fine mountains which I had seen that morning as I arrived, perhaps Berland, Saint-Ange and Taillefer would not have been defeated for ever.

To live in Italy and listen to such music became the basis for all my thoughts.

Next morning, as the six-foot captain and I were walking our horses along, I was childish enough to speak about my happiness; he answered me by coarse jokes about the easy virtue of actresses. The word was a beloved and sacred one to me because of Mme Kubly, and moreover that morning I was in love with Carolina (in the *Matrimonio*). I think we had a serious tiff with some thought of a duel on my part.

I cannot understand my folly, it was like my challenge to that excellent Joinville (now Baron Joinville, Military Intendant in Paris); I couldn't even hold my sword out horizontally.

When I had made peace with the captain I think we became involved in the battle of Tessino, in which, I fancy, we took part, though without danger. I say no more about it for fear of romanticizing; this battle, or scuffle, was described to me in great detail a few months later by M. Guyardet, Major in the 6th or 9th Light, the regiment of that excellent man Macon who died at Leipzig about 1809, I fancy. M. Guyardet's story, which I think he told Joinville in my presence, fills in the gaps in my memory and I'm afraid of mistaking my impression of his story for my own recollection.

I don't even remember whether the battle of Tessino counted in my mind as a second experience of being under fire; in any case it can only have been the fire of cannon, perhaps we were afraid of being cut down if we got amongst cavalrymen being driven back by the enemy. I can see nothing clearly save the smoke of the cannon or of the musket volleys. It's all confused.

Except to mention the keenest and wildest happiness, I have really nothing to tell from Ivrea to Milan. The sight of the landscape enraptured me. I did not think of it as the embodiment of beauty but when, between Tessino and Milan, the frequency of the trees and the strength of the vegetation – and even the maize-stalks, I seem to remember – prevented one from seeing a hundred yards to right or left, then I felt that *here indeed was Beauty*.

That's what Milan has meant to me for twenty years (1800 to 1820). Even now I can barely separate this adored picture from my conception of beauty. My reason tells me : but real beauty is, for instance, Naples and Pausilippo, the neighbourhood of Dresden, the ruined walls of Leipzig, the Elbe below Rainville's place at Altona, the Lake of Geneva, etc. My reason tells me this, my heart feels only Milan and the luxuriant countryside around it.[1]

1. 8 April 1836. This third volume finishes at my arrival in Milan. 796 pages will be all right, when increased by the corrections and guards against critics, 400 pages in 8vo. Who will read 400 pages of heart throbs?
26 March 1836, announcement of leave FOR Lutèce. Imagination flies off

I ENTERED Milan on a delightful spring morning – and what a springtime! – and what a country! – and I saw Martial three paces from me, to the left of my horse. I think I can still see him, it was in the *Corsia del Giardino*, a little beyond the Via dei Bigli, at the top of the Corsia di Porta Nova.

He was wearing a blue coat and the braided hat of an Adjutant-General. He was delighted to see me. 'We thought you were lost,' he said to me.

'The horse was sick in Geneva,' I replied. 'I only left on the . . .'

'I'll show you the house, it's near here.'

I took my leave of Captain Burelviller; I never saw him again. Martial turned back and took me to the Casa d'Adda, at D.

The façade of the Casa d'Adda was still unfinished; the greater part of it at that time was built of rough bricks like San Lorenzo in Florence. I went into a magnificent courtyard. I got off my horse in great amazement, admiring everything. I went up a superb staircase. Martial's servants took off my portmanteau and led my horse away.

---

elsewhere. This work is interrupted thereby. Boredom numbs the spirit, which has suffered too many ordeals between 1832 and [18]36 at Omar. The writing, continually interrupted by professional work, no doubt suffers from this numbness,

This morning saw the Fesch gallery with the prince, and Raphael's 'loggie' – Pedantry: nothing is wrong in Dante's and Raphael's work, as Goldoni said more or less, 8 April 1836, Omar.

Boredom freezes the mind. I cannot hide from myself the fact that complete privation of any exchange of ideas has thrown me into the bad mood of 1832 to 1836. Writing what follows was a consolation. I have always been against writing lies, but have I not communicated to the friendly reader something of the boredom which made me fall asleep in the middle of my work, instead of the heart flutterings of no. 71, Richelieu? 6 April 1836.

6 April 1836, letter from Kolo [Colomb] about such curious things; saw paintings at the tombs of Cornet[to]. Chap. 42 will begin the 4th volume. 8 April 1836. No more work after the gé-kon [*congé* – leave] 26 March.

I went upstairs with him and soon found myself in a superb drawing-room overlooking the Corsia. I was enraptured, it was the first time that architecture had impressed me. Soon they

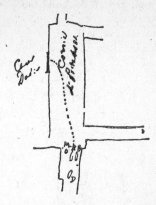

M. Martial – H. Myself, on horseback – B. Captain Burelviller, on horseback – D. The Captain's servant. [*Casa d'Adda – Corsia di Porta Nova.*]

brought us some excellent cutlets fried in breadcrumbs. For several years this dish reminded me of Milan.

This town came to be the finest place on earth for me. My homeland has no charms for me, and for the place where I was born I feel a repulsion amounting to disgust (to seasickness). From 1800 to 1821 Milan was for me the place where I constantly longed to live.

I spent a few months there in 1800, the finest time in my life. I went back to it as often as possible in 1801 and 1802, when I was in garrison at Brescia and Bergamo, and finally I lived there by choice from 1815 to 1821. Even in 1836 it is only my reason that tells me Paris is better. In 1803 or '4, in Martial's study, I used to avoid looking at a print which showed the dome of Milan Cathedral in the distance, because the memory was too tender and hurt me.

It may have been at the end of May or the beginning of June that I first entered the Casa d'Adda (a name I still hold sacred).

Martial was extremely good to me, and indeed always remained so. I am sorry I did not realize this during his lifetime;

since he had an amazing amount of petty vanity, I used to play up to it.

But what I said to him in those days because of the social tact that I was just beginning to develop and from friendship, I ought to have said from passionate friendship and from gratitude.

He was not romantic, while I carried that weakness to the point of folly; I despised him for his lack of it. My romanticism extended to love, to bravery, to everything. I dreaded the moment when I should have to tip a porter, for fear of not giving him enough and of offending his delicate feelings. It has often

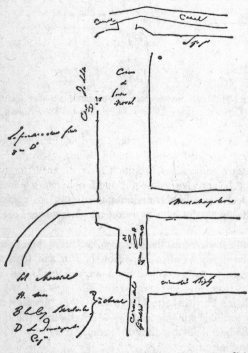

[*Canal – Canal – Via della Spiga – Corsia di Porta Nova – Casa d' Adda. The façade was only finished at D'. – Monte Napoleon – Via dei Bigli – Corsia del Giardino – M. Martial – H. Myself*

                B. Capt. Burelviller   }   *on horseback.*]
                D. The captain's servant.   }

happened to me not to dare offer a tip to a man who is too well-dressed for fear of offending him, and I must have been thought miserly. This is just the opposite fault from that of most of the sub-lieutenants I have known, whose one thought was how to dodge giving a *mancia*.

Then came an interval of utter crazy happiness; I shall probably rave a little when I talk about it. Perhaps I'd do better to stick to the preceding line.

From the end of May until October or November when I was admitted as a sub-lieutenant to the 6th Regiment of Dragoons at Bagnolo or Romanengo, between Brescia and Cremona, I experienced five or six months of heavenly and absolute happiness.[1]

The part of the sky nearest the sun cannot be seen distinctly, and in the same way I shall find it very hard to give a rational account of my love for Angela Pietragrua. How can I give an account of so many follies that is at all rational? Where should I begin? How could I make it at all understandable? Now I'm already forgetting how to spell, as happens to me during any great transport of passion, and yet these things took place thirty-six years ago!

Deign to forgive me, kind reader! Or rather, if you are over thirty or if, being under thirty, you belong to the prosaic order, close this book!

It will hardly be believed – but then, everything will seem absurd in my account of that year 1800 – this heavenly, passionate love which had entirely carried me out of this world and transported me to the land of illusions, but the most heavenly, delicious, utterly satisfying illusions, did not attain what is known as success until September 1811.

A mere eleven years! – not of faithfulness but a sort of constancy.

The woman I loved and who, I believed, in a way loved me, had other lovers, but she would prefer me to the rest, I told myself. I had other mistresses.

1. On 26 March 1836, at half past ten, a very polite letter about gé-kon [*congé*]. Since having this new great influence in my ideas I haven't done a stroke of work.

1 April 1836. Proof of 31 March. Vignaccia: *Stabat Mater*, barbaric old couplets in rhyming Latin but at least no sign of wit *à la* Marmontel.

('I've been walking about for a quarter of an hour before writing this.)

How can I give a rational account of those times? I'd rather put it off to another day.

By confining myself to rational forms of expression I should do too great an injustice to what I want to tell.

I don't want to say what things were like, which I'm discovering for the first time, more or less, in 1836; but on the other hand I cannot write down what they meant to me in 1800; if I did the reader would throw the book away.

What shall I do? How can I describe frantic happiness?

Has the reader ever been madly in love? Has he ever had the good fortune to spend a night with the mistress he loved best in the world?

I declare I can't go on, the tale is too great for the teller.

I realize that I am ridiculous, or rather, unbelievable. My hand can no longer write; I'll put it off till tomorrow.

Perhaps it would be better to skip those six months completely.

How can I describe the excessive happiness that everything gave me? It's impossible for me.

All I can do is to trace a summary so as not to interrupt my story completely.

I am like a painter who lacks the courage to go on painting one corner of his picture. So as not to spoil the rest he sketches out, *alla meglio*, what he cannot paint.

O unfeeling reader, forgive my memory, or rather skip fifty pages. Here is the summary of what, thirty-six years later, I cannot recount without spoiling it horribly. Even if I had to spend the remaining five, ten, twenty or thirty years I have to live in horrible agony, I should not say as I died: 'I don't want to begin again.'

For one thing, the happiness of having done what I wanted to do. The self with whom I lived was a man of moderate, of perhaps less than moderate merit, but kind and gay, or rather happy himself at that time.

All these things are discoveries which I am making as I write. Not knowing how to paint what I then felt, I am now analysing it.

Suggested titles for

THE LIFE OF HENRY BRULARD
from the opening pages of Stendhal's MS volumes

1.
> *Life of Hy. Brulard*
> written by himself, LIFE. Nov. '35.

2.
> *Life of Henry Brulard*
> written by himself. Novel imitated from the *Vicar of Wakefield*.

Vol. 1.
3.   *Life of Henri Brulard*

To Messieurs the Police. This is a novel imitated from the *Vicar of Wake-field*. The hero, Henry Brulard, writes his life, at the age of fifty-two, after the death of his wife, the celebrated Charlotte Corday.

Beginning of the work, vol. 1. I, *Henry Brulard*, I wrote what follows while at Rome between 1832 and 1836.

Vol. 2.
4.
> *Life of Henry Brulard*
> written by himself, a moral novel.

To Messieurs the Police, there is nothing political in it. The hero of this novel ends by becoming a priest, like Jocelyn.

5.
> *Life of Henry Brulard*
> written by himself, vol. 2.

A novel imitated from the *Vicar of Wakefield* particularly in the purity of its sentiments.

6.   *Life of Hy. Brulard*
Vol. III.

Third volume begun 20 January 1838 with page 501, finished 10 March 1836 at Civita-Vecchia with page 796.

The Life of Henry Brulard, written by himself. A novel with details, imitated from the *Vicar of Wakefield*.

To Messieurs the Police. There is nothing political in this novel. It is about an enthusiast in every sphere who, gradually disillusioned and en-lightened, ends by devoting himself to the *culte des hôtels*.

I am in a cold mood today, the weather is grey and I am rather unwell.

Nothing can cure my folly.

As an honest man who loathes exaggeration, I don't know what to do.

I'm writing this, and I have always written just as Rossini writes his music, I think about it, and write down every morning what I find before me in the libretto.

I read in a book I received today: 'This result is not always apparent to contemporaries, for those who bring it about or who experience it; but at a distance and from the point of view of history, it can be noticed at what period a nation loses the originality of its character,' etc., etc. (M. Villemain, preface, page x).

Tender feelings are spoilt by being set down in detail.[1]

---

1. *In the margin on back of last sheet:* Plan, 27 March. Journey: steamboat as far as Marseilles. Buy six scarves at Livorno and twenty pairs of yellow gloves at Gagiati's in Rome. Continuation of journey: definitely the mail coach at Marseilles, whether the Toulouse coach or the Bordeaux one, to avoid the tedium of Valence and Lyons, Semur and Auxerre too well known to me.

Bad b[eginning]. I shall probably not like the detour by Florence, arriving at Livorno. Perhaps go to England, at any rate to Brus[sels], perhaps to Edinburgh. Make the most of my time during this journey to Paris. Never say Omar has changed a great deal. 2nd. Diet, so as to avoid supper parties at the Tour de Nesle. See a lot of M. de La Touche, Balzac, if I can, for literature; a little of M. Chasles through Levavasseur; Mmes d'Anjou (assiduously) [Cas]tellane, Tasche, and Jules, Ancelot, Menti, Coste, 7 Julia. Assiduity is what's needed. If I stayed in Paris, it would be in the first two months that I should gain access to the salons which would last me for the rest OF MY LIFE.

I feel carried away by no one except Giul[ia]. A lodging facing south in rue Taitbout. What's an extra 200 francs for lodgings, for three months?